BASIC PROBABILITY

1. **Single Events** $= \dfrac{f}{p}$

2. **Conjunction of Independent Events** $= \dfrac{f_1}{p_1} \times \dfrac{f_2}{p_2}$

3. **Conjunction of Dependent Events** $= \dfrac{f_1}{p_1} \times \dfrac{f_2}{p_2}$

4. **Mutually Exclusive Alternative Events** $= \dfrac{f_1}{p_1} + \dfrac{f_2}{p_2}$

BAYESIAN CONFIRMATION

$$\Pr(h \mid e) = \frac{\Pr(h) \times \Pr(e \mid h)}{[\Pr(h) \times \Pr(e \mid h)] + [\Pr(\sim h) \times \Pr(e \mid \sim h)]}$$

ENUMERATIVE INDUCTION

Types	Criteria
Simple Enumeration	Total Evidence Diverse Sample
Inductive Generalization	Sample Size Diverse Sample
Argument from Analogy	Relevancy of Analogy
Statistical Syllogism	Sample Size Total Evidence
Appeal to Authority (Consensus)	Expertise General Consensus
Appeal to Experience (Testimony)	Reliability General Consistency

Critical Reasoning
and
Logic

Critical Reasoning and Logic

Robert Boyd
Fresno City College

Prentice
Hall

Upper Saddle River, New Jersey 07458

Library of Congress Cataloging-in-Publication Data

Boyd, Robert.
   Critical reasoning and logic/ Robert Boyd.
     p. cm.
   Includes bibliographical references and index.
   ISBN 0-13-081221-8
   1. Reasoning—Study and teaching. 2. Critical thinking—Study and teaching.
  3. Logic—Study and teaching. I. Title.
  BC177 .B677 2003
  160—dc21

                                                    2002032654

Editorial director: *Charlyce Jones Owen*
Production editor: *Joe Scordato*
Senior Acquisitions editor: *Ross Miller*
Manufacturing buyer: *Sherry Lewis*
Manufacturing manager: *Nick Sklitsis*
Cover art: *Clark Dunbar Studio/CORBIS*
Cover design: *Bruce Kenselaar*
Marketing manager: *Chris Ruel*
Assistant editor: *Wendy Yurash*
Editorial assistant: *Carla Worner*

This book was set in 10/12 Times Roman by TSI Graphics and was printed and bound by Hamilton Printing Company. The cover was printed by Coral Graphics.

 © 2003 by Pearson Education, Inc.
Upper Saddle River, New Jersey 07458

Printed in the United States of America
10 9 8 7 6 5 4 3 2 1

ISBN 0-13-081221-8

Pearson Education Ltd.
Pearson Education Australia Pty. Ltd.
Pearson Education Singapore, Pte. Ltd.
Pearson Education North Asia Ltd.
Pearson Education Canada, Ltd.
Pearson Educación de Mexico, S.A. de C.V.
Pearson Education-Tokyo, Japan
Pearson Education Malaysia, Pte. Ltd.
Pearson Education, Upper Saddle River, New Jersey

To
SKW
A teacher and a colleague,
but more importantly,
a friend

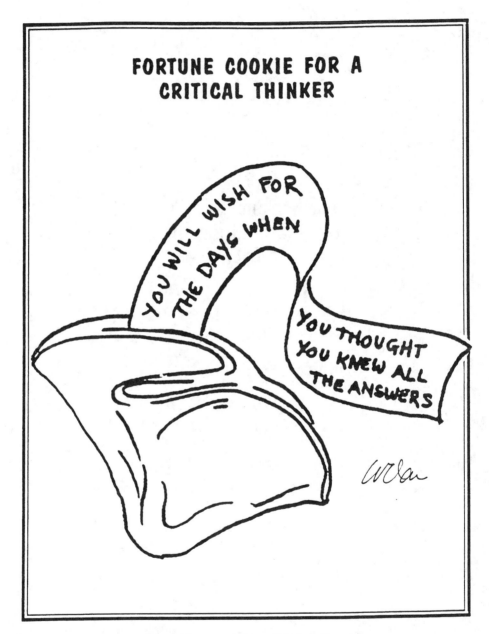

Reprinted by permission of Wendy Oxman.

Contents

8 Propositional Logic 189

PART FOUR: APPLICATION

Preface

Critical reasoning requires the criteria provided by logic. It requires a critical reasoner who is sensitive to the context of the materials being examined. Critical reasoning requires an evaluation process by which revision is possible, of both the reasoning being examined and the critical reasoner him- or herself. Furthermore, I have been influenced by my belief that critical reasoning must be practical. Students will use logic only when they are shown that it is relevant to them. Also, I have kept in mind that the role of critical reasoning is not to *end* discussion, but to *stimulate* it, for, in discussion, new insights are gained. Critical reasoning is best learned when students observe instructors doing it and allowing students to engage in it. As a result, some of the positions taken in this text are open to debate. For example, does one's attitude toward truth affect one's approach to critical reasoning? Or can *some* arguments reflect both deductive and inductive reasoning? Finally, the text reflects my belief that an adequate system of critical reasoning must have a balanced emphasis between deductive and inductive reasoning. Induction, which is the most practical form of reasoning, cannot be relegated to a single chapter or two. Nor should the presentation of deductive reasoning leave the student with the idea that a valid argument renders truth. Depending upon the nature of the course, the interests of the instructor, and the abilities of the students, some sections of the text will be more relevant than others.

While critical reasoning is an art and a science that requires both the discipline and practical application of logic, there is no single approach to teaching the subject. Some instructors prefer to approach critical reasoning from a more formal and rigorous angle, even in their introductory courses in logic. Others—especially those who do critical thinking—prefer a *very* informal approach that deals only with arguments in natural language. In writing this text, I have kept both approaches in mind. I have maintained the precision and rigor, to the extent possible in an introductory text, that is required by the more formal approach. I also have preserved the flexibility of the informal strategy. It is important both to make critical reasoning relevant to students and to understand how much material can be realistically covered in a term, while meeting the requirements and objectives of the course. *This text covers more ground than any instructor could cover in a single semester with undergraduates.* The following lists illustrate four possible approaches to critical reasoning and relevant corresponding sections of the text.

Informal-logic emphasis	*Critical-thinking emphasis*
Chapters 1, 2, 3, 4, 5, 6, 7	Chapters 1, 2, 3, Application Part I, 5, Application Part II, 7, Application Part III, 10

Inductive-Reasoning emphasis	*Deductive-Reasoning emphasis*
1, 3, 4, 5, 6	1, 3, 7, 8, 9

As with any major writing project, this work is the product of many individuals, and I want to acknowledge my gratitude publicly. When I began graduate work in philosophy, Dr. Spencer Wertz piqued my interest in logic. He taught me that logic is not a dead discipline, but a field in which much more work needs to be done. Since then, he has been a constant source of advice, encouragement, and criticism. I dedicate this work to him. I want to thank Dr. Louis Pojman for his steadfast support. By example, he taught me what it means to be a teacher at heart. I have fond memories of the University of Texas–Dallas because of the courses I took from Professor Pojman. The late Dr. Neil Daniel (of the English Department at Texas Christian University) had more patience than most people I know. I want to publicly express my thanks to him for helping me improve my writing skills. Also, I wish to thank Tony Cantu, Dean of Instruction at Fresno City College, for his encouragement. While this text owes a debt to all my critical reasoning students at Texas Christian University (TCU) and now at Fresno City College (FCC), I especially want to thank David Williams (TCU), Joel Bush (TCU), Gail Mayberry (FCC), Linda Calandra (FCC), and Kristine Snow (FCC). As always, I must acknowledge the important role my family played in writing this text: They allowed me to pursue my dream. Thanks, Kath, Brian, and Mandie.

Others to whom I wish to express gratitude include Danney Ursery (St. Edwards University), Mary Landers (TCU), Mark Pressman (FCC), John Clifford (University of Missouri–St. Louis), and Jim Druley (State Center Community College District–North Centers). The help of the staff at Prentice Hall was indispensable. Special thanks must be extended to Ross Miller, Karita France, Jennifer Ackerman, Carolyn Smith, Susanna Lesan, Susan G. Alkana, and the rest of the staff at Prentice Hall, as well as the numerous reviewers whose comments helped improve this project. They include Robert G. Pielke, El Camino College; Charles F. Kielkopf, The Ohio State University; Glenn C. Joy, Southwest Texas State University; Dolores Miller, University of Missouri, Kansas City; Michael Coste, Front Range Community College; Marina Banchetti, Florida Atlantic University; Frank X. Ryan, Kent State University; Pedro Amaral, Calif State University, Fresno; John Halpin, Oakland University; Priscilla Sakezles, Univ of Akron; Peter Hutcheson, Southwest Texas State University; Kenneth Stern, SUNY, Albany; A.C.W. Bethel, Calif Polytechnic State University, San Luis Obispo; Royce P. Jones, Illinois

College; Joseph J. Tarala, Ocean Community College; Thomas G. Morrow, Richland Community College; Bruce K. Hanson, Fullerton College; Adam D. Moore, Columbus State Community College; Milton C. Moreland, University of LaVerne; Ann J. Cahill, Elon College; Joel Lindsey, Pennsylvania State University; Frances Lozano, Gavilan College.

PART ONE

Introduction

Preface to Introduction

Anyone who pursues truth is never a scholar, but always a student.

As a college student, you have already shown that you are able to *reason*—that is, to think logically—and to express your thoughts in writing. The objective of this text is to help you improve your reasoning and writing skills.

Good reasoning is *critical* reasoning; it produces statements that are consistent and justifiable, statements derived from the application of the rules of logic. **Logic** may be defined as the identification, classification, and evaluation of arguments (facts or statements). Like any skill, the skills associated with logic do not develop overnight. They require practice. This text will give you many opportunities to practice applying the rules of logic. Through such practice, you will improve your ability to ask relevant questions, make correct inferences, understand what you believe and why you believe it, understand someone else's point of view, and communicate effectively.

Critical reasoning should not be confused with criticism, which implies a negative judgment. Rather, critical reasoning is a process that enables us to examine and evaluate material presented to us in order to make an informed decision based on that material. It also is a process that enables us to present our own beliefs logically and coherently. People who employ critical reasoning are concerned with using rational beliefs to motivate proper actions.

CHAPTER ONE

Introduction to Critical Reasoning

1.1 TWO EXAMPLES OF REASONING

As examples of how different ways of thinking affect the strength of a person's arguments, consider these introductory paragraphs from essays written for an English composition class:

1.1a

Censorship of literature is wrong; however, I guess there are times that it might be okay. But no one has the right to tell me what I can read and what I cannot. I remember reading James Joyce's *Ulysses*, and I really enjoyed it. I must admit, there are parts that were a little different, but how could this work be considered obscene? We can all be thankful that the district court ruled that this book should be permitted into the United States.

1.1b

While there are some types of literature that are harmful to readers and possibly should not be promoted, censorship of any type of literature should not be tolerated. I would like to propose that censorship is morally wrong, as is murder, rape, child abuse, and so forth. First, it is wrong to do something if it is morally wrong. Furthermore, John Milton, in his essay "Areopagitica," showed that licensing of the press was morally wrong. Finally, an analogy can be developed between licensing of press and censorship, so that if licensing is morally wrong, then so is censorship, and if censorship is morally wrong, then we should not do it.

Which of these paragraphs lays the most persuasive foundation for an essay on censorship? What is the reasoning in the first paragraph, and what is it based on? What is the reasoning in the second paragraph? The first example clearly is problematic. Why? Because the student does not offer any evidence to support the claim that censorship is wrong. A key element of logic is determining the relationship between the claim being made and the evidence offered in support of that claim.

Frank and Ernest

© 1988 Thaves / Reprinted with permission. Newspaper distribution by NEA, Inc.

1.2 WHY STUDY CRITICAL REASONING?

At first glance, the study of logic may not seem very important to how we live our everyday lives. If we look more closely, however, we find that logic can be applied to a wide variety of situations. Whenever we think, communicate, or make decisions, logic enters the picture. In fact, it is almost impossible to communicate effectively without logic.

In a work titled *Rhetorica*, the ancient Greek philosopher Aristotle (see box) pointed out that persuasive communication and logic are closely connected:

> Of all the modes of persuasion furnished by the spoken word there are three kinds. The first kind depends on the personal character of the speaker; the second on putting the audience into a certain frame of mind; the third on the proof, or apparent proof, provided by the words of the speech itself.[1]

> Aristotle, born in 384 B.C., was a student at Plato's Academy in Athens. In addition to writing on a wide variety of topics, he is reputed to be the first individual to develop precise rules to distinguish good reasoning from bad. Aristotle became the tutor of Alexander the Great in 342 B.C., a position he held for only a couple of years. In 335 B.C., Aristotle started his own school, the Lyceum.

By "proof," Aristotle means the use of logic. His comments apply not just to philosophy, but to any discipline: Whether one is studying philosophy, literature, mathematics, or business management, persuasive communication and logic play an important role.

Critical reasoning is at the core of a persuasive essay. Consider the following cartoon:

Reprinted by permission of Wendy Oxman

Junior's letter must have shown that he is fair minded and that he understands his father—his audience. He also must have presented his reasoning in a logical fashion.

Despite the clear advantages of applying logical rules to communication, "few persons care to study logic, because everybody conceives himself to be proficient enough in the art of reasoning already."[2] Unfortunately, this belief is usually incorrect.

Not only can the study of logic improve a person's writing; it also improves the ability to read written material from a critical perspective. As mentioned earlier, this does not mean "criticizing"; it means reading with discerning judgment. As educated individuals, we realize that we cannot believe everything we read. We must evaluate the evidence and then make decisions on the basis of our evaluation.

Critical reasoning can help us understand the role of *presuppositions* in arriving at a conclusion. By understanding our own and other people's assumptions, we gain a greater understanding of the reasoning behind a particular argument and the potential flaws in that reasoning.

In sum, the study of logic disciplines the mind. It establishes the habit of critical reasoning and is essential to any effort to improve the mind.[3]

1.3 HOW SHOULD WE STUDY CRITICAL REASONING?

The key to developing critical-reasoning skills is *practice*. This text contains numerous exercises that require you to apply various rules of logic. In Chapter 3, for example, after learning how to identify arguments, you will have an opportunity to apply your newfound knowledge to a number of passages in order to determine whether they present an argument. You will also have an opportunity to practice writing simple arguments. Later, you will be able to practice using more difficult passages. Finally, in the "Application" section of Part I, you will be asked to identify the arguments presented in a published article.

As you work your way through this text, keep in mind that the discipline of logic involves more than just applying formulas. Critical reasoning is an art as well as a science. Just as it takes years of practice to become a concert pianist, it takes considerable practice to know which rules of logic to apply in a given situation. As you listen and talk to other people, as you read and study, and as you observe the world around you, practice critical reasoning. As the following chart illustrates, critical reasoning is a process that enables us to examine and evaluate written and other communications in order to make informed judgments about the arguments presented therein.

Finally, practice using critical reasoning as you write and communicate.

DILBERT reprinted by permission of United Feature Syndicate, Inc.

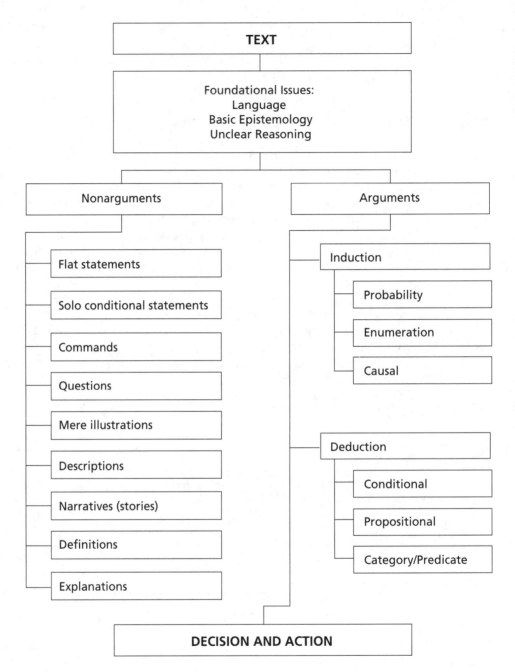

CHAPTER TWO

Foundations

Critical reasoning does not occur in a vacuum; it requires a *text*—that is, a set of words. Hence, since words are part of language, critical reasoning requires an understanding of language and its use as a means of communication. In this chapter, we will discuss the purpose of language, the reasons for failures of communication, and the central role of definitions. We will also explore the benefits of effective use of language.

How we use language depends in part on our attitude toward truth. Therefore, the second section of the chapter introduces four basic attitudes toward truth—and since our quest for truth may be hindered by unclear thinking, the final section briefly introduces three criteria for clear thinking. These criteria will then be developed further in Chapter 3.

2.1 LANGUAGE: A SOURCE OF PROBLEMS AND INSIGHTS

The primary purpose of language is to communicate: to convey a message or get an idea across. Language does not do so directly, however; instead, it makes use of symbols/signs.[4] Words are symbols/signs: They stand for something other than the series of letters they contain. Thus, they can be problematic, for reasons that we will explore shortly. At the same time, words can be extremely powerful. As Aldous Huxley points out in *Brave New World*, "Words can be like X-rays, if you use them properly—they'll go through anything."[5]

Various kinds of signs or symbols are used to communicate. One type is *natural signs*. The dark, billowing clouds one often sees in spring are a natural sign; they communicate the fact that a thunderstorm is approaching. Another natural sign is the smog one sees when approaching many large cities; it communicates the fact that the air over the city is polluted. Since we are focusing on human reasoning, we will not concern ourselves with natural signs.

There are also *artificial signs*—the dots and dashes of the Morse code and the logical notations used later in this text, for example. Words, also, are artificial signs. When we write a series of words in a proper format, we have written a sentence. While some sentences, such as exclamations or questions, are not declarative sentences, most sentences are declarative. "A declarative sentence, punctuated at the end with a period, makes a statement."[6] What a statement *means* is its **proposition**. To properly identify the proposition of a statement is to properly identify what the statement means. Unfortunately, we frequently misunderstand a statement and, as a result, we experience communication failure.

Failures of Communication

In an ideal world, the sender and the receiver of a message would understand the symbols contained within it in the same way. That is, the words making up the message would have the same meaning for both the sender and the receiver. Unfortunately, however, this is not always the case, and the communication process breaks down as a result. There are several reasons for such failures of communication. Some of these are described in the paragraphs that follow.

Complexity. A major source of communication failures is the complexity of language as a system of symbols. Consider the many possible relationships between symbols. How are the symbols "couch" and "sofa" related? Do they refer to the same thing or to the same *type* of thing? Moreover, what is the relationship between an object and a word that refers to that object? Alternatively, consider a case in which two objects—say, two chairs—are referred to by the same symbol—that is, the word *chair*. What is the relationship between the objects? This becomes especially problematic when we consider two different types of chairs, such as a desk chair and an armchair.

Complexity can also take the form of vagueness and ambiguity, especially in ordinary language—in languages like English, French, and Spanish. Consider the phrase "holy cow." In what way is it ambiguous? Can you think of other examples of ambiguity in everyday language?

Cultural Differences. Communication may also fail because of cultural differences of various kinds. The same word may refer to different things in different cultures, just as the same thing may be expressed by different words. In the United States, for example, the word *napkin* refers to a piece of cloth or paper used to wipe one's lips when eating. In Britain, it refers to a diaper. We are not surprised by such differences when the two cultures are on different continents. But even within a culture, there can be regional differences. A person from the east coast may have difficulty communicating certain ideas to a person from the west coast, even though both speak English. For example, a person on the east coast may say that he or she is going down to the shore, whereas a person on the west coast would say that he or she is going down to the beach. While there are similarities, "the shore" does not convey the same meaning as "the beach." Can you think of any other examples?

Cultural differences extend to differences between the sexes. Much has been written about the different ways in which men and women may interpret the same statement. We might even smile when we see books like John Gray's *Men are from Mars, Women are from Venus: A Practical Guide for Improving Communication and Getting What You Want in Your Relationships*. But consider the simple sentence, "I need some love." Does its meaning change with the gender of the speaker?

Linguistic Change. Other problems of communication arise because language is dynamic; it changes over time. Consider the following passage:

	"No baet yoe byo
to befleonne,	fremme se be wille,
ac ges can sceal	sawl-berendra,
nyde genydde,	niboa berna,
grund-buendra	gearwe stowe,
baer his lic-homa	leger-bedde faest
swefep aefter symle."[7]	

Believe it or not, the language of the passage is English—not the English spoken today, but Old English, the language of England in the eleventh century. The English language has changed radically in the centuries since *Beowulf* was written—so much so that it is almost impossible to understand passages like this one without some knowledge of linguistics.

Other changes are less obvious. For example, in the 1600s, the word *perfect* did not have the same meaning that it does today. Then, it meant "mature." The word *let*, which today means "to allow," formerly meant its opposite, "to hinder" (a meaning that persists in the language of tennis, where *let* refers to a serve that has been hindered by the net). Such *historical distancing* can cause communication problems.

Although we obviously cannot communicate with people from other historical periods, the fact that language is constantly changing often leads to failures of communication. This may occur when members of different generations interpret words in different ways. During the 1950s, the term "reds" was used to refer to communism. However, during the 1970s, the term was used to identify a recreational drug. Today, if we refer to someone as a red, we might be identifying his or her allegiance to a particular gang.

The Way We Learn Language. A fourth reason for communication failures is the way we learn language. Usually, we learn a language by listening to other people and imitating them. However, the language of the people we imitate may be different from that used by most members of the larger society. If the people from whom we learn a language use it incorrectly, we are likely to use it incorrectly as well. Frequently, we hear someone say, "I'm going to lay down," as opposed to "I'm going to lie down." In most cases, they have used the grammatically incorrect term (lay) because they grew up hearing others use incorrect grammar.

Misinterpretation. Communication may also break down because of misinterpretation by the recipient of the message. The recipient may misinterpret a word or fail to understand language that is used in a *figurative* or *metaphorical* way. Have you ever been in a class when a student raises his or her hand and says, "I have a question" to which the teacher responds, "Shoot." Or maybe "Fire away!" Most communication failures result from some form of misinterpretation.

For correct interpretation to occur, six elements of a message must be understood:

1. Context: As critical reasoners, we must understand the context in which the communication has taken place. The context may include the intended audience of the communication or the surrounding paragraphs in a printed text. As writers, one of the first things we are told that we must take into consideration when we write is the context in which we are writing.

2. Grammar: Verb tenses, parts of speech, and other aspects of grammar have a significant effect on the meaning of a message. Notice how the following two sentences have different meanings, and we see this through the grammar: (1) "I went to the store." (2) "I had gone to the store." The second implies that I went to the store before doing something else.

3. Genre: The genre of, for example, a literary text—that is, the type or category of literature represented—affects the interpretation of the text. Statements in a satirical essay, such as Jonathan Swift's "A Modest Proposal," which suggests eating babies in order to control the indigent population of Ireland, cannot be interpreted in the same way as statements in a serious political treatise.

4. Figurative language: The recipient of a communication must be sensitive to the possible use of figurative language and not interpret such language literally. When, for example, a fellow actor tells you to "break a leg," it would be inappropriate to take him literally. He is wishing you good luck.

5. Historical setting: The historical setting of a text can be extremely important in interpreting a message. Political cartoonists, for example, depend upon their readers to understand the historical context of their work.

6. Definitions: Finally, as critical reasoners, we must be sensitive to the definitions of words. As we shall discover, definitions can be complicated, but we must be aware of accepted, standard meanings of a word. Frequently, the meaning of a word changes as its context changes. For instance, the context is the workplace and the word "boss" is used, we understand that the term probably refers to someone in charge. But if two individuals are admiring a car and the term is used to describe the car, then, as critical reasoners, we need to understand that the word means something different.

Types of Definitions

The last element in the preceding list, definitions, may be the most important of all. As critical reasoners, we must be sensitive to the meanings of individual words. Since definitions

Six Basic Elements of Interpretation

1. Context
2. Grammar
3. Genre
4. Figurative language
5. Historical setting
6. Definitions

are the primary tool used in interpreting a text, it is important to realize that there are different types of definitions. We therefore devote this section to a discussion of the various types of definitions.

The most basic type of definition is the **contextual** or **synonymous definition**. Such a definition equates a word with another word or phrase that, in an appropriate context, is its equivalent. Following are two examples:

'round' = [df.] 'circular'
'desert' = [df.] 'forsake'

A second type of definition is the **ostensive definition**, also known as the **nonverbal extensional definition** or demonstrative definition. Often, we define a word by presenting examples of what it refers to. Consider how you might teach children a concept such as "circle" or "smiley face." You might show the child a circle and say, "Circle":

Or you might point to a smiley face and say "Smiley face":

These are ostensive definitions. Such definitions usually rely on perceivable, concrete experiences. The experience, of course, need not be visual; other senses may be used to present the example. Touch, for instance, may be used to define the concept "hard," and taste may be used to define "sweet."

Denotative definitions, also called **verbal extensional definitions** or definitions by subclass, provide a list of things or types of things that are referred to be the word being defined. For example, to define the word *carnivorous*, you might present a list of meat-eating animals such as dogs, cats, tigers, wolves, and vultures. Unlike ostensive definitions, denotative definitions do not require the physical presence of the objects used to illustrate the word's meaning. In fact, most people would probably prefer to have *carnivorous* defined denotatively rather than ostensively!

A fourth type of definition is **connotative** or **intensional**. This type of definition consists of a complete list of the essential properties of the word. It includes all and only the properties that pinpoint the word being defined. Aristotle provides an example in his *Categories*. In discussing the concept "an individual man," he says, "For instance, the individual man is included in the species 'man,' and the genus to which the species belongs is animal."[8]

A complete intensional definition identifies both the genus and the difference. The *genus* is the general class or category to which the thing being defined belongs (e.g., animal). The *difference* is what distinguishes the thing being defined from other objects in the same category. Aristotle, for example, offers rationality as the difference between man and other members of the genus animal.

A final type of definition is the **operational definition**. Such a definition provides a test or other formal procedure to be used in deciding whether the word or term applies to a particular object. For example, a *passing grade* may be defined as "a score of sixty or above." This definition now provides a test to be used in determining whether a particular grade is a passing grade.

Five Types of Definitions

1. Contextual (synonymous)
2. Ostensive (nonverbal extensional)
3. Denotative (verbal extensional)
4. Connotative (intensional)
5. Operational

When you are doing the exercises in this book, bear in mind that what is important is not obtaining *the* answer to a particular question, but going through the *process* of critical reasoning. Only by going through this process many times can you develop the habit of discriminating between good arguments and poor ones. By doing so—as well as by reading the text and completing the course—you will lay the foundations for the development of good critical-reasoning skills.

Like all the exercises in this book, those which follow progress from easier questions to more difficult ones. (Problems marked with an asterisk are worked out in the appendix.)

To gain the maximum benefit from these exercises, first do the problems on your own; that is, try to find the answers yourself. Then—and this is crucial—discuss your answers with others to learn how they obtained their answers. Again, it is the process of *arriving at the answer*, rather than the answer itself, that is the key to building critical reasoning skills.

2.1A EXERCISE: IDENTIFYING TYPES OF DEFINITIONS
Identify the following definitions by their basic type:

1. This ball, which I am holding in my hand, illustrates what I mean by 'spherical.'
*2. "What is truth?" "How accurate is our perception?" and "How do I know anything?" are all questions of epistemology.
3. 'Freedom' = [df.] 'liberty.'
*4. Milk is considered to be whole milk if, when it is tested, it is found to contain a butterfat level of at least 3.25.
5. By 'carnivorous,' I mean animals such as dogs, cats, tigers, wolves, and so forth.
6. A piece of material is considered elastic if it can be stretched without ripping.
7. 'Quote' = [df.] 'cite.'
*8. That bag of rotten potatoes gives us a vivid understanding of the term 'stink.'
9. That is truly a philosophical question.
*10. 'Abandon' = [df.] 'desert.'
11. Any milk with an acid measurement of over 0.16 is considered to be high-acidity milk.
12. The simplest way to explain a smile is to point one out on smiling people.
13. Night refers to that period of darkness between sunset and sunrise when it is not light, but instead dark outside.
*14. Chopsticks are a pair of narrow sticks held between the thumb and fingers and used in East Asian countries for lifting food to the mouth.
15. This part of the tennis racket is called the head. It is the part of the racket designed to hit the ball.
16. A hat is a type of head covering with a shaped top and a brim, unlike a hood or a veil.
*17. By 'joint,' we mean connections between the various parts of a body. As examples, we might cite the joint between the shoulder and the arm or the joint between the hand and the arm.
18. A motto is a phrase or statement that expresses one's guiding principle. The Boy Scouts' motto is "Be prepared."
19. 'Happy' = [df.] 'gay.'
*20. These are the type of things I mean by 'junk.' Look at this broken food processor or this weed eater that does not work.

21.   By 'fast-food restaurants,' I mean places such as McDonald's, Wendy's, Kentucky Fried Chicken, Jack in the Box, and Arby's.

*22.   If a student is taking at least twelve semester hours of classes, then he or she is considered to be a full-time student.

*23.   A man is a member of the male sex, is at least eighteen years of age, and has achieved an appropriate level of mental and emotional maturity.

24.   Love is that which exists between two or more persons and exhibits consideration, giving, trust, honesty, and emotions.

25.   You can tell if a car is a true sports car if it has more than 450 horsepower and can exceed speeds greater than 150 mph.

Uses of Definitions

Not only are there different types of definitions; there are also different ways of using definitions. The most basic use of a definition is **lexical** or **reportive**. When we define a word in this way, we give the meaning of the word that is generally understood by most members of a specific group. The group may be very limited in scope (e.g., most logicians) or very broad (e.g., most English speakers). A lexical definition is **propositional** in that it can be judged as true or false, depending on whether it accurately represents the way most members of the specified group use the word. For example, a group of young people discussing last weekend's concert may claim that the band was "really bad." For this group of speakers, "bad" might mean what another group of speakers would term "good." Since no definition can cover all the possible shades of meaning that a given word can have, there is no such thing as an absolutely true or absolutely false lexical definition.

A second use of definitions occurs when we create a new symbol, give an old symbol a new meaning, or combine old symbols in a new way. This is referred to as a **stipulative** use of a definition. Such a definition cannot be judged as true or false. After a new symbol or word has been created or an existing one has been given a new meaning, it may be absorbed into general usage or into the standard vocabulary of a particular group of people. It is then used in a lexical or reportive fashion.

Sigmund Freud (1856–1939) provided numerous examples of the stipulative use of definitions in developing his psychoanalytic theory. He gave new meanings to existing words such as *transference* and *repression*. In so doing, he was using these definitions in a stipulative way. Over time, however, they were absorbed into the general vocabulary and came to be used in a lexical manner. Freud also created new words, such as *neurosis* and *sublimation*. Again, these words began by being defined stipulatively, but now are defined lexically. We see the same process at work in the case of words created by the computer revolution, such as *byte*, *window*, and *microprocessor*.

A third use of definitions is called **precising** and involves defining a word or term in precise language. The purpose is to eliminate ambiguity and vagueness from the definition. For example, we might define a *traffic accident* as "any contact between vehicles causing more than $100 in damage." Again, such a definition cannot be judged as true or false; it can be judged only by its success in eliminating ambiguity or vagueness without distorting the word's generally accepted meaning.

Definitions may also be used **persuasively**—that is, to change people's attitudes or feelings toward a specific thing or subject. Consider the subject of abortion. Some groups define the word in terms of "women's rights." This approach is designed to elicit positive feelings, because few people approve of infringing on individual rights. Other groups define abortion in terms of "murder of an innocent human being," thereby producing negative attitudes. As with precising definitions, it is generally inappropriate to judge persuasive definitions as true or false; they can be evaluated only on the basis of whether they succeed or fail in accomplishing their intended purpose.

Dear God, please save me from the sin of intellectual arrogance.... Oh, and God, intellectual arrogance is defined as...

Reprinted by permission of Wendy Oxman

Definitions can also be used in a **theoretical** fashion. A theoretical definition is similar to a reportive definition in that it indicates the meaning of the word or term within a particular theory. However, theoretical definitions are less arbitrary than lexical definitions. They are especially helpful when the term being defined has a different meaning in a given theory than it does in normal usage. An example is the famous equation $E = mC^2$. Here, *energy* (E) is defined according to Einstein's theory of relativity, not according to the way we generally understand the word. While theoretical definitions are especially evident in the sciences, they also occur in the humanities.

Finally, there are **legal** definitions. A term that is defined legally is given meaning by the laws determined by a legislative, judicial, or executive body. The legal use of definitions tends to be arbitrary. (This is not to suggest that legal definitions are totally arbitrary in the sense that there is no good reason for having them. Rather, legal definitions must provide some sort of demarcation, and the point of demarcation is not crisp.) The legal speed limit, for example, is defined as the speed limit that is posted beside the road. Why is the legal speed limit 55 miles per hour on one portion of a road and 65 miles per hour on another portion of the same road? Because those are the posted limits. Notice, however, that in each case the term "legal speed limit" is both described and prescribed: Not only does the speed sign *describe* the legal speed limit, but it *prescribes* that limit.

Six Ways of Using Definitions

1. Lexical (reportive)
2. Stipulative
3. Precising
4. Persuasive
5. Theoretical
6. Legal

2.1B EXERCISE: IDENTIFYING USAGE OF DEFINITIONS

For each of the following definitions, identify the way in which it is probably being used:

1. Professors are those squinty-eyed, hollow people who live in ivory towers and have no conception of the real world.
2. By 'wakalle,' I mean that warm, fuzzy feeling one gets when he or she is kissed.
*3. Love is that strong and deep feeling of attachment that exists between two or more persons.
4. A quark in quantum physics is the actualization of the unexpected.
5. A good ole boy is someone just like you and me.
*6. For lack of another word, let's name our new invention a blyfixus.
7. When I say 'old,' I am referring to anyone over thirty years of age.
8. According to the law, anyone driving over 55 mph is a speeder.
*9. Allow me to clarify what I mean by metaphysics. Metaphysics is that branch of philosophy which is concerned primarily with the nature of reality.
10. When I think of philosophical questions, I think of those questions which deal with issues of ultimate concern, such as the existence of God or the nature of beauty.
11. Most Americans think of freedom as the right to do whatever they please.
12. We must stop thinking of 'pagan' in terms of its old meaning and must understand that it now means "that which is against the accepted norm."
13. Within the context of our given hypothesis, 'elasticity of the world' refers to the ability of the rock tables to shift.

14. A minor is any person under the age of twenty-one.

15. A persons on welfare is simply someone who is lazy and does not try to get a job.

16. (When the computer revolution first began) A bug is an error within a computer program that prevents the program from working as it was intended.

17. Now, in tennis, the term 'love' means "zero."

18. By 'Reaganomics,' we simply mean supply-side economics.

19. Given the theory of ontonation, 'gilmorae' refers to the connections that are claimed to exist between philmeusee and dormatia.

20. Ontonation is the science of collecting sound waves from wind blowing through the trees.

Evaluating Definitions

When we are evaluating a definition, we must realize that no single definition will be best for a given term for all purposes and under all situations in which the term may be used. *Typically, definitions are formulated to satisfy a specific purpose and are designed for a specific audience.* Clearly, if one were to define 'energy' for a group of first graders as an advanced physics textbook might, the definition would not work. However, we can identify some general criteria for a good definition. First of all, a good definition should be **noncircular**. A circular definition is a definition in which the term being defined is also used in its definition. For example, *Webster's New American Dictionary* defines 'terrorism' as "the action of terror; a system of terror." A good definition is noncircular and should be given in an **affirmative** fashion. Consider the following definitions of 'textbook': "A volume used in schools as a basis for instruction in a given subject" (*Webster's*). "A volume that no one would read unless required to do so." "A volume that is not easily read." Many students would say that all three definitions are accurate and therefore good. However, notice that the last two violate the criterion of affirmativeness. (Some terms, such as 'baldness,' cannot be defined in the affirmative, but most terms can.) A good definition also must be **accurate**. In requiring a definition to be accurate, one must remember that no single definition will cover all the various shades of meaning a given term may have. Hence, the criterion of accuracy must be understood to be dependent on context. For example, consider Webster's definition of 'valid': "resting upon fact, sound, logical." In the context of a logic-oriented class, this definition would not be accurate, although it might be in another context. Finally, a definition must be **clear**. If a definition is ambiguous or vague, then it is not a good definition. Just as with accuracy, the criterion of clarity is also dependent on context. To see that this is so, consider a situation in which Professor Smith is introduced to a fifth-grade class as a chemagonist. One of the students asks what a chemagonist is and is told that a chemagonist is "a physiologist who believes that the nerves act by chemical means" (*Webster's*). For most fifth graders, such a definition would not satisfy the criterion of clarity. The ability to define words in relation to a specific purpose or audience illustrates the flexibility of language—a flexibility that is both welcome and problematic.

Why is it problematic? Because using language requires us to manipulate symbols (words), which refer to objects. Yet any object is itself a symbol that points to another object, which in turn points to another; the sequence goes on forever. Thus, for any symbol, there is an infinite set of referents. Most words invoke a *chain of association*. Sometimes, the chain varies from one speaker to another. Consider, for example, the word "fire." For some readers, the word invokes memories of a campfire, hot dogs, and good times visiting a ranch as a child. For others, the word carries memories of an awful night when the house burned down. It reminds them of their lost childhood toys, especially that stuffed, ragged dog they always went to bed with—before the fire. Note that, although words or symbols do point to a chain of associations, we intuitively reject Humpty Dumpty's claim that a word means whatever the user decides it means—nothing more, nothing less. If, however, there is an infinite number of possible referents for any symbol, any of which can be the definition of that symbol, how can we hope to avoid Humpty Dumpty's claim?

To avoid having a word mean whatever we choose, we focus on the *relationship* between a symbol and its referent—that is, the word and the object it points to. A symbol is connected with an object only by this relationship, which holds true regardless of how the word is being used. Let's go back to the term "fire." Suppose I am visiting a friend who is preparing to barbeque some steaks, and she says, "The fire is perfect!" Even though the term "fire" does remind me of my neighbor's home burning down and the family's loss of everything, as a critical reasoner, I am able to understand my friend's use of the term. The referent—the charcoals in the black Weber—and the symbol—a proper charred look and appropriate heat—are related to the task of cooking the steaks. In this situation, the relationship is positive; thus, I understand which chain of associations I should use to interpret my friend's statement.

2.1C EXERCISE: EVALUATING DEFINITIONS

Indicate which if any, criterion or criteria are violated by each of the following definitions:

*1.   A logician is a person who does logic.
 2.   A passing grade is not sixty percent or below.
*3.   By 'American,' I mean a person who is not a European.
*4.   A carcinogen is any substance that may produce cancer.
 5.   When I say an argument is valid, I mean that it is justifiable.
 6.   A kilt is a knee-length skirt.
*7.   A partridge is a game bird.
 8.   'Vanity' refers to someone who is characterized as being vain.
 9.   One who practices science is a scientist.
10.   An irreligious person is a person who is not religious.
*11. A student is someone who sits behind a desk in a classroom.
12.   A lyrebird is a ground-dwelling bird of Australia.
13.   A preface to a paper explains what is to come.
14.   A circular argument is an argument that goes around in circles.
15.   A judge is a man who is overseeing an event and who passes judgment upon that event.
16.   Adherence is the act or state of adhering to.
*17. A raccoon is a small, carnivorous animal.
18.   The concept of goodness applies to that quality of being good.
19.   A hazardous person is a person who is not cautious.

*20.   Hemophilia means that one's blood will not clot properly.

21.   A chair is a seat with legs and a back.

*22.   By 'appropriate dress,' we mean a person who is attired appropriately.

23.   An extraordinary event is an event that is not common.

24.   The denarius was a coin used in early Greece.

25.   In this passage of Homer, Phoebe is a Greek goddess.

2.2 BASIC EPISTEMOLOGY

Now that we have explored some fundamental characteristics of language, we turn to **epistemology**, the branch of philosophy that is concerned with belief, knowledge, and truth. Critical reasoning and epistemology are closely related. Critical reasoning provides a method for examining a text. Epistemology is essential for determining whether truth exists, and if so, where it exists and whether it can be known. These questions can be approached from any of four basic perspectives:

1.   A **skeptic** claims that truth probably does not exist and that even if it does, we can never know what it is.

2.   A **relativist** claims that truth exists, that there are many truths, and that these truths are dependent on those who know them. The individual's or society's belief that something is true makes it true.

3.   A **naive objectivist** claims that truth exists, that it exists independently of those who know it, and that we can and do know precisely what it is.

4.   A **critical objectivist** also claims that truth exists and that it exists independently of those who know it. However, it is possible that we will never know what it is.

Skepticism

The third-century Greek physician and philosopher Sextus Empiricus (see box) tells us that

> the skeptical ability is the ability to set in opposition appearances and ideas in any manner whatsoever, the result of which is first that, because of the equal force of the opposed objects and arguments, final suspension of judgement is achieved. . . . The main principle of the skeptical system is that for every argument another argument of equal weight is opposed.[9]

Trained as a medical doctor during the last half of the second century A.D., **Sextus Empiricus** studied and classified all of the Greek skeptics. Since many of the ancient Greek writings are no longer available, much of our understanding of Greek skepticism is dependent upon Sextus Empiricus.

Skepticism does not necessarily claim that there is nothing to be known, but it questions our ability to know whether something is true. For example, consider the philosophical paradox of a brain in a vat.[10] Imagine that you are merely a brain in a vat in some scientific laboratory. Someone is stimulating your brain in such a fashion that makes you think you are reading this text. The skeptic will point out that, regardless of whether you are merely a brain in a vat, you will never know for sure. The very proof by means of which you think you are not merely a brain in a vat could be produced by the scientist who is stimulating you! In other words, skepticism claims neither that truth does not exist nor that it does exist; skepticism simply expresses the position that humans do not ever have the ability to know something, even if they are confronted by it.

Cratylus (see box) represents *radical* skepticism; he claimed that communication between people is impossible. Since everything is constantly changing, including words, the meaning of a word may change between the time it is spoken or written and the time the communication is received. Cratylus reportedly would move a finger to show that he had heard something spoken to him, but he would not reply, because he was unsure of the meaning of what he had heard. This form of skepticism is inconsistent with the goal of a critical reasoner. However, there is a form of skepticism that is not inconsistent with that goal; in fact, it is necessary. In its more constructive form, known as *methodological* skepticism, skepticism can prevent us from embracing a position prematurely or can cause us to examine beliefs that we have not previously examined critically. Methodological skepticism is crucial for the critical reasoner and does not necessarily conflict with relativism or objectivism.

Relativism

Relativism affirms the existence of truth. For the relativist, however, truth is dependent on what a group of people happen to believe is true. Truth thus is dependent on a society whose members share a particular belief. For example, is it true that "freedom of speech" implies no constraints on speech? Some in the United States advocate this, but in Canada one has freedom of speech as long as it does not inflict harm on others. What is meant by "freedom of speech" is relative to the society being discussed. For this reason, relativism is sometimes referred to as *societalism*. Applied to individuals, it is termed *subjectivism* or *individualism*.

During periods like the present, when members of different societies are increasingly likely to come into contact, relativism is very attractive. When we encounter members of other societies, we discover that they do not have the same beliefs that we do: Facts that we consider true they may not believe to be true. We then realize that we actually *create* truth by holding certain facts to be true.

Because of the large number of different societies, there is a temptation to maintain that what our society perceives as true may be true for us, but may not be true for members

Cratylus, a disciple of Heracleitus, who died around 480 B.C., taught that the world of sense perception was always changing and that it therefore was not a good source for discovering truth. Plato, born in 427 B.C., was influenced by Cratylus, a younger contemporary of Socrates, the teacher of Plato.

of another society. In its subjective form, this view is echoed in the claim, "What is true is true for me, and what you think is true is true for you." Attractive though such a claim may appear to be, critics point out that it is incoherent: It says, in effect, "There is no such thing as reality, but there are realities." However, if there are real*ities* (plural), then there must be *a* real*ity* (singular), just as, if there are philoso*phers*, then there must be a philosoph*er*. Also, some critics claim that it is difficult to keep relativism from collapsing into self-contradiction. A relativist might claim, for example, that the doctrines of Christianity are true because they are held to be true in a given society and that the doctrines of Buddhism are true because they are held to be true in a different given society. The one religious tradition, however, is theistic (i.e., it has a concept of god), whereas the other may be non-theistic (i.e., it does not have a concept of god). But then the relativist is claiming that both theism is true and nontheism is true, which is a contradiction. Moreover, both relativism (societalism) and subjectivism (individualism) make it impossible to evaluate alternative beliefs by means of any external criteria.

If, then, on the one hand, by 'relativism,' we mean that *all* truths are relative, relativism is incompatible with objectivism. Relativism is compatible with skepticism, but the objections just noted still hold. If, on the other hand, by 'relativism,' we mean that *some* truths are relative, the foregoing objections do not stand up, and relativism is compatible with objectivism. The term 'compatible' simply means that both positions can be true at the same time. Again, if we assert, "All truth is relative" and see this claim to be true, then we must reject any objectivist position. However, if we embrace "some truth is relative," then it is possible also to embrace an objectivist position.

Naive Objectivism

A third possible response to the question of whether truth exists is naive objectivism. This position claims that there is such a thing as truth and that human beings can and do attain or know it. Truth is something objective; the qualities that make it true are not dependent on any particular knower. Truth is also recognizable. Thus, we can be totally objective in the search for truth: If we satisfy certain criteria, we will discover truth. For example, consider the bumper sticker seen on some automobiles: "The Bible said it; I believe it; that settles it." The two criteria are the Bible saying it and my believing it. Now, if the Bible says it and I believe it, then the case is closed. There is nothing to question; the truth is obvious.

The "objectivity" espoused by naive objectivists was questioned by the German philosopher Immanuel Kant. (See box.) According to Kant, we all wear rose-colored glasses; that is, our presuppositions influence what and how we perceive. In the example of the bumper sticker, which Bible are we talking about? The Judeo–Christian Bible? The Quran? The Bhagavad-Gita? Depending on which it is, what we hold to be true will differ.

Immanuel Kant (1724–1804) claimed that our experiences of the world are influenced by our understanding. Our minds, to some extent, influences how we perceive the world around us. As a result, we never grasp something in our experience the way it really is.

Critical Objectivism

A fourth perspective on the existence of truth is critical objectivism. In this view, truth is external and objective. It exists independently of our knowledge of it, and it is possible that we never attain it. That is, although truth exists, we may fail to find it. While we are always operating within our own theories or worldviews, which may interfere with our ability to recognize truth, truth exists outside of our theories. Accordingly, even when scholars were claiming that the earth was flat, it was spherical. As critical objectivists, we recognize the possibility that we might be wrong; hence, we carefully examine and reexamine that which we claim to be true. Furthermore, unlike relativism, critical objectivism allows alternative beliefs to be evaluated by the use of external criteria. Moreover, a truth embraced by critical objectivists is true for all societies and individuals, even if they do not recognize it as true.

Because critical objectivism realizes that we operate within our own worldview, it recognizes the potential for error. In this respect, it is consistent with certain forms of relativism,

THE FAR SIDE® By GARY LARSON

"Say ... *you're* not Bob! ... You look like him, but
you're certainly not him!"

in that both hold that some truths are universal and others are relative. Critical objectivism presupposes methodological skepticism; however, it is inconsistent with naive objectivism.

Of the four perspectives we have examined, critical objectivism is most consistent with the goals of critical reasoning. Because it readily acknowledges the fallibility of human knowledge, critical reasoning is not consistent with naive objectivism; and because it accepts the use of external standards for examining some statements, critical reasoning denies total relativism. Unlike radical skepticism, critical objectivism holds hope for the discovery of truth.

In sum, the pursuit of truth is not a chase after an illusionary butterfly. The pursuit of truth is meaningful because it is possible to attain the goal. We can both pursue and attain truth, even if we do not attain all possible truths, but the pursuit will begin with our imagination, which is what frees us to pursue truth. As Charles Peirce expresses it,

> When a man desires ardently to know the truth, his first effort will be to imagine what that truth can be. He cannot prosecute his pursuit long without finding that imagination unbridled is sure to carry him off track. Yet, nevertheless, it remains true that there is, after all, nothing but imagination that can ever supply him an inkling of truth.[11]

Four Attitudes toward Truth

1. Skepticism
2. Relativism
3. Naive objectivism
4. Critical objectivism

2.3 CLEAR THINKING: CLARITY, RELEVANCE, AND CONSISTENCY

All good reasoning must be clear, relevant, and consistent.

These criteria will be examined closer in Chapter 3; however, some preliminary comments can be made at this point.

Clarity does not necessarily mean that every person should be able to understand what is being communicated. Many readers of this text will have failed to understand some of the reasoning in the preceding section, but that does not necessarily constitute a violation of clarity. A violation of clarity occurs when an ambiguity arises due to the author's failure to use correct grammar or syntax or failure to choose the correct word. A violation of clarity also occurs when the accenting of a word or phrase changes its intended meaning. An argument is clear when the intended audience can examine it and understand what the author intended to communicate.

Good reasoning should have *internal* relevance, meaning that the evidence offered for a claim must be about that claim. This criterion may be violated by replacing rational evidence with emotionalism[12] or with evidence that does not actually support the claim. Much, though not all, advertising exhibits violations of relevance. (Bikini-clad females or muscle-bound males are not reasons for purchasing a particular beverage!) The criterion of relevance is met only if the evidence helps support the claim. However, when an individual is unfamiliar with the subject of the reasoning or with the type of reasoning used, it is easy to conclude that a certain piece of reasoning violates relevance when in fact it does not.

The final criterion, consistency, simply requires that the statements included in the reasoning not contradict one another. For example, one cannot simultaneously assert both "It is raining here and now" and "It is not raining here and now." In good reasoning, all of the statements can be true simultaneously.[13]

The opinions which you bring to the study of logic comprise among them a system of logic all made. . . . Every reasoner, then, has some general idea of what good reasoning is. . . . He, therefore, comes to the study of logic handicapped by a conceit that he knows something about it already. . . . It is foolish, therefore, to study logic unless one is persuaded that one's own reasonings are more or less bad.[14]

CHAPTER THREE

Introduction to Arguments

Imagine a world without arguments. Would it be a better place than the world as it is?

When we think of an argument, what usually comes to mind is a verbal battle, the kind of conflict we might have experienced when we disagreed with our parents or friends. Arguments also occur between nations, sometimes going beyond verbal battles to actual armed conflict. From this perspective, a world in which arguments do not exist definitely would be a better place than the one we live in. For a logician, however, a world without arguments would be uneventful and sterile, a far worse place than the one we live in. This is because the logician's definition of the term *argument* differs from the everyday use of the word. In logic, an **argument** is a set of statements in which one or more statements provide support for another statement in that set. Since this is a technical definition, we will devote the first portion of the chapter to explaining it in detail.

3.1 CHARACTERISTICS OF ARGUMENTS

Basic Terms

To understand the definition of an argument, it is necessary to understand several other terms. The first of these terms is *statement*. In logic, a **statement** is a simple sentence that can be judged to be either true or false. Any declarative sentence can be a statement; however, such a sentence can contain more than one statement. For example, the sentence "John is using his computer and working on his term paper" contains two statements: "John is using his computer" and "John is working on his term paper."

Examine the following sets of sentences. The sentences in Set A are statements because they are simple sentences and can be judged to be either true or false.[15] The sentences in Set B are also simple sentences, but they are not statements, because they cannot be judged as either true or false.

Set A	*Set B*
It is raining.	Go close the window.
John is wearing a ring.	Is John wearing a ring?
Saturn has many rings.	How ridiculous he looked!

The sentences in Set B are a command, a question, and an exclamation, respectively. They are not statements. The sentences that are of interest to logicians are statements or are sentences composed of statements.

It is important to note that, when we identify a sentence as a statement, we are not making a claim about its truth-value. A sentence that has been identified as a statement can be judged to be either true or false. In other words, we can claim that a particular sentence *has* a truth-value without necessarily *deciding* or even *knowing* its truth-value (i.e., judging it to be true or false). Thus, a statement about the future has a truth-value, although at present we do not know what it is.

Statements can be linked together by grammatical or logical connectors. Two basic *grammatical* connectors are illustrated in the following examples:

1.   Tahita practices law in Texas, and Kathy works in California.
2.   Tahita practices law in Texas; Kathy works in California.

In the first example, the connector is a comma followed by a coordinating conjunction. In the second, the connector is a semicolon.

There are four basic *logical* connectors:

1.   Statements can be linked together with the word *and*. For example, the sentences "Peter attended Ubany University" and "Mary attended Ubany University" can be linked together to create a single statement, "Peter and Mary attended Ubany University."

2.   The word *or* can serve as a logical connector: "Peter or Mary attended Ubany University."

3.   Conditional sentences can serve as logical connectors: "If Peter attended Ubany University, then Mary also attended Ubany University."

4.   The phrase "if and only if" reflects a biconditional relationship between two statements: "Peter attended Ubany University if and only if Mary did." This concept is a little more difficult. In this case, if Peter attended Ubany, then Mary did, and if Peter did not attend Ubany, then Mary did not attend. Furthermore, if Mary attended, then Peter did, and if Mary did not attend, then Peter did not attend.

In sum, if a sentence contains one or more statements that are properly linked together with a grammatical or logical connector, it can be analyzed in logical terms.

A *proposition* is an extension of a statement. A **proposition** is the *meaning* of a statement. Often, the proposition contained in a statement is equivalent to the statement itself, as in "It is raining." However, a statement may express many different propositions.

Consider the statement, "I am hungry." Each time a new speaker utters this statement, it takes on a new meaning (i.e., it refers to that speaker's hunger and not the previous speaker's) and therefore expresses a new proposition.

Sometimes it is impossible to determine the proposition expressed by a statement without further information. Consider the statement, "Every race has a beginning." While the statement is clear, its meaning is not. Depending on the context, it could be referring to an athletic event or perhaps to an ethnic group. Whenever possible, logicians prefer to analyze *propositions* rather than statements.[16] Can you think of why logicians prefer to analyze propositions? What are some problems with this preference?

Components of Arguments

Now that we have examined some related terms, we can return to our definition of **argument**: *a set of statements in which one or more statements provide support for another statement in that set.* Note that while this is a technical definition used in logic, it is not really a new idea. English composition courses teach students that a good essay contains a thesis statement and evidence to support that thesis. This is, in effect, an argument.

It is also important to remember that, although arguments are made up of statements and propositions, arguments themselves do not have a truth-value. That is, there is no such thing as a true or false argument. Depending on the type of reasoning, an argument may be evaluated as either valid or invalid, or as strong, moderate, or weak. These kinds of evaluations are the focus of much of this text.

An argument *always* has two parts, one of which provides the evidence or support for the other. The part that offers the evidence is the **premise(s)**. At least one premise, either explicit or implicit, must be present for an argument to exist. Premises are statements and therefore can be judged to be either true or false. The part of an argument that presents the claim supported by the premise or premises is the **conclusion**. It, too, is a statement and therefore has a truth-value.

An argument exists if and only if both premise(s) and conclusion, whether explicit or implicit, are present. Moreover, in order for a conclusion to exist, there must also be a premise. Conversely, without a conclusion, there cannot be a premise. In other words, both a premise *and* a conclusion must be present for either to exist, and both must be present for an argument to exist. For example, I might say, "Spring has finally arrived." While I am making a claim, I have not presented a conclusion because I have not offered any evidence for the claim. However, an argument would exist if I said, "Spring has finally arrived because I saw a couple of robins building a nest yesterday." Notice that I have both a conclusion (Spring has finally arrived) and a premise (I saw a couple of robins building a nest yesterday).

Standard Form

After identifying an argument, logicians express it in what is termed **standard form**, a form of presentation in which it is easy to "see" the argument and its components. The standard form of an argument serves as the basis for all further analysis of that argument. To express an argument in standard form, the logician first lists all the premises separately and then draws a solid line to separate them from the conclusion, which is placed below the line and preceded by the symbol for "therefore" ($\therefore$).

Consider the following passage, which is an argument, but not in standard form:

> If an individual wishes to communicate effectively, then the study of logic is essential. This is clear because, if an individual wishes to communicate effectively, then certain ideas such as clarity, relevance, consistency, appropriate form, variety, and adequate information, must be understood. Furthermore, if these ideas are to be understood, then the study of logic is essential.

Clearly, the main point of this passage is "If an individual wishes to communicate effectively, then the study of logic is essential." This statement is supported by two others:

> If an individual wishes to communicate effectively, then certain ideas, such as clarity, relevance, consistency, appropriate form, variety, and adequate information, must be understood.
>
>   and
>
> If these ideas are to be understood, then the study of logic is essential.

In standard form, this argument would be presented as follows:

> If an individual wishes to communicate effectively, then certain ideas, such as clarity, relevance, consistency, appropriate form, variety, and adequate information, must be understood.
> If these ideas are to be understood, then the study of logic is essential.
> $\therefore$ If an individual wishes to communicate effectively, then the study of logic is essential.

Just as writers use transitional words to guide their readers, arguments can contain words that provide guidance. Often, they contain **indicator words** that aid in the identification of premises and conclusion and alert the reader to the presence of an argument. Some of these words point to premises and are called **premise indicators**. Following are some common premise indicators:

as indicated by	given that
as shown by	inasmuch as
assuming that	in view of
because	in view of the fact that
can be inferred from	insofar as
due to	may be deduced from
for	on the assumption that
for the reason that	since

There are also **conclusion indicators**, which suggest the presence of a conclusion. The following are the most common conclusion indicators:

accordingly	it follows that
allows us to infer that	leads me to believe that
as a result	points to the conclusion that
bears out the point that	proves that
consequently	so
entails that	suggests very strongly that
hence	then
I conclude that	therefore
implies that	we may deduce that
indicates that	which shows that

Technically, indicator words are not part of the argument. We therefore omit them when we present an argument in standard form.

While indicator words are helpful in identifying the components of arguments, their presence or absence is not meaningful in itself and in fact can be misleading. In the following example, there are no indicator words, yet the passage is an argument:

> If John attends class and works hard, then he will pass his logic course. Unfortunately, John eitherxz did not attend class or he did not work hard. John did not pass logic.

It is also important to note that sometimes indicator words are present, but do not in fact indicate a premise or conclusion. A prime example is the word *since*, which may be used as a premise indicator, as in "Since John studied logic, he had no problem on the LSAT," or in a temporal sense, as in "Since studying logic, John has improved his grades." The latter sentence is not an argument.

3.2 RECOGNIZING ARGUMENTS

Steps in Identifying Arguments

The most basic skill in logic—and in many ways one of the most difficult—is that of properly identifying an argument. There are several steps that can be taken in developing this skill. The first is to realize that the process of identifying arguments is not limited to logic; many reading and writing tasks require the identification of a main point and the evidence for it. Most college students already have the skill and can build on it. The second step is to pay close attention to grammar, punctuation, and key words such as indicator words; these can help in identifying a writer's reasoning process. Even when the reader is totally unfamiliar with a topic, if an argument is written carefully, it is possible to identify its premise and conclusion. Consider two slightly modified lines from *Beowulf*:

þāra ðe cwice hwyrfaþ. Thus, ðā driht-guman.

Ne gefeah hē þære fæhðe, because ac hē hine feor forwræc.

In the first line, which phrase represents the conclusion? In the second, which phrase may represent evidence?

While we cannot analyze the reasoning in these lines unless we can read Old English, we can still present the arguments in standard form:

þāra ðe cwice hwyrfaþ.   ac hē hine feor forwræc
∴ [ðā driht-guman.   ∴ Ne gefeah hē þære fæhðe

The third step, which cannot be emphasized enough, is *practice*. Whether reading a textbook, a professional journal, or the newspaper, a student of logic needs to practice looking for arguments.

Common Hurdles in Identifying Arguments

Before practicing the identification of arguments, we should note several common hurdles. First, *conditional sentences ("If . . . , then . . .") may be part of an argument, but do not by themselves form an argument*. Such a sentence may be a premise or a conclusion. However, the *antecedent* (the material between "if" and "then") and the *consequent* (the material that follows "then") cannot be separated by making the antecedent a premise and the consequent a conclusion. "If the bough breaks, then the cradle will fall" is not an argument, because no evidence is offered in support of any claim; the sentence simply describes how the world works.

Second, *since not all sentences are statements, not all sentences can be parts of arguments*. Questions, for example, cannot be parts of arguments. Note, however, that rules such as "questions are not parts of arguments" must be applied judiciously, for some apparent questions are not really questions. Imagine the following conversation between two college students:

S1: "Did you understand the assignment in physics last night?"

S2: "Is snow white?"

The second student's response is probably a rhetorical question and represents the proposition, "Yes, I understood the assignment."

Commands also are not statements. Generally, it is obvious when one has a command rather than a statement, as in the sentence "Don't drive the car today!" Since this is clearly just a command, with no evidence to support it, it is not an argument. Now consider what happens when we expand the sentence:

The roads are bad, and the car doesn't have snow tires; don't drive the car today.

Is *this* an argument? It appears that the two sentences could be presented in standard form as follows:

```
        The roads are bad.
        The car doesn't have snow tires.
        ∴      Don't drive the car today.
```

On the one hand, the statements about the roads and the lack of snow tires seem to offer evidence of the "conclusion." On the other hand, there are two clues suggesting that an argument is *not* present. First, in spite of the apparent connection between the first two statements and the sentence "Don't drive the car today," there is actually no connection. The two statements may provide evidence for some claim, but they do not provide evidence for the third sentence. Therefore, an argument is not present.

The second clue lies in the last sentence. This sentence is merely a command; it is not a statement. As we have seen, for an argument to be present, both the premise(s) and the conclusion must be statements. Therefore, even the expanded sentence (now three sentences) is not an argument.

This introduces a third hurdle to be overcome in identifying arguments: *All written material is subject to interpretation*. To the extent possible, logicians should take into consideration the author's meaning. If one is working with statements, one works only with the text as written. At that level, it is correct to say that the sentences "The roads are bad, and the car doesn't have snow tires; don't drive the car today" do not constitute an argument. However, if one is working with propositions—that is, with the *meanings* of statements—a question arises: Did the author mean exactly what is said, or can the sentence be interpreted as "The roads are bad; the car doesn't have snow tires, so it would be best if you did not drive today"? If we decide that this is an accurate or at least plausible interpretation, then an argument does exist and can be presented in standard form as follows:

```
        The roads are bad.
        The car does not have snow tires.
        ∴      It would be best if you did not drive today.
```

Whenever a logician takes the liberty of supplying an interpretative translation, an error is possible because the interpretation is an assumption and it becomes the basis for analyzing the passage. However, if we do not take such liberties, often no analysis is possible. When we interpret a passage for its meaning, analysis can proceed, possibly leading to new insights; this process of interpretative translation is known as the **principle of clarity**. The principle allows us to make explicit ideas that we believe are implied in the materials being examined. The principle is for the purpose of clarifying the author's point or intention. The principle of clarity should never be used in a fashion that clearly changes the author's meaning. More will be said about assumptions in Section 3.4.

A fourth hurdle to be overcome in identifying arguments concerns *explanations, examples, and illustrations*. Consider the following passages:

1. Statistics tell us that few people become farmers unless they grew up on a farm. Several explanations for this phenomenon are possible, but I believe the best explanation is that the training required to be a farmer cannot be taught in a four-year college program, but requires ten to fifteen years of hands-on experience.

2. A diamond is the hardest substance. For example, a diamond can cut even steel.

3.   Most of our prelaw majors benefit from taking "Introduction to Logic." To illustrate, last year's prelaw graduates who had taken logic averaged a 173 on their LSAT.

Logicians generally do not think of explanations, examples, and illustrations as arguments. In an explanation like (1), the reasoning process is the reverse of that which takes place in an argument. Whereas in an argument the conclusion follows from or is supported by the evidence (i.e., the evidence leads to the conclusion), in an explanation we discover a fact and then seek a principle which explains that fact. Similarly, examples and illustrations may appear to be arguments, but they contain no evidence. In passages (2) and (3), the "evidence" simply highlights the claim.

Here is another example: "Shakespeare wrote many famous tragedies, including *Hamlet, Romeo and Juliet*, and *King Lear*." Observe that the three titles do not provide evidence that Shakespeare wrote many famous tragedies; they merely are examples of tragedies written by Shakespeare.

There are, however, times when we generalize from cases or examples. Consider the following passage:

Example A is a home in Forest Hill and it is brick.
Example B is a home in Forest Hill and it is brick.
Example C is a home in Forest Hill and it is brick.
Example D is a home in Forest Hill and it is brick.
Example E is a home in Forest Hill and it is brick.
Example G is a home in Forest Hill and it is brick.
Example H is a home in Forest Hill and it is brick.
Therefore, most homes in Forest Hill are brick.

This passage is composed of numerous examples. Is an argument present? Yes: We can generalize from the examples to reach a conclusion. Just because a passage contains examples does not mean that no argument exists.

Consider the following two similar passages:

I have just claimed that Jonesville has the lowest crime rate of any city in the county. There are only half as many robberies as in North Adams, for instance.

I have just claimed that Jonesville has the lowest crime rate of any city in the county. To illustrate this, I have prepared this overhead transparency that lists all the categories of crime within the county and the number of crimes in each category for each city in the county.

Is either of these passages an argument? In the first passage, the illustration was probably included not to provide evidence, but "merely" to illustrate a point; no argument is present. In the second passage, an argument exists. Examples and illustrations may be part of an argument if the author clearly intended them to serve as evidence.

Finally in relation to explanations, it is possible to *reconstruct* a passage that contains an explanation. Such a reconstruction enables the critical thinker to evaluate the reasoning process exhibited in the explanation. Here is a reconstruction of the explanation concerning farming presented earlier:

> The training required to be a farmer cannot be taught in a four-year college program, but requires ten to fifteen years of hands-on experience. Therefore, few people become farmers unless they grew up on a farm.

The relationship between explanation and argument is discussed further in Section 3.6.

A fifth reason that arguments may be difficult to identify is that *some arguments are not fully stated*. That is, sometimes one or more premises or the conclusion is not explicitly stated. As a case in point, examine the following passage:

> The construction of an atom smasher in Texas would have greatly benefited our state. Not only would it have enhanced our status in the academic community and made us a world leader in the field; it also would have meant an increase in employment for our fellow Texans. It would have brought into our communities some leading scientists and technicians and, of course, their money.

While this passage contains a minor conclusion, note that the major conclusion, "We should have built the atom smasher in Texas," is not explicitly stated. The statement is clearly implied, however, and thus an argument does exist. If the argument were presented in standard form, the implied conclusion would be made explicit by being placed below the line.

The final common hurdle faced in identifying arguments stems from our desire to evaluate them. We want to know whether an argument is "good." Unfortunately, we have a tendency to try to evaluate the argument even before we properly identify it. The process of *identifying* an argument must always remain separate from the process of *evaluating* the argument. Even if the author of the following passage intended it to be an argument, and we identified the passage as an argument, it would not necessarily be considered a "good" argument:

> I have just claimed that Jonesville has the lowest crime rate of any city in the county. There are only half as many robberies in Jonesville as in North Adams, for instance.

Identification and Evaluation are Different Activities

Only after an argument has been identified does the logician evaluate it to determine whether it is a "good" argument.

In sum, the process of identifying arguments is not simply a matter of following a set of rules. Often, interpretation or reconstruction is needed as well. Thus, logic is as much an art as it is a science.

3.3 EXERCISE: IDENTIFYING ARGUMENTS

Examine each of the problems that follow, and decide whether an argument is present. If an argument is present, rewrite the argument in standard form. If an argument is not present, briefly explain why you think it is not.

Six Common Hurdles

1. Conditional sentences may be <u>part of</u> an argument, but, by themselves, do not <u>form</u> an argument.
2. Not all sentences are statements; therefore, not all sentences can be part of an argument.
3. Frequently, the identification of an argument requires interpretation.
4. Illustrations, examples, and explanations may or may not be part of an argument.
5. There are times that one or more premises or the conclusion of an argument is not explicitly stated.
6. Identification and evaluation are different activities.

1. If it rains, then I will take my umbrella.
*2. John received an A in logic, as did Betty and Peter. We can conclude that Paula also received an A in logic, because the four of them were in the same class and usually receive the same grades.
3. A bird in the hand is better than two on wing.
*4. Don't forget your umbrella—it's raining.
5. Since he received his Ph.D., he surely will have a job.
6. If logic is essential for good writing, then a person who wants to be a good writer must study logic. Logic is essential for good writing. Therefore, John, who wants to be a good writer, must study logic.
7. "A moment can be eons of separation if love is involved." (Gibran)
8. When mixed with water, sulfuric acid creates a violent reaction; consequently, one must take care not to mix acid with water.
*9. Since he received his Ph.D., he has been teaching at Shelton University.
10. When mixed with water, sulfuric acid creates a violent reaction.
11. Every person is a self-made person, but only the successful admit it.
12. If salt is mixed with water, it will dissolve. This pan is full of water, so if I put salt in it, the salt will dissolve.
13. Since thirteen is my unlucky number, I probably should avoid this problem.
*14. If salt is mixed with water, it will dissolve.
15. Winners concentrate on winning, but losers concentrate on just getting by. Coach Sullivan does not concentrate on just getting by. He is a winner.
*16. Last year I visited the Fort Worth Zoo, the Dallas Zoo, and the Fort Wayne Zoo. I especially enjoyed the exotic-bird section at each zoo. Consequently, next week when I visit the Miami Zoo, I will be looking forward to the exotic-bird section.
17. "Every new opinion at its start is precisely in the minority of one." (Thomas Carlyle)

*18.   "The man who never reads will never be read; he who never quotes will never be quoted. He who will not use the thoughts of other men's brains proves he has no brain of his own. You need to read." (Charles Spurgeon)

19.   Next semester, Mandie hopes to take either metaphysics or epistemology. She will take epistemology only if Professor Holms teaches the class. It seems that Mandie will be taking metaphysics, since I just heard that Professor Holms will be on leave next semester.

20.   Please help keep the park clean—others may want to use it.

21.   "Maturity is the capacity to face unpleasantness and frustration, discomfort and defeat without complaint, collapse, or attempting to find someone to blame." (Ann Landers)

*22.   Jonesville has the lowest crime rate in this area. For example, its murder statistics are over 50% lower than those of any other city in the area.

23.   "America's a free country, kid! That means, if you don't get a haircut, I can kick the crap out of you." (Cochran)

24.   New Jersey farmers rejected the first successful cast-iron plow, which was invented in the United States in 1797, because they believed that cast iron poisoned the land and that it stimulated the growth of weeds.

25.   "There is no peace in the world today, because there is no peace in the minds of men." (U Thant)

26.   If Peter and Joan had attended the party and had dressed in their usual fashion, the party would have been a great success. Unfortunately, neither Peter nor Joan attended.

27.   Don't forget to buy the required texts for this class. Of course, I am assuming that you want to pass.

28.   "I have only been a child gathering shells and pebbles on the shore of the great ocean of truth." (Leonardo da Vinci)

*29.   Listen, the statistics prove that such a building as the one proposed has provided durable housing in other parts of the country. It is highly energy efficient and relatively inexpensive to construct and maintain. Furthermore, it would be adequate for both our present needs and our projected future needs.

30.   "He that to what he sees, adds observation, and to what he reads, reflection, is on the right road to knowledge, provided that in scrutinizing the hearts of others, he neglects not his own." (Charles Colton)

31.   "It is not enough to give theoretic assent to a truth clearly formulated, for example, by Aquinas; we must also do for our time the great work which he did for his. This means that we shall have to understand our time in its living continuity with the whole past. The historical consciousness of the true Christian is an indispensable condition of fulfilling the role of a Christian philosopher." (Father P. Hug)

32.   "If you would learn anything of lasting benefit, seek to be unknown and little esteemed of men. For a true knowledge and understanding of himself is man's highest and most profitable lesson." (Thomas à Kempis)

33. "The presumption that any current opinion is not wholly false, gains in strength according to the number of its adherents. . . . ; we must admit that the convictions entertained by many minds in common are most likely to have some foundation." (Herbert Spencer)

34. "As, therefore, we can have no dependence upon morality without religion—so, on the other hand, there is nothing better to be expected from religion without morality." (Laurence Sterne)

35. "It is not that I am afraid to fail; it's that I fear succeeding at that which does not matter." (Howard Hendricks)

36. "I put modern history aside, not only because there is a lack of distinctive character about men nowadays, but because our historians are so much concerned with producing an impression that they aim mainly at making highly colored portraits, often representing nothing much." (Jean Jacques Rousseau)

37. "A man was more precious than gold to the guards. If one head was missing behind the barbed wire, a guard would take his place." (Aleksandr Solzhenitsyn)

3.4 ASSUMPTIONS

Imagine the following argument:

Julie is a Maltese.
Sammy is a Manx.
Mandie is a tabby.
David is a Persian.
∴   Brian probably loves cats.

This argument does not make sense without the reader making some type of connections almost without realizing it, because the evidence does not seem to support the conclusion. That is, it is unclear how the premises are related to the conclusion. For the argument to work, the "bridge" that connects the evidence to the conclusion must be made explicit. Such a "bridge" is an assumption.

Assumptions are evidence or conditions that must be true for an argument to make sense; they are portions of the argument that are *assumed* by the reasoner. When we identify assumptions, we are interested only in conditions that are necessary for an argument to work. In the example just given, two assumptions are made. First, a Maltese, a Manx, a tabby, and a Persian are all types of cats. If "Maltese" referred to a bird and "Persian" to a person's ethnic heritage, the argument would not make sense. Second, Brian is the proud owner of these four cats. If the cats referred to belonged to anyone else, the argument would fail to make sense.

Every reasoner makes some assumptions when presenting an argument. However, not every assumption is crucial for a given argument, and those which are not crucial need not be made explicit. A test for determining whether an assumption is crucial is the **denial test**. In this test, the statement that is thought to be an assumption is logically denied. For example, suppose that we are considering the statement "The four cats named in the previous argument all meow softly" as an assumption underlying the argument. Then we would restate it as "The four cats named in the previous argument do not all meow softly." If this new statement (i.e., the negation of the original) is true, does it affect the argument? It does not; therefore, the original statement is not a crucial assumption.

Notice however, what happens to the argument when we apply the denial test to the two assumptions we made earlier:

At least one of Maltese, a Manx, a tabby, and a Persian is not a type of cat.
Brian is not the proud owner of these four cats.

If either of these statements is true, the argument fails. Hence, the original statements are crucial assumptions.

Once we identify a crucial assumption, we can consider the first step in evaluating an argument. This step consists of asking, Is this assumption warranted? That is, are there good reasons for accepting or not accepting the assumption? An argument can be strengthened by shoring up the crucial assumption, but the argument can also be weakened by eroding the assumption. The assumption is shored up by supplying additional evidence for it. Conversely, the assumption can be eroded by offering evidence against it.

3.5 EXERCISE: IDENTIFYING ASSUMPTIONS

Examine each of the arguments that follow. First, identify the premise(s) and conclusion. Then, using the denial test, determine the crucial assumption made in the reasoning. Finally, write the argument, including its crucial assumption, in standard form.

1. During the first class meeting, Professor Smith promised to curve the grades at the end of the semester. However, ten people failed the course, so Professor Smith could not have curved the grades as promised.

2. A citizen's group is protesting the local police department's response to the large number of accidents resulting from high-speed chases by police officers. To address the problem, the police department increased the hours of classroom instruction dealing with such chases. The citizen's group claims that the police department should rethink its approach to this problem.

*3. Recently, a large number of elm trees on our street died. Two explanations for the demise have been offered. First, the trees died because of the lower-than-average rainfall for the past three years. Second, in trying to combat fire ants, someone on the street must have used a chemical that poisoned the trees. However, other elm trees in our immediate area have not been harmed by the lower-than-average rain falls. Therefore, someone has poisoned the trees.

4. Miracle Drug X is not safe for human consumption. Even though the drug has been approved in France, England, and Germany, the U.S. Food and Drug Administration has not given its approval.

5. The trip this summer to Lansing, Michigan, should be a breeze. For the past six summers, I have made the trip without the slightest hitch. Furthermore, this year I will have my new car to drive, instead of that old bucket of bolts I have driven before.

3.6 EXPLANATIONS VERSUS JUSTIFICATIONS

In Section 3.2, we indicated that logicians generally do not consider explanations to be arguments. Rather, logicians maintain that explanations and arguments perform different roles in reasoning. We can understand these roles by noting the distinction between an explanation and a justification. An **explanation** presents evidence *why* something has taken place. A **justification**, in contrast, presents evidence *that* something is the case. Consider the following story:

> Recently, a student approached me after class, saying. "I must apologize. I did not turn in my research paper today. My kid brother has a gerbil that will eat anything that is sweet. Well, after printing my paper, I laid the diskette, which contained my paper, and the hard copy on the table. Would you believe that the gerbil got out and accidentally spilled honey on my paper and the diskette? As I said, that gerbil will eat anything sweet! I'll have to start my research all over. Can I take an incomplete for the semester?"

This story illustrates both explanation and justification. While the gerbil's action does not *justify* the student's failure to turn in the required paper, it does *explain* the failure: It tells us *why* the student failed to submit the paper. On the other hand, the gerbil's eating of the diskette and hard copy *is* a justification. Since the gerbil will eat anything that is sweet, and the honey on the diskette and hard copy was sweet, we find reasons that the gerbil ate the paper and diskette. Thus, we have a justification for the gerbil's action (though, again, not for the student's failure to submit the paper). Explanations focus on showing *why* an action occurred, whereas justifications focus on showing *that* it occurred. The distinction between them depends on their purpose.

While there are no hard-and-fast rules for distinguishing explanations from justifications, there are some steps that can help in the process. After carefully reading a passage and looking for indicator words, ask the following questions: (1) What claim, if any, is being made? (2) If a claim is being made, what evidence is offered for that claim? (3) Is the evidence intended to show *why* (explanation) something happened or *that* (justification) it happened? If an argument exists, the first question will identify the conclusion, the second will identify potential premises, and the third will clarify the relationship between the evidence and the claim. However, this distinction may be too narrow for the critical reasoner. At the beginning of this chapter, an argument was defined as a set of statements, one or more of which provide support for one of the other statements. An argument presents the *reasoning* process that connects premises with conclusion. Whether a passage contains a justification or an explanation, if the passage presents a reasoning process, then an argument is present. Furthermore, as pointed out earlier, in some cases an explanation may be interpreted and presented as an argument.

3.7 EXERCISE: IDENTIFYING AND INTERPRETING ARGUMENTS

Paying close attention to indicator words, analyze each of the selections that follow, and decide whether an argument is present. If an argument is present, write it in standard form. Remember, the task here is to *identify* an argument if one is present, not to evaluate it.

3.7A

1. The treatment of Afghan women is so brutally horrific; in fact, they're being denied the necessities of life. A July 1997 edict prohibits women from picking up food at distribution centers; a male relative must fetch it for them. As a result, the many thousands of women whose husbands, sons, fathers, and brothers were killed fighting Soviet invaders from 1979 to 1989—and in the four-year civil war that began in 1992—must resort to begging to survive. Another decree, issued in September 1997, limits medical care for women and girls. ("The Country That Has Declared All-Out War on Women," *Glamour*)

*2. There is a difference between a need for information during a period of uncertainty and an almost vulturelike picking over of the bodies afterward. For example, it was important to know that Carolyn Bessette Kennedy's prescription bottle and her sister Lauren's luggage tag had washed upon the beach because they confirmed the plane had gone into the ocean. ("Why We Want the Dirty Details," *Cosmopolitan*)

3. All road users, be they motorists, pedestrians or cyclists, are subject to the same rules of the road, dictated by the laws of physics. No two bits of matter can occupy the same space at the same time. If you want others to keep out of your way when it's your turn, then you must keep out of their way when it's their turn. Therefore you must adhere to the rules of the road. (*Bicycling Magazine*)

4. Whatever the case, with the biotech revolution we find ourselves in the ironic situations of becoming empowered to alter our genetics—and eventually these ethical inclinations—more swiftly and more dramatically than ever before, acquiring this power just as we are beginning to understand the genetic roots and original survival advantages of those same ethical inclinations. Thus we gain a capacity to change that which we don't yet fully understand and run the risk of doing what we have mistakenly done in the past: upset the balance of nature, suffer the consequences then scramble to fix our errors. (*The Humanist*)

5. It is illogical to assume that the average American congregation will endorse significant social changes through consensus. There are ultimately too many [people in] positions of leadership within the church who want to retain the status quo. A church desirous of growth must be willing to face confrontation of issues brought by the few. Consequently, the church must see the minority at work within it as precious to it's life. (*The Humanist*)

6. Every group and organization has some kind of power structure. A power structure that is never challenged ultimately leads to sterility. The "pressure group," or minority in most situations, comes nearer to representing the voice of conscience. The maturity of a congregation is measured, therefore, to the degree that the possibilities of controversy are made real. (*The Humanist*)

7.   At any age, teasing and bullying are harmful and can create a classroom cli-mate that negatively affects children's ability to learn and teachers' ability to teach. Therefore, it seems critical for teachers and parents to address this behavior in early childhood before it becomes ingrained. ("On Purpose: Addressing Teasing and Bullying in Early Childhood," *Young Children*)

8.   In ordinary mind we perceive the stream of thoughts as continuous. You will discover for yourself that there is a gap between each thought. When the past thought is past, and the future thought has not yet arisen, you will always find a gap in which the Rigpa is revealed. So, the work of meditation is to allow thoughts to slow down, to make that gap become more and more apparent. (Sogyal Rinpoche, *Glimpse after Glimpse: Daily Reflections on Living and Dying*)

9.   The basis on which Buddhists accept the concept of rebirth is principally the continuity of consciousness. If you trace our present mind or consciousness back, then you will find that you are tracing the origin of the continuity of mind into an infinite dimension. It is beginningless. Therefore, there must be successive rebirths that allow that continuum of the mind to be there. (Sogyal Rinpoche, *Glimpse after Glimpse: Daily Reflections on Living and Dying*)

10. We cannot hope to die peacefully if our lives have been full of violence. Also if our minds have mostly been agitated by emotions like anger, attachment, or fear. So if we wish to die well, we must learn to live well. (Sogyal Rinpoche, *Glimpse after Glimpse: Daily Reflections on Living and Dying*)

3.7B
The following selections are from the work of Roger Boscovich. (See box.)[17]

1.   But my theory differs in marked degree from that of Leibniz. For one thing, because it does not admit the continuous extension that arises from the idea of consecutive, non-extended points touching one another. . . . For another thing, it admits homogeneity amongst the elements, all distinction between masses depending on relative position only, and different combinations on the ele-ments. (p. 19)

After receiving his primary and secondary education at the local Jesuit col-lege, **Roger Boscovich** (1711–1787) became a member of the Jesuit order and was sent to Rome to study philosophy, physics, and mathematics in 1725. As a teacher, a scientist, and a diplomat for the Church of Rome, Boscovich traveled extensively. Because of his scientific reputation, he was allowed into countries that had closed their borders to members of the order. Many of Boscovich's views regarding physics have only recently been fully appreciated. For example, he sug-gested that space, time, and motion are relative. Also, Boscovich's concept of molecular structure was studied by scientists such as Faraday and Maxwell, who contributed so much to our modern understanding of electricity and magnetism.

*2. If matter is continuous, it may and must be subject to infinite divisibility; but actual division carried on indefinitely brings in its train difficulties that are truly inextricable; however, this infinite division is required by those who do not admit that there are any particles, no matter how small, in bodies that are perfectly free from, and incapable of, compression. (25)

3. So that there is only an infinity of possible points, but not of existing points; and with regard to these possible points, I usually term the whole series of possibilities a series that ends at finite limits at infinity. This for the reason that any of them that exist must be finite in number; but there is no finite number of things that exist so great that other numbers, greater and greater still, but yet all finite, cannot be obtained. (46)

4. But as a matter of fact, there cannot possibly be a last stage or a first; just as there cannot be a last ordinate or a first in the curve. . . . Given any short line, no matter how short, there will be others shorter than it, less and less in infinite succession without any limit whatever; and in this, as we remarked also above, there lies the nature of continuity. Hence anyone who brings forward the idea of a first or a last in the case of a line, or a force, or a degree of velocity, or an interval of time, must be ignorant of continuity. (50)

5. For long ago it was observed that, when a ray of light is reflected, it is not reflected entirely in such a manner that the angle of reflection is equal to the angle of incidence, but that a part of it is dispersed in all directions. For this reason, if a ray of light from the Sun falls upon some part of a mirror, anybody who is in the room sees where the ray strikes the mirror; and this certainly would not be the case, unless some of the solar rays reached his eye directly issuing from the mirror in all those directions that reach to all positions that the eye might be in. (62)

*6. If universal gravity obeys the law of a force inversely proportional to the square of the distance . . . , sensibly unchanged only throughout the planetary and cometary system, it will certainly be the case that the curve of forces will not have the last arm PV asymptotic with the straight line AC as the asymptote, but will again cut the axis and wind about it. (69)

7. If the three points do not lie in a straight line, then indeed without the presence of an external force they cannot be in equilibrium; unless all three distances, which form the sides of the triangle, are those corresponding to the limit-points. For, since the mutual forces do not have opposite directions, either a single force from one of the remaining two points acts on the third, or two such forces. Hence, there must be for that third point some motion, either in the direction of the straight line joining it to the acting point, or along the diagonal of the parallelogram whose sides represent those two forces. (91)

8. Draw a straight line from the beginning to the end of this motion, and take any plane perpendicular to this line produced beyond all the points; then the center of gravity would approach towards the plane, in the second part of the continuous time, through an interval equal to the straight line, but in the first part of the time there would have been no approach at all; hence the approaches would not have been proportional to those parts of the continuous time. Hence the center of gravity is always at rest, or is always in motion. (103)

9.   The third kind of law agrees with the mutual law of points in the fact that it
      pertains to local motion of the mind itself, to a definite position which it has
      with regard to the body, and to the definite arrangement of the organs. Thus,
      while the arrangement persists, upon which life depends, the mind must of
      necessity change its position, as the body changes its position, and that on
      account of some connection of the necessary type, and not a free connection.
      (189)

*10.   When either objects external to us, or our organs change their modes of exis-
       tence in such a way that the first equality of similitude does not remain con-
       stant, then indeed the ideas are altered, and there is a feeling of change; but the
       ideas are the same exactly, . . . In every case our ideas refer to the difference
       between the new state and the old, and not to the absolute change, . . . Thus,
       whether the stars move around the Earth, or the Earth and ourselves move in
       the opposite direction around them, the ideas are the same, and there is the
       same sensation. (203)

3.7C
The following selections are from Joseph Le Conte. (See box.)[18]

1.   The process pervades the whole universe, and the doctrine concerns alike
      every department of science, yea, every department of human thought. It is lit-
      erally one half of all science. Therefore, its truth or falseness, its acceptance or
      rejection, is no trifling matter, affecting only one small corner of the thought
      realm. (3–4)

2.   As society advances, the constituent members begin to diverge, some taking
      on one social function and some another, until in the highest stages of social
      organization this diversification or division and subdivision of labor reaches its
      highest point, and each member of the aggregate can do perfectly but one
      thing. Thus, the social organism becomes more and more strongly bound
      together by mutual dependence, and separation becomes mutilation. (25)

*3.   Let us again remind the reader that evolution means, first of all, continuity.
       The law of evolution, although it doubtless means much more, means, first of
       all, a law of continuity, or causal relation throughout Nature. It means that,
       alike in every department of Nature, each state or condition grew naturally out
       of the immediately preceding. (53)

> **Joseph LeConte** (1823–1901) is remembered for his contributions to educa-
> tion and the natural sciences. He was instrumental in organizing the University
> of California. In 1892, LeConte joined forces with John Muir and helped orga-
> nize the Sierra Club. Joseph LeConte's *Elements of Geology* was considered a
> standard text in the field for many years. His contributions to science led to his
> election to the National Academy of Sciences in 1874.

4.   Evolution, therefore, is no longer a school of thought. The words "evolutionism" and "evolutionist" ought not any longer to be used, any more than "gravitationism" and "gravitationists"; for the law of evolution is as certain as the law of gravitation. (66)

5.   Natural selection is a theory of origin of adaptive structures rather than of origin of species. Comparing to a growing tree, once admit lateral buds started, and natural selection completely accounts for the growth in different directions, and therefore for the profuse ramification; but the origin of the lateral buds is not explained. (76)

*6.   Organic evolution is by necessary law, human progress by free or at least by freer law. Organic evolution is by a pursuing upward and onward from above and in front by the attractive force of ideals. In a word, organic evolution is by the law of force, human evolution by the law of love. (88)

7.   If individual or race gets off the straight, narrow way toward the highest—the divine ideal—it is hard, very hard to get back on the track. Hard, I say, but not impossible, because man's conscious voluntary effort is the chief factor in his own evolution. (91)

8.   In all these the physical factors are at first powerfully operative; these become subordinate to organic factors, and these, in their turn, to psychical and rational factors. Therefore, as the individual in its early stages—i.e., in embryo and infancy—is peculiarly plastic under the influence of the physical environment, and afterward become more and more independent of these; so a species when first formed is more plastic under the influences of Lamarckian factors, and afterwards become more rigid to the same. (95)

9.   In all vertebrates, and in none other, the axis of this skeleton is a jointed backbone (vertebral column) inclosing and protecting the nervous centers (cerebra–spinal axis). These, therefore, may well be called backboned animals. (111)

*10.   Long experience has shown that very close breeding of the same variety for a long time fixes the kind but weakens the stock, especially in fertility, while judicious crossing of varieties strengthens the stock, increasing its fertility, and especially producing plasticity or variability. Therefore, breeders, if they wish to preserve a valuable variety, breed close; but, if they wish to make new varieties, cross-breed. (236)

3.7D
The following selections are from Herbert Spencer. (See box.)[19]

*1.   But this is not true. For a belief which gains extensive reception without critical examination, is thereby proved to have a general congruity with the various other beliefs of those who receive it. (4)

2.   Later in the progress of civilization, as during the middle ages in Europe, the current opinions respecting the relationship of rulers and ruled are further changed. For the theory of divine origin, there is substituted that divine right.

> **Herbert Spencer** (1820–1903) attempted to apply the theory of evolution to all areas of knowledge. Spencer accepted the Kantian distinction between experience and reality itself. Hence, when we have an experience, we cannot know whether it is real, since knowledge is limited to the realm of experience.

No longer god or demigod, or even god-descended, the king is now regarded as simply God's vice-regent. (6)

3.   As, to the religious, it will seem absurd to set forth any justification for Religion; so, to the scientific, will it seem absurd to defend Science. (18)

4.   For some centuries we have been asserting in practice, and have now established in theory, the right of every man to choose his own religious beliefs, instead of receiving such beliefs on State-authority. Within the last few generations we have inaugurated complete liberty of speech, in spite of all legislative attempts to suppress or limit it. And still more recently we have claimed and finally obtained under a few exceptional restrictions, freedom to trade with whomsoever we please. Thus our political beliefs are widely different from ancient ones. (8)

*5.   Hence if knowledge cannot monopolize conscious—if it must always continue possible for the mind to dwell upon that which transcends knowledge; then there can never cease to be a place for something of the nature of Religion; since Religion under all its forms is distinguished from everything else in this, that its subject matter is that which passes the sphere of experience. (17)

*6.   Making a more rational estimate of human authority, we shall avoid alike the extremes of undue submission and undue rebellion—shall not regard some men's judgments as wholly good and others as wholly bad; but shall rather lean to the more defensible position that none are completely right and none are completely wrong. (12–13)

7.   In thus excluding the idea of any antecedent cause, we necessarily exclude the idea of a beginning; for to admit the idea of a beginning—to admit that there was a time when the existence had not commenced—is to admit that its commencement was determined by something, or was caused; which is a contradiction. (32)

8.   We have no state of consciousness answering to the words—an inherent necessity by which potential existence became actual existence. To render them into thought, existence, having for an indefinite period remained in one form, must be conceived as passing without any external or additional impulse, into another form; and this involves the idea of a change without a cause—a thing of which no idea is possible. Thus the terms of this hypothesis do not stand for real thought; but merely suggest the vaguest symbols incapable of any interpretation. (33–34)

9.   And if the religious sentiment, displayed habitually by the majority of mankind, and occasionally aroused even in those seemingly devoid of it, must be classed among human emotions, we cannot rationally ignore it. (15)

10. Thus as Space and Time cannot be either non-entities, nor the attributes of entities, we have no choice but consider them as entities. (49)

3.7E
The following selections are from Bernard Ramm. (See box.)[20]

1. Sometimes he was woefully ignorant of the simplest facts of science. It must be kept in mind that university training up to the early part of the twentieth century was principally literary and classical. Science courses and scientific laboratories on the grand scale now found in the modern university are strictly phenomena of the twentieth century. Most clergy were trained in the classics, and were strangers to the sciences. Therefore, they did not even have the facts to create a telling strategy. (18)

2. We conclude that it is impossible for us to follow the pattern set by the hyper-orthodox in their proposed relationship of Christianity to science. Their efforts in the past have increased the gap between Christianity and the scientists, have embittered the scientists, and have done little to provide a working theory of any creative dimensions for the rapprochement of science and evangelicalism. (25)

3. If we believe that the God of creation is the God of redemption, and that the God of redemption is the God of creation, then we are committed to some very positive theory of harmonization between science and evangelicalism. God cannot contradict His speech in Nature by His speech in Scripture. If the Author of Nature and Scripture are the same God, then the two books of God must eventually recite the same story. Therefore, in place of resentment or suspicion or vilification toward science and scientists, we must have a spirit of respect and gratitude. (25)

*4. The theological, the ethical, and the practical are so conjoined in the Bible with the statements about Nature or creation that it is impossible to separate them, and to impugn one is to impugn the other. It is therefore suicidal for the hyper-orthodox to pass by the findings of science which cannot but have a most important bearing on the Biblical references to Nature and matters of fact; and it is inconsistent for the neo-orthodox to try to separate neatly the theological elements of the Bible from the statements about Nature and facts. (26)

5. We, therefore, in speaking of science mean to emphasize that body of knowledge dealing with the structure and causal or functional relationships of the

Bernard Ramm (1916–1992), one of the foremost American evangelical theologians of the twentieth century, sought to defend the historical Christian faith while openly conducting a dialogue with the modern world. As an evangelical theologian, Ramm attempted to maintain a balance between fundamentalists, on the one hand, and liberals, on the other.

physical and space–time aspects of the universe. Hence, our emphasis is on that which is external in contrast to the internal; on that which is causal or determined in contrast to that which is free or novel or spontaneous; on that which is capable of description by law in contrast to that which is unique; and on that which is based on the continuous or uniform or regular in contrast to that which is novel, vertical, and occasional. (34–35)

6.   The first feature of the Biblical view of Nature is that it is very frank creationism. God is the Almighty Creator of heaven and earth. Therefore, Nature exists fundamentally for spiritual purposes, and is capable of teleological explanation. (56)

7.   In that the Hebrew people had such a magnificent view of Nature due to their revealed knowledge of God, and because they were observant and conversant with Nature, we can expect some of their inferences and statements to accord with modern science. (86)

8.   However, we prefer the interpretation of Delitzsche. First of all he rejects the interpretation that the ocean girdles the earth, as the radical critical scholars have so imagined. He claims that this is an importation into the text. . . . Next, he says that the meaning of the verse is that God has set a boundary to the extent of the ocean. . . . So interpreted the verse does not refer to the sphericity of the earth, but to the divinely drawn boundaries of the ocean. (92)

9.   The ocean is the world's thermostat. It takes a large loss of heat for water to pass from liquid to ice, and for water to become steam quite an intake of energy is required. Hence the ocean is a cushion against the heat of the sun and the freezing blast of the winter. (102)

*10.   During each day the logical development of the creative act were carried out. For example, whatever processes necessary to bring the light through to the earth or gather waters into one place or make the ocean teem with fish, were inaugurated and over a period of time realized. (146)

3.8 EXTENDED ARGUMENTS

The arguments we have considered up to this point are **simple arguments**. They may have more than one premise, but they contain only one conclusion. By contrast, arguments which contain several simple arguments that support the major argument are termed **extended arguments** or **chain arguments**. An extended argument may contain several minor conclusions or intermediate arguments, which serve as premises for the major conclusion. Here is an example:

Whenever John has logic, he must go to class because if he loses his scholarship, then he will have to leave school, and he does not want to leave school. Furthermore, if his G.P.A. drops, then he will lose his scholarship, and the only way that he can maintain his G.P.A. is always to attend class. Since John has logic Thursday and today is Thursday, we can conclude that John must go to logic class today.

The major claim of this paragraph is "John must go to logic class today." However, the first sentence is also a claim supported by evidence; it is used as a premise to support the major claim. The minor conclusion links the two arguments together, as follows:

> If he loses his scholarship, then John will have to leave school.
> John does not want to leave school.
> If his G.P.A. drops, then he will lose his scholarship.
> The only way John can maintain his G.P.A. is always to attend class.
> ∴   Whenever John has logic, he must go to class.

> Whenever John has logic, he must go to class.
> John has logic Thursday.
> Today is Thursday.
> ∴   John must go to logic class today.

Often, it is helpful to number the individual sentences in an extended passage and then draw a diagram that shows how they fit together:

> [1] Whenever John has logic, he must go to class because [2] if he loses his scholarship, then he would have to leave school and [3] he does not want to leave school. Furthermore, [4] if his G.P.A. drops, then he would lose his scholarship and [5] the only way he can maintain his G.P.A. is always to attend class. Since [6] John has logic Thursday and [7] today is Thursday, we can conclude that [8] John must go to logic class today.

$$2 + 3 + 4 + 5$$
$$|$$
$$\underline{1 + 6 + 7}$$
$$\therefore 8$$

We can illustrate the process of identifying arguments within an extended passage with the following discussion of film by Siegfried Kracauer. (See box.)[21]

Films . . . tend to weaken the spectator's consciousness. Its withdrawal from the scene may be furthered by the darkness in moviehouses. Darkness automatically reduces our contacts with actuality, depriving us of many environmental data needed for adequate judgments and other mental activities. It lulls the mind. . . . Devotees of film and its opponents alike have compared the medium to a sort of drug and have drawn attention to its stupefying effects. . . . Doping creates dope addicts. It would seem a sound proposition that the cinema has its habitues who frequent it out of an

> **Siegfried Kracauer** (1889–1966) was best known for his studies of film as a portrait of the social scenery and a medium for presenting attitudes and ideas of the time. He sought the deeper psychological foundation behind film.

all but physiological urge. They are not prompted by a desire to look at a specific film or to be pleasantly entertained; what they really crave is for once to be released from the grip of consciousness, lose their identity in the dark, and let sink in, with their senses ready to absorb them, the images as they happen to follow each other on the screen.

To support his major argument (**MA**), "Films . . . tend to weaken the spectator's consciousness," Kracauer uses three intermediate arguments (**IA**). If each sentence in the passage were numbered (including the sentence after the semicolon), the following diagram could be drawn:

```
                 8 + 9
(IA-1)             |
                 7 + 6  3 + 4
(IA-2)             |      |      (IA-3)
                 5   +   2
                     |          (MA)
                     1
```

The chain of reasoning is as follows:

IA-1

Some habitues of film are not prompted by a desire to look at a specific film or to be pleasantly entertained.
What they really crave is to be released from the grip of consciousness, lose their identity in the dark, and let sink in, with their senses ready to absorb them, the images as they happen to follow each other on the screen.
Therefore, the cinema has its habitues who frequent it out of an all but physiological urge.

IA-2

Some habitues of film frequent it out of an all but physiological urge.
Doping creates dope addicts.
Therefore, devotees of film and its opponents alike have compared the medium to a sort of drug and have drawn attention to its stupefying effects.

IA-3

Darkness automatically reduces our contacts with actuality, depriving us of many environmental data needed for adequate judgments and other mental activities.

Darkness lulls the mind.
Therefore, the withdrawal of consciousness from the scene may be furthered by
the darkness in movie houses.

MA

Devotees of film and its opponents alike have compared the medium to a sort
of drug and have drawn attention to its stupefying effects. The withdrawal of
consciousness from the scene may be furthered by the darkness in moviehouses.
Therefore, films . . . tend to weaken the spectator's consciousness.

"Decomposing" extended arguments in this way has two benefits. First, it allows
us to "see" the reasoning process and enhances the identification stage of critical reasoning. Critical reasoners often disagree on the validity or strength of an argument
because they disagree on the chain of reasoning within the passage. For example, some
may claim that Kracauer's main conclusion is found in sentences 8 and 9. *When the
source of such a disagreement is understood, critical reasoners can discuss it and
attempt to find a resolution.*

The second benefit of this approach is that it aids in the evaluation of
arguments.[22] "Seeing" how the argument is put together tells us something about the
argument: how it stands in relation to other arguments or how it is dependent upon
other arguments. If we see that a particular argument is crucial to some bigger argument, then we might want to spend much more time carefully examining the crucial
reasoning. However, if the argument is a side issue of the bigger argument and we are
interested in the main argument, then we might spend less time examining the intermediate argument.

The chain of reasoning is as follows: Extended arguments usually follow one of
two patterns. In the *pyramid approach*, each argument in the chain presents another
premise to support the major conclusion, with the major conclusion presented last. In
the *inverted pyramid*, the main conclusion is presented first, followed by the evidence
that purportedly supports it. The difference between the two patterns can easily be seen
when one writes an essay. Some writers present their thesis statement close to the
beginning of the essay and offer the support in subsequent paragraphs. This approach
illustrates the inverted pyramid. Others begin with the supporting evidence and lead up
to the thesis, which is presented near the end of the essay. This approach illustrates the
right-side-up pyramid.

3.9 EXERCISE: EXTENDED ARGUMENTS

Examine the following passages and identify the arguments. For each argument you find,
number each statement that is part of the argument. Then draw a diagram that illustrates
the chain of reasoning within the passage. Be sure to include implied premises when you
present the argument in standard form. *Remember that there is a difference between identification and evaluation!* (The passages are used with the permission of the *Fort Worth
Star-Telegram.*)

1.   Day of the long knives

Have you ever really looked at a 5½-inch knife blade? It doesn't sound very long. But it is dangerously long. It is Texas' legal limit for a knife.

Under Texas law, a knife becomes an illegal weapon if it is longer than 5½ inches (Section 46.02, Penal Code). This does not include double-bladed knives and throwing knives, which are illegal to carry no matter what the length.

Do you know how much damage a 5½-inch blade can do? It can go through heavy clothes and even body armor. It can slice and dice and flay open skin and muscles and do damage that bullets cannot do. I remember an FBI agent demonstrating how a 5½-inch blade can go through most doors.

Cops have shot knife-wielders who kept coming forward and still stabbed the officer to death. Cops hate confronting people with guns, but they hate confronting people with knives even more.

That homeless man who was recently shot in front of the White House had a fairly good-sized knife. Unless the blade was more than 5½ inches long, that man could have carried it around the streets of Fort Worth, and he would have been within his rights.

Have we lost our minds letting people carry something that big and dangerous around? In the rush to do something about guns, we may just have done that.

2.   Shelve these standards

How would you like your schoolchildren to study history that makes no mention of Paul Revere, Daniel Webster, Robert E. Lee, Thomas Edison, Albert Einstein or the Wright brothers? Imagine an outline for teaching American history in which George Washington makes only a fleeting appearance and is never described as our first president. Or in which the founding of the Sierra Club and the National Organization for Women are considered noteworthy events but the first gathering of the U.S. Congress is not.

This is the version of history in the soon-to-be-released National Standards for U.S. History. If they are approved by the bureaucracy created by the Clinton administration's Goals 2000 Act, students nationwide in the fifth through 12th grades may begin to learn their history according to these standards.

What is included is as alarming as what is omitted. For instance, McCarthyism is mentioned 19 times and the Ku Klux Klan 17 times.

Preventing certification will be a formidable task, but the battle is worth taking on. We are better people than the national standards indicate, and our children deserve to know it.

The federal government has no business imposing politically correct curriculums—or any national curriculum—on our children. Write or call your members of Congress and tell them to put Goals 2000 on the shelf—permanently.

3.   No Church of the U.S.A.

Alan Moore's Dec. 22 letter, "Respecting religion," said that the First Amendment suggests "that Congress will not 'respect' any religion by way of legislation."

The word *respecting* in the amendment means *concerning*, and the phrase "an establishment of religion" refers to an establishment of a national religion, such as the Anglican Church in England at that time.

Persecution of dissident Christians by the official church set in motion the events that led to the first settlements in New England by the Pilgrims and, later, the Puritans. Established state churches were the norm in most European countries at that time.

The First Amendment can be properly paraphrased to say, "Congress will never adopt legislation to establish a 'Church of the U.S.A.' or to prohibit the free exercise of religion." The concern of the Founding Fathers was to keep the government out of the church's business, not to keep the moral influence of the church out of government and public life.

The Bible was the principal textbook in schools in this country in the 1780s. The writers of the Constitution never intended the First Amendment to be used to take prayer or the teachings of the Bible out of schools. The First Amendment was written to protect the free exercise of religion, not suppress it.

4.   J-O-B-S

You'd think a program whose acronym is "JOBS" would hold finding employment for participants to be its primary goal. Acronyms sure can be deceiving.

Poor, single parents on Aid to Families with Dependent Children alone won't make or break the nation's economy. But the AFDC's relatively small education and training program should be helping put people to work. Instead, the education and training program, called Job Opportunities and Basic Skills, has set itself up as a big, slow target for reformers looking for scapegoats.

According to a recent report by the General Accounting Office, only 11 percent of the 4 million parents on AFDC from 1991 to 1993 participated in the JOBS program. JOBS cost $1.1 billion last year, but getting people trained and employed was not the program's priority. Reaching people most likely to remain jobless—teen-agers and people with learning disabilities and emotional problems—was never emphasized.

This is a monumental failure, but not a failure of welfare. Rather, it is a failure of a program to do what it was designed to do: chip away at dependence.

Our country spends $41 billion on public assistance each year, most of which goes to people who have dropped out of high school. It's not enough to require that they get vocational training. They must also be in a better position to earn a living wage. This program failed to do either.

The answer to true welfare reform is not to push people who are most likely to remain unemployed from the precarious plank that public assistance provided. Any effort to train and educate the poor should help people in a position to work. That's not too much to ask of a job—excuse us, JOBS—program.

*5.   Bloody 'Beauty'

Assuming the National Rifle Association is wrong, and there really is a "Rhino-Ammo" bullet that fragments on impact and leaves a grapefruit-sized hole in a human body, and a "Black Rhino" bullet that penetrates bullet-proof vests and *then* fragments, the outcry is justified.

Police chiefs and other law enforcement officials around the nation are alarmed, especially as police are the ones wearing the vests. Sen. Pat Moynihan, D–N.Y., said he will introduce legislation to ban such bullets if regulators with the federal Bureau of Alcohol, Tobacco, and Firearms do not stop their manufacture.

Why? Well, harken to the promotional claims of David Keen, whose Huntsville, Ala., company wants to make and market the bullets: "The beauty

HERMAN®

1-16   © 1988 Jim Unger/dist. by LaughingStock Licensing Inc.

"I've proven I don't exist."

behind it," he told the Associated Press, "is that it makes an incredible wound. There's no way to stop the bleeding. I don't care where it hits. They're going down for good."

The packaging for the Rhino bullets says each of the fragments "become lethal shrapnel and is hurled into vital organs, lungs, circulatory system components, the heart and other tissues. The wound channel is catastrophic. Death is nearly instantaneous."

Attractive, no? We think a society already awash in violence, and suspicion does not need the "beauty" of "incredible wounds." We don't think loonies should be lured by the appeal of "catastrophic" wound channels and "instantaneous" death.

Somebody—the ATF, Congress, whoever—needs to head this one off at the pass.

6. Using the method of numbering statements presented in this exercise, and organizing the argument, identify the reasoning in an editorial in either your school paper or the local newspaper.

3.10 BASIC CRITERIA FOR ALL ARGUMENTS

Now that we have learned how to identify arguments, we can begin to evaluate them. While we may consider many criteria in evaluating a specific argument, three are required of all arguments: clarity, relevance, and consistency. We encountered these fundamental criteria in Chapter 2 in discussing clear reasoning.

All arguments must be clear, relevant, and consistent; a violation of any of these criteria results in a fallacy, and all fallacies are poor arguments.

Just as communication can fail because of unclear language, reasoning can fail because of unclear thinking. The study of how unclear thinking interferes with reasoning focuses on **fallacies**, or faulty reasoning. There are various approaches to the description of fallacies; the one we use here classifies fallacies into "families," or types, of faulty reasoning.

One family of fallacies consists of **formal fallacies**, fallacies that are always incorrect because they fail to satisfy certain formal or structural criteria. Because these occur in deductive reasoning, they are discussed in Part III. A second family of fallacies consists of **conditional fallacies**. These fallacies fail to satisfy certain conditions that are required by specific types of arguments; they are discussed in Part II because they are related to inductive reasoning. A third family consists of fallacies that fail to satisfy basic criteria of good reasoning. This family, referred to as **fallacies due to unclear reasoning**, applies to all types of reasoning. Because they are fundamental to a proper understanding of good reasoning, they are discussed in detail in the remainder of the chapter.

Before looking more closely at the various fallacies within the latter family, it is important to be aware of the basic criteria for good reasoning. As indicated in the first paragraph of this section, those criteria are clarity, relevance, and consistency. First, all good reasoning is **clear**, meaning that the reasoning process is not confusing in any way. It is the reasoner's responsibility to write in a fashion that enables the reader to understand the reasoning presented in an argument. Second, the evidence offered to support a claim must be **relevant** to that claim. A good piece of reasoning includes *only* evidence that is relevant to the claim. Finally, good reasoning is **consistent**. This means that all the parts of an argument are coherent and uniform: The evidence and claim do not contradict one another.

Using these three criteria, we will divide our discussion of fallacies due to unclear thinking into three subsections: fallacies that violate clarity, fallacies that violate relevance, and fallacies that violate consistency.

Fallacies That Violate Clarity

There are several categories of fallacies that violate clarity. When clarity is violated, *ambiguity* results. In ambiguous reasoning, the meanings of terms are doubtful or uncertain, or the terms are open to more than one interpretation. There are three fallacies in this group: the fallacy of accent, amphiboly, and equivocation.

The Fallacy of Accent. The **fallacy of accent** occurs when improper emphasis is given to a particular part of the evidence or claim, causing the meaning of the argument to be distorted. This fallacy is possible because one can give different meanings to a statement by emphasizing different words. Consider a student who has been accused of copying a classmate's paper. Notice the varying meanings that result from simply changing the emphasis (indicated by italics) in the student's statement:

1. "*I* didn't copy her paper." (Her paper was copied, but not by me.)
2. "I didn't *copy* her paper." (I made use of her paper, but I did not copy it.)
3. "I didn't copy *her* paper." (I copied someone's paper, but not hers.)
4. "I didn't copy her *paper*." (I copied something else of hers, but not the paper.)

While these statements do not necessarily illustrate the fallacy of accent, they do show that meaning can be altered simply by emphasizing different words. When meaning is altered in such a way that it creates ambiguity, then the fallacy of accent is committed.

The fallacy of accent can be properly identified only when the statement being examined is compared with the statement that it purports to be quoting. When the fallacy of accent occurs, it is usually an intentional action by the person formulating the argument. One of the most common occurrences of this fallacy takes the form of a quotation that fails to reproduce the emphasis of the original source. For example, a word or phrase may be italicized to support a particular point being made by the person quoting the text when, in fact, that word or phrase was not italicized in the original source. Have you ever, when quoting a source while writing a research paper, added italics to a particular point within that source to emphasize it? If you have, and if you did not point out that the italics did not occur in the original source, then you have committed the fallacy of accent. Of course, the fallacy also occurs when the original source contains italicized words or phrases that are *not* reproduced in the quotation.

Amphiboly. A second fallacy of ambiguity is **amphiboly**. In this case, the ambiguity arises because of a problem of grammar or syntax that makes it possible to derive more than one meaning from a statement when in fact only one meaning is accurate. Consider the sentence "Lacking good sense, the text was not clear to the critics." What lacks good sense, the text or the critics? We cannot answer this question because of the way the sentence is constructed. Or consider this sign outside an exclusive restaurant: GOOD FOOD EVERY NIGHT BUT MONDAY. While we know the meanings of the individual words, it is unclear exactly what proposition they are attempting to express. If either of these sentences were part of an argument, a critical reasoner would identify the argument as fallacious. The source of the problem is that the information provided does not allow us to formulate a clear proposition.

Equivocation. A third fallacy of ambiguity is **equivocation**. Equivocation occurs because of a muddled usage of words, but it is slightly different from amphiboly. In an equivocation, we will find a word or phrase that allows for two or more different meanings. However, whereas in an amphiboly only one interpretation is correct, in an equivocation *both* meanings are correct. For example, in "Peter is a poor salesman," *poor* can have more than one meaning. Or consider "While shooting at the burglars, Peter missed his friends."

Equivocations make delightful, but fallacious, arguments. Here are some examples:

1. Somebody arrived at the party at six o'clock.
    Somebody left the party at nine o'clock.
    Therefore, somebody stayed at the party for three hours.
2. Man is an inventor.
    No woman is a man.
    Therefore, no woman is an inventor.
3. Love is blind.
    God is love.
    Hence, God is blind.
4. A ham sandwich is better than nothing.
    Nothing is better than God.
    Thus, a ham sandwich is better than God.

In each argument, we find a single word being used in such a way that it has more than one meaning in the argument, even though its usage in each sentence is correct. Equivocations are common when relative terms, such as *bad, difficult, good, heavy, major*, and *small*, are used.

Fallacies That Violate Relevance

The second type of fallacy stemming from unclear thinking arises when the evidence given is irrelevant to the conclusion. Fallacies of this type are known as fallacies of irrelevance, and they occur in a wide variety of ways.

The Fallacy of Appealing to Force. The **fallacy of appealing to force** occurs when the persuasive power of the argument lies not in its reasoning and presentation of facts, but in intimidation. In other words, persuasion occurs not through reason, but through fear. The appeal to force may consist of physical violence or may take the form of nonphysical pressure. The following are some examples:

Reprinted by permission of Jimmy Margulies

1.   "You had better vote for me, or I'll break your arm!"
2.   "You had better vote for me, or I'll make sure your project does not receive the needed funding!"
3.   "Continuing to disagree with my interpretation of inductive reasoning could be risky when it comes to exam time. After all, you do want to pass—don't you?"

In each of these cases, the evidence offered is irrelevant to the claim that is being made.

The Fallacy of Appealing to the People. The **fallacy of appealing to the people**, also known as the *bandwagon effect*, attempts to persuade a person to accept a position by claiming that all people of a particular type believe the same thing. This fallacy can be seen in advertisements that identify a specific audience and claim that everyone in that audience needs the product being advertised: "You—one of the beautiful people—need this car stereo!" The advertiser hopes that the audience will want to be like the type of person represented.

For years, ads for Camel cigarettes were based on this fallacy, proclaiming, "Everyone else smokes Brand X, but you, the individualist, smoke Camels." The ads were effective because everyone wants to be an individualist. In recent years, the same approach has been used to sell Coors light beer. Notice the people drinking "the Silver Bullet" in the ads. We all want to be like these people. However, the evidence being offered is irrelevant to the claim being made.

The Fallacy of Appealing to Pity. A third fallacy of irrelevance is the **fallacy of appealing to pity**. This fallacy brings emotion into play. While proper reasoning is not inconsistent with emotion, the fallacy of appealing to pity attempts to *replace* reasoning with emotion and thereby influence the listener's decision. Here are two examples:

1. "But Bob, you just can't give me *that* grade—my parents will disown me!"
2. "Glutz is a quadriplegic because of the accident. Therefore, we ought to believe him when he says that he was not at fault."

In considering the first example, remember that even if the parents would respond in such a fashion, the argument is still fallacious: It offers no relevant evidence for changing the grade!

The Fallacy of Abusiveness. The **fallacy of abusiveness**, or the *fallacy against the person* (Latin name: *ad hominem*), occurs when a person is attacked by means of disparaging remarks and the remarks are offered as evidence that we should reject any position advocated by that person. At times, it is easy to be deceived into accepting such a claim, especially when the remarks, though irrelevant, happen to be true.

Consider, for example, a gubernatorial election campaign in which each candidate takes a shot (verbally) at his or her opponent:

1. "How can you even think of voting for a man like that; after all, he even made use of a prostitute when he was in college!"
2. "Can you really trust my opponent with your vote? She won't even tell us if she has ever tried marijuana!"

In both cases the discrediting comments may happen to be true, but how relevant are they to the question of who would be a better governor?

Here is another example:

"My rival, Mr. Jay—who happens to be notorious for mismanaging funds—thinks he deserves the position."

This statement contains an abusive charge: "happens to be notorious for mismanaging funds." But let us consider a specific situation. The position Mr. Jay is seeking is that of honorary chairperson for the local parade. The charge is not relevant in this situation, and the argument therefore is fallacious. If, however, Mr. Jay were seeking the position of treasurer of an affluent, but loosely governed, organization, the abusive charge might be relevant, and the argument would not be fallacious.

The Fallacy of Accident. The **fallacy of accident**, also known as the fallacy of exception, occurs when one attempts to apply a general rule to a situation to which the rule was not intended to apply. Let us assume that the laws of a particular state call for capital punishment in cases in which a person is convicted of killing another person with a handgun. This is a general rule. Now suppose that Ms. Jones admits that she shot Mr. James with a handgun and that he died as a result. It may appear that the general rule applies in this situation; therefore, Ms. Jones should be sentenced to death for killing Mr. James. The problem is that Ms. Jones is a police officer and the shooting occurred during a drug bust in which Mr. James was shooting at the officers. The general rule was not intended to apply to this type of situation, so any attempt to apply it in that fashion would be fallacious.

In another case, suppose that a professor states in a course syllabus that students must take each exam on the date indicated or fail the exam. One morning Peter is driving to school to take one of the exams. Another car runs a stop sign and hits Peter's car; Peter is hospitalized as a result. Most people would agree that the general rule set forth by the professor was not meant to apply in this type of situation and that any attempt to do so would be fallacious.

The Fallacy of Argument from Ignorance. In the **fallacy of argument from ignorance,** the evidence offered in support of a claim is lack of knowledge, or ignorance: "Since I don't know that X is not the case, I will assume that X is the case." For many years, this type of fallacious reasoning was applied to smoking: "Since there is no real proof that cigarette smoking causes cancer, it is safe to conclude that cigarette smoking does not cause cancer." Another version of this fallacy takes the form, "Since I don't know that X is true, it must be false." Can you think of something that people often conclude to be false simply because it has not been proven to be true? This type of reasoning is fallacious because the evidence being offered is not relevant to the claim. It fails to make the required connection between the evidence and the conclusion.

The Fallacy of Begging the Question. Also known as *circular reasoning*, the **fallacy of begging the question** occurs when we claim to know X to be true because we know Y to be true and we know the truth of Y because we know X. Imagine yourself in a sports bar. It's Monday night, early November, and you overhear someone at the table next to you say, "That Deion Sanders is the greatest defensive back ever to play football." Someone else at that table challenges the claim: "How can you say that he is the greatest? He's nothing but a showman!" The first person replies, "Not the greatest? Of course he is! He plays for the Redskins, and we know they are the best because they attract players like Deion!" Although it is not as easy to see how this fallacy violates relevance as it is with the other fallacies described in this section, it does violate relevance. Also, as frequently happens, when one fallacy occurs, others may also. In this dialogue at the sports bar, the fallacy of division occurs. (The fallacy of division is discussed later in the section.) The evidence offered does not really address the claim being made. Once we realize what is taking place, we readily reject the reasoning (even though the original claim about Deion is true), acknowledging that it is fallacious. Still, the fallacy can be hard to spot. The longer and more detailed a circular argument becomes, the greater is the likelihood that we will not see its circularity and will in fact accept the reasoning. Remember the first time you asked your parents for permission to stay out all night. They said "No" and spent the next half an hour justifying their position. They probably went into great detail why it would be unsafe and why "good" kids don't stay out all night. This time, unlike the second or third time you made the same request, you walked away disappointed and overwhelmed by your parents' response. You were more persistent the next time, because you realized that the only justification your parents really gave for their response was that they did not want you to stay out all night. When you next listen to a political candidate answering questions, pay close attention to the candidate's line of reasoning. Occasionally, you will be able to identify circular arguments—especially as election time comes closer.

The Fallacy of a Complex Question. Some logicians view the **fallacy of a complex question** as a form of circular reasoning. However, it is distinct from circular reasoning in that it has two parts. A *complex question* raises a particular type of issue and attempts to provide a response. The issue raised, however, is divisible into subissues and is raised in a fashion that demands a single, simple response. As a case in point, consider a nominee to the Supreme Court being asked whether he or she believes that abortion is justified. The abortion issue comprises many subissues: the rights of women, the rights of the fetus, the time at which life begins, the medical implications for the woman, the circumstances in which conception occurred, and so forth. The question being asked therefore involves many issues, not just one. Moreover, the issue is raised in a fashion that seems to demand a simple "yes" or "no" response: Either abortion is justified or it is not. If the nominee attempts to give such a response, the fallacy of a complex question has occurred. Thus, for this fallacy to occur, both a question and a response are needed. If the nominee either refused to answer the question or attempted to deal with each issue in turn, the fallacy would not occur.

Can you think of any other issues that might give rise to this fallacy? Capital punishment? Desegregation? Capitalism? Grading systems? Most of the important issues that confront us daily are more complex than we generally realize. Beware of oversimplified questions and answers; they may be fallacious.

The Fallacy of Composition. The fallacy of composition is best understood when seen in contrast to the fallacy of division (discussed next). The **fallacy of composition** consists of a claim about an entity, considered as a whole, that is based on evidence concerning various components of that entity. The fallacy occurs when we take a characteristic that is common to all the parts of an entity and assume that it is also a characteristic of the entity as a whole. For example, suppose we know that no member of the Texas Boys Choir is more than 21 years old. From this, we conclude that the choir itself is not more than 21 years old. Similarly, since a feather weighs less than one ounce, we conclude that a ton of feathers weighs less than one ounce.

The Fallacy of Division. In contrast to the fallacy of composition, which lies in reasoning from the part to the whole, the **fallacy of division** consists of reasoning from the whole to its parts. The following line of reasoning is an example: Since the Texas Boys Choir is the best such musical group in the nation, its members are the best soloists. In another example, we reason that because the choir is over 50 years old, each of its members is over 50.

In both the fallacy of composition and the fallacy of division, the evidence offered is irrelevant to the claim being made. The key to identifying these fallacies is not the *direction* of the reasoning, but the *relationship* between the evidence and the claim. That is, just because an argument moves from the part to the whole does not mean that the fallacy of composition has occurred. Consider a case in which we could examine every single cell in a particular individual and determine that each one is healthy. It would not be fallacious to conclude that the individual is healthy. Nor would an argument that moves from a whole to its parts necessarily be fallacious. The Bon-Bon Club admits only males. It would be safe to infer that all its members are male.

The Fallacy of Irrelevant Conclusion. The final fallacy that violates relevance is the **fallacy of irrelevant conclusion**. This fallacy occurs when the conclusion of an argument entirely misses the point of the evidence; that is, there is no connection between the evidence and the conclusion. Anyone would identify the following argument as fallacious:

John is tall. Peter is tall. James is tall.
Therefore, Mary is going shopping.

The conclusion, or claim about Mary, is totally irrelevant to the premises.

However, we must be careful in assuming that a line of reasoning is fallacious simply because we fail to see the relevance of the conclusion. Consider this example:

$$P \supset [(Q \lor R) \,\&\, \sim (Q \,\&\, R)]$$

Therefore, if Joe passes, then either Mary passes or John does.

To some people, it might not be obvious that the claim made in the sentence in English is relevant to the evidence offered for it. The failure to see how the claim is relevant may be a result of ignorance and not a problem with the reasoning. In fact, we will discover later in this text that $P \supset [(Q \lor R) \,\&\, \sim (Q \,\&\, R)]$ might be relevant to the claim "If Joe passes, then either Mary passes or John does."

Fallacies That Violate Consistency

As noted earlier, a good piece of reasoning is consistent. This characteristic will be addressed more fully in the discussion of propositional logic in Part 3. Here, it suffices to say that a claim ought to be based on evidence that can all be true at the same time. This means that the evidence offered in support of a conclusion should not be contradictory. For example, imagine how your English composition instructor might respond to the following paragraph:

> My Christmas vacation was the best vacation I've ever had! Joan, the girl I dated in high school, but had not seen for several years, was home to visit her parents. By accident, we ran into each other at the grocery store, and our relationship picked up just the the way it was in high school. She is a great person, and her folks really like me. In fact, her mother called and told me that Joan was going to the store to buy some red peppers. I had dreamed of the time we would meet again. Someone once said that anything worth having is worth planning and waiting for—they were right!

Can all of the statements in this passage be true at the same time? Can the meeting between Joan and the writer be accidental, yet planned? The passage clearly violates consistency.

3.11 EXERCISE: IDENTIFYING FALLACIES CAUSED BY UNCLEAR THINKING

Examine the following pieces of reasoning, identify the fallacy that is committed (if one is, in fact, committed), and then write a brief explanation as to why it offends clear thinking.

1.   Shakespeare is a better writer than Zola, because people with good taste prefer Shakespeare. We know those who have good taste in literature, because they are the ones who prefer Shakespeare to Zola.

*2.   (A politician speaks to a gathering back home). "Listen to me you hicks! I'm a hick just like you, and that means I know what you got what you ain't got. Trust me."

3. We know that there is no planet inside the orbit of Mercury, because astronomers looked hard for one a hundred years ago and couldn't find it, although they did find a lot of asteroids.

*4. The dean's threat to disband the Humanities Division is good news. My mother always said, "No news is good news," and we all know the dean's threats are nothing new!

5. What do you mean, "Should we fight in Iraq?" You're an American, aren't you?

6. The alarmists have not proven that apple juice is harmful for children to drink. Therefore, I believe we can safely conclude that it is okay for our children to drink it.

7. The underlying assumption of the antislum program seems to be that if people are given better homes, they will become better and more productive citizens. But the people who live in slums are shiftless and lazy to begin with. This is evident from the fact that they are willing to live under such conditions.

8. The world must be well ordered, because it is the work of divine wisdom; and we know that God is wise from the admirable disposition of His works.

*9. A man who has been divorced four times can hardly be a good lawyer.

10. I've never seen God, and that's proof enough for me that he doesn't exist.

11. Only lowbrows listen to Sterne, so Sterne's claims are probably false.

12. Dean Cantu must be inefficient, because we all know that administrators are notoriously inefficient.

*13. The woman Glutz married fifty years ago had a great figure and loved to dance. Glutz is still married to that same woman. Therefore, the woman who Glutz is married to now has a great figure and loves to dance.

Unclear Thinking: Violations of Clarity, Relevance, and Consistency

I. *Fallacies of Ambiguity*
   1. Accent
   2. Amphiboly
   3. Equivocation

II. *Fallacies of Irrelevance*
   1. Appeal to Force
   2. Appeal to the People
   3. Appeal to Pity
   4. Abusiveness
   5. Accident
   6. Argument from Ignorance
   7. Begging the Question
   8. Complex Question
   9. Composition
   10. Division
   11. Irrelevant Conclusion

III. *Fallacy of Inconsistency*

14.   The mind is an immaterial thing. The body is a material thing. No material thing can be moved by an immaterial thing. The mind can move the body. Therefore, God exists.

15.   Smoking is bad for your heart and lungs. No one with any sense wants to injure his or her heart or lungs. Therefore, smoking ought to be illegal.

16.   No one has ever proved that we cannot create utopia, so probably we can.

17.   Please, officer, don't think that I took the money. Why, it would break the heart of my poor, sweet old mother if anyone were to suppose me to be a thief.

18.   The team consists of fifty-five players. None of the players are over forty years old. Hence, the team cannot be over forty years old.

19.   Genuine miracles never occur, for miracles are impossible, and impossible things just do not happen.

20.   You are wrong to accuse me of being lazy just because I sleep fourteen hours a day. Why, you, yourself, never get up from in front of that television set from noon till midnight.

21.   Scientists agree that there are laws of nature, such as the law of gravitation. Now, there cannot be a law unless there is some authority, some lawgiver, who promulgates the law. Therefore, there must be someone who promulgated the law of gravitation and the other natural laws. This person can only be God.

22.   Peter and Mary spent last summer working on a film documentary dealing with the late chancellor and his role in the university community. The film covers almost every aspect of the chancellor's life from 1962 to 1990 and it is called *Chancellor Smith*. *Chancellor Smith* was shot with cooperation from the university's faculty.

23.   The process of playing a piano sonata consists of depressing the keys of the piano in the order and for the length of time that the printed score of the sonata indicates. If a person has no difficulty in depressing any one of the keys singly for any given length of time, and his or her hands are large and strong enough to depress simultaneously the keys of such chords as the sonata includes for any given length of time, the person should have no difficulties in playing a piano sonata.

24.   Dear Neighbor,

   I have noticed that you have a dog. While pets can add a great deal of joy to one's life, they are also a big responsibility. For instance, do you know that every time you leave the house, your dog barks constantly until you return? I hope your trip out of the house for the entirety of last weekend was fun for you. I had to study for an important chemistry exam. I understand that people become very attached to their pets and often grieve terribly when they lose their beloved animals. I'm sure that you would be very upset if anything were to accidentally happen to your dog. I'm also certain that everyone would be happier if this problem could be solved without anyone else getting involved. Suffering the loss of a loved one, especially when the death was preventable, is an awful thing to have to endure. Take my advice and take responsibility. Have a nice day.

                                                                                 Your Concerned Neighbor

25.   "Why should people who cover sports figures (who are turning out to be not so great in character) be of a better ability than the 'characters' they describe and analyze? While sports in general become more popular and lucrative to participants, the personal qualities of sports participants become less admirable. Therefore, there is no need for announcers and commentators to necessarily be 'better' than the sports figures they present." {*Dallas Morning News*}

26.   "The governor responded less than jovially to reporters' questions about Dallas lawyer A. Don Crowder's accusation that White was 'one of the first nerds in Texas.' Crowder charged that White strongly supports the school 'no pass–no play' rule because he didn't participate in extracurricular activities in high school." {*Fort Worth Star Telegram*}

*27. "Education Openers: Percent of Japanese high-school graduates who have taken at least six years of English: 100%. Percent of American high-school students who have studied three years of Japanese: .02%." {*The Wall Street Journal*}

28.   "The peddlers of sex harassment advice have, of course, their own moneymaking agenda. Equally suspect are those extremists who would politicize all of American life and seek to regulate human behavior to suit their private prejudices. These people want to impose stringently moralistic standards on private industry that are not met in any other environment." {*Forbes*}

29.   "Gumbel goes after Abernathy on 'Today': Gumbel, who'd questioned the author about the book in Atlanta last week, showed Abernathy roughly the same deference a coroner shows a corpse he's about to dissect. The session began with Gumbel feeding Abernathy two potential excuses: Perhaps his publisher had insisted on highlighting the King-sex material, he suggested. Or, perhaps Abernathy's own health problems—including two mild strokes—had impaired his memory and thus muddied the historical waters. When Abernathy denied both hypotheses, Gumbel brought out the heavy artillery. 'You say it was 'common knowledge,' says Gumbel of the controversial passages, rolling his eyes toward the ceiling, 'but isn't it better to say it was common accusation? This has never been confirmed by someone as close to Dr. King as you were.'" {*The Boston Globe*}

30.   "By now, everybody knows that the earth's protective ozone shield is wearing thin and even has a hole in it over the South Pole. Some people actually believe they have already suffered from the resulting increase in ultraviolet sun rays, however tiny. . . . Unfortunately, the popular press, abetted by scientists whose grants demand a public outcry, has painted ozone depletion in such apocalyptic terms that it's hard for most people to distinguish scientific facts from hysterical fears." {*Forbes*}

31.   "Want to avoid a heart attack? Eat olive oil and oat bran—they'll lower your cholesterol. Need to strengthen your bones? Drink calcium-fortified orange juice. Want to fight off cancer? We've got just the cereal for you. These days, the supermarket food aisles look like a modern medicine show. With the American public increasingly anxious about diet and disease, food companies are claiming health benefits everywhere." {*Business Week*}

32. **"Criticism of Perot rises with gain in polls."** "My own judgment is [that Ross Perot] is a little dictator."—Democratic National Chairman Ron Brown in a speech in Kentucky on Thursday. Perot's refusal to explain his positions on major issues makes it hard to criticize him, but "being afraid of the unknown may soon make people ask, 'What kind of monster are we buying here?'"—White House spokesman Marlon Fitzwater . . . Perot, a "barefoot billionaire from Texas," is a "frightening . . . demagogue" who could foster "authoritarianism in America."—House Republican Leader Rober H. Michel of Illinois, in a speech Thursday at the Capital Hill Club. "I don't know Ross Perot from a load of coal . . . and I suspect most Americans don't know him from a load of coal."—Louisville, Ky., Mayor Jerry Abramson at a meeting with Brown and other Democratic leaders." {*Fort Worth Star-Telegram*}

33. "When was the last time you were really excited about an election? For most Americans it was long ago. This fall two-thirds of potential voters will stay home. More and more people no longer feel they can affect the political process on the national level. Many Americans seem to think that inside the Beltway is alien territory as remote from everyday life as Mars." {*The Wall Street Journal*}

34. "A Northwest Airlines pilot on trial with two crew-mates on charges of flying while intoxicated was an alcoholic who had 17 rum and Cokes the night before the flight, attorneys and witnesses say. . . . All three pilots had blood-alcohol levels higher than .04 percent, the FAA limit, according to test results admitted as evidence. Prouse (the pilot) had the highest reading, .131 percent. Prouse's attorney, Peter Wold, said in his opening statement that Prouse is an alcoholic and thus has a high tolerance for alcohol. The pilot had no trouble flying the Boeing 727 with 91 passengers, his lawyer said." {*Fort Worth Star-Telegram*}

35. **PROJECT**: From materials you are reading outside of this class—for instance, magazines, newspapers, and professional journals—find ten examples of unclear thinking. Explain briefly why you think your examples illustrate unclear thinking, and try to identify the fallacies by name.

3.12 ONE ADDITIONAL STEP

Up to this point, our concern has been with understanding what constitutes an argument, the identification of arguments, and the difficulties sometimes encountered in identifying them. But while the identification of arguments is crucial, it is not an end in itself. Logicians use the identification process as a step to another process that is much more enlightening and fruitful. The critical reasoner's goal is to evaluate arguments in order to respond to them in an informed manner. Through evaluation, new insights can be obtained and errors corrected.

Before embarking on the evaluation of arguments, we must take one additional step. Imagine the following situation:

Peter was asked by his friends, the McCarthers, to help paint the exterior of their Victorian home. They would supply the paint, ladders, food, and beverages, but they requested Peter to bring his own paintbrush. Since the McCarthers were popular and had asked many friends to help, Peter thought it would be fun. The day came and Peter showed up with his brand new 18/0 paintbrush. All who were present stood in shock as Peter scaled a ladder; in one hand he had a bucket of paint and in the other his brush.

This story illustrates a major mistake: An 18/0 brush is an extremely fine one that an artist might use to do detailed work on a canvas. Peter's willingness to help is to be commended, but he chose the wrong tool for the task. Imagine a carpenter who tries to use a saw to drive a nail!

Logicians can make a similar mistake if they choose methods of evaluation that are inappropriate for the reasoning they are examining. After identifying an argument and examining it for clarity, relevance, and consistency, the logician must determine the best method for evaluating the argument. This task is important, because there are two basic types of reasoning, each of which requires a different method of evaluation. One of them, *deduction*, focuses on the structure or form of the argument, while the other, *induction*, focuses on the content of the argument.[23]

The distinction between deductive and inductive reasoning is often difficult to grasp because of commonly taught misconceptions. One such misconception stems from the meanings of the words *deduce* and *induce*. Since *deduce* means "bring or draw from" and *induce* means "bring or draw into," it is mistakenly assumed that the distinction between deduction and induction lies in the location of the conclusion. This mistake can be found in some English composition texts,[24] which claim that if a writer introduces a thesis statement early in an essay and then provides points of support for it, the reasoning used in the essay is deductive, whereas if the writer offers the support first and does not introduce the thesis statement until the last paragraph, the reasoning used is inductive. This notion is incorrect; the position of a conclusion in relation to the evidence supporting it has nothing to do with the type of reasoning used. Just as the topic sentence of a paragraph can be located at the beginning, the middle, or the end of the paragraph, a conclusion can appear at any point in an argument.

Another common error is to distinguish between the two types of reasoning on the basis of the movement within an argument.[25] If the premises are general in nature (e.g., "All dogs bark") and the conclusion involves a particular item (e.g., "Snooper barks"), the reasoning is deductive. If the premises are particular in nature (e.g., "Alex is a good student") and the conclusion is a generalization (e.g., "All males are good students"), the reasoning is inductive. Although in these examples the types of reasoning are correctly identified, this approach will not always yield the correct answers. Consider a slight change in each argument:

Most dogs bark.	Alex is a good student.
∴ Snooper barks.	∴ Pete is a good student.

In the first case, the reasoning is not deductive, but inductive. In the second case, the reasoning is still inductive, but does not illustrate movement from the particular to the general.

The following lists provide a means for distinguishing correctly between deductive and inductive reasoning.[26]

Deductive reasoning has the following characteristics:
1.   The scope of the conclusion does not exceed the scope of the premises.
2.   The premises provide conclusive grounds for the conclusion.
3.   The conclusion must be true if the premises are true.

Inductive reasoning has the following characteristics:
1.   The scope of the conclusion transcends the scope of the premises.
2.   The premises do not provide conclusive grounds for the conclusion.
3.   The conclusion might be false even if the premises are true.

These characteristics will be illustrated and explained in further detail in later sections of the text: Part II is devoted to inductive reasoning, and Part III focuses upon deductive reasoning.

Like many other aspects of logic, the ability to distinguish between induction and deduction is both a science and an art. The characteristics just listed are accurate, but applying them correctly requires practice. Only after spending considerable time with each of the two reasoning methods can one expect to distinguish between them without difficulty.

Note, also, that there are times when an argument can be rewritten in standard form to reflect either deductive or inductive reasoning. In such cases, we can choose between evaluating the argument on the basis of its content (induction) or evaluating it on the basis of its structure (deduction). Ideally, an argument should be both deductively valid and inductively strong. (These two concepts will be explained in subsequent sections of the text.)

3.13 EXERCISE: BASIC TYPES OF REASONING
Examine the arguments that follow. Rewrite each in standard form, and state whether the reasoning is deductive or inductive and why.

*1.   No fish can write novels. All bluegills are fish. Therefore, no bluegill can write novels.

2.   David has done well on all his history exams, so he will do well on his history exam today.

3.   The Cowboys have a 10–0 win–loss record and the Jets have a 4–6 record, so the Cowboys probably will win, even though the game will be played on the Jets' home field.

*4.   A ballad is a form of verse presenting a dramatic episode in narrative form and is to be sung or recited. The song "Hang Down Your Head, Tom Dooley" is a form of verse that depicts a dramatic episode. Hence, it is a form of the ballad.

5.   We should have a good volleyball game Saturday, since it's not supposed to rain and enough people have promised to come.

6.   The Greeks used *hamartia* for reversing the fortunes of heroes in their tragedies. Oedipus's very desire to do good became his undoing and thus his *hamartia*.

7. Robert Frost must be the most widely read poet, because he has won the Pulitzer prize for poetry four times since 1924.

8. The baroque style stressed energy, movement, and a realistic treatment of its subject. Nabokov's *Pale Fire* neither illustrates nor stresses these elements, so it is safe to conclude that it was not written in baroque style.

*9. I have read all of the best-sellers for the past ten years, plus many of the classics. Consequently, I am sure that I have read *Tristram Shandy*.

10. The main character in Wright's *Native Son*, known as Bigger, depicts an outlook on life that can be viewed as jargon to many middle-class white Americans. His outlook and actions seem confusing and foreign to many. Jargon, in its broadest sense, is or seems to be confusing and strange to the listener.

3.14 A CLOSING COMMENT

This chapter opened by asking whether an imaginary world in which arguments do not exist would be better or worse than the world as it is. Given the definition of an argument set forth in the chapter, it is clear that a world without arguments would not be the best of all possible worlds. In fact, it would be a world of chaos and irrationality. Arguments performs the valuable task of illustrating the reasoning process. The study of arguments enables us to think critically about that process. As a result, we become better able to examine, evaluate, question, assess, and respond to the world around us.

Part I Application

Critical reasoning is a process that we can use to examine and evaluate how well premises support a claim. The process has five key elements.

First, we must analyze what a piece of textual material is saying. To do that, we must be aware of the nature of language and its use of symbols.

Second, we must determine whether a claim is being made and whether evidence is offered to support that claim. To identify claims for which evidence is offered is to identify an argument. The identification of arguments often requires considerable skill.

Third, we must arrange information found in the textual material in a coherent fashion that makes a distinction between the claim and the evidence offered in support of it. This arrangement makes explicit the connections and assumptions that link the evidence with the claim. Asking questions about the relationship between the evidence and the conclusion helps us identify assumptions.

Fourth, we must identify the type of reasoning used and then evaluate it by means of appropriate objective standards. The process of evaluating an argument is explored in detail in Parts II and III.

Fifth, we must make a decision concerning the subject of the argument. The purpose of critical reasoning is to make a decision that is based on the best available information. The decision may change as we discover new information, but critical reasoning is not intended to make us so skeptical that we do not make decisions at all. Once we have made a decision, we can present it in the form of an extended argument. This new argument could include the original evidence, along with the logic that connects the evidence with the claim.

In sum, the elements of critical reasoning are as follows:

1. analysis of textual material, focusing on language and meaning
2. identification of arguments
3. arrangement of information in a coherent form
4. evaluation of the information and arguments
5. arrival at a decision based on the evidence

COURSE PROJECT

Part I

Choose an article from a professional journal that presents an argument about an issue that interests you. (See "Example of an Article," to follow.) While such articles may be difficult to read, they typically are better written than articles appearing in nonprofessional journals, and their line of reasoning is easier to follow. *Your instructor may modify this assignment, so be sure to follow his or her directions.* Make at least three copies of the article. Give one unmarked copy to the instructor; the other two copies are for you to use as you carry out the project.

Begin by identifying the main claim made by the article and the evidence offered to support that claim. Also, identify the minor claims and their premises. Rewrite these arguments in standard form. Present some of the arguments in a three- to four-page essay. Be sure to have an introduction and conclusion to your essay. The body of your essay should be a presentation of the major argument and several of the minor or intermediate arguments. You will probably need transitional sentences between the minor arguments to help the reader follow your essay. Be sure to cite and document the source of the arguments properly. (See "Example of Part I: Application," to follow.) This is the first of four stages that will result in a ten- to twelve-page research paper at the end of the course.

EXAMPLE OF AN ARTICLE

DEATH AND JUSTICE:

How Capital Punishment Affirms Life

Last December a man named Robert Lee Willie, who had been convicted of raping and murdering an 18 year old woman, was executed in the Louisiana state prison. In a statement issued several minutes before his death, Mr. Willie said: "Killing people is wrong . . . It makes no difference whether it's citizens, countries, or governments. Killing is wrong." Two weeks later in South Carolina, an admitted killer named Joseph Carl Shaw was put to death for murdering two teenagers. In an appeal to the governor for clemency, Mr. Shaw wrote: "Killing is wrong when I did it. Killing is wrong when you do it. I hope you have the courage and moral strength to stop the killing."

It is a curiosity of modern life that we find ourselves being lectured on morality by cold-blooded killers. Mr. Willie previously had been convicted of aggravated rape, aggravated kidnapping, and the murders of a Louisiana deputy and a man from Missouri. Mr. Shaw committed another murder a week before the two for which he was executed, and admitted mutilating the body of the 14 year old girl he killed. I can't help wondering what prompted these murderers to speak out against killing as they entered the death-house door. Did their newfound reverence for life stem from the realization that they were about to lose their own?

Life is indeed precious, and I believe the death penalty helps to affirm this fact. Had the death penalty been a real possibility in the minds of these murderers, they might well have stayed their hand. They might have shown moral awareness before their victims died, and not after. Consider the tragic death of Rosa Velez, who happened to be home when a man named Luis Vera burglarized her apartment in Brooklyn. "Yeah, I shot her," Vera admitted. "She knew me, and I knew I wouldn't go to the chair."

During my 22 years in public service, I have heard the pros and cons of capital punishment expressed with special intensity. As a district leader, councilman, congressman, and mayor, I have represented constituencies generally thought of as liberal. Because I support the death penalty for heinous crimes of murder, I have sometimes been the subject of emotional and outraged attacks by voters who find my position reprehensible or worse.

I have listened to their ideas. I have weighed their objections carefully. I still support the death penalty. The reasons I maintain my position can be best understood by examining the arguments most frequently heard in opposition.

(1)   The death penalty is "barbaric." Sometimes opponents of capital punishment horrify with tales of lingering death on the gallows, of faulty electric chairs, or of agony in the gas chamber. Partly in response to such protests, several states such as North Carolina and Texas switched to execution by lethal injection. The condemned person is put to death painlessly, without ropes, voltage, bullets, or gas. Did this answer the objections of death penalty opponents? Of course not. On June 22, 1984, *The New York Times* published an editorial that sarcastically attacked the new "hygienic" method of death by injection, and stated that "execution can never be made humane through science." So it's not the method that really troubles opponents. It's the death itself they consider barbaric.

Admittedly, capital punishment is not a pleasant topic. However, one does not have to like the death penalty in order to support it any more than one must like medical surgery, radiation, or chemotherapy in order to find necessary these attempts at curing cancer. Ultimately we may learn how to cure cancer with a simple pill. Unfortunately, that day has not yet arrived. Today we are faced with the choice of letting the cancer spread or trying to cure it with the methods available, methods that one day will almost certainly be considered barbaric. But to give up and do nothing would be far more barbaric and would certainly delay the discovery of an eventual cure. The analogy between cancer and murder is imperfect, because murder is not the "disease" we are trying to cure. The disease is injustice. We may not like the death penalty, but it must be available to punish crimes of cold-blooded murder, cases in which any other form of punishment would be inadequate and, therefore, unjust. If we create a society in which injustice is not tolerated, incidents of murder—the most flagrant form of injustice—will diminish.

(2)   No other major democracy uses the death penalty. No other major democracy—in fact, few other countries of any description—are plagued by a murder rate such as that in the United States. Fewer and fewer Americans can remember the days when unlocked doors were the norm and murder was a rare and terrible offense. In America the murder rate climbed 122 percent between 1963 and 1980. During that same period, the murder rate in New York City increased by almost 400 percent, and the statistics are even worse in many other cities. A study at M.I.T. showed that based on 1970 homicide rates a person who lived in a large American city ran a greater risk of being murdered than an American soldier in World War II ran of being killed in combat. It is not surprising that the laws of each country differ according to differing conditions and traditions. If other countries had our murder problem, the cry for capital punishment would be just as loud as it is here. And I daresay that any other major democracy where 75 percent of the people supported the death penalty would soon enact it into law.

(3)   An innocent person might be executed by mistake. Consider the work of Adam Bedau, one of the most implacable foes of capital punishment in this country. According to Mr. Bedau, it is "false sentimentality to argue that the death penalty should be abolished because of the abstract possibility that an innocent person might be executed." He cites a study of the 7,000 executions in this country from 1893 to

1971, and concludes that the record fails to show that such cases occur. The main point, however, is this. If government functioned only when the possibility of error didn't exist, government wouldn't function at all. Human life deserves special protection, and one of the best ways to guarantee that protection is to assure that convicted murderers do not kill again. Only the death penalty can accomplish this end. In a recent case in New Jersey, a man named Richard Biegenwald was freed from prison after serving 18 years for murder; since his release he has been convicted of committing four murders. A prisoner named Lemuel Smith, who, while serving four life sentences for murder (plus two life sentences for kidnapping and robbery) in New York's Green Haven Prison, lured a woman corrections officer into the chaplain's office and strangled her. He then mutilated and dismembered her body. An additional life sentence for Smith is meaningless. Because New York has no death penalty statute, Smith has effectively been given a license to kill.

But the problem of multiple murder is not confined to the nation's penitentiaries. In 1981, 91 police officers were killed in the line of duty in this country. Seven percent of those arrested in the cases that have been solved had a previous arrest for murder. In New York City in 1976 and 1977, 85 persons arrested for homicide had a previous arrest for murder. Six of these individuals had two previous arrests for murder, and one had four previous murder arrests. During those two years the New York police were arresting for murder persons with a previous arrest for murder on the average of one every 8.5 days. This is not surprising when we learn that in 1975, for example, the median time served in Massachusetts for homicide was less than two-and-a-half years. In 1976, a study sponsored by the Twentieth Century Fund found that the average time served in the United States for first degree murder is ten years. The median time served may be considerably lower.

(4) Capital punishment cheapens the value of human life. On the contrary, it can be easily demonstrated that the death penalty strengthens the value of human life. If the penalty for rape were lowered, clearly it would signal a lessened regard for the victims' suffering, humiliation, and personal integrity. It would cheapen their horrible experience, and expose them to an increased danger of recurrence. When we lower the penalty for murder, it signals a lessened regard for the value of the victim's life. Some critics of capital punishment, such as columnist Jimmy Breslin, have suggested that a life sentence is actually a harsher penalty for murder than death. This is sophist nonsense. A few killers may decide not to appeal a death sentence, but the overwhelming majority make every effort to stay alive. It is by exacting the highest penalty for the taking of human life that we affirm the highest value of human life.

(5) The death penalty is applied in a discriminatory manner. This factor no longer seems to be the problem it once was. The appeals process for a condemned prisoner is lengthy and painstaking. Every effort is made to see that the verdict and sentence were fairly arrived at. However, assertions of discrimination are not an argument for ending the death penalty but for extending it. It is not justice to exclude everyone from the penalty of the law if a few are found to be so favored. Justice requires that the law be applied equally to all.

(6) Thou Shalt Not Kill. The Bible is our greatest source of moral inspiration. Opponents of the death penalty frequently cite the sixth of the Ten Commandments in an attempt to prove that capital punishment is divinely proscribed. In the original Hebrew, however, the Sixth Commandment reads, "Thou

Shalt Not commit Murder," and the Torah specifies capital punishment for a variety of offenses. The biblical viewpoint has been upheld by philosophers throughout history. The greatest thinkers of the 19th century—Kant, Locke, Hobbes, Rousseau, Montesquieu, and Mill—agreed that natural law properly authorizes the sovereign to take life in order to vindicate justice. Only Jeremy Bentham was ambivalent. Washington, Jefferson, and Franklin endorsed it. Abraham Lincoln authorized executions for deserters in wartime. Alexis de Tocqueville, who expressed profound respect for American institutions, believed that the death penalty was indispensable to the support of social order. The United States Constitution, widely admired as one of the seminal achievements in the history of humanity, condemns cruel and inhuman punishment, but does not condemn capital punishment.

(7)   The death penalty is state-sanctioned murder. This is the defense with which Messrs. Willie and Shaw hoped to soften the resolve of those who sentenced them to death. By saying in effect, "You're no better than I am," the murderer seeks to bring his accusers down to his own level. It is also a popular argument among opponents of capital punishment, but a transparently false one. Simply said, the state has rights that the private individual does not. In a democracy, those rights are given to the state by the electorate. The execution of a lawfully condemned killer is no more an act of murder than is legal imprisonment an act of kidnapping. If an individual forces a neighbor to pay him money under threat of punishment, it's called extortion. If the state does it, it's called taxation. Rights and responsibilities surrendered by the individual are what give the state its power to govern. This contract is the foundation of civilization itself.

Everyone wants his or her rights, and will defend them jealously. Not everyone, however, wants responsibilities, especially the painful responsibilities that come with law enforcement. Twenty-one years ago a woman named Kitty Genovese was assaulted and murdered on a street in New York. Dozens of neighbors heard her cries for help but did nothing to assist her. They didn't even call the police. In such a climate the criminal understandably grows bolder. In the presence of moral cowardice, he lectures us on our supposed failings and tries to equate his crimes with our quest for justice.

The death of anyone—even a convicted killer—diminishes us all. But we are diminished even more by a justice system that fails to function. It is an illusion to let ourselves believe that doing away with capital punishment removes the murderer's deed from our conscience. The rights of society are paramount. When we protect guilty lives, we give up innocent lives in exchange. When opponents of capital punishment say to the state: "I will not let you kill in my name," they are also saying to murderers: "You can kill in your own name as long as I have an excuse for not getting involved."

It is hard to imagine anything worse than being murdered while neighbors do nothing. But something worse exists. When those same neighbors shrink back from justly punishing the murderer, the victim dies twice.

Mayor Edward I. Koch.

The New Republic, April 15, 1985, 13–15. Reprinted by permission of THE NEW REPUBLIC, (c) 1985, The New Republic, Inc.

EXAMPLE OF PART I: APPLICATION

CAPITAL PUNISHMENT AFFIRMS LIFE (?)

Capital punishment is a crucial contemporary issue that confronts us today. Edward I. Koch, former mayor of New York City, presents an intriguing argument in support of capital punishment ("Death and Justice: How Capital Punishment Affirms Life," *The New Republic*, April 15, 1985: 13–15). In this section, I will present some of the arguments set forth by Mayor Koch to support his position.

Major Argument

Mayor Koch's position is that we should support capital punishment. His evidence is basically a denial of each of the premises used to argue against capital punishment. One way of rewriting his argument is as follows:

> If the death penalty is barbaric, and no other major democracy uses the death penalty, and an innocent person might be executed by mistake, and capital punishment cheapens the value of life, and the death penalty is applied in a discriminatory manner, and the Bible says, "Thou Shall Not Kill," and the death penalty is state-sanctioned murder, then we must not support capital punishment. However, the death penalty is not barbaric, and it is not relevant that no other major democracy uses the death penalty, and the execution of an innocent person by mistake is improbable, and capital punishment does not cheapen the value of life, and the death penalty is not applied in a discriminatory manner, and "Thou Shall Not Kill" does not apply to the issue of capital punishment, and the death penalty is not state-sanctioned murder.
> ∴   We must support capital punishment.

The following is another way to rewrite Mayor Koch's overall argument:

> The death penalty is not barbaric.
> It is not relevant that no other major democracy uses the death penalty.
> The execution of an innocent person by mistake is improbable.
> Capital punishment does not cheapen the value of life.
> The death penalty is not applied in a discriminatory manner.
> "Thou Shall Not Kill" does not apply to the issue of capital punishment.
> The death penalty is not state-sanctioned murder.
> ∴   We must support capital punishment.

Minor Arguments

1.   Mayor Koch claims that capital punishment is not barbaric. To support his claim, he offers two arguments:

We are faced with either letting cancer spread or trying to cure it with available methods.
The available methods may one day seem barbaric, but are the only options currently available.
It is more barbaric to do nothing today than to treat illnesses by available methods.
∴   We perform radical surgery, radiation, chemotherapy, etc.

(and)

Radical surgery, etc., are not liked by anyone, but are currently necessary as attempts to cure cancer.
Capital punishment is not pleasant.
∴   Capital punishment must be supported for certain crimes.

(furthermore)

(Certain crimes =$_{df.}$ cases in which any other form of punishment would be inadequate and unjust.)

(also)

Furthermore, he states that if we create a society in which injustice is not tolerated, incidents like murder and other forms of injustice will diminish.

2.   Koch claims that it is not relevant that no other major democracy uses the death penalty:

No other major democracy has the murder rate of the United States.
Between 1963 and 1980, the murder rate increased 122%.
On the basis of 1970 homicide rates, a person living in a large city ran a greater risk of being murdered than a U.S. soldier ran of being killed in World War II.
Each country's laws ought to reflect the different conditions and traditions of that country.
If other countries had our problem, they would want the death penalty also.
∴   The claim that no other democracy uses the death penalty is not relevant to the argument.

3.   The mayor's position is that the death penalty should not be abolished because of some abstract possibility, and furthermore, he claims that innocent persons might be killed if we do not have a death penalty. To support his position he offers two arguments:

Adam Bedau (one of the most implacable foes of capital punishment) says that it is "false sentimentality to argue that the death penalty should be abolished because of the abstract possibility that an innocent person might be executed."

Bedau cites a study of the 7,000 executions carried out between 1893 and
<u>1971 and concludes that records fail to show any such occurrence.</u>

∴   The death penalty should not be abolished because of some mere
       abstract possibility.

(and)

If government functions only when the possibility of error does not exist,
government would not function at all.
Human life deserves special protection, and one of the best ways to
guarantee that protection is to make sure that convicted murderers do
not kill again. The only way to accomplish this is via the death penalty.
Examples of Biegenwald and Smith.
Example of 91 police officers killed in 1981; 7% of those arrested in cases
that were solved had been arrested for previous murders.
Example citing 85 persons arrested in New York City for homicide in 1976
and 1977 who had previous arrests for murder. During those two years,
New York police arrested for murder persons with a previous arrest for
<u>murder an average of one every 8.5 days.</u>

∴   Innocent persons might be killed if we do not have capital
       punishment.

While Mayor Koch presents other arguments to support his position, the ones just listed make up his main line of reasoning and several internal or minor arguments. Note that we have not evaluated the mayor's reasoning, but rather have simply identified some of the arguments that (I believe) are crucial to his case.

***

We will evaluate these arguments in the application sections of Parts II and III. The application section of Part IV will lead to the completion of a term paper.

Notes for Part 1

[1]Aristotle, *The Basic Works of Aristotle*, ed. Richard McKeon (New York: Random House, 1941); 1329. *The Oxford Translation of Aristotle*, ed. W. D. Ross (Oxford, U.K.: Clarendon Press). Reprinted by permission of Oxford University Press.

[2]Charles Peirce, "The Fixation of Belief," *Philosophical Writings of Peirce*, ed. Justus Buchler (New York: Dover Publications, 1955), p. 5.

[3]Critical reasoning, as developed in this text, involves us in the "five eminent means or methods whereby the mind is improved in the knowledge of things, and these are observation, reading, instruction by lectures, conversation, and meditation (study)" [Isaac Watts, *Improvement of the Mind*, edited and abridged by Stephen B. Helfant and J. David Coccoli (Groton, MA: Helfant Publishing House, 1987), p. 23]. *Improvement of the Mind* was first published in 1741. Isaac Asimov provides an additional five characteristics that he deems important for the creative thinker in his essay, "Those Crazy Ideas." I have modified his points to apply directly to the critical reasoner: (1) A critical reasoner must accumulate as much information as possible in as many fields as possible (i.e., avoid becoming overly specialized). (2) A critical reasoner must be able to combine information in new ways and recognize patterns of thought. (3) A critical reasoner must be able to see consequences of new combinations. (4) A critical reasoner must be willing to take a stance, even if it is an unpopular stance, assuming that the evidence best supports the stance. (5) A critical reasoner must be somewhat lucky.

[4]For our purposes, we will not distinguish between a symbol and a sign.

[5]Aldous Huxley, *Brave New World* (New York: Bantam Books, 1962), p. 47.

[6]Neil Daniel, *A Guide to Style and Mechanics* (Fort Worth, TX: Harcourt Brace Jovanovich College Publishers, 1992), p. 235.

[7]*Beowulf: A Dual-Language Edition*, trans. Howell Chickering, Jr. (Garden City: Anchor Books, 1977), p. 106. The modern-English translation is:

No man escapes easily from death—let him try who will—but all soul-bearers walking the earth, each son of man, driven by need, must enter his place made ready from birth, where the body-covering deep in its earth-bed sleeps after feast. (107)

[8]Aristotle, *op. cit.*, 9.

[9]*Hellenistic Philosophy*, translated by Inwood and Gerson (Indianapolis: Hackett Publishing Company, 1988), pp. 185–186.

[10]John Pollock, *Contemporary Theories of Knowledge* (Savage, MD: Rowman and Littlefield, 1986), pp. 1–4.

[11]Charles S. Peirce, "The Scientific Attitude and Fallibilism" (1896), in *Philosophical Writings of Peirce* (New York: Dover Publications, 1955), p. 43.

[12]This does not mean that an argument must be emotionally neutral in order to be relevant. The emotional element is part of being human, just like the rational element, and both can complement each other.

[13]Consistency, although a standard of good reasoning in basic logic, may be abandoned in more advanced forms of reasoning. For example, fascinating work that is

important for fuzzy logic (see Chapter 9) is being done in paraconsistent logics. See Jim MacKenzie and Graham Priest, "Paraconsistent Dialogues; or, how to start talking to Cretans," *Logique & Analyse* 131–132 (1990): 339–357; and Anthony Bloesch, "A Tableau Style Proof System for Two Paraconsistent Logics," *Notre Dame Journal of Formal Logic* 34, p. 2 (Spring 1993): 295–301.

[14]Charles S. Peirce, "The Criterion of Validity in Reasoning" (1902), in *Philosophical Writings of Peirce, op. cit.*, 126.

[15]Notice the claim being made. "The sentences in Set A . . . can be judged to be either true or false." Consider the sentence "John is wearing a ring." Gottfried Leibniz (1646–1716) claims that this sentence is true if John exists and he is wearing a ring, and it is false if John exists, but he is not wearing a ring. However, what if John does not exist? While Aristotle and Bertrand Russell assume that he does in evaluating the truth or falsity of the sentence, other logicians (e.g., Boole, Frege, and Strawson) do not. For example, Strawson maintains that a sentence has a truth-value if and only if the subject exists. Thus, if John does not exist, then the sentence "John is wearing a ring" is neither true nor false. Hence, while it is meaningful, it lacks a truth-value.

[16]The terms *statement* and *proposition* are not without controversy. In 1879, Gottlob Frege ("*Begriffsschrift*") pointed to difference between a sentence and its proposition. Peter F. Strawson [*Introduction to Logical Theory* (New York: John Wiley & Sons, 1952)] uses the term 'statement' to refer the meaning of a sentence: "A particular statement is identified, not only by reference to the words used, but also by reference to the circumstances in which they are used, and, sometimes, to the identity of the person using them" (p. 4). However, the controversy is much deeper than whether we use the term statement or proposition. Some maintain that, because propositions are abstract entities, they "occupy no space, reflect no light, have no beginning or end, and so forth." [Benson Mates, *Elementary Logic*, 2d ed. (New York: Oxford University Press, 1972), p. 11).] W. V. Quine ["Meaning and Truth," in his *Philosophy of Logic* (Englewood Cliffs, NJ: Prentice-Hall, 1970), pp. 1–14] presents an excellent argument against the use of the notion of a *proposition*. Mates chooses to avoid the problem with propositions and speaks only of *sentences*. However, "we shall avoid sentences like 'It is raining' and 'He is here,' which contain . . . 'egocentric' words . . . and depend for their truth or falsity upon when, where, and by whom they are uttered. This sort of dependence can usually be obviated by using a sentence in which person, times, places are specified . . . " (p. 13). This is essentially the definition we gave to the term *proposition*. Our usage of the term does not imply any ontological status; rather, a proposition merely provides clarity.

[17]Roger Boscovich, *A Theory of Natural Philosophy* (Cambridge, MA: MIT Press, 1966); originally published in 1763.

[18]Joseph Le Conte, *Evolution: Its Nature. Its Evidence, and Its Relation to Religious Thought* (New York: D. Appleton and Company, 1892).

[19]Herbert Spencer, *First Principles* (New York: D. Appleton and Company, 1898).

[20]Bernard Ramm, *The Christian View of Science and Scripture* (Grand Rapids, MI: Eerdmans Publishing Company, 1981). Reprinted by permission of Eerdmans Publishing Company.

[21]Siegfried Kracauer, *Theory of Film* (Oxford, U.K.: Oxford University Press, 1960), p. 159.

[22]For example, in the passage from Kracauer, the major argument is flawed because it is based upon a minor conclusion arrived at by faulty reasoning, namely, a fallacious argument from analogy.

[23]Historically, logicians assigned the terms "deduction" and "induction" to types of arguments. For example, Charles Peirce claimed that four types of arguments exist: deductive, inductive, abduction, and mixed. Although using these terms to refer to types of arguments normally is not problematic, it is misleading, since some arguments can be evaluated by both inductive and deductive methods. However, for the beginning student of logic, the distinction is helpful. As this text progresses, the demarcation between "deduction" and "induction" will become extremely gray, for both approaches to reasoning have similar roots.

[24]See, for example, Michael E. Adelstein and Jean G. Pival, *The Reading Commitment* (New York: Harcourt Brace Jovanovich, Inc., 1978), p. 337; and Sheridan Baker, *The Complete Stylist* (New York: Thomas Y. Crowell Company, 1966), p. 45.

[25]Examples of this kind of error abound: See Andrea Lunsford and Robert Connors, *The St. Martin's Handbook* 2d ed. (New York: St. Martin's Press, 1992), pp. 81–83; Winifred Bryan Horner, Suzanne Strobeck Webb, and Robert Keith Miller, *Harbrace College Handbook* 12th ed. (Fort Worth, TX: Harcourt Brace College Publishers, 1994), pp. 296–298; and Laurie G. Kirszner and Stephen R. Mandell, *Patterns for College Writing*, 5th ed. (New York: St. Martin's Press, 1992), pp. 527–531.

[26]Note that the lists give *characteristics*, not essential properties. This is important, since if they stated essential properties of the arguments they encompass, then the two sets of arguments would be mutually exclusive. However, they are not mutually exclusive and may overlap, so some guidance is provided for beginning logic students.

PART TWO

Inductive Reasoning

Preface to Induction

In Chapter 3, we noted that not all reasoning is the same. Some reasoning is fallacious; the evidence offered as premises does not provide any real justification or support for the claim, due to unclear thinking. Reasoning that is not fallacious is deductive or inductive. If it is deductive, it has the following characteristics:

1.   The scope of the conclusion does not exceed the scope of the evidence.
2.   The evidence provides conclusive grounds for the conclusion.
3.   The conclusion must be true if the evidence is true.

These characteristics highlight the fact that proper deductive reasoning preserves truth. That is, if the premises are true and the argument is in the proper form, the conclusion also must be true. This guarantee of truth is possible because the conclusion does not provide any new information. The premises contain all the information that is found in the conclusion. The conclusion does not extend our knowledge beyond the evidence provided in the premises.

On the other hand, if reasoning is inductive, it has the following characteristics:

1.   The scope of the conclusion transcends the scope of the evidence.
2.   The evidence does not provide conclusive grounds for the conclusion.
3.   The conclusion might be false even if the evidence is true.

In inductive reasoning, the conclusion contains new information. Because the conclusion extends our knowledge beyond the scope of the premises, inductive reasoning does not preserve truth.

Our focus in this part of the text will be on inductive reasoning, which does not claim to preserve truth. Our examination of inductive reasoning will be selective, however; we will concentrate on aspects of induction that are relevant to everyday reasoning and that provide a foundation for making basic decisions. The first chapter, dealing with induction, will examine probability theory, and the next chapter will examine enumerative arguments and develop a method for evaluating such arguments. Finally, we will look briefly at causal reasoning.

THE PROBLEM OF INDUCTION

Although inductive logic is as old as deduction, the study of induction is still in its infancy. One reason for this is the so-called problem of induction. The Scottish philosopher and historian David Hume (see box) described this problem in his *Treatise of Human Nature:*

> If reason determin'ed us, it wou'd proceed upon that principle, *that instances, of which we have had no experience, must resemble those, of which we have had experience, and that the course of nature continues always uniformly the same. . . .*
>
> Our foregoing method of reasoning will easily convince us, that there can be no *demonstrative* arguments to prove, *that those instances, of which we have had no experience, resemble those, of which we have had experience.* We can at least conceive a change in the course of nature; which sufficiently provides, that such a change is not absolutely impossible.[1]

He restates the problem in *An Enquiry Concerning Human Understanding:*

> If we be, therefore, engaged by arguments to put trust in past experience, and make it the standard of our future judgement, these arguments must be probable only, . . . But that there is no argument of this kind, must appear, if our explication of that species of reasoning be admitted as solid and satisfactory. . . . It is impossible, therefore, that any arguments from experience can prove this resemblance of the past to the future; since all these arguments are founded on the supposition of that resemblance.[2]

The problem Hume is pointing to is this: How can the conclusion of an inductive argument be said to provide new information based on its premises? On what basis can the conclusion be allowed to go beyond the scope of its premises? While a certain event in the past may have produced a particular result, there is no guarantee that tomorrow's experience will be the same. It is possible that things have changed or may change. For example, consider the following scenario:

> For the past 30 days I visited the San Diego Zoo daily and on each visit I observed only white swans. On the basis of this experience, I conclude that during tomorrow's visit the third swan I observe will be white.

David Hume, born in Scotland in 1711, maintained that all knowledge comes through sensory experience and that sensory experience is founded upon customs and not necessarily the real world.

Clearly, this argument is not "solid" or "satisfactory" if, by these terms, we mean that the premises guarantee the conclusion or, in other words, the argument preserves truth. It is conceivable that tomorrow's visit may take me to the section of the zoo that houses Australian swans, which are black. Even if the premise is true, it is still possible for the conclusion to be false. Yet the kind of reasoning illustrated in this scenario occurs daily and typically is quite adequate. (Consider your evidence for believing that the sun will set tomorrow evening.)

The question Hume raises is, How can we justify a method of reasoning that may result in incorrect conclusions? More broadly, how can we justify inductive reasoning? Given the evidence presented, how can I justify the conclusion, "I know or believe that the third swan I see tomorrow will be white"? Such conclusions are usually justified by the **principle of uniformity**, which states that if certain experiences lead to a given result, then similar experiences in the future will lead to the same or at least a similar result. If this principle always held, inductive reasoning would not be problematic. However, if it is possible that the principle of uniformity does not always hold, there may be a problem with induction. And obviously, the principle does *not* always hold: It is possible that the third swan I observe tomorrow will be an Australian swan, in spite of my past experiences.

Since this is an introductory text, we are not concerned with a complete answer to the problem. However, as critical reasoners, we need to be aware of the problem and of the more important responses to it. And we should realize that the problem itself may be problematic; that is, Hume may not have identified a real problem. Let us examine these issues in more detail.

RESPONSES TO THE PROBLEM

In light of induction's potential for error, the most typical reaction a person has upon first considering the problem is simply to reject it. After all, if inductive reasoning is so susceptible to error, why be concerned with it? If it does not always provide us with the truth, why even bother with this type of reasoning? Induction does indeed have these problems, but in almost all disciplines except mathematics and philosophy, the major type of reasoning used is induction. In everyday life, too, our ordinary reasoning processes are largely inductive. For example, I just got home from a three-night backpacking trip in the high Sierra mountain range, and my wife concludes that I am tired when she sees me. She used induction to draw her conclusion. Can you think of other examples in which induction is used in everyday life? In spite of its weaknesses, induction is important simply because it is the way we normally reason.

If deduction is the reasoning method that preserves truth, induction is the method that expands our knowledge. To have a thorough system of critical reasoning, we need both methods.[3] Also, it seems that deductive reasoning is dependent on induction for the *content* of its arguments: The premises used in deductive reasoning ultimately are based on inductive reasoning. John Stuart Mill, a famous English philosopher and economist (see box), recognized this fact:

> I grappled at one with the problem of Induction, postponing that of reasoning [meaning deduction], on the ground that it is necessary to obtain premises before we can reason from them.[4]

John Stuart Mill (1806–1873) began learning Greek at the age of three. By eight, he was reading Plato and Herodotus. Mill was not only influential in the development of utilitarian ethics, but also crucial in the establishment of the first women's rights organizations.

A second frequent response to the problem of induction is to use *inductive support for induction*—in other words, to use induction to justify induction:

> To the layman the most natural way of defending belief in induction is that it has worked in the past. Concealed in this reply, of course, is the assumption that what has already worked will continue to do so . . . .[5]

Two problems with this approach appear immediately. First, the reasoning used is fallacious; it is circular and thus begs the question. However, it can be argued that it is not really circular. As the American philosopher Max Black (see box) points out, "the appearance of circularity arises only from overhasty application of criteria applied to deduction."[6] That is, this approach appears to be simply a version of "P; therefore, P." But Black insists that it is not. While one may question whether this is so, there is a second, possibly more serious, problem: The approach is dependent on the principle of uniformity, which, as we have seen, may not always hold true.

A third response related to the first one described earlier, is *converting inductive reasoning into deductive reasoning*. This is done by adding a premise that would link the existing premises to the conclusion in a deductive fashion. An example is the use of "covering laws" in scientific explanations. These "laws" connect premise and conclusion in such a way as to make the reasoning deductive rather than inductive. For example, imagine

Max Black (1909–1988) was born in Russia, was educated in England, and moved to the United States in 1940. He is best known for his work in philosophical analysis in which he emphasized the value of ordinary language.

that you are asked to investigate an airplane accident. You begin by reviewing the data. While the runway was of minimal length, Mr. Smith, the pilot of the Cherokee 140, had flown in and out of the small private runway outside of Denver many times before. However, on this particular day, instead of lifting off of the runway, the plane simply ran off the end of the runway. After interviewing the pilot, you determine that he used the same procedures he always had and that the engine did not malfunction. Furthermore, you discover that the day of the accident was abnormally hot and extremely humid. As the investigator, you conclude that the plane failed to produce adequate lift, and you structure your reasoning as follows:

> Mr. Smith was familiar with the short runway and had used it successfully before.
> There was no problem with the plane's engine.
> There was no change in takeoff procedures.
> The weather conditions were abnormally hot and extremely humid.
> ∴ The plane failed to produce adequate lift.

The data presented as evidence do not deductively support the conclusion. However, explanatory information can be made explicit that would convert the inductive reasoning into deductive reasoning. This explanatory information is known as a *covering law*. The covering law may state that on a hot, humid day, at altitude, it takes longer to attain a speed sufficient to produce adequate lift than on a cold, dry day. You take this covering law and add it to your premises:

> Mr. Smith was familiar with the short runway and had used it successfully before.
> There was no problem with the plane's engine.
> There was no change in takeoff procedures.
> The weather conditions were abnormally hot and extremely humid.
> On a hot, humid day, at altitude, it takes longer to attain a speed sufficient to produce adequate lift than on a cold, dry day.
> ∴ The plane failed to produce adequate lift.

As the philosopher of science Carl Hempel (see box) pointed out, the explanatory information (i.e., the covering laws) provided implies the conclusion deductively and thus offers logically conclusive grounds for the conclusion.[7]

If the covering law is true and the other premises are also true, then the conclusion must be true. However, the notion of covering laws itself is questionable. In this example, other covering laws are possible that would equally support the conclusion. Possibly when Mr. Smith flew in and out of the small runway in the past, the grass had been mown short, but on this particular day the grass was tall and the ground soggy. These conditions would create additional drag, thus deductively supporting the conclusion that the plane failed to produce adequate lift. But which covering law is the correct explanation? Unless we checked every possible explanation and eliminated all but one, the selection of a covering law is dependent upon inductive reasoning.

It should also be noted that attempts to solve the problem of induction by transforming inductive reasoning into deductive reasoning may be based on a misunderstanding of the nature of inductive reasoning. Consider the following remarks by the British philosopher of science Karl Popper (see box):

> It is usual to call an inference "inductive" if it passes from singular statements (sometimes also called "particular" statements), such as accounts of the results of observations or experiments, to universal statements, such as hypotheses or theories.
>
> Now it is far from obvious, from a logical point of view, that we are justified in inferring universal statements from singular ones, no matter how numerous; for any conclusion drawn in this way may always turn out to be false: no matter how many instances of white swans we may have observed. This does not justify the conclusion that all swans are white.[8]

Popper is assuming that we cannot check every single swan, even though we might be able to examine most of them. This passage illustrates some of the problems raised by attempts to convert induction into deduction. First, Popper assumes that the only appropriate logical point of view is that of deduction. Second, the passage seems to ignore the nature of inductive reasoning: Inductive reasoning does not claim to preserve truth; it readily admits that its conclusions may be false. A third problem is the characterization of inductive reasoning as moving from the particular to the general or universal; as we have seen, this is a common error in the conceptualization of induction.

A fourth possible response to the problem of induction as stated by Hume is known as the *pragmatic justification of inductive reasoning*. This response was introduced by Hans Reichenbach (1891–1953), a German philosopher and educator, and expanded by his pupil Wesley Salmon (see box). It is described in the following passage:

> **Sir Karl Popper** (1902–1994): Although Popper, was friends with several of the logical positivists, he was extremely critical of their position on verification. His *Logic of Scientific Discovery* (1959) is considered a classic in the field of philosophy of science. Sir Karl Popper was knighted in 1965.

> **Wesley Salmon** (1925–2001) was University Professor Emeritus of Philosophy at the University of Pittsburgh. He joined the faculty there in 1981. His main interests were scientific explanation and causality, probability, confirmation, induction, and the philosophy of physical science.

This approach accepts Hume's arguments up to the point of agreeing that it is impossible to establish, either deductively or inductively, that any inductive inference will ever again have true conclusions. Nevertheless, Reichenbach claims, the standard method of inductive generalization can be justified. Although its success as a method of prediction cannot be established in advance, it can be shown to be superior to any alternative method of prediction.[9]

Salmon goes on to point out that if any method of prediction works, it will be the inductive method, since any method of prediction must move from known data to unknown data. "As a result, we have everything to gain and nothing to lose by adopting the inductive method."[10] Salmon does not try to defend the principle of uniformity. He simply claims that the inductive method is the best method for prediction, even if it occasionally does not work.

Earlier, we suggested that the problem of induction may itself be problematic. Note that, like Popper, Hume apparently assumed that deductive reasoning is the only appropriate method of reasoning, because only deduction preserves truth. If the preservation of truth is what makes an argument good, then both Hume and Popper are correct. But it is a questionable practice to evaluate one thing by the standards of another.

Even so, to say that it is inappropriate to evaluate inductive reasoning by the standards of deductive reasoning is not to deny that the problem of induction exists. The problem does exist, but it does not mean that induction has no value. The real problem of induction is this: *Under what conditions can inductive reasoning be a good argument? What conditions must be satisfied if the premises of an inductive argument are to offer support for, or a justification of, the conclusion of the argument?* Those conditions will be discussed in the chapters that follow, but as we explore them, we must never lose sight of the fact that even if the premises of an argument are all true and the argument satisfies all the stipulated conditions, it is still possible for the conclusion to be false. *That's the nature of induction!*

CHAPTER FOUR

Introduction to Probability

Developing a theory of probability can be dangerous. Consider the case of Girolamo Cardano (1501–1576). A rogue by nature, Cardano wrote one of the first books for gamblers; it described how to cheat, using a probability theory. Cardano also predicted the day of his own death on the basis of probabilities. But on the fateful day he was not ill, so he reportedly took poison just to prove that his calculations were accurate. For today's critical reasoner, probability theory is not necessarily life threatening, but it is nonetheless important. This chapter therefore presents a brief introduction to the subject.

4.1 PROBABILITY THEORY

Probability presents a conclusion *relative to* the evidence and thereby attempts to bridge gaps or shortcomings in our knowledge of ourselves and the world about us. It is concerned with the degree of likelihood that an event will take place, given the evidence. Thus, when we claim the likelihood of an event or the probability of an event occurring, we are citing the degree of justification the evidence gives for that event. For example, if we ask the likelihood of rolling a deuce on a fair die, the degree of justification or probability is 1/6. (How this answer is arrived at will be explained later in the chapter.) Probability provides a foundation for inductive reasoning, also termed **plausible reasoning**. Although probability is an aspect of mathematics, it differs from the **demonstrative reasoning**[11] often associated with mathematics. (In demonstrative reasoning, also termed deductive reasoning, the conclusion is conclusive, given the evidence. For example, in a base-ten system, three plus five equals eight. So if you have three apples and you are given five more, you now have eight apples. The answer is conclusive, given the evidence. Demonstrative reasoning is not interested in "the likelihood of"; it seeks a definite answer.)

Although a theoretical discussion of probability is beyond the scope of the text, it is important to understand the theoretical assumptions underlying this chapter. To begin with,

> **Bruno de Finetti** (1906–1985), the Italian mathematician, had an interesting response to the question "What is probability?" De Finetti's response was that probability does not exist; it is not a property of the world. Rather, probability, expresses a relationship between us and our view of the world.

the purpose of introducing probabilities is pragmatic: Probabilities are used in decision making. When confronted with a situation requiring a decision that is not deductive in nature, we calculate probabilities to aid in the decision-making process. Suppose, for example, that you are in the process of registering for your classes and you want to take English 3. However, you have been told that two of the instructors are really bad; unfortunately, you have forgotten their names. You look at the course offerings and discover that there are only three sections of English 3 being offered. The odds (probability) are against you, so you decide not to take English 3 this time around. Our focus thus is on **epistemic probability**, or the degree of justification for a particular decision. Unlike physical probabilities, which deal with the structure of the universe or universally applicable assignments, such as "Whenever anyone is confronted with the opportunity to tell a lie, he or she ought to always tell the truth," epistemic probabilities deal with the individual decision maker in a particular situation. They treat definite, specific instances and do not claim to address entire classes of events.

The pragmatic orientation of this text gives rise to a **subjectivist** emphasis; that is, it acknowledges that the assignment of a degree of likelihood is rooted in the beliefs of the decision maker.[12] According to Bruno de Finetti (see box),

> *the notions of uncertainty and probability do not apply to the facts as such* (distinguishing those which are "determined" from those which are not and have a "less or greater chance" of occurring). Rather, they become relevant in the particular situations of a decision-maker who may ignore certain facts (and it is immaterial whether his uncertainty is due to the impossibility of foreseeing the future, or to an incomplete knowledge of the past, or for any other reason).[13]

This emphasis can be problematic if we assign a probability merely on the basis of personal feelings of confidence.[14] If the decision maker had no guidelines or boundaries to operate within, then his or her decisions could be irrational. But while a subjectivist approach allows two reasoners to examine the same evidence and assign different degrees of likelihood to it, it places certain constraints on the reasoners. First, the axioms of probability calculus hold true. Second, as we will see in the next chapter, the subjective evaluation process is guided by rational criteria.

The pragmatic orientation of this text also influences its presentation of probability calculus. Since many people are not comfortable with mathematical formulas and tend to avoid using them, we present this material in a very elementary form. In spite of its simplicity, however, the discussion will provide an adequate foundation for understanding plausibility.[15]

NANCY ® by Jerry Scott. NANCY reprinted by permission of United Feature Syndicate, Inc.

4.2 BASIC PROBABILITY

Four basic principles guide the study of probability:

1. If a conclusion or event is true, it will have a probability of 1.
2. If a conclusion or event is false, it will have a probability of 0.
3. If a conclusion or event has a probability of either 1 or 0, we test the argument by deductive methods. (See Part III of the text.)
4. If a conclusion or event has a probability greater than 0, but less than 1 (i.e., $0 \le \times \le 1$), we apply probability calculus.

In addition, there are four basic formulas that will usually satisfy the needs of a decision maker. (Two additional formulas will be introduced in Section 4.11.) In these formulas, f stands for "number of favorable instances" and p for "total number of possible instances." Favorable instances are instances that satisfy the required conditions. If you ask what is the probability of drawing a queen of hearts from a standard deck of playing cards, the condition being sought is "the queen of hearts." The total number of possible instances is "the total number of cards in a standard deck of cards." The formulas of classical probability are as follows:

1. **single events** $= \dfrac{f}{p}$

2. **conjunction of independent events** $= \dfrac{f_1}{p_1} \times \dfrac{f_2}{p_2}$

3. **conjunction of dependent events** $= \dfrac{f_1}{p_1} \times \dfrac{f_2}{p_2}$

4. **mutually exclusive alternative events** $= \dfrac{f_1}{p_1} + \dfrac{f_2}{p_2}$

These formulas represent the four most common types of situations in which probability aids in the decision-making process. For example, suppose you are considering whether you can pass a particular course if you take it next semester. This is an example of a **single-event probability**, since it involves just one event: passing the course. Or you might be wondering what the likelihood is of passing both advanced calculus and chemistry III. In this case, you have two independent events, neither of which is dependent upon the other—an example of a **conjunction of independent events**. There are other times, however, when the likelihood of one event is dependent upon another event. For example, suppose you are wondering what the probability is of drawing two cards from a standard deck of cards and both cards being an ace. If you do not put the first card drawn back in the stack, then the likelihood of the second card being an ace is different from what it would be if you had replaced the first card. That is, with replacement, you are drawing from fifty-two cards, but without replacement, you are drawing the second card from a deck of fifty-one cards. The second card's probability is dependent upon the first draw. This is an example of a **conjunction of dependent events**. Finally, there are times when we see the likelihood of one result or a second result, and the two events cannot both occur. For instance, the NFL football season starts up, many fans declare which team will win the Super Bowl. Someone might claim that either the Dallas Cowboys or the San Francisco 49ers will win. Both teams cannot win, so the probability of either the Cowboys or the 49ers winning is mutually exclusive: If one wins, the other is automatically a nonwinner, but the claim is that one of these teams will win. So what is the probability that either the Dallas Cowboys or the San Francisco 49ers will win? This is an example of **mutually exclusive alternative events**. Now, to better understand these four types of probabilities, we will focus on each one separately, giving further examples and then an exercise composed of several problems that can be solved using the foregoing formulas.

4.3 SINGLE-EVENT PROBABILITIES

The following problems are examples of **single-event probabilities**:

4.3a

What is the probability of tossing a fair die and rolling a three?

$$\frac{f}{p} = \frac{1}{6}$$

Given the question, only one situation will count as a favorable instance—that is, the die rolling up a 3. Since there are six possible ways a fair die could land, we replace p with 6. Hence, there is a 1/6 probability of rolling a 3 on a fair die.

4.3b

What is the probability of tossing a fair coin and its landing tails up?

$$\frac{f}{p} = \frac{1}{2}$$

4.3c

What is the probability of drawing a king of hearts from a new deck of cards?

$$\frac{f}{p} = \frac{1}{52}$$

4.4 EXERCISE: SINGLE-EVENT PROBABILITIES

In solving these problems, always start with the formula and show all your work:

1. Determine the probability of tossing a fair coin and its landing tails up.
*2. What is the probability of blindly drawing a king of hearts from a new deck of standard cards?
3. What is the probability of blindly drawing an ace from a new deck of standard cards?
4. What is the probability of rolling a two on a fair die?
*5. What is the probability of blindly opening a 400-page book to page 251 or page 301 in a single try?
6. What is the probability of rolling an even number on a single toss of a fair die?
7. You are a contestant on a game show. You have before you four doors, and you do not know what is behind each door. However, you do know that behind one door is an empty box, behind another is a copy of Hacking's *The Emergence of Probability*, behind a third is a new Mercedes 560SL, and behind a fourth is a 1971 Ford Pinto (which does not run). You are told that you will receive whatever is behind the first door you choose to open. What is the probability that you will be stuck with the Pinto?
8. You are registering for classes and want to take critical reasoning. There are eight offerings of the course, each with a different instructor. In talking with your friends, you learned that the school has only three instructors who are really good in this subject, but you have forgotten which three are good. You must make your decision now! What is the probability of getting one of those three good instructors?
9. In looking over your assignment for tomorrow's class, you find that you are to read pages 50 through 100. However, you forgot to write down which text the assignment comes from. You have ten books for the course, but three of them do not have 100 or more pages in them. You do not have time to read 50 pages in all of the books, so you blindly choose one and read pages 50 through 100. What is the probability that you selected the wrong text?

4.5 CONJUNCTION OF INDEPENDENT EVENTS

The following problems are examples of the **conjunction of independent events**:

4.5a

What is the probability of tossing two fair coins and both landing heads up?

$$\frac{f}{p} \times \frac{f}{p} = \frac{1}{2} \times \frac{1}{2} = \frac{1}{4}$$

  ↑ ↑
first coin second coin

4.5b

What is the probability of tossing four dice together and all rolling up threes?

$$\frac{f}{p} \times \frac{f}{p} \times \frac{f}{p} \times \frac{f}{p} = \frac{1}{6} \times \frac{1}{6} \times \frac{1}{6} \times \frac{1}{6} = \frac{1}{1,296}$$

4.5c

What is the probability of tossing five fair coins and all of them landing heads up?

$$\frac{f}{p} \times \frac{f}{p} \times \frac{f}{p} \times \frac{f}{p} \times \frac{f}{p} = \frac{1}{2} \times \frac{1}{2} \times \frac{1}{2} \times \frac{1}{2} \times \frac{1}{2} = \frac{1}{32}$$

4.5d

What is the probability of rolling eight dice and none turning up three?

$$\frac{f}{p} \times \frac{f}{p} \times \frac{f}{p} \times \frac{f}{p} \times \frac{f}{p} \times \frac{f}{p} \times \frac{f}{p} \times \frac{f}{p} =$$
$$\frac{5}{6} \times \frac{5}{6} \times \frac{5}{6} \times \frac{5}{6} \times \frac{5}{6} \times \frac{5}{6} \times \frac{5}{6} \times \frac{5}{6} = \frac{390,625}{1,679,616}$$

4.6 EXERCISE: CONJUNCTION OF INDEPENDENT EVENTS
Again, be sure to show all your work.

1. What is the probability of tossing two fair coins and both landing with heads up?

*2. What is the probability of tossing five fair coins and all of them landing with heads up?

3. What is the probability that four fair dice thrown together will all turn up twos?

4. What is the probability of eight fair dice thrown together and none will turn up a three?

*5. What is the probability that four fair dice thrown together will all turn up an even number?

6. You have three jars, each containing ten marbles. Jar one contains three white marbles, two black marbles, and five red marbles. Jar two contains one white marble, eight black marbles, and one red marble. Jar three contains three white marbles, four black marbles, and three red marbles. You select one marble from each jar blindly.
    a. What is the probability that all three marbles are white?
    b. What is the probability that all three marbles are black?
    c. What is the probability that all three marbles are red?

4.7 CONJUNCTION OF DEPENDENT EVENTS

The following problems are examples of the **conjunction of dependent events**:
   Note that the formulas for the conjunctions of independent and dependent events are the same. The difference is that in independent events the various events do not influence or affect the other events, whereas in dependent events one event affects subsequent events.

4.7a

Given a jar with three black, four white, and three red marbles, what is the probability in two blind draws (i.e., draws without replacement) of both marbles being black?

$$\frac{f}{p} \times \frac{f}{p} = \frac{3}{10} \times \frac{2}{9} = \frac{6}{90} = \frac{1}{15}$$

$$\uparrow \quad \uparrow$$

first draw second draw

Notice that the first draw affects the second draw. That is, since there is no replacement after the first draw, there no longer are three black balls left. We now have only two black balls; hence, only two favorable instances are possible. Moreover, after the first draw there no longer are ten marbles in the jar. Only nine marbles are left, and this fact needs to be reflected in the replacement of p for the second draw.

4.7b

What is the probability in two blind draws of drawing two white marbles?

$$\frac{f}{p} \times \frac{f}{p} = \frac{4}{10} \times \frac{3}{9} = \frac{12}{90} = \frac{6}{45}$$

4.7c

What is the probability in three blind draws of obtaining three black marbles?

$$\frac{f}{p} \times \frac{f}{p} \times \frac{f}{p} = \frac{3}{10} \times \frac{2}{9} \times \frac{1}{8} = \frac{6}{720} = \frac{1}{120}$$

4.8 EXERCISE: CONJUNCTION OF DEPENDENT EVENTS

1. You have a jar that contains three black, four white, and three red marbles.
    *a. You have two blind draws. What is the probability that both marbles drawn will be black?
    b. Given two blind draws, what is the probability that both marbles drawn will be white?
    c. Given two blind draws, what is the probability that both marbles drawn will be red?
    *d. You have three blind draws. What is the probability that all three marbles are black?
    e. Given three blind draws, what is the probability that all three marbles drawn will be white?

2. You have a fresh deck of standard cards that are adequately shuffled and face down.
    a. You cut the deck and then draw the top two cards. What is the probability that both cards are spades?
    b. After cutting the deck, you randomly, but blindly, draw four cards. What is the probability that all four cards will be red?

3. You have a bag that contains four black marbles and one white marble. You draw one marble; if it is black, you draw another marble. If it is white, you must stop. If the second marble is also black, you have another draw. If the third marble is black, you have a fourth draw. What is the probability of drawing all four black marbles if you do not replace any marbles?

4. You have a jar with twenty-five marbles in it, five of each of the following colors: black, white, red, green, and purple. You have five blind draws without replacement. What is the probability that you will draw five purple marbles?

4.9 MUTUALLY EXCLUSIVE ALTERNATIVE EVENTS

Sometimes a favorable result may be obtained in more than one instance or in more than one way. For example, suppose that your main goal is to pass your course in critical reasoning. If you pass, you will be happy. Thus, you will be happy if you receive a grade of D. You will also be happy if you receive a C, a B, or an A. There are four different possible results, and you will be happy if any of them occur. Moreover, the results are mutually exclusive, since they cannot all occur at once. That is, if any one of them occurs, none of the other three can occur. In these types of situations, we use the formula for **mutually exclusive alternative events**, illustrated in the following problem:

4.9a

What is the probability of rolling an even number in a single throw of a die?

$$\text{Pr } 2 = \frac{1}{6}$$

$$\text{Pr } 4 = \frac{1}{6}$$

$$\text{Pr } 6 = \frac{1}{6}$$

$$\frac{f}{p} + \frac{f}{p} + \frac{f}{p} = \frac{1}{6} + \frac{1}{6} + \frac{1}{6} = \frac{3}{6} = \frac{1}{2}$$

This situation has three different, mutually exclusive, possible outcomes. We might roll a two, a four, or a six, but not more than one of these would be rolled in a single toss. Therefore, we find the probability of each single event and then apply the formula for mutually exclusive alternative events. This example illustrates the fact that before we can apply this formula, we often need to apply another formula first.

Interestingly, the problem can also be worked as a single-event probability. Remember the question that this problem presents: "What is the probability of rolling an even number in a single throw of a die?" Since there are three even numbers on the die, there are three favorable instances. As a result, we might approach the problem as follows:

4.9b

$$\frac{f}{p} = \frac{3}{6} = \frac{1}{2}$$

Which approach is correct? Both are acceptable.

Not all problems involving mutually exclusive alternative events can be worked more than one way. Consider this problem:

4.9c

What is the probability of tossing two coins and both landing with the same face up?

$$\text{both heads} = \frac{1}{2} \times \frac{1}{2} = \frac{1}{4}$$

$$\text{both tails} = \frac{1}{2} \times \frac{1}{2} = \frac{1}{4}$$

$$\frac{1}{4} + \frac{1}{4} = \frac{2}{4} = \frac{1}{2}$$

It is possible that you calculated that there are two possible ways to satisfy the question and four total possible combinations, thus giving you 2/4, which reduces to the correct answer. But sometimes it is too easy to make mental mistakes, and it is just easier to work through the problem using the formula.

4.9d

> *What is the probability of tossing three coins and obtaining two heads and one tail (not necessarily in that order)?*

There are three alternatives:

$$h, h, t = \frac{1}{2} \times \frac{1}{2} \times \frac{1}{2} = \frac{1}{8}$$

$$h, t, h = \frac{1}{2} \times \frac{1}{2} \times \frac{1}{2} = \frac{1}{8}$$

$$t, h, h = \frac{1}{2} \times \frac{1}{2} \times \frac{1}{2} = \frac{1}{8}$$

$$\frac{1}{8} + \frac{1}{8} + \frac{1}{8} = \frac{3}{8}$$

4.10 EXERCISE: MUTUALLY EXCLUSIVE ALTERNATIVE EVENTS

1. What is the probability of rolling an even number in a single throw of a die? (This problem could be worked as a single-event probability.)
2. What is the probability that if we toss two coins, both will land with the same face up?
3. Find the probability of drawing an ace and a ten in two draws from a standard deck with replacement.
*4. What is the probability of obtaining a total of ten in a single toss of two dice?

4.11 TWO ADDITIONAL FORMULAS

While the four basic probability formulas presented are generally adequate, two additional formulas may be useful for decision makers.

1. **Subtraction Principle** = Not $\left[\dfrac{f_1}{p_1}\right] = 1 - \left[\dfrac{f_1}{p_1}\right]$

2. **General Alternative Principle** = $\left[\dfrac{f_1}{p_1}\right]$ or $\left[\dfrac{f_2}{p_2}\right]$ =

$$\left[\frac{f_1}{p_1} + \frac{f_2}{p_2}\right] - \left[\frac{f_1}{p_1} \times \frac{f_2}{p_2}\right]$$

As a decision maker, you may at times be looking for the probability of an event *not* occurring. For example, suppose you are planning an outdoor event three weeks from now, but you are currently in the rainy season. You are interested, not in the likelihood of rain, but the likelihood of it *not* raining. If you know the probability of rain, given that time of the year, then the **subtraction principle** enables you to calculate the probability of not getting wet. Furthermore, when we are confronted with alternative possibilities, the formulas presented in Section 4.2 presuppose that we can distinguish between mutually exclusive and nonexclusive events. Consider, for example, taking a poorly designed exam (not by your instructor, of course). A question is asked, "What is the probability of drawing an ace in two draws from a standard deck of cards?" As a student who has mastered probability, you realize that your answer depends upon whether the first card drawn is placed back in the stack, and since you are taking an exam, you cannot ask for clarification. Given this situation, you should use the **general alternative principle**.

4.12 EXERCISE: MIXED PROBABILITIES

In solving these problems, indicate the type of probability involved and show all work, including the formula used:

1. What is the probability of randomly glancing at your watch and seeing that the second hand will be on twelve seconds after the hour?

*2. What is the probability of drawing a queen, a four, and a king in three draws from a standard deck of cards? The order in which you draw the cards does not matter, and you will replace each card after you have drawn it.

3. Of the 100 students in your class, thirty-three are seniors, forty are juniors, seventeen are sophomores, and ten are freshmen. What is the probability of two separate persons looking at the class roll and blindly selecting a freshman?

*4. You have a standard fair deck of cards. You have two blind draws. What is the probability that both cards now in your hand are red?

5. Sixteen pool balls on a table are set up in such a fashion that one ball will go in some pocket on every shot. What is the probability that you sink two solid colored balls, not counting the eight ball, on successive (blind) shots? (There are equal numbers of solid and striped balls.)

*6. What is the probability of spinning an odd number on a single spin of a wheel with numbers from one to ten?

7. What is the probability of being dealt identical five-card poker hands twice in a row? (Assume that you are the only player.)

*8. You are playing basketball and you have two free throws. What is the probability that you will make both of them if the likelihood of your making the shots is the same as the likelihood of your missing them?

9. Suppose there are four flavors of ice cream (chocolate, vanilla, chocolate chip, and "pralines-'n'-cream"). Three people will each choose one flavor for dessert. What is the probability that all will select the same flavor?

10. Your closet has fifteen differently styled shirts, eight of which are short sleeved. What is the probability that you could blindly pick out all of the short-sleeved shirts in succession?

11. A friend will take you out to dinner at the restaurant of your choice if you can draw a king, a queen, and a jack of the same suit, but in any order, from a standard deck of cards. You will have only three draws and will not be replacing any cards. What is the probability that the friend will take you out to dinner?

12. There is a jar with five white marbles, seven red marbles, and four black marbles in it on the table. You will chose one marble, but you must close your eyes and withdraw only one marble. The marble you get is the marble you keep. What is the probability that you will obtain either a white marble or a purple one?

13. You are at a picnic with your friends. In the cooler you have six cans of Budweiser, twelve Miller Lites, and six Coors Extra Gold Drafts. What is the probability of blindly pulling three Coors out of the cooler? (I assume that you will not replace them!)

14. There are five pieces of bread on a plate on the table. Each is buttered only on one side. Your two-year-old nephew comes along and "accidentally" pulls the plate off the table. What is the probability that all five slices of bread will land with the buttered side down?

15. You are about to get married, and you have requested that your parents buy you a dining room table. You have asked them to buy you either an oak table or a maple table. What is the probability that you will receive the oak table? (Your parents have no obligation to buy what you request.) (What problems does this exercise raise? Given these problems, can the exercise be worked?)

16. If you are dealt five cards from an honest deck of cards, what is the probability that you will be given four aces and a king of hearts? You may receive these cards in any order.

17. You have three jars that each contain five snakes. Jar one contains one short snake, three medium snakes, and one long snake. Jar two contains three short, one medium, and one long snake. Jar three has one short, one medium, and three long snakes. You are blindfolded, and then you remove one snake from each jar. What is the probability that all three snakes you selected are short?

18. What is the probability of blindly picking a short straw when there are twenty-five straws, three of which are short and the rest are long?

19. Each of a total of twenty-six cards has a different letter of the Roman alphabet on it. What is the probability of blindly drawing a "Z"?

20. You are fishing in a tank that has four bass and six trout in it. You are using a bait which guarantees that you will catch a fish every time you cast your line. What is the probability that you will catch two bass for supper in two casts?

4.13 BAYESIAN CONFIRMATION

The problems we have considered so far deal with the likelihood of a particular event occurring in the future. However, there are times when we are interested in the probability that a certain event occurred in the past. For example, suppose that you are reading Rene

> Nature also teaches me by these sensations of pain: hunger, thirst, etc., that I am not only lodged in my body as a pilot in a vessel, but that I am very closely united to it, and so to speak so intermingled with it that I seem to compose with it one whole. For if that were not the case, when my body is hurt, I, who am merely a thinking thing, should not feel pain, for I should perceive this wound by the understanding only just as the sailor perceives by sight when something is damaged in his vessel; and when my body has need of drink or food, I should clearly understand the fact without being warned of it by confused feelings of hunger and thirst. For all these sensations of hunger, thirst, pain, etc. are in truth none other than certain confused modes of thought which are produced by the union and apparent intermingling of mind and body.[16]

Descartes' Sixth Meditation. You come upon his illustration of the sailor in the ship, published in 1641. (See box.)

Remembering what you learned in your course on medieval literature, you recall that John Buridan, who died around 1358, used the same illustration. So you ask, "Is it possible that Descartes borrowed his illustration from Buridan?"

Or maybe you are not reading Descartes, but instead want to know the likelihood that your car's engine was built in Canada rather than in Detroit, given that you have had a particular kind of problem with that engine. To determine such "posttrial" or "after-the-fact" probabilities, we can use **Bayesian confirmation** if we have enough information. The formula is as follows:

4.13a

$$\text{Pr}\,(h \mid e) = \frac{\text{Pr}\,(h) \times \text{Pr}\,(e \mid h)}{[\text{Pr}\,(h) \times \text{Pr}\,(e \mid h)] + [\text{Pr}\,(\sim h) \times \text{Pr}\,(e \mid \sim h)]}$$

In this formula, "Pr" stands for probability, h stands for the proposed hypothesis, e stands for the evidence offered, $\sim$ means "not", and | means "given." The key to using the formula is to identify the following items:

1. the proposed hypothesis
2. the evidence given to support the hypothesis
3. the probability of the hypothesis being true and the probability of its being false
4. the probability of the given evidence occurring if the hypothesis is true and the probability of the evidence occurring if the hypothesis is false

With this information, we can calculate the probability that an event occurred in the past. Consider the following example:

4.13b

> *We have two jars before us. In jar one, we have twelve marbles; ten are black and two are white. In jar two, there are also twelve marbles, six of which are black and the remainder white. You are blindfolded and are directed to draw one marble from one of the jars. After drawing the marble, someone rotates the jars such that you have no idea from which jar you drew the marble. The blindfold is removed, and you see you are holding a white marble. You are then asked, "Given the evidence, what is the probability that you drew that marble from jar two?"*

The first step in solving this problem is to determine what information can be derived immediately, as follows:

4.13c

Pr of drawing from $J1 = \dfrac{1}{2}$

Pr of drawing from $J2 = \dfrac{1}{2}$

Pr of drawing a black marble from $J1 = \dfrac{10}{12}$

Pr of drawing a white marble from $J1 = \dfrac{2}{12}$

Pr of drawing a black marble from $J2 = \dfrac{6}{12}$

Pr of drawing a black marble from $J2 = \dfrac{6}{12}$

The second step is to clearly identify the question and insert it into the formula. The question in the formula reads as follows: "What is the probability of the hypothesis being true, given the evidence?" [Pr $(h \mid e) =$.]

In this situation, the evidence we have is that you are holding a white marble. The hypothesis to be tested is that you drew the marble from jar two. Hence, the problem can be presented as Pr($J2 \mid$ white). Once we have completed this step, the next step becomes quite easy, for we have determined that $J2$ is to stand for h and white for e. In step three we make these substitutions, producing the following formula:

$$\text{Pr } (J2 \mid \text{white}) = \frac{\text{Pr } (J2) \; \times \text{Pr } (\text{white} \mid J2)}{[\text{Pr } (J2) \times \text{Pr } (\text{white} \mid J2)] + [\text{Pr } (\sim J2) \times \text{Pr } (\text{white} \mid \; \sim J2)]}$$

In step four, we insert the information from step one into the appropriate positions on the right side of the formula and complete the calculation. The result is as follows:

4.13d

$$\text{Pr}\,(J2\mid \text{white}) = \frac{\dfrac{1}{2}\times\dfrac{6}{12}}{\left[\dfrac{1}{2}\times\dfrac{6}{12}\right]+\left[\dfrac{1}{2}\times\dfrac{2}{12}\right]} =$$

$$\frac{\dfrac{6}{24}}{\dfrac{6}{24}+\dfrac{2}{24}}=\frac{\dfrac{6}{24}}{\dfrac{8}{24}}=\frac{6}{8}=\frac{3}{4}.$$

Thus, given that you are holding a white marble, the probability that you drew the marble from jar two is $\dfrac{3}{4}$.

4.13e

Let's add a third jar to the problem. This jar contains twelve marbles, of which three are black and nine are white. *Now* what is the probability that the white marble you are holding came from jar two?

$$\text{Pr}\,(J2\mid \text{white}) = \frac{\text{Pr}\,(J2)\times\text{Pr}\,(\text{white}\mid J2)}{[\text{Pr}\,(J2)\times\text{Pr}\,(\text{white}\mid J2)]+[\text{Pr}\,(\sim J2)\times\text{Pr}\,(\text{white}\mid \sim J2)]}=$$

$$\frac{\dfrac{1}{3}\times\dfrac{6}{12}}{\left(\dfrac{1}{3}\times\dfrac{6}{12}\right)+\left(\dfrac{2}{3}\times\dfrac{11}{24}\right)}=\frac{\dfrac{6}{36}}{\dfrac{6}{36}+\dfrac{22}{72}}=\frac{\dfrac{12}{72}}{\dfrac{12}{72}+\dfrac{22}{72}}=\frac{12}{34}=\frac{6}{17}$$

The key to solving this problem is to understand the last part of the formula in the denominator—that is, Pr (~J2) × Pr (white | ~J2).

We can readily see that the probability of the marble not coming from jar two is $\dfrac{2}{3}$. However, we must calculate the probability of drawing a white marble, given a jar other than jar two. Hence, we need to calculate the probability of drawing from jar one and the probability of drawing a white marble from that jar. Then we have to calculate the probability of drawing from jar three and the probability of drawing a white marble from that jar. Since we now have only two possible jars to draw from (J1 and J3), the probability of drawing from J1 is $\dfrac{1}{2}$. The probability of drawing a white marble from J1 is $\dfrac{2}{12}$. Hence, we have $\dfrac{1}{2}\times\dfrac{2}{12}=\dfrac{2}{24}$. We also could have drawn from J3, in which case we have

$\frac{1}{2} \times \frac{9}{12} = \frac{9}{24}$. Since both alternatives satisfy the condition, we will add them:

$\frac{2}{24} + \frac{9}{24} = \frac{11}{24}$. Hence, Pr (white | ~J2) = $\frac{11}{24}$.

4.14 EXERCISE: BAYESIAN CONFIRMATION

Evaluate the problems that follow. Be sure to show all work, including the formulas used.

1. You operate a small family-owned grocery store in a rural community. Four small farms supply you with eggs daily. Farmer Jones brought in his eggs in the basket you supplied, and it contained thirty-six eggs. Twelve of these eggs were large, twelve were medium, and twelve were small. Furthermore, all were white except twelve of them. Farmer Smith brought in his eggs in the same type of basket. He brought in forty-two eggs, 20 of which were medium size and the rest small. Half the eggs supplied by Smith were brown. Farmer Bruce brought his eggs in a box. (He had accidently run over your basket with a tractor.) In his box were four dozen eggs; all were large and only six were brown. Your fourth supplier, Farmer Klein, brought three dozen eggs in the basket you supplied. Two dozen of those were large and the rest were medium size. Twelve of his eggs were brown. You took each container of eggs and placed them in your cooler. Whenever a customer asked for eggs, you would go to the cooler and sort the eggs according to the customer's request. (Assume that the eggs are white unless indicated to be brown.)

    *a. Mr. Philips comes in and requests one dozen large eggs. You go to the cooler and fill his request from a single basket. Later that day, Mr. Philips calls and complains that all of the eggs he purchased were rotten. What is the probability that these eggs were supplied by Farmer Jones?

    b. Given the same situation as in Part a, what is the probability that the eggs came from the Klein farm?

    c. Mrs. Richards comes in and requests six brown eggs. You fill her order from a single basket. What is the probability that those six brown eggs came from the Smith farm?

    d. What is the probability that Mrs. Richards's eggs originated from the Bruce farm? Explain.

    e. You have just filled an order for three dozen large white eggs. You do not remember from which container you took the eggs. What is the probability that those eggs came from the Bruce farm?

2. You are a doctor, and a patient comes to you with a rash on her left knee. She wants you to find the cause of the rash. After studying the rash and your patient's medical history, you have narrowed the causal candidates to two. Given her history, you conclude that there is a 30% chance of the rash being caused by XYZ and a 50% chance of it being caused by XWW. However, in cases of XYZ, there is a likelihood of 90% that a rash as exhibited will occur, while in cases of XWW, the likelihood of a rash is only 50%. Unfortunately,

the treatment for the two possible causes is not similar, and both treatments are expensive. You know that your patient does not have medical insurance, and you do not wish to inflict a large medical bill upon her; hence, you wish to treat her for the the most probable cause.

a. Given the rash, what is the probability that your patient is suffering from XYZ?

b. What is the probability that your patient is suffering from XWW?

c. Which treatment will you recommend for your patient?

3. You currently own a Honda Prelude that has a problem with the transmission. After talking to your mechanic, you find out that transmissions such as yours are built in three plants, two in Japan and one in Kentucky. There is an equal prior probability that your transmission was built in any of the plants. However, the transmissions being produced by the plants do not have the same percentage of problems. Plants A and B are in Japan, and only 10% of the transmissions from Plant A have the problem you are encountering, but 30% of the transmissions from Plant B have the problem. In the Kentucky plant, only 15% of the transmissions develop the problem you are encountering. Since you have no way of knowing for sure at which plant your transmission was built, what is the probability of your transmission having been built in Kentucky?

4. Some philosophers of religion have suggested that the existence of God has a higher degree of probability than the nonexistence of God, given the order found in the universe. While it is not clear exactly how the various probabilities are derived, let us suppose the following: If God does exist, then there is

"I JUST DID PROVE IT!"

© 2000; Reprinted courtesy of Bunny Hoest and *Parade Magazine* an 85% chance of order existing in the universe. However, if God does not exist, then there is only a 15% chance of order existing. Furthermore, let us assume that the existence of God and the nonexistence of God have equal probabilities and that order does exist.

a. What is the probability that God exists, given the actual disposition of the universe—that is, that an ordered universe does exist?

b. What is the probability that God does not exist, given that order does exist in the universe?

c. What are some problems you find with this type of reasoning?

4.15 LOOKING AHEAD

This last exercise raises several important points for the critical reasoner. First, the process of critical reasoning does not cease when the text includes scientific or mathematical material. In such situations, we need to ask, "Where did these numbers come from?" This question may become the basis for further research. Second, if the subject of the argument is important to the reasoner, the data should be analyzed and interpreted. This often leads to further questions: Is the sample size large enough to justify or support the claim? Can we really count on that analogy? Is this the real cause? How was the information or data obtained? Frequently, when making a decision, we must ask whether we have all the necessary information and whether the information provided is accurate.

If we carefully analyze inductive arguments and pursue the many questions that arise, we often discover useful qualitative data. When the new information obtained through further research is combined with the information contained in the original argument, a new argument emerges. Chapter 5 focuses on the process of raising questions and seeking adequate qualitative information.

CHAPTER FIVE

Enumerative Induction

Will the sun rise tomorrow morning? What evidence is there for this belief? What argument could be given to support the claim that the sun will rise tomorrow morning? One possibility is as follows:

> The sun rose tomorrow minus *n* days.
>
> .
>
> .
>
> .
>
> The sun rose tomorrow minus 4 days.
> The sun rose tomorrow minus 3 days.
> The sun rose tomorrow minus 2 days.
> The sun rose tomorrow minus 1 day.
> ∴   The sun will rise tomorrow.

Even if the sun did rise this morning and has risen on every morning back through day *n*, does this evidence guarantee that the sun will rise tomorrow? Not at all: It is possible that the order of the universe could change during the night, causing the sun not to rise tomorrow.

In this chapter, we examine a form of inductive reasoning that we use every day. Whether our concern is the sun rising tomorrow or whether it is that the running shoes we just purchased be satisfactory because they are like the last pair we owned, we continually employ *enumerative* induction.

5.1 INTRODUCTION TO ENUMERATIVE INDUCTION

An **enumerative induction** is an argument that has as its premises a *listing of information* concerning either individuals or classes of individuals; the information is offered as evidence for the argument's conclusion, which also deals with either an individual or a class of individuals.[17] This reasoning process attempts to use observations of individuals or classes of individuals in support of some claim regarding them that has not been observed. The following arguments are classic examples of enumerative reasoning (note, however, that this type of reasoning is much broader than these two examples suggest):

5.1a	5.1b
Swan A is white.	Swan A is white.
Swan B is white.	Swan B is white.
Swan C is white.	Swan C is white.
∴ Swan D is white.	∴ All swans are white.

In both examples, the evidence consists of a list of things that have been observed. These are offered as evidence for a claim about something that has not been observed.

Since inductive reasoning does not intend to preserve truth, enumerative induction is not judged by its ability to guarantee the preservation of truth. Evaluations of such arguments—that is, attempts to determine whether they are good or bad arguments—are based on the four basic criteria discussed in the next section.

5.2 CRITERIA FOR EVALUATING ENUMERATIVE REASONING

Sample Size. The first criterion used in assessing an enumerative argument is *sample size*. Is the sample of items listed large enough to support the claim? An ideal sample might be 100 percent of the entities being considered. However, for purposes of inductive reasoning, such a sample size is impractical—even if it were possible. When an argument is assessed in terms of sample size, a larger number of observed items listed as evidence typically increases the likelihood that the conclusion is true. Hence, the argument is stronger.

5.2a

Swan A is white.
Swan B is white.
∴   Most swans are white.

5.2b

Swan A is white.
Swan B is white.
Swan C is white.
.
.
.
Swan Y is white.
∴   Most swans are white.

Notice that in Example 5.2a the evidence of observed swans is limited to swans A and B, whereas in example 5.2b the evidence includes swans A *through* Y. Because of the larger number of items in the second example, there is a greater likelihood that its conclusion is true. The phrase "greater likelihood" does not make a definitive claim concerning the truth of the conclusion; it simply states that it has a greater *probability* of being true.

The size of the sample offered in the premises should reflect the total number of items represented in the conclusion. However, because of advances in polling techniques, this ratio may be smaller than was formerly considered necessary. Moreover, one does not have to determine the exact number of items required to satisfy this criterion, since the dialogue approach is used to assess it. The notion of a dialogue approach to assessment may be a new concept to the reader. It is an approach that is fluid and developing. It provides a context and then tells a developing story that addresses key points within the said context. Since it is fluid and developing, it is not necessary to determine the exact number of items required for a sample size to be "large enough." And since inductive reasoning is evaluated in terms of a continuum from strong to weak, it is not necessary to establish a precise point of demarcation between strong and weak: Even without such a precise point, an argument can be placed somewhere between the two extremes with relative accuracy.

To illustrate the points we have made about sample size, consider the claim, "Most Sheldon College (SC) students are interested in improving their critical-thinking skills." (Assume that the college has slightly fewer than 9,000 students.)

5.2c

Yesterday I arbitrarily stopped 15 SC students and asked them whether they were interested in improving their critical-thinking skills.
Each responded in an affirmative fashion.
∴   Most SC students are interested in improving their critical-thinking skills.

Clearly, the size of the sample in this argument is much too small to warrant such a conclusion. The argument therefore must be considered weak. However, another argument using the same conclusion could be formulated as follows:

5.2d

Yesterday, by means of my fantastic abilities, I arbitrarily polled over 4,000 SC students, asking them whether they were interested in improving their critical-thinking skills.
All said yes, they were interested.
∴   Most SC students are interested in improving their critical-thinking skills.

It appears that this sample is large enough to warrant the claim being made. This argument, therefore, may be considered strong.

The two arguments just set forth illustrate the two ends of the continuum in relation to sample size. However, they give rise to an interesting problem: Given that these arguments represent opposite ends of the continuum and that the two poles can be clearly identified, how can the middle, or "moderate," region be identified? That is, at what point does an argument cease to be strong and become moderate? If 3,000 students had been polled, would the argument still have been strong? What about 2,500? 2,000? In the first argument, what if 20 students had been polled instead of 15? Would the argument still be weak, or would it be moderate? Or would we have to question 50 students to move from "weak" to "moderate"?

Fortunately, such decisions are not necessary. In the final assessment of an enumerative argument, the judgment of "strong," "moderate," or "weak" is always accompanied by an explanation, qualification, or justification. Hence, it is possible for different logicians to examine the same argument and place it at different points on the continuum. Qualitative assessments of probability are necessarily vague. Consider a glass of water sitting on a table. Some might say that it is half full, while others might claim that it is half empty. Whether they emphasize "full" or "empty" is not as important as the fact that they have qualified their label: It is somewhere in the middle of the range. Again, remember that inductive reasoning makes no claim to the rigidity that is found in deductive reasoning.

A final note concerning the criterion of sample size: If the criterion is clearly violated—that is, if the sample is obviously too small—a fallacy has been committed. This violation of proper reasoning is termed as **hasty generalization**. It is also known as leaping to a conclusion.

Sample Diversity. A second criterion by which enumerative arguments are evaluated is *sample diversity*: Is the sample varied enough to be representative of all the items in the group being sampled? The principle behind this criterion is that, generally, the greater the variety or diversity of the items listed in the premises, the greater is the likelihood that the conclusion is true. Consider the following argument:

5.2e

Swan A, which is at the Chicago Zoo, is white.
Swan B, which is at the Chicago Zoo, is white.
Swan C, which is at the Chicago Zoo, is white.

.
.
.

<u>Swan Y, which is at the Chicago Zoo, is white.</u>
∴   All swans are white.

Contrast this argument with the following:

5.2f

Swan A, which is at the Chicago Zoo, is white.
Swan B, which is at the London Zoo, is white.
Swan C, which is at the Melbourne Zoo, is white.
                        .
                        .
                        .
Swan Y, which is at the Moscow Zoo, is white.
∴   All swans are white.

Notice the diversity of the items listed in Example 5.2f, in contrast to the lack of diversity in Example 5.2e. While such diversity does not guarantee the truthfulness of the conclusion, it does increase its likelihood of being true. The lack of diversity in Example 5.2e, on the other hand, weakens the argument. After all, it is possible that, for some strange reason, whenever a swan breathes the air at the Chicago Zoo, it turns white. The criterion of diversity is meant to protect the reasoning process from any quirks that may occur in the polling process.

As with sample size, it is difficult to state exactly how diverse a sample must be. Again, arguments can be developed to illustrate the two extremes.

5.2g

In a recent poll at Michigan State University (MSU), students who are currently enrolled in either critical reasoning or symbolic logic were asked if they wanted to improve their critical-thinking skills.
In addition, any student who has checked a book out of the library from the BC section was asked the same question.
All of the students polled responded "yes."
∴   Most MSU students are interested in improving their critical thinking skills.

Notice the lack of diversity in this argument. All of the students polled are already involved in activities that will improve their critical-thinking skills, and it is quite possible that these students are the only ones at MSU who are interested in doing so. After all, it is possible that the rest of the MSU student body is interested solely in developing the skill of using one-liners to pick up members of the opposite sex at parties. The sample, therefore, lacks sufficient diversity.

Now consider the following argument:

5.2h

In a recent poll, we randomly selected an equal number of students from each major represented at MSU. Furthermore, we made sure that our sample included a fair representation of each class, of each sex, married and unmarried, etc.
In this poll, the students were asked whether they were interested in improving

their critical-thinking skills. Each person polled responded affirmatively to the question.

∴   Most MSU students are interested in improving their critical-thinking skills.

By increasing the diversity of the observed instances listed in this argument, we have minimized the chance that our sample merely reflects a particular group of students whom we just happened to interview. Therefore, there is a greater likelihood that the conclusion is true, and the argument has been strengthened.

If the list of observed instances does not represent the *scope* identified in the conclusion—that is, if it lacks appropriate diversity—the argument is fallacious. It is an example of **biased statistics**.

What exactly do we mean by *scope*? Here, the term refers to the range or extent suggested by the conclusion. Notice how the scope becomes increasingly smaller in each of the following sets:

5.2i

all MSU students
all MSU students who use the library
all MSU students who take Symbolic Logic II

5.2j

all Americans
all homeowners in America
all homeowners in America with no mortgages

In sum, the diversity of the sample, or evidence, in an argument must reflect the range suggested by the conclusion if the argument is to be considered strong.

Relevance of Analogy. A third criterion by which enumerative arguments are evaluated is *relevance of analogy:* Is the evidence in the premises sufficiently similar to the instance cited in the conclusion to justify the conclusion? This criterion has two aspects: positive and negative. In the case of **relevant positive analogy**, the greater the number of *relevant* similarities between the observed and unobserved instances, the greater is the likelihood that the conclusion is true. In the case of **relevant negative analogy**, the greater the number of relevant *dis*similarities between the items listed in the premises and the item cited in the conclusion, the less is the likelihood that the conclusion is true.

5.2k

Item 1 is a swan, and it is white.
Item 2 is a swan, and it is white.
Item 3 is a cat.

∴   Item 3 is white.

Contrast Example 5.2k with the following argument:

5.2l

Item 1 is a non-Australian swan, and it is white.
Item 2 is a non-Australian swan, and it is white.
Item 3 is a non-Australian swan.
∴   Item 3 is white.

Notice that is example 5.2k there is a similarity between the observed and unobserved instances: In both cases, they are presented as "Item" followed by a number. It is highly doubtful, however, that this qualifies as a *relevant* similarity. On the other hand, there is clearly a relevant dissimilarity. If we examined the properties "swanness" and "catness," their dissimilarities would be evident. Because of the high level of relevant dissimilarity it contains, Example 5.2k is a weak argument. In contrast, in Example 5.2l, there is a great amount of relevant similarity and no apparent relevant dissimilarity. Hence, there is a greater likelihood that the conclusion is true.

As with the criterion of sample size, in considering the number of relevant similarities or dissimilarities in an argument, both quantitative and qualitative aspects must be addressed. For example, suppose that we are comparing two pieces of jewelry. One is a copy and the other an original. From a quantitative standpoint, the comparison may be good, but from a qualitative standpoint (depending on the purpose of the comparison), it may be bad. While a fake diamond may have the same number of facets as a real diamond, the real diamond generally will be more valuable. Thus, comparing a copy with a real diamond would be a bad comparison.

Moreover, as with the criterion of sample diversity, the conclusion of an analogy dictates what counts as relevant. In Example 5.2m, for instance, the dissimilarities between a man and a rat are quite relevant:

5.2m

Rats are living, breathing things that run on four legs.
Men are living, breathing things.
∴   Men run on four legs.

In Example 5.2n, by contrast, the dissimilarities are less relevant:

5.2n

In the lab, nicotine smeared on the skin tissues of rats produces cancer.
Humans have similar skin tissues.
∴   Nicotine smeared on the skin tissues of a human being will produce cancer.

In like fashion, sometimes similarities may be relevant, while at other times they may be irrelevant.

If the instances cited as evidence contain more relevant dissimilarities than relevant similarities, or the dissimilarities qualitatively outweigh the similarities, we will consider the argument fallacious. The fallacy, which violates relevance of analogy, is known as **false analogy**.

Total Evidence. The fourth basic criterion for evaluating enumerative induction is **total evidence**. Would our evaluation of an argument change if additional information were provided? Do the premises present an adequate picture of the argument? Inductive reasoning can be strengthened by additional information. Note that the criterion of total evidence does not require that *all* possible information be contained in the argument. Rather, it focuses on the withholding of *relevant* information that might alter the assessment of the argument.

Consider the following argument:

5.2o

Swan A is black.
Swan B is black.
∴   Swan C is black.

Does this argument satisfy the criterion of total evidence? Is any information readily available, either in the domain of general human knowledge or in the specific audience to whom the argument is addressed, that, if it were included, would alter the assessment of the argument? Has the author intentionally or unintentionally withheld relevant information? While all the criteria we have discussed require an active reader, the criterion of total evidence demands critical reading and listening. A critical reader and listener must practice methodological skepticism, as referred to in chapter two. It is true that the author of an argument should include all relevant information, and the reader or listener is responsible for examining the information provided before embracing the claim put forth in the argument.

In the case of Example 5.2o, the reader must ask, Is there anything about swan C that might suggest that the argument is weak? Has any information been withheld? Often, this requires research. Assume that, in seeking answers to these questions, the reader discovers that swan C is a non-Australian swan. This piece of information should be added to the list of premises, because it is important to the assessment of the argument. Therefore, Example 5.2o could be rewritten as follows:

5.2p

Swan A is black.
Swan B is black.
Swan C is a non-Australian swan.
∴   Swan C is black.

The information that swan C is a non-Australian swan is crucial, because Australian swans typically are black, whereas all other swans generally are white. Example 5.2o thus violates the criterion of total evidence, and as a result, it is an example of the fallacy of **incomplete evidence**. Example 5.2o violates the criterion because it withholds some critical information that would enhance our evaluation of the reasoning. With the new information, we can easily see that something is wrong with the reasoning in Example 5.2p.

A word of caution is in order here. Because of the nature of inductive reasoning, additional evidence may always be added to an argument to strengthen it. This does not mean that all inductive reasoning commits the fallacy of incomplete evidence. This fallacy is limited to arguments that *intentionally* or *obviously* omit facts, thereby creating a faulty scenario. For example, the following argument is not an illustration of the fallacy of incomplete evidence, even though it is logically (and physically) possible that some new kind of living thing will be discovered that does not have carbon as part of its molecular structure:

5.2q

All living things, past and present, have carbon as part of their molecular structure.
∴   In the future, any living thing that we can identify also will have carbon as part of its molecular structure.

This argument does not illustrate the fallacy of incomplete evidence because the evidence stated seems to be given in good faith and no facts are intentionally or obviously omitted.

5.3 ADDITIONAL OBSERVATIONS

When evaluating enumerative arguments, the critical thinker's most important activity is asking questions. The analysis of an enumerative argument should produce many questions. Some can be answered by examining the argument more closely. Others will require research, while still others will go unanswered. The analysis process described in this section is designed to engage the critical thinker in a dialogue with the argument.

Note that the fact that questions can be raised does not necessarily make an argument weak. Enumerative induction is a form of logic that can expand our knowledge of the world. If we are to benefit from this expansion, we must become involved with the argument by asking questions. The premises in the argument *should* provide reasons for believing or accepting the conclusion. By asking specific questions, we learn whether the evidence provides good reasons for accepting the claim. Moreover—and perhaps more important—we may learn whether there are good reasons for *not* accepting the conclusion. (For more on this, see the excellent article by Geoffrey Hunter cited in the Appendix.)

Fallacious Arguments versus Weak Arguments

As discussed in the preceding section, the four basic criteria used in evaluating enumerative inductive reasoning are sample size, sample diversity, relevance of analogy, and total evidence. Whenever an argument *obviously* violates one of these criteria, the violation results

Reprinted by permission of Wendy Oxman

in a fallacy. Violation of the criterion of sample size results in the fallacy of **hasty generalization**; violation of sample diversity results in **biased statistics**; violation of relevance of analogy results in **false analogy**; and violation of total evidence results in **incomplete evidence**. Each of these fallacies can occur only when the appropriate criterion is violated.

It is important to note the relationship between a weak argument and arguments that are fallacious. *All* fallacious arguments are weak arguments. However, not all weak arguments are fallacious. An argument may be weak for reasons other than the clear violation of a particular criterion.

The Role of Relevance

In Chapter 3, we stated that a basic criterion for all arguments is that premises and conclusion must be relevant to each other. In dealing with enumerative induction, this criterion can easily be overlooked. It is easy to decide that an argument violates relevance when, in fact, adequate relevance is present. Beware of prematurely rejecting an enumerative argument just because the premises and conclusion are not obviously relevant to each other.

For example, as critical thinkers, we might question the relevance of information about swans A and B as evidence for any claim about swan Z. In Example 5.2a, it is unclear whether the evidence is relevant; however, it also is not clear that relevance is violated. Therefore, since there is *no clear* violation, the argument should not be judged to be fallacious simply because it *appears* to violate relevance. In our earlier discussion of Example 5.2a, we identified other problems with that argument. The point here is that critical thinkers must beware of prematurely rejecting an argument just because it does not have the type of relevance they expect. Many times, in dealing with inductive reasoning, the relevance will be *assumed* to be adequate.

The Role of Assumption

The last sentence suggests another important observation about enumerative induction. In evaluating such arguments, it often is not clear whether the reasoner has satisfied a particular criterion. If the issue is important enough to us, we may engage in additional research that may shed light on the problem. However, there are times when we do not need to do more research, even when questions arise. In the case of a textbook problem, for example, a student probably would not do additional research to determine whether some hypothetical argument satisfies the criterion of sample size. Moreover, some issues are not important enough to warrant additional research. In both cases, we might simply *assume* that the argument satisfies the criterion. (Remember, this does not mean that the argument is strong; it simply means that no violation has occurred.) By contrast, an individual striving to survive must make assumptions on a daily or even hourly basis. For example, few of us carefully examined the chair in which we are currently sitting. We assumed that it would support our weight and not collapse as we sat down. One things that distinguishes us as critical thinkers from noncritical thinkers is that we are aware of our assumptions. We boldly state, "Assuming that the size of the sample is adequate, then. . . ."

Strength of Claims

Still another observation concerns the relative strength of the conclusion. Generally, *the stronger the claim made in the conclusion, the weaker is the argument*. If, for example, the conclusion claims that "Swan A is white," the claim is very strong, and the likelihood of its being true diminishes—or at least it is more difficult to justify. However, if the conclusion claims that "Swan A is possibly (or might be) white," the claim is weaker, but the likelihood of its being true increases. Such a claim would be easier to justify.

This general rule is not without problems, however. First, there is the problem of interpretation. Is the author of the claim merely weakening the claim "Swan A is white," or is the inclusion of "possibly" intended to suggest the author's own misgivings concerning the claim? Second, while an argument's persuasive power is usually related to its strength as an argument, this is not always true. Occasionally, even if a line of reasoning is strong, the argument's ability to persuade may be weak. For example, consider an argument in which the conclusion states "It might just possibly be true that walking on air is possible." Because of the hedging words, the line of reasoning might be strengthened, but the persuasiveness of the argument is diminished. As critical thinkers, we must be sensitive to the relative strength of the conclusion and to the problems that arise when claims are very strong or very weak.

Types of Enumerative Arguments

A final observation is that there is more than one type of enumerative argument. The remainder of this section presents a brief overview of four basic types of enumerations, which will be examined more closely later in the chapter.

    Simple Enumeration. The first basic type of enumerative argument is **simple enumeration**. This is the most straightforward form of enumeration: The conclusion makes a claim about some additional examples of the same type of thing as those listed in the premises. For example,

5.3a

Swan A is white.
Swan B is white.
Swan C is white.

.

.

.

Swan Y is white.
∴   Swan Z is white.

    In a simple enumeration, the conclusion will not necessarily be falsified by the identification of a counterexample in the premises. That is, even if we were to discover that swan D is not white, this would not necessarily mean that swan Z is not white. Note that the reasoning process in this type of enumeration moves from particular entities to a claim about another particular entity. Frequently, we use the movement within the argument to help us identify the type of enumerative induction we are examining. For example, if the reasoning moves from particulars to a conclusion that is also particular, then we might have a simple enumeration. But if the conclusion is a generalization based on particulars, then the argument is an inductive generalization. (See next.)

    Inductive Generalization. A second basic type of enumerative induction is **inductive generalization**. In arguments of this type, the conclusion makes a generalized claim concerning things of the same type as the things listed in the premises.

5.3b

Yesterday, by means of my fantastic abilities, I arbitrarily polled more than 4,000 SC students, asking them whether they were interested in improving their critical-thinking skills. All of them said yes, they were interested.
∴   Most SC students are interested in improving their critical-thinking skills.

    In an inductive generalization, the discovery of a counterexample could falsify the conclusion. In Example 5.3b, if the 4,001st student said "No!" the conclusion would not be falsified, because it contains the word "most." However, if we were to replace "most" with "all," the response of the 4,001st student *would* falsify the conclusion. The line of reasoning in arguments of this type moves from evidence concerning particular entities to a generalized claim about such entities.

Argument from Analogy. A third basic type of enumerative induction is **argument from analogy**. Arguments of this type are extensions of simple enumeration. In simple enumeration, the conclusion makes a claim about the same kinds of items as those listed in the premises. However, an argument from analogy is dependent on various characteristics of the items cited. The argument develops a comparison and draws a conclusion based on that comparison. Moreover, in a simple enumeration, the subject of the conclusion is not introduced until the conclusion, whereas in an argument from analogy, the subject of the conclusion is introduced in the premises, and the conclusion says something new about that subject.

5.3c	5.3d

5.3c	5.3d
Swan A is white.	Swan A is white.
Swan B is white.	Swan B is white.
Swan C is white.	Swan D is similar to swans A and B.
∴ Swan D is white.	∴ Swan D is white.

Example 5.3c is a simple enumeration; Example 5.3d is an argument from analogy.

5.3e

In the lab, nicotine smeared on the skin tissues of rats produces cancer.
Humans have skin tissues similar to those of rats.
∴   Nicotine smeared on the skin tissues of a human being will produce cancer.

In Example 5.3e, the discovery of a counterexample will not necessarily falsify the conclusion, but it may weaken the argument.

Statistical Syllogism. The fourth basic type of enumerative induction is **statistical syllogism**. In arguments of this type, the claim is specified in quantitative terms in relation to a particular thing and with respect to the evidence offered, which includes a statement concerning the class of things to which that thing belongs. The reasoning moves from evidence that includes a generalization to a conclusion that is particular.

5.3f

Most MSU students are interested in improving their critical-thinking skills.
Paula is a student at MSU.
∴   Paula is interested in improving her critical-thinking skills.

The conclusion of a statistical syllogism may be, but is not necessarily, falsified by the discovery of a counterexample. This is so because statistics are collective in nature and therefore cannot tell us what an individual will do. For example, the statistic that the average American family has 2.3 children does not tell us how many children any individual family has.

5.4 ANALYSIS

In analyzing and evaluating enumerative inductive arguments, we follow five steps that form a logical progression. First, we express the argument in standard form. Included in this step is the initial examination of the argument to determine its clarity, relevance, and consistency. The second step is to name the specific type of enumerative induction represented by the argument. This typically involves examining the way the argument moves from premises to conclusion. Third, we make an initial assessment of the argument on the basis of the criteria that are relevant to the type of argument identified in the second step. (As we will see in the sections that follow, each type of argument has its own set of criteria for assessment.) The third step should give rise to several questions. It should also result in a statement of the assumptions, if any, used in the analysis, and lead to a brief dialogue explaining how the argument satisfies or fails to satisfy each of the criteria for assessment of that type of argument.

The following list of "relative" or "hedging" terms is helpful in analyzing the likelihood that a criterion has been satisfied:[18]

5.4a

About as often as not	Once in a while
Almost never	Often
Always	Rarely
Frequently	Rather often
Generally	Seldom
Hardly ever	Sometimes
Never	Usually
Not often	Usually not
Now and then	Very often
Occasionally	Very seldom

Next, if a fallacy is present, we identify it. For example, if, in the preceding step, we found that the argument violates the criterion of sample size, we note that it commits the fallacy of hasty generalization. If no criterion for assessment has obviously been violated, no fallacy can be identified.

The fifth step in the analysis is the final evaluation and the justification of that evaluation. In this step, we judge the argument as "strong," "moderate," or "weak" and set forth the justification for our assessment. The justification will consider insights gained from Step 3, as well as other observations we may have made about the argument and its subject matter. Since the conclusion of any inductive argument is a proposed hypothesis, the justification for labeling the argument as strong, moderate, or weak should include an assessment of the hypothesis that goes beyond just considering the criteria for assessment. For example, it may be relevant to address the relative strength of the conclusion, or possibly

Frank and Ernest

research was done because of questions raised in Step 2, and the results of the research can add further insight into the argument.

Unless a fallacy is present, the justification will typically consist of at least a brief paragraph. If a fallacy is identified in Step 4, then in Step 5 we can simply say that the argument is weak because it is fallacious.

In sum, the analysis consists of the following five steps:

1. presentation of the argument in standard form
2. identification of the type of argument present
3. assessment of the argument according to the criteria for that type
4. identification of fallacies if any
5. final evaluation and justification

While each of these steps is essential in that it builds upon the preceding one, Steps 3 and 5 are most crucial. If these two steps are carried out correctly, at least one of two results will ensue. First, the discussions associated with those steps should advance our knowledge and understanding of the reasoning used in the argument. Second, the discussions should propose ways to expand our knowledge and understanding. That is, they should suggest questions that require further research and study.

A Word of Caution. Seldom does reasoning occur in a vacuum the way textbook exercises do. Moreover, seldom does a textbook exercise motivate us to do further research. However, such exercises are extremely valuable. They help us develop the habits necessary for critical reasoning, they teach us how to manipulate the analysis by telling a story that might weaken or strengthen or even make the reasoning fallacious, they expand our understanding, they provide practice in thinking critically, and they foster creative thinking.

When we work through textbook exercises, we have an opportunity to create our own scenarios. Some of these scenarios will supplement and strengthen the reasoning; others will weaken it. I recommend that sometimes, instead of doing several different exercises, you do the same exercise several different ways. For example, create a scenario in which the criteria are clearly adequate for the claim and in which the argument is strong. Then create a scenario in which the argument is moderate or weak without being fallacious. Finally, create a scenario in which the criteria are violated, making the argument weak because it is fallacious. In short, approach a textbook exercise as if it were a chemistry experiment: Try a little of this and a little of that, and see what happens.

5.5 SIMPLE ENUMERATION

As indicated earlier, **simple enumeration (SE)** is a form of inductive reasoning that has as its premises a listing of observed particular things and as its conclusion a statement about an unobserved thing that is of the same type as those listed in the premises. The following argument is a model for simple enumeration:

5.5a

X is p.
Y is p.
Z is p.
∴   W is p.

In this model, the uppercase letters stand for individual things and the lowercase letters indicate some characteristic of the subject. For example,

5.5b

Swan 1 is white.
Swan 2 is white.
Swan 3 is white.
∴   Swan 4 is white.

The movement in this type of argument is from particular to particular. That is, the premises deal with particular items or entities, and the argument presents a conclusion concerning another particular item.

A simple enumeration is evaluated in terms of two basic criteria: total evidence and sample diversity. The fallacies that occur when these conditions are violated are those of incomplete evidence and biased statistics, respectively. The following examples illustrate the evaluation process for simple enumerations.

5.5c

John was in Mr. Towns's advanced math class last year, and he is currently attending North Texas University (NTU). Joan was in the same class, and she is attending NTU. Peter, Paul, and Mary also had Mr. Towns for math last year, and they are attending NTU this year. We can conclude that it is possible that Greg is also attending NTU.

Step 1

John was in Mr. T's math class and is attending NTU.
John was in Mr. T's math class and is attending NTU.
Peter was in Mr. T's math class and is attending NTU.

Paul was in Mr. T's math class and is attending NTU.
<u>Mary was in Mr. T's math class and is attending NTU.</u>
∴   Possibly Greg is also attending NTU

(No apparent violation of clarity, relevance, or consistency.)

Step 2

movement: particular to particular
Simple enumeration

Step 3

Sample Diversity. Without some specific context in which to place this argument, it is unclear whether it has adequate diversity. Is the context a group of friends that stuck together in high school? Is the diversity of individuals presented in the premises adequate to include Greg? Without any possible clarification of the context, let's assume that the six individuals are best friends who did everything together in high school, including taking all their classes. Furthermore, all six idolized Mr. T, who graduated from NTU. Given this story, the six friends might stay together. Hence, it appears that the argument's diversity is adequate. However, as often as not, high school friends attend different colleges.
Total Evidence. Was Greg in Mr. T's math class? Even if Greg had Mr. T for math and was friends with the other five individuals, does NTU offer the major wanted by Greg? While the argument does leave a few questions, given the assumption presented under the other criterion, let's assume that no information has been withheld.

Step 4

In spite of the questions raised, the accepted assumptions reveal no violation. Hence, the argument does not commit any fallacies.

Step 5

This argument seems to be a *moderate* argument. We base our assessment on two factors. First, the context of the argument is extremely questionable: Even if the argument does not violate any criteria of critical thinking, the evidence provides very little support for the claim. Second, however, the conclusion is extremely weak ("*possibly* Greg . . . "). This weakness in the conclusion strengthens the general argument. Because of the lack of context and the weakness of the conclusion, I view this argument as moderate.

5.5d

Shakespeare's Macbeth *is more than 300 pages, since Joyce's* Ulysses *is longer than 300 pages and Kazantzakis's* The Odyssey *is more than 300 pages. Furthermore, Mitchell's* Gone with the Wind *is also longer than 300 pages.*

Step 1

Joyce's *Ulysses* is longer than 300 pages.
Kazantzakis's *The Odyssey* is longer than 300 pages.
<u>Mitchell's *Gone with the Wind* is longer than 300 pages.</u>
∴   Shakespeare's *Macbeth* is longer than 300 pages.

(no apparent violations of clarity, relevance, or consistency)

Step 2

movement: particular to particular
Simple enumeration

Step 3

Sample Diversity. Is the sample diverse enough? Given the number of books in existence, three books do not provide a sufficient diversity, because frequently books are *not* longer than 300 pages. Furthermore, the three books mentioned are all novels. Hence, the argument does not satisfy this criterion.
Total Evidence. Do we have total evidence? This is unclear. If the person presenting the argument does not know anything about Shakespeare's work, then we cannot charge him or her with intentionally withholding evidence, such as the actual length of *Macbeth* or the nature of the book.

Step 4

Are there any fallacies? In Step 3, we indicated that the sampling is not diverse enough; therefore, we do have the fallacy of biased statistics. It is not clear whether the fallacy of incomplete evidence is present.

Step 5

This argument is extremely weak. First, notice the strength of the conclusion. Because of its strength, the overall argument is weakened. However, the real reason we consider this argument weak is that it is fallacious. (See Step 4.)

5.5A EXERCISE: SIMPLE ENUMERATION
Evaluate the following arguments:

*1. Joe received an A in British literature. Betty received an A in British literature. John also received an A in British literature. So we can conclude that Bill received an A in British literature.

2. Rhodes College believes that it has a winning combination when it comes to its orientation program for incoming freshmen. The college took a poll three weeks into the fall semester and found some pleasing information. Eighty-five percent of the freshmen polled said that they really enjoyed and learned from the freshman orientation program. From this, they have already concluded that next year's freshman class also will enjoy freshman orientation.

3. We can assume that Paula enjoyed the football game, since both John and Bill enjoyed it.

4. In a recent study, it was found that the Ford Escort is a well-built car. The same study said that the following vehicles were also well built: Dodge Stealth, BMW 318i, Honda Accord, Mercedes–Benz 190E, Chevy Lumina Z34, and Volvo 940. Given this evidence, I am confident that the 1988 Yugo also was a well-built car.

5. Most of the homes we have looked at were dumps, so probably the next house we look at will be a dump.

6. A report in the *Texas Monthly* claims that the following cities are exciting places to live: Austin, Texas; Dallas, Texas; Fort Worth, Texas; and Houston, Texas. While the magazine failed to mention it, I am sure that we can conclude that Boyd, Texas, is also an exciting place to live.

7. The state bird of Michigan is the robin and it probably cannot fly, since neither the Baltimore orioles nor the St. Louis cardinals can fly.

8. We have examined 45 penguins, and all of them were black and white. Therefore, the next penguin also will be black and white.

9. Over the last month, we have been visiting different churches. We have visited four separate churches. In two of those churches, the song "Amazing Grace" was sung. Hence, there is a very good chance that the church we will visit next week will sing "Amazing Grace."

10. For the last three weeks, interviews have been taking place in an attempt to find a new chancellor. To date, fifteen candidates have been questioned, and each had a proposal that would result in an increase in the number of faculty members and simultaneously lower tuition costs. Dr. James is scheduled to be interviewed next week. We can assume that he will have a similar proposal.

5.5B EXERCISE: WRITING SIMPLE ENUMERATIVE ARGUMENTS

Write a brief paragraph that presents a simple enumerative argument regarding either the value of athletics for the college community or the importance of the Internet for today's college student. First, develop your topic sentence (claim); this should be a statement that is particular in nature. Then develop three or more points that support the claim; these, too, should deal with particular issues. Finally, structure your paragraph, including both the topic sentence and the supporting points.

5.6 INDUCTIVE GENERALIZATION

Many **inductive generalizations (IGs)** have as their conclusions a universal statement such that if at least one premise were falsified, the conclusion would be falsified as well. Some, however, have a conclusion that is statistically qualified such that even if one premise were falsified, the conclusion would not necessarily be falsified. Thus, while all IGs move from the particular to the general, they may take two forms: **universal generalization (UG)** and **statistical generalization (SG).** The following examples illustrate these two forms.

UNIVERSAL GENERALIZATION (UG)

5.6a

X^1 is p.
X^2 is p.
X^3 is p.
∴   All X's are p.

5.6b

Swan 1 is white.
Swan 2 is white.
Swan 3 is white.
∴   All swans are white.

and

STATISTICAL GENERALIZATION (SG)

5.6c

X% of observed P's are Q's.
∴   X% of all P's are Q's.

5.6d

85% of observed swans are white.
∴ 85% of all swans are white.

An IG of either form must satisfy two basic criteria. The first of these is sample size: Is the sample large enough to support the generalization being made? If this criterion is clearly violated, the fallacy of hasty generalization has occurred. The second criterion is that of sample diversity: Is the sample diverse enough to support the claim made in the conclusion? As with simple enumerations, if this criterion is violated, the fallacy of biased statistics has occurred. The following examples illustrate the evaluation of inductive generalizations.

5.6e

A recent study released by Texas Christian University (TCU) concluded that there are no U.S. university students interested in improving their critical reasoning skills. The study was based on four separate polls. In April of this year, the research team traveled to Austin and polled a representative number of students at the University of Texas (UT). None of those polled expressed an interest in improving their critical-reasoning skills. Later, the same team traveled to Southern Methodist University (SMU), then to Baylor University, and finally to Rice University. The polls at these schools indicated the same results as those obtained from UT.

Step 1

A representative sample of students at UT expressed the fact that they had no interest in critical reasoning.
A representative sample of students at SMU expressed the fact that they had no interest in critical reasoning.
A representative sample of students at Baylor expressed the fact that they had no interest in critical reasoning.
A representative sample of students at Rice expressed the fact that they had no interest in critical reasoning.
∴   No university students are interested in critical reasoning.

(no apparent violations of clarity, relevance, or consistency.)

Step 2

movement: particular to general
Inductive generalization (universal generalization)

Step 3

Sample Size. Is the sample large enough? Although the actual number of students is relatively small, it is possible that, since at each university a representative number of students was polled, this criterion may not be violated. It is possible that the total number is sufficient. However, even if this criterion is not violated, obviously it would be desirable to poll a greater number of students.
Sample Diversity. Is the sample sufficiently diverse? No, this criterion is violated. Notice that each university is located in Texas, and seldom can one geographical

area be presented as representing the entire world. Texas may be the only state with students not interested in improving their critical-reasoning skills.

Step 4

Are there any fallacies? While it is possible that we have a hasty generalization, as we indicated in Step 3, it is not clear that the sample-size criterion has been definitely violated. Whether it has is actually a moot issue, since the second criterion is violated, resulting in a fallacy. In other words, we do have the fallacy of biased statistics.

Step 5

This argument is weak because it is fallacious.

5.6f

A recent poll conducted at Texas Christian University (TCU) provided some startling facts. A questionnaire was sent to one faculty member, randomly chosen, in each department. The study showed that 95% of those polled were content with their teaching positions and salaries at TCU. On the basis of this result, the chancellor concluded that 95% of all TCU faculty members are satisfied with their positions and salaries.

Step 1

95% of TCU faculty polled was satisfied with p and s.
∴   95% of all TCU faculty are satisfied with p and s.

(no apparent fallacies)

Step 2

movement: particular to general
Inductive generalization (SG)

Step 3

Sample Size. Is the sample size large enough? Given that each department has at least four or more members, it is questionable whether the sample is large enough. In fact, I believe this criterion has been violated.

Sample Diversity. Is the sample diverse? Given the random nature of the selection and the fact that each department was represented, the sample was probably sufficiently diverse.

Step 4

Are there any fallacies? In Step 3, we find that the sample size was not sufficient for the conclusion; hence, a violation of that criterion occurs. As a result, this argument is fallacious. It is a hasty generalization. The fallacy of biased statistics does not occur.

Step 5

The argument is weak because it is fallacious.

Note that a statistical generalization may be made stronger if the percentage suggested in the conclusion is reduced. For example, if the premise states, "Ninety-five percent of observed X's are p," we can weaken the conclusion by lowering the percentage; the conclusion might then read, "Ninety percent of all X's are p." In short, by weakening the conclusion, we can strengthen the argument.

5.6A EXERCISE: INDUCTIVE GENERALIZATION
Evaluate the following inductive generalizations:

1.   It has rained during the last five homecoming games. Therefore, it probably will rain during all future homecoming games.
2.   Most of the students I have had at TCU have been a pleasure to work with. Given this, I am confident that all future students will be a pleasure to work with.
3.   I have read the last five books written by Karl Popper and have found them all to be very stimulating, so I am sure that every book he has written is equally stimulating.
*4.   With 95% of the votes in, 90% of those votes are for Bozo to be the next governor of Texas. It is possible that Bozo will win the gubernatorial race with 80% of all the votes.
5.   Since Peter is going to Africa and Paul is going to Africa, as are Philip and Perry, it is possible that all males with their first names beginning with "P" will go to Africa.
*6.   The last time we had ants in the house, I sprayed the house with XYZ and it took care of the ant problem. Furthermore, I have used XYZ ten times previously, each time with the same results. Therefore, every time in the future when ants invade the house, XYZ will take care of them.
7.   The polls tell us that Bozo will receive 95% of the votes cast by rural voters. Therefore, she may receive 80% of all votes cast.
8.   Senator X was afraid of Bork's conservatism. Senator Y and Senator Z also were afraid of Bork's conservatism. We might conclude that the reason Bork was not confirmed to a Supreme Court position was that all liberal senators were afraid of his conservatism. (Senators X, Y, and Z were all liberals.)

9. The court-ordered treatment of pregnant women is often unjustified. Evidence for this includes the fact that court orders concerning medical treatment usually are granted without the opportunity for the individual involved to receive adequate legal representation. Furthermore, legal precedent says that one person cannot be forced to undergo surgery for the sake of another. Finally, the American College of Obstetricians and Gynecologists has announced that it feels that court-ordered treatment is almost never justified. {based on Katie Sherrod, "Is a Pregnant Woman less a Person . . . ," *Fort Worth Star Telegram*}

10. During a test performed on an undisclosed number of young adult Sprague–Dawley rats, amiodarone was administered to these laboratory animals. On the basis of the results of the test, it was concluded that amiodarone treatment of young adult rats will always lead to changes in the lungs of those treated. {based on a study by M. F. Heath et al. and reported in the *British Journal of Experimental Pathology*}

5.6B EXERCISE: WRITING INDUCTIVE GENERALIZATIONS

Write a brief paragraph that presents an inductive generalization argument regarding either the value of athletics for the college community or the importance of the Internet for today's college student. This is the same topic used earlier in the exercise on writing a simple enumerative argument. In this case, however, the topic sentence should be a generalization drawn from the sample or from points of support.

5.7 ARGUMENT FROM ANALOGY

An **argument from analogy** involves a comparison of two or more types of things. The basic model of such an argument is as follows:

5.7a

Things of type X have the properties of α, β, γ, etc., and ω.
Things of type Y have the properties of α, β, γ, etc.
∴   Things of type Y also have property ω.

5.7b

Snooper is a Labrador retriever, is three years old, and loves kids.
Jock is a Labrador retriever and is three years old.
∴   Jock also loves kids.

The movement in this type of argument is the same as that in simple enumerations: It proceeds from a set of particulars to a particular. The difference between the two types of argument lies in the subject of the conclusion. If that subject is not introduced in the premises, the argument is a simple enumeration (unless the reasoning is clearly meant to be understood as a process based on a comparison, in which case the implied premise must be supplied). If the subject of the conclusion is introduced in one of the premises, the argument is an argument from analogy.

The criterion used to evaluate an argument from analogy is that of relevance of the analogy. When examining an argument of this type, we must be careful not to assume that the evidence is irrelevant to the conclusion. That is, after the argument has been expressed in standard form, it is examined for obvious violations of clarity, relevance, and consistency.

In examining an argument from analogy, it is extremely easy to simply claim that the conclusion is irrelevant to the evidence offered, and that the argument is therefore fallacious, when in fact it is not.

5.7c

Peter and John both took critical reasoning last semester, and, as is typical of many students in that course, both received F's on the first exam. However, both worked hard, turning in all their homework assignments, and received B's on the next four exams. Peter, we know, received a B for the semester, so we may conclude that John may have also received a B in critical reasoning.

Step 1

Peter received an F on his first exam in critical reasoning, but on the remaining four he achieved B's. He did all his homework and received a B in the course.
John received an F on his first exam in critical reasoning, but also received B's on the remaining four. He did all his homework, too.
∴   John may have also received a B in critical reasoning.

(no apparent fallacies)

Step 2

movement: particular to particular
Argument from analogy

Step 3

Relevance of Analogy. Is the analogy relevant? It would appear that there are several relevant similarities between Peter and John. They took the same course the same semester. The letter grades they received on the various exams were the same, and both did the assigned homework.

There are no clear relevant dissimilarities, although some may exist. For example, Peter and John may not have attended the same college, and even if they did, they could have had different instructors, which could be a significant dissimilarity. Another possible relevant dissimilarity could be that while the letter grades each received were the same, it is possible that each time Peter's were at the top of the scale and John's were at the bottom. However, these are mere speculations and probably are not warranted in a normal context in which such an argument would be presented. Therefore, the criterion of relevant analogy is not violated.

Step 4

No fallacies are committed in this argument.

Step 5

The argument is a strong argument. Although it would have been nice to know whether Peter and John had attended the same school and so forth, in a normal context for such an argument we can evaluate the argument somewhere in the range between strong and moderate. However, due to the weakness of the conclusion (i.e., "John may have . . . ") the argument is definitely strengthened. Hence, I believe this argument can be assessed to be a strong argument from analogy.

5.7A EXERCISE: ARGUMENT FROM ANALOGY

Evaluate the following arguments:

1. In 1974, there was an oil shortage that resulted in higher prices for gasoline, long lines at gas stations, and short tempers. In 1990, there was another oil shortage that resulted in higher prices and gas lines. I guess there were probably some short tempers.

2. Richard recently came to me for some advice concerning a purchase he is contemplating. It seems that he has the opportunity to acquire the original "Promenading" by the artist Edward Clifford, but he had no idea how much to offer. When I suggested $25.00, Richard was stunned and asked how I had arrived at that figure. I pointed out to him that four years ago I purchased a copy of that particular work, and I paid only $20.00 for it then. With the price of everything going up, I figured he could get the original for $25.00.

3. While I am not familiar with Professor Smith of Haberding College, I surmise that he is an excellent teacher. I know several other members of the Haberding faculty, plus their academic dean, personally. On the basis of my knowledge of them, I would put my money on the claim that Professor Smith is an excellent teacher.

4. This murder must have been committed by the same individual who we believe killed those three young women last month. Of course, I might be

wrong, but I don't think so. After all, the three young women were all blonds in their twenties, and all lived in the same apartment complex. The victim in this murder also fits that description.

5.   "I am the father of two daughters. When I hear this argument that we can't protect freedom in Europe, in Asia, or in our own hemisphere and still meet our domestic problems, I think it is a phony argument. It is just like saying that I can't take care of Luci because I have Lynda Bird. We have to take care of both of them and we have to meet them head on." {President Lyndon Johnson}

6.   The perfect candidate for President of the Student House of Representatives would be someone who has been an active member of a variety of campus organizations. That person must possess proven leadership abilities, and must be a capable communicator. Frosty Tempel has been active in many organizations on campus. He has held leadership positions in several of those organization and his track record in those positions speaks for itself. Furthermore, when it comes to communications Tempel knows that there must be two channels of communications. Students need to be able to communicate with their leaders, and those in leadership must be able to communicate with the administration. Tempel has proven that he can do this. Therefore, Frosty Tempel is the perfect candidate for President of the Student House of Representatives. {based on article in the *TCU Daily Skiff*}

7.   "Many sociologists have argued that similarities in value system between some ethnic minorities and the American middle class are responsible for high rates of social mobility and economic success. Strodtbeck (1957), for example, contrasted the value of systems of Jews and Italians to explain their different rates of social mobility, . . . Caudill and DeVos (1956) emphasized the similarities in value system between Japanese Americans and the American middle class to explain the high achievement made by second-generation Japanese. Hill (1977) also claims that value congruity, along with ethnocentrism and community organization, is a crucial variable which explains differential responses between the Japanese and the Jews on the one hand and other non-middleman minorities on the other." {*Sociology and Social Research*}

*8.   In 1985, megacuries of KR-85 were produced by the USSR from weapons tests. In that same year, the United States also produced megacuries of KR-85 from weapons tests. Several major Western European countries performed weapons tests in 1985, as did Japan. We can assume that those Western European countries and Japan also produced megacuries of KR-85.

9.   "Developed by Joseph A. Gause, a sculptor and painter, the boat usually clips along at 4 to 5 mph. That she travels at all amazes most onlookers. Gause's concept, which involves fixed fins, is so simple that he often wonders why the Phoenicians did not think of it thousands of years ago. While watching maneuvering fish one day, Gause noted that they push their bodies in a forward motion with a slight up-and-down movement of the fins. Applying this idea to the water, he reasoned that wave action could be used to create an undulating movement of fins to propel a boat. In his view, the fins would be fixed and the water would move, a reversal of nature." {*Mechanix Illustrated*}

10. "The stock market correction of Oct. 13, 1989, was a grim reminder of the Oct. 19, 1987 market collapse. Since, like earthquakes, stock market disturbances will always be with us, it is prudent to take all possible precautions against another such market collapse." {*Wall Street Journal*}

5.7B EXERCISE: WRITING ARGUMENTS FROM ANALOGY

Write a brief paragraph that presents an argument from analogy. Choose any subject you wish. Remember that when writing arguments from analogy, you are making a comparison; the details must show that the items being compared are similar. Moreover, the evidence must show that the first item has a characteristic that is currently unobserved in the second item. Finally, the topic sentence should state that the second item may have the additional characteristic observed in the first item.

5.8 STATISTICAL SYLLOGISM

The fourth type of inductive enumeration is the **statistical syllogism (SS)**. This type of argument moves from statistical claims about a general class of things to a conclusion about a particular member of that class. The following is a basic model of such an argument:

5.8a

X% of all P's are Q's.
s is a P.
∴   s is a Q.

5.8b

95% of all TJC graduates are employed.
Sue is a TJC graduate.
∴   Sue is employed.

In examining arguments of this type, we find that they embody a reasoning process that is contrary to the stereotype about inductive arguments. Clearly, the argument just presented is intended to be inductive, for there is no guarantee that the conclusion is true even if the premises are true. However, the reasoning process moves from a generalization to a particular.

The generalization made in the premises is statistical, although the percentage may not always appear as a number. As we mentioned in relation to inductive generalizations, the statistic or percentage may be expressed in the form of words such as "most," "many," and "some." Moreover, the percentage must be less than 100 percent, or less than "all," for if the argument states that 100 percent of P's, or all P's, are Q's, we have a deductive argument, not an inductive one. However, the closer the percentage is to 100, the greater is the likelihood that the conclusion might be true and, hence, the stronger is the argument. Thus, our analysis must take into consideration how close the percentage is to 100 percent.

The criteria for evaluating statistical syllogisms are sample size and total evidence. The analysis of sample size focuses on the percentage expressed in the premise, while the analysis of total evidence is concerned with whether the particular cited in the conclusion is a typical member of the class specified in the premises. If the argument violates the criterion of sample size, the fallacy of hasty generalization has occurred. If it violates the criterion of total evidence, the fallacy of incomplete evidence has occurred.

The following example illustrates the analysis of statistical syllogisms:

In 1984, seventy-five percent of all homeowners were male. Kelly was a homeowner in 1984. So Kelly definitely is male.

Step 1

Seventy-five percent of all homeowners in 1984 were male.
Kelly was a homeowner in 1984.
∴   Kelly definitely is a male.

(no apparent fallacies)

Step 2

movement: generalization to particular
Statistical syllogism

Step 3

Sample Size. Is the criterion of sample size satisfied? The first premise tells us that seventy-five percent of homeowners were male. While seventy-five percent does not seem to be a violation, of the sample-size criterion, we might desire a greater percentage to support the claim of the conclusion.

Total Evidence. Do we have the total evidence? Given the limited nature of this argument, there is no indication that the total evidence criterion has been violated. However, it would be nice to know more about Kelly; even the name does not help in deciding Kelly's sex.

Step 4

Are there any fallacies? Although the criteria are not satisfied the way we would like, they do not seem to be violated. Therefore, there are no fallacies.

Step 5

Despite the fact that the argument does not appear to be fallacious, it must be evaluated as weak. Given the seventy-five percent of homeowners, there is still a twenty-five percent chance for the conclusion to be false. While this does not by itself warrant an assessment of "weak," it does when it is combined with the conclusion. Notice that the conclusion is an extremely strong statement, weakening the overall argument even more. Hence, we would assess this argument as weak.

There are two subtypes of statistical syllogisms: appeal to authority and appeal to experience. Because these types of arguments must be assessed according to different criteria, they are discussed separately in the next two sections.

5.8A EXERCISE: STATISTICAL SYLLOGISM

Evaluate the following statistical syllogisms:

1. Since most Americans do not speak German, the U.S. ambassador to Germany probably doesn't speak German.

*2. "Now, let's see, I think I'll place my bet that the top card is black because the chances are twenty-six to one that it is black." {Wertz's reasoning at the semipack table at the gambling casino in Las Vegas. In a "semipack," all the red cards except one have been removed.}

3. Presently, all known living things, past and present, have carbon as part of their molecular structure. In the future, the first living thing that we identify on another planet also will have carbon as part of its molecular structure.

4. Agricultural systems are both the most sensitive and the most important to humans. Without any agricultural productivity, at least ninety to ninety-nine percent of the current world population could not be maintained. Therefore, starvation may be the single greatest cause of death following a nuclear exchange. This conclusion is also based on the fact that a nuclear exchange would cause a chronic climatic disruption resulting in little or no agricultural productivity for the first several years afterwards. Furthermore, experts say that even in the best of times natural ecosystems could never feed the earth's 5 billion people. {based on Janet Raloff, "Nuclear Winter: Shutting Down the Farm?"}

5. Sixty percent of prime-time shows contain alcohol, 10.65 drinking acts per hour occur on prime-time television shows, and one out of every ten scenes in a prime-time show contains alcohol. On the basis of this frequent usage of alcohol on prime-time television, a misconception develops: Alcohol is taken for granted, it is conceived as routine and even necessary that most people drink and that drinking is part of everyday life, and alcohol-related problems are seen to be relatively rare. {based on Wallack and Breed, "Alcohol on Prime-Time Television," *Journal of Studies on Alcohol*}

6. Since only about 26 percent of the American adult population smokes and Richard is an adult American, we can conclude that Richard does not smoke.

7. "Smoking by pregnant women may result in fetal injuries, premature birth, and low birth weight." {Surgeon General's warning on a pack of cigarettes} Susan is a 95-year-old smoker. Probably, her next child will be born premature.

8. A recent study claimed that children who are sexually abused can rise above the situation without any long-term psychological damage. Peter was a sexually

abused child. So it is at least possible that he will not have any long-term
psychological damage.

9.   "There are tens of millions of emotionally handicapped children and adults in
     our society who need help, aren't getting it and, as things stand, never will get
     it." Paula is an adult who is emotionally handicapped, so she may never
     receive the help she needs. {quote from *Psychology Today*}

10. "First identified only in 1962, the condition until quite recently was considered
     extremely rare, and even today only about 350 to 400 individuals throughout the
     world have been positively identified as XYY. But recent studies have shown
     that the syndrome occurs about once in every 800 births. Based on a world pop-
     ulation of 3.2 billion and the assumption that half the human race is male, this
     would mean roughly 2 million males alive today. At least an equal number car-
     rying a mirror-image of this gene pattern—XXY or Klinefelter's Syndrome—
     are also believed to exist, most of them unidentified." {*Corpus Christi Times*}

5.8B EXERCISE: WRITING STATISTICAL SYLLOGISMS

Write a brief paragraph that presents a statistical syllogism. The topic sentence should deal
with a particular item in relation to the evidence, and the evidence must include a generalization about the class of things to which the subject of the topic sentence belongs.

THE FAMILY CIRCUS.   By Bil Keane

2-10

Copyright 1984
The Register and Tribune
Syndicate, Inc.

"Does it bovver you when people keep askin'
questions, Daddy? Does it, Daddy?
Daddy?..."

5.9 APPEAL TO AUTHORITY

The **appeal to authority**, a type of statistical syllogism, takes the following form:

5.9a

X% of what P says about q is correct.

P says s about q.
_____

∴   s is correct.

5.9b

Most of what Spencer says about the philosophy of sports is correct.

Spencer says that cheating is commonly accepted, if not expected, in most

sports.
_____

∴   Cheating is commonly accepted, if not expected, in most sports.

An **appeal to consensus** is a type of appeal to authority. It has the same form as an appeal to authority and is analyzed according to the same criteria.

A good argument that appeals to authority must satisfy two criteria. First, the individual cited as an authority must actually be an *authority or expert* in the field about which the statements are made. The issue is not whether the individual is an authority in *some* field, but whether he or she is an authority in the *area of specialization* about which the claim is made. For instance, in Example 5.9b, Spencer is cited as an authority on the philosophy of sports. Let us assume that this is true, but does that make him an expert on cheating in sports? Not necessarily: As with most fields, one can properly be an expert in one aspect of a discipline and know a great deal about other aspects of that discipline without being an expert in those aspects. If it is discovered that the individual cited is not really an expert on the topic, this criterion has been violated.

The second criterion is that there must be a *general consensus* among other experts in the field that the position claimed by the authority is plausible. This is not to say that all experts in the area must agree with that position. Experts are likely to disagree on any issue of interest. The criterion merely requires that there be some general agreement on the issue. For example, consider an argument in which a well-known economist who advocates the need for a governmental agency to be charged with the responsibility for stabilizing the stock market is cited as an authority, and this expert's position is the sole evidence for the claim that we need a market-stabilizing agency. In other words, this economist is an expert, but all of his fellow experts disagree with him, and they do not believe that such an agency is even viable. In this case, general consensus is violated. Obviously, the greater the degree of consensus on the issue, the stronger is the argument. Citing an authority on a point about which other authorities disagree violates the general-consensus criterion because important contrary evidence is omitted. If either criterion is violated, the argument is a fallacious appeal to authority.

5.9A EXERCISE: APPEAL TO AUTHORITY

Evaluate the following appeals to authority:

1. Karl Popper, the well-known philosopher of science, claimed that the major problem with science was its attempt to use inductive reasoning. He maintained that all proper reasoning was performed by means of deduction. As a result, we should reject any model of science that incorporates inductive reasoning.

2. Thomas Kuhn, the author of *The Structure of Scientific Revolutions*, claimed that all normal science is performed within a paradigm. As a result, when we see scientific formulas such as $E = mc^2$, we would be wise to ask in which paradigm this equation is true.

3. Paul Feyerabend, the noted philosopher from MIT and author of *Against Methods*, advocates a total anarchy in the area of scientific knowledge. He maintains that there is no such thing as truth, in the objective sense. Therefore, any pursuit of truth is ridiculous.

4. Mr. Heller, now at VISA International, was a governor of the Federal Reserve Board from 1986 until earlier this year. He claimed that "the mere existence of a market-stabilizing agency helps to avoid panic in emergencies." Therefore, we need a market-stabilizing agency. {*Wall Street Journal*}

5. "Smoking by pregnant women may result in fetal injuries, premature birth, and low birth weight." {Surgeon General's warning on a pack of cigarettes} Susan is a 95-year-old smoker. Probably, her next child will be born premature.

The last argument illustrates the fact that a passage may be analyzed in more than one way. Earlier (Problem 7 under statistical syllogisms), we viewed this argument as a statistical syllogism and concluded that it was a weak argument because it appeared to violate total evidence. (Very few 95-year-olds have children.) If we now view the same passage as an appeal to authority, Susan's age is irrelevant.

5.9B EXERCISE: WRITING APPEALS TO AUTHORITY

After doing some research, write a brief paragraph containing an appeal to authority on the subject of national health care. The key to writing a successful appeal to authority is to provide adequate information showing that the authority you cite is an expert on the issue and that his or her position is at least considered viable by other experts.

5.10 APPEAL TO EXPERIENCE

The second subtype of statistical syllogism is the **appeal to experience**. Arguments of this type have the following basic form:

5.10a

X% of what P says is correct.
P says s.
∴   s is correct.

5.10b

John, who has flown for over twenty years, first in the military and now as a commercial pilot, claims to have seen a UFO.
John is not one to exaggerate; in the past, he has always been extremely accurate when reporting anything about aviation.
∴   UFOs exist.

While appeals to experience are similar to appeals to authority, the criteria by which they are evaluated are different. In arguments of this type, the concern is with the general reliability of the individual cited, not whether that person is an expert. Is the person generally known for accurately reporting his or her experiences? Or is he or she generally known to exaggerate or hallucinate? This information will be provided by the argument itself and may be supported by means of another argument that considers evidence concerning the reliability of the person who had the experience.

The second criterion for evaluating appeals to experience is that the reported experience must be consistent with general knowledge of human experience. For example, consider a member of the International Flat Earth Research Society proclaiming, "I have scaled the 150-foot-high wall of ice that provides the outer edge of our earth, and as I peered over the edge, all I saw was nothing. Since I have been to the ends of the earth, the earth must be flat!" Most of us recognize that this individual's experience is not consistent with the general knowledge of human experience. **Appeals to testimony**, commonly found in advertising, such as one of the commercials for Miller Genuine Draft beer, are a form of appeal to experience and are evaluated by the same criteria.

5.10A EXERCISE: APPEAL TO EXPERIENCE

Evaluate the following appeals to experience:

*1.   Of course, air walking is possible! Just the other night I was in my office, on the second floor in Reed Hall, quite late. When I was ready to leave, I decided not to take the stairs, so I simply opened my window and walked down to the ground. Since I did it, it must be possible!

2.   "Officer, would you please tell the jury what you saw as you entered the room?"

      "I saw the defendant hit a woman over the head with a beer bottle. After a brief scuffle, I was able to handcuff the defendant, but by the time I got to the woman, it was too late."

3. "Mr. Boyd, you have claimed under oath that you received three threatening phone calls on the day in question and that you were so frightened that you sped out of the parking garage doing over 60 miles per hour. You claimed that it was those phone calls and your fear that made you drive that fast, hitting the child who was walking on the sidewalk. Mr. Boyd, I have here a stack of twenty-five speeding tickets issued to you just this past year, five of which you received upon leaving the parking garage. Did you receive threatening calls on those days also?"

4. "I must boast; there is nothing to be gained by it, but I will go on to visions and revelations of the Lord. I know a man in Christ who fourteen years ago was caught up to the third heaven—whether in the body or out of the body I do not know, God knows. And I know that this man was caught up into Paradise—whether in the body or out of the body I do not know, God knows—and he heard things that cannot be told, which man may not utter. On behalf of this man I will boast, but on my own behalf I will not boast, except of my weaknesses. Though if I wish to boast, I shall not be a fool, for I shall be speaking the truth." {II Corinthians 12:1–6, Revised Standard Version}

5. "God is quite real to me. I talk to him and often get answers. Thoughts sudden and distinct from any I have been entertaining come to my mind after asking God for his direction. . . . I don't think I ever doubted the existence of God, or had him drop out of my consciousness. God has frequently stepped into my affairs very perceptibly, and I feel that he directs many little details all the time." {William James, *The Varieties of Religious Experience* (New York: Collier Books, 1961), p. 72.}

5.10B EXERCISE: WRITING APPEALS TO EXPERIENCE

Write a brief paragraph claiming that some event is possible because you have experienced it. (If you wish, you may make up an experience.) Be sure to provide information about your reliability and to address the issue of whether the event conforms to known facts about the world.

5.11 OVERVIEW OF ENUMERATIVE INDUCTION

Type	Movement	Criteria	Fallacies
Simple Enumeration	particular to particular	1. Total evidence 2. Diverse sample	1. Incomplete evidence 2. Biased statistics
Inductive Generalization	particular to general	1. Sample size 2. Diverse sample	1. Hasty generalization 2. Biased statistics
Argument from Analogy	particular to particular	Relevance of analogy	False analogy
Statistical Syllogism	general to particular	1. Sample size 2. Total evidence	1. Hasty generalization 2. Incomplete evidence
Appeal to Authority		Authority	False appeal to authority
Appeal to Experience		Experience	False appeal to experience

5.12 EXERCISE: MIXED ENUMERATIVE INDUCTION

For those of the passages that follow which contain enumerative arguments, evaluate the arguments, using the appropriate procedure. Be aware that some arguments can be evaluated in more than one way. If a passage does not contain an enumerative argument, explain why this is the case.

*1.   "The first model of the finned boat was just 2½ ft. long and was tested by Gause in his swimming pool. It worked . . . though at a speed of 3/4 ft. per second. And the waves were only 4 in. high. A second boat was twice the length of the original and the pair were placed together in the pool. The result was a surprise: the 5-ft. craft covered the same distance as the 2½-footer . . . but in half the time! Gause concluded that if the length of the boat was multiplied, the speed would go up accordingly." {*Mechanix Illustrated*}

2.   "Little is known about the prevalence of anabolic–androgenic steroid use in the United States. To obtain some initial information, the authors sent questionnaires to male students at three U.S. colleges. Of the 1,010 respondents, 17 (2%) reported using steroids. Most were competitive athletes, but four used steroids primarily to improve personal appearance." {Pope, Katz, and Champoux, "Anabolic–Androgenic Steroid Use among 1,010 College Men," *The Physician and Sports Medicine*}

*3.   "Lawyers, labor leaders and hospital officials said they don't know of any hospitals or other health care facilities that require their employees to be tested for AIDS or hepatitis. . . . They said the cost of testing every worker—as much as a concern for employees' privacy and federal laws that ban discrimination against people with AIDS—plays an important role in that decision." {Mayer, "Court Upholds Ban on AIDS Tests for Workers," *Health Week*}

4.   "The evidence that we presented in support of McCleskey's claim of racial discrimination left nothing out. [Warren McCleskey, a black man, was sentenced to die for the murder of a white man in Georgia. At issue here was his appeal, which claimed racial discrimination.] Our centerpiece was a pair of studies conducted by Professor David Baldus, of the University of Iowa, and his colleagues, which examined 2,484 cases of murder and non-negligent manslaughter that occurred in Georgia between 1873, the date when its present capital murder statute was enacted, and 1979, the year after McCleskey's own death sentence was imposed. . . . Through a highly refined protocol, the [Baldus] team collected information regarding more than five hundred factors in each case . . . What did it show? The death sentences were being imposed in Georgia murder cases in a clear, consistent pattern that reflected the race of the victim and the race of the defendant and could not be explained by any non-racial factor." {Amsterdam, "Race and the Death Penalty," *Criminal Justice Ethics*}

5.   "Today many industries are reaching capacity levels and enjoying increased sales and profits. This resurgence cuts across industrial, geographic, and company boundaries. A common element among the leaders, however, is a significantly changed manufacturing environment characterized by increased automation and computerization, reduced levels of direct labor and inventory, increased attention to product and production planning, and shorter product

life cycles. . . . The revolution taking place in our factories might be expected to bring significant accounting changes with it. After all, the traditional cost accounting approach was designed for a prior era of manufacturing when labor often was the most significant component of product cost and was used as the primary method of allocating overhead and other indirect costs. Today, overhead itself often is the most significant product cost, and labor could be characterized as an indirect cost. . . . Labor costs or hours no longer are an accurate basis for allocating overhead, and cost accounting techniques based on a disappearing manufacturing environment are no longer appropriate. The traditional cost accounting model gives too little attention to internal and cost controls, matches revenue and expenses improperly, and emphasizes conservative inventory valuation at the expense of management reporting. [We can conclude that] the accounting profession [needs] to adopt new methods of accounting for product costs under generally accepted accounting principles." {Peavey, "It's Time for a Change," *Management Accounting*}

*6.

A Growing Hispanic Market

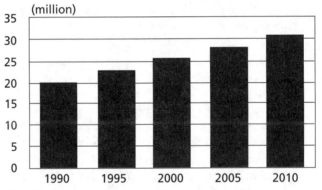

{based on Szabo and Baker, "Hot New Markets of the 1990s," *Nation's Business*}

7.   "Despite excesses, the junk-bond investment back was still a positive force in the economy . . . Granting that dealmaking went to excess, I submit that Drexel still represented a positive force for the U.S. economy. Drexel helped force corporate managers to run more productive and profitable companies . . . What's good for executives is not necessarily good for business or good for America. In the 1960s and 1970s, managerial power was virtually unassailable. The result was that many companies became flabby, leaving them exposed to the tougher times and competition of the 1980s. Drexel's demise may now lead to a new rise in management's power. Like everyone else, executives do a bit better when they know someone is looking over their shoulders. Corporate America needs to be held accountable for its performance. And if Drexel's disappearance makes it less accountable, we will all ultimately be the losers." {Samuelson, "The Demise of Drexel," *Newsweek*}

*8.   "Board members need policies, training activities, guidelines to ensure that if and when sexual harassment occurs, school officials are prepared to deal with it. . . . Furthermore, if a sexual harassment case reaches the courts, the grievance and rectifying procedures provide some legal protection, proving that your board made a good-faith effort to prevent sexual harassment among employees. You also might find your efforts make it possible to prevent it." {Decker, "Can Schools Eliminate Sexual Harassment?" *The Education Digest*}

9. "People (obviously) use different criteria to judge credibility of TV news than they do to judge newspaper credibility. Television news credibility has relentlessly outscored newspaper credibility for nearly three decades. By 1984, respondents asked by the Roper organization which medium they would select when confronted with conflicting news reports chose television 46% of the time versus 22% for newspapers. The idea that television is perceived as a more credible news source than newspapers, however, seems to contradict the notion that the print medium is more deliberate and thorough in its reporting, [and has] more time and space, which allows more detailed and precise coverage of the news." {Newhagen and Nass, "Differential Criteria for Evaluating Credibility of Newspapers and TV News," *Journalism Quarterly*}

10. "The extension or decline of democracy has implications for other social values, such as economic growth, socioeconomic equity, political stability, social justice, and national independence. In societies at one level of development, progress toward one or more of these goals may be compatible with a high level of democracy. At another level of socioeconomic development, conflicts may exist. The question of the appropriateness of democracy for poor countries is, in this context, a central issue. But even highly developed societies may achieve their democracy at some sacrifice of other important values, such as national security." {Huntington, "Will More Countries Become Democratic?" *The Center Magazine*}

11. "Nor can the U.S. trade deficit be blamed on 'excessive imports.' Manufactured-goods imports account for a smaller share of America's GNP— 9%—than they do in any other developed country except Japan. And the Japanese are now 'outsourcing' at such a furious rate that the import share of manufactured goods in Japan's GNP is likely to match the U.S. figure within four or five years." {Drucker, "Help Latin America and Help Ourselves," *Wall Street Journal*}

*12. "**CONDOMS NOT WHAT SCHOOLS NEED**. The American people have lost their minds. I'm referring to passing out condoms in our public schools to our children to help combat AIDS. Did it ever occur to anyone to have a class teaching our young people that it is morally wrong to have sex outside of marriage and that there are guidelines in the word of God for people to follow? Those guidelines have been around for about 2,000 years, and no one has ever been able to improve upon them!" {*Fort Worth Star-Telegram*}

13. "The real success of summer music study for teacher or student lies in rediscovering the joy of music without the usual distractions found during the regular school year. The music student can strengthen technical skills, learn the nuts and bolts of music theory, experiment on the piano, compose on the computer, or learn another instrument. Instrumentalists can learn to sing; singers can learn to conduct. Above all, summer music should be fun—something

different and interesting from both the student's and the teacher's point of view. So, while they're still under your wing, encourage your students at all levels to participate in some aspect of summer music." {Hadley, "Summer Music Programs," *Music Educators Journal*}

14. "Finally, if we examine the potential of each of the great power blocs to expand over the next fifty years, I have to say that I believe the Greater European economic community will have the edge. The Pacific will win the silver medal and the Americas the bronze. This is because I believe that it will be easier to integrate Eastern Europe and Russia into the West European system, of which it was always an integral part until 1917, than it will be to integrate Latin and South America into the U.S. system." [Closing remarks of a paper presented at the thirty-first annual meeting of the National Association of Business Economists, September 24–27, 1989, in San Francisco, California, by Brian Reading. Brian Reading is London Partner and International Economist, HME International Advisory Associates, Inc.] {Reading, "Europe in 1992: Threat or Promise?" printed in *Business Economics*}

15. "The recent upsurge of interest in so-called near death experiences, or NDEs, is no doubt a consequence of the fact that more than ever before, people can be "brought back from death's door." Personal tales of NDEs make fascinating reading, and there is no reason to doubt the honesty or accuracy of these accounts. But many take a further leap and interpret these experience as a glimpse into 'the other side.'" {Kurtz, *Psychology Today*}

16. "A number of the existing laws written by the APB and the FASB are inappropriate and should be changed. The bad laws were written in spite of the fact that the APB and FASB, throughout their existence, have been composed of intelligent, competent people with good intentions. Many of the bad laws result from the lack of some form of accounting constitution in which the accounting profession and business world agree at least on the basic issues discussed here. . . . What is needed . . . is not a paper with no authority approved by only seven (or less) members of a select committee. Instead, we need an authoritative document approved by thousands." {Snavely, "Needed: An Accounting Constitution," *The Accountants Digest*}

17. "Japanese children may be no smarter than those elsewhere, but they undoubtedly work harder. They spend more time in school than do Americans—an average of 220 days a year, vs. 178—and they have more homework. They memorize more too." {Mikami, "A Look Inside a Japanese School," *Fortune*}

18. "The rewards of pursuing the high-investment choice are clearly superior: GNP in constant 1982 dollars would reach $7.3 trillion by 2008, the end of the forecast period—over $1 trillion more than the U.S. would get by muddling through. National debt would fall as a percentage of GNP from 42% to 12.9%—a far more manageable load for taxpayers to handle. . . . Real interest rates would decline dramatically. . . . Investment would rebound. . . . Living standards would climb. . . . Corporate profits would soar 70% above the level of the baseline economy, to a total of $518 billion in 1982 dollars." {Richman, "How America Can Triumph," *Fortune*}

19. "Physicians believe that professional liability is one of the most severe problems they face today. (Quoting Dr. Hryniuk:) 'Doctors tend to undertreat in this country [the United States] because they fear complications will lead to lawsuit. People are suing themselves into second-class medicine by pursuing this mentality. They are binding their physicians' hands.' Further evidence of the effects of professional liability comes from the latest national survey of the American College of Obstetricians and Gynecologists. According to the college, almost one in eight obstetricians has stopped performing deliveries, and two thirds of those who have stopped did so before the age of 55, solely because of the risk of malpractice suits. . . . The American College of Surgeons, in a survey of its members, found that 40 percent were no longer accepting high-risk cases in consultation and 28 percent were not performing certain procedures solely because of the risk of malpractice suits." {Manuel, "Professional Liability—a No-Fault Solution," *New England Journal of Medicine*}

20. "Japanese banks enjoyed virtual free rein to pursue market share. Greater capital requirements held no terror for the Japanese banks, which could repeatedly turn to the Tokyo capital markets for the necessary funding, confident that Japanese investors would continue to view other measures of corporate vitality, such as market capitalization, as more important than operating profitably. . . . Moreover, the runaway bull market in Japanese equities raised the banks' own valuations, reflecting the higher values of their equity portfolios, and lowering their cost of capital. Not least, the buoyant Tokyo bourse allowed banks to report appreciably higher income by recognizing as current income some of the appreciations in their stock portfolios. For those very reasons, the damage that a prolonged bear market in Tokyo would inflict on the Japanese banking industry is potentially staggering." {Kreps, "Behind the Bamboo Curtain," *Barron's*}

21. "This on-site registration tactic was effective. Before the voter registration only 37 percent of the 552 people signed up to receive commodities were registered to vote. This increased to 59 percent after registrars worked the cheese lines on several different commodity-distribution days. . . . Since the increases occurred only after registration days and since the drives occurred at different times at the two centers, we can conclude that the on-site registration—and not something else going on–produced the change." {Fawcett, Seekins, and Silber, "Agency-Based Voter Registration: How Well Does It Work?" *Social Policy*}

22. "The authors investigate whether a manager's home culture significantly influences his or her international marketing decisions. They also examine whether the impact of home culture diminishes in an open economy with intense exposure to international markets, giving way to a process of 'globalization.' Decision making in four simulated international marketing situations was studied with executives from the People's Republic of China, Hong Kong, and Canada. The findings confirm that home culture has predictable, significant effects on the decision making of executives from the People's Republic of China and Canada. Chinese executives from Hong Kong were influenced by a

combination of Western and Chinese cultural norms." {Tse, Lee, Vertinsky, & Wehrung, "Does Culture Matter? . . . " *Journal of Marketing*}

23. "IBM could be the market leader with products less impressive than competitors whose machines sell at lower prices. That is because IBM just doesn't sell machinery—it delivers a product with a back-up service no competitor matches. There is also the shining light of the service industry, American Express, whose commitment to customer service is unparalleled. . . . Two things must happen, preferably together, for other companies to shine. First they must find out exactly what customers want. . . . Second, they must deploy a systematic approach to the elimination of all failures within order processing. . . . " {Knapton, "Without Quality, Profits Disappear," *USA Today*}

24. "Alvin Ailey was a giant among men. It wasn't his tall, broad-shouldered physique alone, however, that made him so, but his creative spirit, generosity and intellect. . . . In the history of American dance, there have been only a handful of figures of comparable moment to Ailey. . . . 'Revelations' alone—the Ailey company's signature work almost since its creation in 1960—forged a significant chapter in the evolution of 20th-century American choreography. . . . But Ailey was more than a choreographer and, in his younger years, a dancer whose brilliance illuminated Broadway and Hollywood as much as the dance stage. . . . Ailey and his company have served as a beacon and advocate not just for Dunham, but for a larger contingent of choreographers working in the African-American tradition. . . . The Ailey troupe remains the most all-encompassing dance company the nation has seen." {Kriegsman, "Alvin Ailey: A Giant Chapter in American Dance History," *Ballet International*}

25. "And speaking of Jerry Falwell, it is a pleasure, I must admit, to share with you opposition to him and others of his ilk—those who are opposed to what we consider fundamental needs and fundamental rights for all individuals on this earth—those who would impose upon us all their bigoted views, their moralistic codes, and their inhumane policies. The thrust of their attacks is to destroy the delicate balance we have achieved in this country between church and state and to destroy the principles, strengthened over the past two hundred years, of tolerance, justice, and individual freedom. They are the apostles of ignorance. . . . We are thus confronted by a political force that is waging an all-out war against civil and human rights and is giving sanctimonious support for the historic patterns of sex and race discrimination." {Wattleton, "Reproductive Rights for a More Humane World," *The Humanist*}

26. "I understand from the press that the Democrats have decided to make America's failing competitiveness the main theme of their attack on the Republicans. The reply that Speaker Thomas Foley made to President Bush's State of the Union address certainly gave top billing to America's lost competitiveness. The president has been more circumspect, but competitiveness is clearly high on his agenda. This becomes most obvious when he talks about education. He wants Americans to be better educated so that America will be more competitive. We are to race with others in education so that we can race better with them in economic performance—not so that we can be better people or better citizens. . . . In a nutshell, being Number One is not necessary for

leadership and is not sufficient for dominance. One could write off all this competitiveness and Number One talk as only talk. But it does have some real significance. It is a distraction from our real problem, which is not to get richer than someone else or to get richer faster than someone else but to be as good as we can be, and better than we have been, in the areas of our serious deficiencies, such as homelessness, poverty, ignorance and crime." {Stein, "Who's Number One? Who Cares?" *Wall Street Journal*}

27. "Who shall separate us from the love of Christ? Shall tribulation, or distress, or persecution, or famine, or nakedness, or peril, or sword? . . . No, in all these things we are more than conquerors through him who loved us. For I am sure that neither death, nor life, nor angles, nor principalities, nor things present, nor things to come, nor powers, nor height, nor anything else in all creation, will be able to separate us from the love of God in Christ Jesus our Lord." {Romans 8:35, 37–39, Revised Standard Version}

28. "Those that desire the life of this world with all its frippery shall be rewarded for their deeds in their own lifetime: nothing shall be denied them. These are the men who in the world to come shall be rewarded with Hell-fire. Fruitless are their deeds, and vain are all their works. Are they to be compared with those that have received a veritable word from their Lord, recited by a witness from Him and heralded by the Book of Moses, a guide and a blessing? These have faith in it, but the factions who deny it shall be consigned to the flames of Hell. Therefore do not doubt it. It is the truth from you Lord: yet most men have no faith." {Houd 11:15, *The Koran*, translated by N.J. Dawood (New York: Penguin Books, 1956), p. 134}

29. "And just as the Japanese amuse themselves by filling a porcelain bowl with water and steeping in it little crumbs of paper which until then are without character or form, but, the moment they become wet, stretch themselves and bend, take on colour and distinctive shape, become flowers or houses or people, permanent and recognizable, so in that moment all the flowers in our garden and in M. Swann's park, and the water-lilies on the Vivonne and the good folk of the village and their little dwellings and the parish church and the whole of Combray and of its surroundings, taking their proper shapes and growing solid, sprang into being, town and gardens alike, from my cup of tea." {Proust, *Swann's Way* (New York: Vintage Books, 1970), p. 36}

30. "Moreover, these religionists are moved by the rise of the experimental methods in other fields. What is more natural and proper, accordingly, than they

should affirm they are just as good empiricists as anybody else—indeed, as good as the scientists themselves? As the latter rely upon certain kinds of objects, so the religionists rely upon a certain kind of experience to prove the existence of the object of religion, especially the supreme object, God." {John Dewey, *A Common Faith* (New Haven, CT: Yale University Press, 1936), p. 11}

31. "Telecommuting, or working from home with the aid of telecommunication and computer-based technology, can achieve important management objectives on a broad scale. It allows employees to alter their lifestyles and employers to better manage administrative overhead. Real estate values and infrastructure costs also are affected by telecommuting. Ultimately, these factors may help sustain productivity in the service sector, which has fluctuated in recent times." {J. A. Young, "The Advantages of Telecommuting," *Management Review*}

32. "I do not believe that experimental methods will replace field research. Economies found in the wild can only be understood by studying them in the wild. Field research is absolutely critical to such an understanding. However, the theories and models used in field research necessarily incorporate many judgments about assumptions, parameters and behavioral principles. The simple cases that can be studied in the laboratory can provide the data against which the importance of such judgments can be assessed. Economics is one of the few sciences that is fortunate to have both the field and the laboratory with which to work. The thesis of this paper is that the laboratory methodology, which has historically been absent, will grow and become an important partner in a joint effort to isolate the principles which govern economic behavior." {Charles Plott, "Will Economics Become an Experimental Science?" *Southern Economic Journal*}

33. "There is little disagreement: that media coverage contributes to gambling's popularity. 'Media are flacks for lotto prizes,' says analyst Christiansen, . . . 'The most important reason why people are spending $10.3 billion on lotteries (annually) is because every time people win big, it's on the front page of every newspaper in the state.' Philip J. Cook, professor of public policy and economics at Duke University and co-author of the 1989 book entitled *Selling Hope: State Lotteries in America*, reports that 'the tabloids, especially, focus on people's styles for winning and encourage superstition. . . .'" Newspapers often neglect or downplay the number of losers that are in legalized gambling activities, notes Charles Whiting, editorial writer for the *Star Tribune* in Minneapolis.

At the *Christian Science Monitor*, Keith J. Henderson says too many editors have simply accepted expansion of gambling activities as fact and have not made related issues the subject of strong reporting." {Nancy Davis, "Newspapers Play High-Stakes Games," *Presstime*}

34. "For me the theological basis of rights is compelling. God is the source of rights, and indeed the whole debate about animals is precisely about the rights of the Creator. For this reason in *Christianity and the Rights of Animals* (Crossroad, 1987) I used the ugly but effective term 'theos-rights.' Animal

rights language conceptualizes what is objectively owed the Creator of animals. From a theological perspective, rights are not something awarded, granted, won or lost but something recognized. To recognize animal rights is to recognize the intrinsic value of God-given life." {Andrew Linzey, "The Theological Basis of Animal Rights," *The Christian Century*}

35. "As a child I disliked onions. I could not understand why Mom put them in nearly everything she prepared. Then, in my single life, I made a meatloaf without them. It was so bland I had to throw it out. Manners are like onions: They add flavoring and zest. Too strong, they tend to overpower our society. Not added, they leave it tasteless and semi-barbaric. Just right, they blend in and help us get along with each other." {Carol Torrence, *Modern Maturity*}

36. "The next morning was serene, with a sunrise of warm purple mixed with rose. In the fields around the town the furrows were newly plowed, and very early the tenants were at work setting out the young, deep green tobacco plants. The wild crows flew down close to the fields, making swift blue shadows on the earth. In town the people set out early with their dinner pails, and the windows of the mill were blinding gold in the sun. The air was fresh and the peach trees light as March clouds with their blossoms." {Carson McCullers, *The Ballad of the Sad Café*}

37. "I stand between two worlds. I am at home in neither, and I suffer in consequence. You artists call me a *bourgeois*, and the *bourgeois* try to arrest me. . . . I don't know which makes me feel worse. The *bourgeois* are stupid; but you adorers of the beautiful, who call me phlegmatic and without aspirations, you ought to realize that there is a way of being an artist that goes so deep and is so much a matter of origins and destinies that no longing seems to it sweeter and more worth knowing than longing after the bliss of the common place." {Thomas Mann, *Tonio Kröger*}

38. "My head was heavy. Something seemed to be hovering over me, provoking me, exciting and worrying me. Resentment and black despair were again surging up in me and seeking an outlet. Suddenly, close beside me, I saw two wide-open eyes observing me intently and curiously. The look in those eyes was coldly indifferent and sullen, as though it were utterly detached, and it made me feel terribly depressed.

   A peevish thought stirred in my mind and seemed to pass all over my body like some vile sensation, resembling the sensation you experience when you enter a damp and stale cellar. It seemed somehow unnatural that those two eyes should have been scrutinising me only now. I remembered, too, that for two whole hours I had never said a word to this creature, and had not even thought it necessary to do so; that, too, for some reason appealed to me. Now, however, I suddenly saw clear how absurd and hideous like a spider was the idea of vice which, without love, grossly and shamelessly begins where true love finds its consummation. We went on looking at each other like that for a long time, but she did not drop her eyes before mine, nor did she change her expression, so that in the end it made me for some reason feel creepy." {Fyodor Dostoevsky, *Notes from the Underground*}

39.   "Have you ever really looked at a 5½-inch knife blade? It doesn't sound very
long. But it is dangerously long. It is Texas' legal limit for a knife.

Under Texas law, a knife becomes an illegal weapon if it is longer than
5½ inches (Section 46.02, Penal Code). This does not include double-bladed
knives and throwing knives, which are illegal to carry no matter what the
length.

Do you know how much damage a 5½-inch blade can do? It can go
through heavy clothes and even body armor. It can slice and dice and flay open
skin and muscles and do damage that bullets cannot do. I remember an FBI
agent demonstrating how a 5½-inch blade can go through most doors.

Cops have shot knife-wielders who kept coming forward and still
stabbed the officer to death. Cops hate confronting people with guns, but they
hate confronting people with knives even more.

That homeless man who was recently shot in front of the White House
had a fairly good-sized knife. Unless the blade was more than 5½ inches long,
that man could have carried it around the streets of Fort Worth, and he would
have been within his rights.

Have we lost our minds letting people carry something that big and dangerous around? In the rush to do something about guns, we may just have done
that." {"Day of the Long Knives," *Fort Worth Star-Telegram*}

5.13 EXERCISE: WRITING ENUMERATIVE ARGUMENTS

Write a five-paragraph essay (800–1,000 words) arguing for your position on whether college athletes should be paid. In each paragraph, the topic sentence should be supported by
an enumerative argument.

CHAPTER SIX

Causal Reasoning

Although much inductive reasoning takes the form of enumerative induction, we often make stronger claims than enumeration allows. In enumerative reasoning, as we have seen, the evidence *suggests* the conclusion: It is offered as nonconclusive support for the main point. But there are times when we develop an argument in order to discover what causes a certain event or the causal relationship between events. In such cases, the evidence also *suggests* an explanation: It is offered as nonconclusive support for a possible causal explanation. This type of reasoning is termed **causal reasoning**.

6.1 INTRODUCTION TO CAUSAL REASONING

Philosophers have been debating the nature of causality for millennia, and they continue to do so today. For our purposes, however, we can identify three types of causality: proximate, remote, and probabilistic.

When we identify the **proximate cause** of a given event, we are identifying the cause that is closest to the event in question. Imagine that your father enters the living room and asks what caused the large mirror over the fireplace to break. The proximate cause was that the mirror, a very fragile object, was struck with sufficient force by another object of sufficient rigidity. But your father is not interested in the proximate cause of the mirror's breaking. He is looking for something else.

The second type of cause that we can identify is a **remote cause**. A remote cause of a given event is part of the chain of events that led to the occurrence of that event. Typically, for any given event, there are many remote causes. For example, the remote cause of the broken mirror might have been a shoe flying through the air. This is an event within the chain of events that led to the mirror's breaking. But this does not satisfy your father either. So you tell him that if your sister had not let go of the shoe, the mirror would not have broken. You have identified another remote cause, yet it, too, does not satisfy your father.

The nature of the information sought determines how far back in the chain of events one needs to go in seeking a remote cause. In the case of the broken mirror, your father continues to question you and eventually discovers that you were sitting on the fireplace mantel reading aloud your sister's diary, which she had always kept hidden. Finally, your father has the answer he has been looking for.

There are times when neither the proximate nor the remote causes of an event are known. In such cases, we seek the **probabilistic cause**. We are looking for the cause that, when present, makes it more probable that the event in question will occur than if that cause were absent. For example, suppose that a fire inspector is examining a vacant building that has just burned down. There were no witnesses to the fire, nor is there any evidence that clearly suggests the cause of the fire. In this case, the inspector is looking for the probabilistic cause.

The following diagrams represent the three types of causes just described.

Proximate Cause

* * * * * *X
↑
Proximate Cause

Remote Cause

* * * * * *X
↑
Remote Cause

Probabilistic Cause

? → X
↑
Probabilistic Cause

6.2 CAUSAL FALLACIES

Two major mistakes can occur when causal reasoning is used. The first of these is the fallacy of **ignoring a common cause**. This fallacy occurs when we observe two events that take place in a regular fashion and note that one always precedes the other. We conclude that the first event causes the second. However, it may be that we ignored or overlooked a third event that always occurred when the other two events occurred. This third event may be the actual cause of the other two, neither of which causes the other. Hence, we committed a fallacy when we concluded that the first event was the cause.

Here is an example: Last summer, while I was on vacation, a little red light came on in the dashboard of my car. Shortly after the light appeared, the car lost power. When the light went off, power was restored. This process was repeated many times. After driving about a thousand miles, I concluded that the red light somehow was causing the loss of power. However, after driving another thousand miles I discovered that I had committed the fallacy of ignoring a common cause. It was then that I finally had a mechanic look at the car. He told me of a third event that was the cause of *both* the light coming on *and* the car losing power: The gas filter needed to be replaced.

Reprinted by permission of Jimmy Margulies

When we engage in causal reasoning, we must accurately identify common causes if they exist. Failure to do so results in fallacious reasoning.

The second fallacy that commonly occurs in causal reasoning is the fallacy of **false cause**. This fallacy occurs whenever the cause of a given event is misidentified. Let us consider an example.

Jamie took three philosophy courses and received an F for each one. When her parents asked her for an explanation, she argued most persuasively that the cause of the F's was the abstract nature of philosophy. However, as they helped her pack to go home in the middle of the year, her parents discovered another cause of those F's: three brand-new philosophy texts that had never been opened. Jamie had identified a false cause of her failures.

It is often extremely difficult to identify and name causal fallacies. In some situations, one critical reasoner may claim that a passage exhibits the fallacy of false cause while another may say that it commits the fallacy of ignoring a common cause. Without additional information, it is difficult to determine which reasoner is correct. Because of this problem, in identifying causal fallacies the labeling of the fallacy is not as important as the reasoning behind the label.

6.3 NECESSARY AND SUFFICIENT CONDITIONS

When evaluating causal reasoning, the critical reasoner should focus not only on fallacies, but also on the kinds of conditions that bring about certain events. There are two basic types of conditions: necessary and sufficient.

A **necessary condition** is a condition whose absence makes the event in question impossible. That is, the condition must be present for the event to take place. An analysis that asks whether such a condition is present reveals the complexity of events, which is often overlooked in the search for a specific cause. For example, if we ask about the cause of a fire, we must admit that a fire is too complex an event to have a single cause. However, if we ask what condition or conditions are necessary for a fire to occur, we can identify three separate conditions. First, for a fire to occur, some type of flammable material must be present. Second, there must be enough heat to ignite the material. Finally, for a fire to occur, oxygen must be present. Each of these conditions is a necessary condition, for if any one of them is lacking, a fire cannot occur.

When we claim that a particular condition is the necessary condition for a given event, we mean that that event will occur *only if* that condition is present. Moreover, a necessary condition may sometimes be able to be broken down into one of several alternative conditions. For example, we have identified the presence of a flammable material as a necessary condition for a fire to occur. That material may be a piece of wood, a stack of paper, or an old sweatshirt.

The second type of condition is the **sufficient condition**. When it is present, the event in question will definitely occur. The sufficient condition is the conjunction of all the necessary conditions for a given event. For example, for a fire to occur, three separate necessary conditions must be present. The sufficient condition for a fire, then, is the presence of a flammable material, as well as oxygen and an adequate amount of heat to ignite the material. Whenever this condition is present, a fire will occur.

We can make two general statements about the identification of causal conditions for a given event. First, whenever an event occurs, we know that all of the necessary conditions for its occurrence are present. We also know that at least one of the sufficient conditions for its occurrence is present. (An event may have more than one sufficient condition.) As a result, if we can produce a sufficient condition for an event, we can produce the event. Second, when we attempt to reason back to the cause of an event in the hope of preventing that event from occurring again, we are typically looking for a necessary condition. But when we try to predict or produce a given event, we are generally seeking the sufficient condition for that event.

6.4 EXERCISE: CAUSAL REASONING

1.   In the following scenarios, is the investigator probably interested in discovering the proximate, a remote, or a probabilistic cause?
      *a.   "It is likely that genetic engineering will play an increasing role in the development of immunotoxins. Just as one can eliminate the receptor-binding region of the B chain by manipulating the diphtheria toxin gene, so one can modify toxin genes in other ways to improve the efficacy and safety of toxin molecules." {Collier & Kaplan, "Immunotoxins," *Scientific American*}
      b.   "Since the discovery in the 1950s that antibiotics promote growth of livestock, antibiotics in animal feeds have become a multimillion dollar industry and have undoubtedly helped feed the world's populations. At

the same time there has been a swell of evidence that antibiotics in animal feeds are helping human bacteria build resistance to antibiotics, a trend that might possibly open people to deadly and once-conquered infectious diseases." {*Science News*}

c. "Although the poor readers didn't do particularly well on either type of question, they tended to do better on questions that tapped their reasoning ability than on those that tested their ability to recall details. . . . They seemed better able to grasp the texts' larger meanings, especially on questions about the 'main idea' of a passage, cause–effect relationships and implications." {Meer, "Reading in Stages," *Psychology Today*}

*d. "Americans by the millions have been hiding their salt shakers in the hope of protecting themselves against high blood pressure. But some experts now question whether a high level of sodium chloride in the diet is really all that bad. And last week, in a controversial report that contradicts the diet advice Americans have been getting for many years, researchers sprinkled more doubt on the issue by suggesting that too little calcium and other nutrients rather than too much sodium may be major culprits in hypertension." {Clark, Hager, & Witherspoon, "Salt: Should I or Shouldn't I," *Newsweek*}

e. "'It's strange,' says lab ecologist Ken McLeod, 'but as the arms race prospers, so will the type of research we do.' For three decades, the arms race has flourished, and for three decades it has fallen to researchers like McLeod at Savannah River Ecology Laboratory to understand the tension between the pollutants of the weapons industry and the neighboring land." {Gordon, "Radiation Paradise," *Science*}

2. In the scenarios that follow, has a causal fallacy been committed? If not, can you identify one that might have been committed in the particular scenario? Explain. If a causal fallacy has been committed, identify the fallacy and explain why it is fallacious. (Remember that it is the *explanation* that is most important.)

a. Because it is a well-known fact that many patients with terminal cancer suffer from severe depression and are unusually irritable, some conclude that emotional distress is the major cause of cancer.

b. Recently, a particular educator claimed that students who are ill are so because they misbehave. He cited as evidence the situation in which a normally well-behaving student becomes extremely difficult to deal with and grumpy. The educator continues to point out that a day or two after a student exhibits these traits of misbehavior, he or she also begins to exhibit signs of some sort of illness.

c. Several studies have shown that a significant number of individuals who have won big in a state lottery have died at a relatively early age. Therefore, be careful and never win big in the state lottery if you want to live a long life.

d. "It should not be surprising to find that [a] significant fraction of shelter residents are mentally ill. In fact, a clinical study I designed and implemented last year found at a shelter in Boston [a] 90 percent incidence of diagnosable mental illness . . . The shelter selected for the study . . . was considered demographically representative of Boston-area shelters." {Bassuk, "The Homeless Problem," *Scientific American*}

e.   "The child thinks he or she participates in the actions of nature. Sometimes these feelings are accompanied by beliefs in magic. Interviewer: What makes the clouds move along? Ten year old: It's when you walk." {Stepans & Kuehn, "Children's Conception of Weather," *Science and Children*}

f.   "Professor Derek Price, of Yale, in a recent article, expounded a theory analogous to that used in statistical thermodynamics. He explained that, in asserting the statistics of science, as crudely measured by counts of men and papers they have authored, he found a uniform exponential relationship that established the logarithm of the head counts as a significant number. In other words the number of scientists and engineers, like all other indices, has shown an exponential growth. During the past three centuries world population has doubled every 10 to 15 years. But the portion of the population composed of scientists of all kinds has increased 10-fold. Because of this exponential growth, he concluded that 90 percent of all the scientists who ever lived are alive today." {Zinner, "The Noise Level of Science," *American Scientists*}

g.   "Princeton University researchers have found a strong link between students' future income and spending on teaching at the schools they attend. The study is the latest contribution to a heated debate over the relationship between spending and educational quality . . . " {Putka, "Earning Power, School Spending Linked in Study," *Wall Street Journal*}

3.   List five events and at least one necessary condition for each to occur.

4.   List five additional events and identify at least one sufficient condition for each to occur.

6.5 MILL'S METHODS

Probably the best-known type of causal reasoning is a set of methods known as Mill's methods. Although these methods appear in the work of David Hume (1711–1776) and even earlier in that of Francis Bacon (1561–1626) and others, they are credited to John Stuart Mill (1806–1873) because he was the first to formulate them explicitly. As an aid to understanding Mill's methods, we present his own concise statements concerning them

John Stuart Mill began learning Greek at the age of three. By eight, he was reading Plato and Herodotus. J. S. Mill was not only influential in the development of utilitarian ethics, but also crucial in the establishment of the first women's rights organizations.

and then explain the methods further. Each explanation is accompanied by a chart that emphasizes the causal reasoning embodied in the method in question.

The Method of Agreement

> If two or more instances of the phenomenon under investigation have only one circumstance in common, the circumstance in which alone all the instances agree, is the cause (or effect) of the given phenomenon.[19]

The **method of agreement** tells us that if a particular circumstance (condition) is present whenever a given event occurs, and no other circumstance is present every time that event occurs, then the particular circumstance that occurs in each instance of that event is probably the necessary circumstance or condition for that event. For example, consider an individual doing research on why some students are successful in an especially difficult subject, say, mathematical logic. In reviewing the data, the researcher finds many circumstances in which students are successful in mathematical logic, such as instructors using particular approaches to teaching the subject or assigning particular texts. However, the researcher discovers that in all instances in which students are successful they are highly motivated, and this is the only condition that is common to all instances of student success in mathematical logic. From this observation, using the method of agreement, the researcher concludes that the necessary condition for student success in mathematical logic is high motivation.

In the charts that follow, let A, B, C, D, and E stand for different instances in which an event or phenomenon occurs. P is the event or phenomenon in question. C1 through C7 indicate different circumstances or conditions present in the situation.

As the chart shows, there are five instances in which a particular phenomenon P is exhibited. We ask, "What is the cause of that phenomenon? What condition exists which makes that phenomenon possible in all five instances?" When we examine the various conditions that exist in each instance, we discover one condition that is common to all of them. From this finding, we conclude that the common condition, C1, may be the necessary condition for the phenomenon in question.

Here is an example: John recently determined that whenever an alkaline substance and an oil are mixed, they produce a kind of soap. He arrived at this conclusion after performing four experiments that produced soap. The only condition that was present in all four experiments was that an alkaline substance and an oil were mixed. Since there were no other common conditions, John concluded, using the method of agreement, that the conjunction of an alkaline substance and an oil may be the necessary condition for the production of soap.

6.5a The Method of Agreement

A	B	C	D	E
		all instances exhibit P		
C1	C1	C1	C1	C1
C3	C6	C2	C4	C7
C2	C3	C4	C5	C6

6.5b The Method of Difference

A	B
P	
C1	C1
C2	C2
C3	
C4	C4
C5	C5
C6	C6

The Method of Difference

If an instance in which the phenomenon under investigation occurs, and an instance in which it does not occur, have every circumstance in common save one, that one occurring only in the former; the circumstance in which alone the two instances differ, is the effect, or the cause, or an indispensable part of the cause, of the phenomenon.[20]

The **method of difference** tells us that if the circumstances present in two instances or events appear to be basically the same, except that a particular phenomenon occurs in one and not in the other, a condition that exists in the former but not in the latter may be the sufficient condition for the phenomenon in question.

In this chart, we find two instances that have several characteristics in common. However, the phenomenon P occurs in one instance, but not in the other. Why does the first instance exhibit the phenomenon? What is the cause of P? Upon examining the conditions present in each instance, we find that the two instances have five conditions in common. However, condition C3 is present only in instance A. From this finding, we conclude that C3 is the cause of P and is probably the sufficient condition for P.

Let us return to our example of John making soap. In another series of experiments, John conducts five separate tests. In the first, he mixes an alkaline substance with water and an oil. In the second, he mixes a viscous material with water and an alkaline substance. In the third, he mixes the viscous material with an alkaline substance and an oil. In the fourth, he mixes just the alkaline substance with an oil. In the fifth, he mixes the oil with the viscous material and water. He finds that the first, third, and fourth tests produce soap.

Why was soap produced in tests 1, 3, and 4 and not in tests 2 and 5? Upon examining his notes, John finds that the two sets of tests differed in that, in each of the three tests which produced soap, an alkaline substance and an oil were present. These conditions were not present in the two tests that did not produce soap. He concludes that those conditions were the cause of the soap being produced and that their presence is probably a sufficient condition for the production of soap.

The Joint Method of Agreement and Difference

If two or more instances in which the phenomenon occurs have only one circumstance in common, while two or more instances in which it does not occur have nothing in common save the absence of that circumstance, the circumstance in which alone the two sets of instances differ, is the effect, or the cause, or an indispensable part of the cause, of the phenomenon.[21]

Mill's third method, the **joint method of agreement and difference**, uses both the methods just described. First the method of agreement is used to determine a probable necessary condition. Then the reasoner examines several other situations that are different from those in which the necessary condition was identified. The only thing these other situations have in common is the *absence* of the condition that was identified as necessary. If we can discover a condition that appears *every* time a particular situation occurs and *only* when that situation occurs, we have probably identified both the necessary condition and the sufficient condition for that situation.

6.5c The Joint Method

Step I:

A	B
P	P
C1	C1 ← possible necessary condition
C2	C4
C3	C5

Step II:

C	D	E
C2	C3	C4
C4	C2	C5

The preceding set of charts shows that C1 is both the necessary and the sufficient condition for P. Using the method of agreement, we identify C1 as a probable necessary condition for P. Then, using the method of difference, we identify C1 as a probable sufficient condition for P. In this case, we could add an additional situation in which the condition in question, C1, occurs, and we would expect the desired phenomenon P also to occur.

Let us return to the example of soap production. In Step 1, John has produced soap in three separate experiments. Upon examining his notes, he finds that one condition, and only one, is common to all three situations. He notices that the combination of an alkaline substance and an oil is present each time soap is produced. In this step, he has used the method of agreement.

In Step 2, John attempts to find out whether the observed condition is also a sufficient condition for the phenomenon of soap production. To do so, he conducts several experiments that test different combinations in an effort to produce soap. However, he is careful to ensure that the combinations of an alkaline substance and oil is not present in any of these experiments. None of the experiments results in the production of soap. Hence, he concludes that not only is the presence of an alkaline substance and oil the probable necessary condition, but their combination is probably the sufficient condition for soap production.

To extend his research, John repeats one of the experiments that failed to produce soap, but this time he includes the combination in question. This time the experiment produces soap. John concludes that the combination of an alkaline substance and an oil is both a necessary and sufficient condition for the production of soap. He has used the joint method of agreement and difference to arrive at his conclusion.

The Method of Residue

> Subduct (subtract) from any phenomenon such part as is known by previous inductions to be the effect of certain antecedents, and the residue of the phenomenon is the effect of the remaining antecedents.[22]

The fourth method identified by Mill is the **method of residue**. This method is a variation of the method of difference. Whereas in the method of difference we deal with phenomena and conditions as wholes, in the method of residue we divide them into separate, identifiable units. Then we can use the three methods discussed earlier to identify the particular conditions that are the causes of each phenomenon. If, after completing this process, we find one phenomenon and one condition unexplained, that condition is the cause of that phenomenon.

As an example of the application of the method of residue, consider the phenomenon of traffic accidents. We find that more traffic accidents occur on wet days than on dry days. What is the cause of the accidents on wet days? We go to the local police department to examine the files regarding traffic accidents on wet days, and we discover that over a given period of time ten such accidents occurred. According to the method of residue, we list each accident individually. We also examine the police reports to identify all of the causes cited for the accidents. We might discover that although there were ten separate traffic accidents on wet days, the police reports list only five different causes of them. One accident occurred due to brake failure and subsequently running a stop sign (i.e., the accident was due to mechanical failure). In three accidents, the police determined that the drivers were under the influence of alcohol (i.e., DWI was the cause). Another driver tried to drive through an intersection as the traffic light was changing from yellow to red (i.e., the driver ran a red light). In two cases, the drivers were cited with negligence because they became distracted while talking on their cellular phones. These seven accidents, while actually occurring in wet weather, could have occurred in dry weather. In the remaining three accidents, the cause was unclear. Since no other cause could be found, the police cited "wet road conditions" as the cause of those accidents. The method of residue then claims that wet weather causes traffic accidents.

6.5d The Method of Residue

P		
P1	P2	P3

(Cases of P)

C		
C1	C2	C3

(Cases of C)

We find the following causal relationships:

$$
\begin{array}{c}
C1 \rightarrow P2 \\
\text{and} \\
\underline{C3 \rightarrow P1} \\
\therefore C2 \rightarrow P3
\end{array}
$$

Notice that the method of residue requires that all of the phenomena *except one* be properly linked with a cause and that there must exist *only one* remaining condition. In Example 6.5d, we find that only P3 and C2 are left after the appropriate associations have been made. Hence, we conclude that C2 is the cause of P3.

The Method of Concomitant Variation

Whatever phenomenon varies in any manner whenever another phenomenon varies in some particular manner, is either a cause or an effect of that phenomenon, or is connected with it through some fact of causation.[23]

The **method of concomitant variation** is designed to determine the cause of changes that occur over a period of time or over a continuum. The method claims that if a change occurs in one situation every time a change occurs in a second situation, and the changes in both situations occur consistently, we can reach one of three possible conclusions: Either the first situation is the cause of the second, or the second is the cause of the first, or there exists a third cause that influences both the first situation and the second situation simultaneously.

6.5e The Method of Concomitant Variation

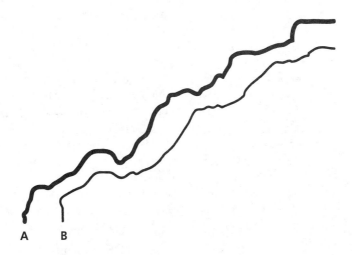

A   B

The preceding chart tracks two phenomena, possibly by means of statistical studies. We notice that the tracking seems to be parallel, so that any time a change occurs in A, we find a change occurring in B.

Before looking at cases in which Mill's methods are used, we must address an objection to them. The methods have been criticized because they do not always make good on their claim of identifying the causal connection that is being sought. Underlying this criticism is the assumption that the methods claim to identify the causal relationship between a given condition and the corresponding phenomenon. It is also assumed that if the methods do not always accurately pinpoint the cause of a given event, they must be flawed.

While it is true that the condition cited as the cause may not be the cause one is seeking, it is important to bear in mind that Mill's methods are a form of inductive reasoning. We must always realize that it is possible for the premises, or evidence, to be true and for the conclusion to be false. Thus, Mill's methods may lead us to commit a causal fallacy, such as false cause. Despite their potential shortcomings, however, these methods can be extremely powerful tools for expanding one's knowledge. Consider a recent outbreak of *Escherichia coli* 0157:H7 at a local county fair. Health officials were able to determine that water was the source of the deadly *E. coli* by using causal reasoning like Mill's.

In evaluating arguments involving Mill's methods, the procedures set forth in Chapter 3 for evaluating all arguments should be followed. If, after examining the text, we conclude that an argument exists, we must rewrite the argument in standard form. We can then ask whether the argument meets the criteria of clarity, relevance, and consistency. As with all arguments, if we identify a fallacy at this point, the reasoning process ends with the claim that the argument is bad because it is fallacious. If no fallacy is identified, we must decide whether the argument is deductive or inductive. Mill's methods are appropriate only for inductive arguments having to do with causation. For this reason, they often occur in scientific investigations, such as the aforementioned outbreak of *E. coli*.

6.6 EXERCISE: MILL'S METHODS

Examine the passages that follow and identify the argument. Also, indicate which of Mill's methods is probably being used.

*1.   "The study involved nine sufferers of severe and frequent attacks of migraine who underwent treatment in 1983. The patients, men and women between the ages of 30 and 64, were first put on a diet avoiding food coloring, additives, . . . , and other substances known to bring on migraine attacks. After showing no improvement, they were then put on diets avoiding, in sequence, milk and milk products; all grain cereals . . . ; meats; and fruit seeds and nuts. The headaches improved on the diets restricting milk products and grains." {*Fort Worth Star-Telegram*}

*2.   "Sleep-inducing drugs that are quickly eliminated from the body can effectively treat the insomnia and daytime sluggishness that afflict shift workers . . . Sleeping pills that remain active for several days, however, cause a loss of mental function and alertness on waking when used after a sudden sleep-schedule change. . . . The study consisted of 24 volunteers with normal sleep patterns. . . . Eight subjects were given the short-acting sleeping pill triazolam, eight received the long-acting medication flurazepam, and the remaining volunteers were given a placebo pill. . . . Subjects given the short-acting pill slept longer than the others, were more alert the next day and performed better on several tests of mental function." {*Science News*}

*3. "Dr. Gerald P. Murphy, . . . , reported that a cross section of men across the U.S. with Kaposi's sarcoma were given interferon for three months and that the sarcoma disappeared in 40 percent of these patients." {*Parade Magazine*}

4. "Rhee coated half her ground beef patties with batter made solely of wheat flour, and the rest in batter made from 50/50 mix of wheat flour and cottonseed flours. After refrigerating these cooked 'chicken-fried steaks' for five days, she found that those in wheat batter registered a thiobarbituric acid (TBA) test value of 10.5 to 10.9—unquestionably and very objectionably rancid. . . . By contrast, 50/50 batter-dipped patties developed a TBA value of just 2.7 in the first test and 4.3 in a second. Rhee attributes the second, higher rancidity score to using meat that had been frozen before cooking, rather than using fresh meat." {*Science News*}

*5. "Despite recognition of the deleterious effects of passive smoking, quantitative information on the intake of environmental tobacco smoke is still lacking. Cotinine is the major metabolite of nicotine found in the urine. We have examined the relationship between urinary cotinine excretion in 472 nonsmokers and the smokiness of their environment. The urinary cotinine levels of nonsmokers who lived with smokers were higher than those of nonsmokers who did not, increasing with the combined daily cigarette consumption of smokers in the family. The urinary cotinine values of nonsmokers who worked with smokers were also higher than those of nonsmokers who did not, increasing with the number of smokers in the workplace. The presence of smokers in both the home and the workplace also increased the cotinine levels. Urban nonsmokers had more cotinine in their urine than rural nonsmokers. We conclude that the deleterious effects of passive smoking may occur in proportion to the exposure of nonsmokers to smokers in the home, the workplace, and the community. {*New England Journal of Medicine*}

6. "A simple blood test can predict who might develop diabetes by detecting the presence of antibodies that destroy insulin-producing cells. . . . In a two-year study of 1,723 first-degree relatives of diabetics, the disease developed in 2 of 16 relatives who had the antibodies and in only 1 of 1,707 relatives who did not have the tell-tale substance." {*U.S. News & World Report*}

7. "It has been suggested that patients with Parkinson's disease might show the same kinds of behavioral impairments as those exhibited by subjects with frontal lesions. Previous tests of this hypothesis have given, at best, equivocal results. Verbal fluency is a measure sensitive to frontal lesions, and data are presented showing that Parkinsonian subjects produce fluency scores similar to those of normal controls and not at all like subjects with left or right frontal lesions." {*British Journal of Clinical Psychology*}

8. "Working in Stockholm through city child welfare centers, which are attended by about 85 percent of the city's children, Dr. Lennart Hamberg has conducted a study on the effectiveness of the addition of sodium fluoride to a solution of

vitamin A and D drops. His findings are reported in the Feb. 27 *Lancet*. Of 705 children taking part in the experiment, 342 received the fluoride treatment and 363 were in a control group. All the children received yearly examinations from the time of their first birthday. After six years the fluoride group had up to 57 percent fewer decayed teeth." {*Science News*}

9. "After weeks or months of regular bingeing the user is 'coked out.' Depression becomes chronic, he starts hallucinating, and signs of psychosis appears. Says Washton, 'Well before psychosis, you see increased irritability, short temper, suspiciousness. . . .' In a survey of 500 callers to the toll-free hotline, 800-COCAINE, researchers found that fully half reported symptoms of this nature. Eighty-three percent of the group, all of whom took cocaine almost daily, told interviewers they felt habitually depressed or anxious. At least half said they had difficulty concentrating or remembering things, were uninterested in sex, and sometimes had panic attacks." {*Discover*}

10. "The latest hypothesis, however, is that cocaine may wreck the brain by slow steps. Charles Schuster, a professor of pharmacology at the University of Chicago, has found that amphetamines lower the overall amounts of some neurotransmitters in the brains of rats, monkeys, and guinea pigs. The reduction persisted for as long as three years after the last time the animals were given the drugs, leading Schuster to believe that the neurons involved may be permanently incapacitated." {*Discover*}

11. "To offer marijuana at a party in the sixties showed you were cool, tuned in, on the cutting edge," says Washton. "The message is different now. We have yuppies instead of hippies. Cocaine is associated with their values—success, mastery, control. It's a self-marketing product." {*Discover*}

12. "Researchers report in the April 29 *New England Journal of Medicine* that they found high levels of nicotine metabolite in babies under 10 months old exposed to cigarette smoke in the home. Researchers from the University of North Carolina at Chapel Hill looked at urine and saliva levels of cotinine, a metabolite of nicotine, in 19 unexposed infants and 32 infants from homes that contained smokers." {*Science News*}

Part II: Application

COURSE PROJECT

In the application section of Part I, you identified arguments in an article of your choice. Now you will evaluate the inductive reasoning in that article. If your article contains many arguments, you may want to evaluate only three or four of the most important ones. In the process, you should raise crucial questions concerning the article. These questions will be the starting point of your research. Instead of going to the library and checking out numerous books about the topic dealt with in your article, focus your research by attempting to find answers to the questions you have raised. Understand that good research does not always find answers; in fact, often the discovery that answers *cannot* be found is fruitful. Failure to find answers while doing research frequently can be attributed to one of three causes.

1. *Researcher failure* occurs when the researcher does not know how or where to look for answers or when the researcher fails to understand the information found. 2. In *resource failure*, a researcher is limited by the available resources. For example, the only library accessible to the researcher may not have adequate resources on the topic of investigation. 3. In *information failure*, either the researcher is asking a question that has not been asked before, so that it has never been researched, or the topic of inquiry needs more research. In this case, discovering that answers are not found is fruitful because it may provide an ongoing research project.

In Part I, we identified several arguments contained in an article by Mayor Edward Koch of New York City. In this section, we will evaluate some of those arguments. Note that although questions are raised, the necessary research is not presented. You will want to include some of your research findings as you present Part II of the semester project. Note also that, as with any inductive analysis, questions may be raised concerning the analysis; not everyone will agree with the analysis of Dr. Koch's article set forth here. That's all right: Any analysis of inductive reasoning should stimulate discussion, not shut it down. The example presented next is followed by an example written by a student.

EXAMPLES

KOCH ARTICLE

In Part I, we identified several arguments contained in the article by Edward Koch. In this section, we will evaluate several of those arguments.

Overall Argument:

> The death penalty is not barbaric.
> It is not relevant that no other major democracy uses the death penalty.
> The execution of an innocent person by mistake is improbable.
> Capital punishment does not cheapen the value of life.
> The death penalty is not applied in a discriminatory manner.
> "Thou Shall Not Kill" does not apply to the issue of capital punishment.
> The death penalty is not state-sanctioned murder.
> ∴   We must support capital punishment.

This overall argument is an inductive generalization; however, analyzing it would be premature, since each premise is the conclusion of an internal argument. If those internal arguments are weak, then the overall argument must be considered weak.

> 1.   Mayor Koch claims that capital punishment is not barbaric. To support his claim, he offers two arguments:

> We are faced with either letting cancer spread or trying to cure it with available methods.
> The available methods may one day seem barbaric, but are the only options currently available.
> It is more barbaric to do nothing today than to treat illnesses by available methods.
> ∴   We perform radical surgery, radiation, chemotherapy, etc.

(and)

> Radical surgery, etc., are not liked by anyone, but are currently necessary as attempts to cure cancer
> Capital punishment is not pleasant.
> ∴   Capital punishment must be supported for certain crimes.

(furthermore)

> (Certain crimes $=_{df.}$ cases in which any other form of punishment would be inadequate and unjust.)

(also)

> Furthermore, he states that if we create a society in which injustice is not tolerated, incidents like murder and other forms of injustice will diminish.

Analysis:

> Argument from analogy (treatment of cancer and treatment for certain crimes)

Criteria: Relevance of Analogy

Relevant Similarities: In both cases, there is a concept of a healthy entity and of an infection. Destroying the infection in both cases results in a healthier entity. (This assumes that Koch is correct when he claims that if we create a society which is not tolerant of injustice, then injustice will diminish.) Is Koch's assumption appropriate? If we accept both of the preceding arguments, then we must question premise two in the first argument. If it may someday seem barbaric to perform radical surgery, isn't it possible that we have already arrived at the point that capital punishment is barbaric?

Relevant Dissimilarities: Cancer is a medical abnormality, but certain crimes have never been shown to be medical abnormalities. Is, say, murder, a physical sickness? If it is not, then does the analogy hold? If it does, then the murderer is the abnormality and that which is infected is society, but is the analogy relevant?

Fallacy: False analogy has been committed, in that the analogy between cancer and murder is not appropriate. In the former case, the infection or abnormality does not possess personhood; in the latter case it does. Furthermore, murder does not seem to be a physical sickness. Mr. Koch does acknowledge that his analogy is "imperfect," but such disclaimers do not change the fact that he makes his case on the basis of this analogy.

The argument is weak because it is fallacious. If Koch's argument, which claims that capital punishment is not barbaric, is fallacious, then is the death penalty barbaric? If the method of death is not the issue, but the policy of capital punishment is, then is there any way of revising the policy to make it nonbarbaric? Just what exactly is barbaric about capital punishment? The desire to create a society that is intolerant of injustices? Or is the putting to death of another individual considered barbaric? If the latter, then is not the toleration of injustices barbaric in that we protect lawbreakers, but not the innocent?

2.   Koch claims that it is not relevant that no other major democracy uses the death penalty:

No other major democracy has the murder rate of the United States. Between 1963 and 1980, the murder rate increased 122%. On the basis of 1970 homicide rates, a person living in a large city ran a greater risk of being murdered than a U.S. soldier ran of being killed in World War II.
Each country's laws ought to reflect the different conditions and traditions of that country.
If other countries had our problem, they would want the death penalty also.
∴   The claim that no other democracy uses the death penalty is not relevant to the argument.

Analysis:

On its surface, this argument does not seem clearly to fit any of the types of enumerative arguments; however, upon closer inspection, we see that premises 2 and 3 are offered as examples or illustrations of the first premise. Since they do not really support premise 1, we must omit them as mere illustrations. Hence, the argument should be as follows:

No other major democracy has the murder rate of the United States.
Each country's laws ought to reflect the different conditions and traditions of that country.
<u>If other countries had our problem, they would want the death penalty also.</u>
∴   The claim that no other democracy uses the death penalty is not relevant to the argument.

With this rewriting, it becomes clear that the premises are generalizations and the conclusion is a particular; hence, the argument is a statistical syllogism.

Criteria:

Sample Size: If the premises are taken at face value, then the sample size should not be problematic. However, can we take the sample sizes indicated in the premises at face value? That is, in each premise there is a universal claim that seems to identify all countries, but can these claims really be extended to all countries?

Total Evidence: As critical reasoners, we must raise several questions. For example, in premise 1, what is meant by 'major democracy'? Is the claim of that premise accurate? The illustrations concerning the U.S. murder rate definitely do not support the premise. The second premise, which suggests that laws ought to reflect the given conditions of a society, makes sense in some cases, but are all laws relativistic? If they are, and there are no universal laws, then it is possible that the death squads of El Salvador are legally and morally correct for that country. In such cases, world opinion would not be appropriate grounds for some type of sanction against El Salvador.

Fallacy: While the foregoing questions do suggest that the argument is problematic, they do not constitute any clear violations of the criteria. Hence, there are no fallacies to be identified.

The assessment of this argument is quite difficult for several reasons. If we could clear up the problems with premise 1 and, in some way, confirm premise 3, then the argument would appear to be strong. However, the relativism that we find in the second premise and that is implied in the conclusion weakens the argument. I am tempted to claim that this argument is moderate; after all, just because no one else is doing a particular thing, the United States is still a great and powerful nation, so we can do as we like! But such provincial thinking has created many atrocities, such as those in Germany during the 1940s. Hence, I suggest that this argument of Koch's is weak, even though it is not fallacious.

3.   Koch's position is that the death penalty should not be abolished because of some abstract possibility, and, furthermore, he claims that innocent persons might be killed if we do not have a death penalty. To support his position, he offers two arguments:

Adam Bedau (one of the most implacable foes of capital punishment) says that it is, "false sentimentality to argue that the death penalty should be abolished because of the abstract possibility that an innocent person might be executed. Bedau cites a study of the 7,000 executions carried out between 1893 and 1971 and concludes that records fail to show any such occurrence.

∴   The death penalty should not be abolished because of some mere abstract possibility.

(and)

If government functions only when the possibility of error does not exist, government would not function at all.
Human life deserves special protection, and one of the best ways to guarantee that protection is to make sure that convicted murderers do not kill again. The only way to accomplish this is via the death penalty.
Examples of Biegenwald and Smith.
Example of 91 police officers killed in 1981; 7% of those arrested in cases that were solved had been arrested for previous murders.
Example citing 85 persons arrested in New York City for homicide in 1976 and 1977 who had previous arrests for murder. During those two years, New York police arrested for murder persons with a previous arrest for murder an average of one every 8.5 days.

∴   Innocent persons might be killed if we do not have capital punishment.

Analysis:

The first argument is an appeal to authority. That is, Mayor Koch appeals to the authority of Adam Bedau.

Criteria:

The first criterion for appeals to authority is that the individual cited be an expert in the area for which he is cited. The only thing that Mayor Koch says about Adam Bedau is that he is one of the most implacable opponents of the death penalty. If Bedau does have the credentials which Koch suggests that he has, then he probably is an expert. Furthermore, the fact that he takes a stance opposite that of the mayor makes Koch's claim even more forceful. Before I could fully accept the point Mayor Koch is making with this argument, however, I would need to do some research to determine Bedau's credentials and whether the mayor has properly presented the expert.

The second criterion is that there must be some consensus amongst experts that the position stated by the individual cited is correct. Of course, this criterion does not require unanimity; it merely requires that the position advocated be viewed as a viable position by other experts. To illustrate that the mayor's argument does satisfy this condition, he states that Bedau cites a study of 7,000 executions between 1893 and 1971 to support his claim. While this citation seems to support the fact that Bedau's position has the required credibility, before we can fully accept it we ought to ask several questions about the study itself. Who conducted it? How thorough was the research? Are there any counterexamples to the study and, if so, how many?

Fallacy: Assuming that further study will support Bedau's credentials and the study he cites, it appears that the argument in question does not violate any required conditions. Hence, no fallacies appear in the argument.

If everything checks out, this argument is clearly at least a moderate argument. For me, the fact that actually makes the argument strong is that Bedau is not an expert who holds the same position as Mayor Koch. The mayor is citing an opponent of his, and the fact that that opponent is making the claim really adds credibility to the argument.

On the basis of the preceding analysis and some very basic research, we can calculate the plausibility of the conclusion, given the evidence. Concerning the expertise of Adam Bedau, we may assign an upper limit of 98% and a lower limit of 95%. Given what Mayor Koch says about Bedau, and given that Koch's argument could easily be undermined by making such claims about Bedau, especially since it is extremely easy to review Bedau's credentials, it is extremely probable that Bedau is an expert. Furthermore, a cursory review of the literature on capital punishment reveals that Bedau is frequently quoted on the issue. The consensus amongst experts, however, is not as probable. Since many of the experts in this area are in academia, and academicians tend to be more liberal, and liberals tend to be against capital punishment, the upper limit may be as low as 85%, with the lower limit around 75%. As far as other considerations are concerned, we can assign the upper limit as 75% and the lower limit as 70%. These assignments are due to the relative strength of the conclusion (i.e., "should not be") and what is at stake. Since it is a human life that is at stake, the possibility of a mistake should weigh heavily. Hence, the plausibility of this argument ranges from 62% to 50%. The argument is not as strong as it initially appeared.

The second argument moves from particulars to a generalization. This means that the argument is an inductive generalization.

Criteria:

Sample Size: It is difficult to assess how to evaluate this argument's sample size. The first premise, dealing with governments functioning only when errors will occur, seems to suggest a large sample. But even here, it is unclear. The second premise is also questionable in terms of its sample size and its relation to the conclusion. Premises 3 through 5 definitely relate to the sample size, but it is unclear whether they satisfy the criterion or whether they violate it.

Sample Diversity: Again, it is unclear whether the evidence satisfies, or even relates to, the criterion. There is diversity in that two persons cited as examples were already in prison and 91 police officers were from various parts of the country. Then, the last premise deals just with New York City.

Fallacy: Without further research, there are no obvious violations of the criteria and hence no fallacies apparent in this argument.

This argument is also strong: Before I state exactly why, let me point out several of its problems. First of all, it is unclear how the evidence satisfies the criteria. The evidence does not appear, to violate the conditions, but we need more information to show that it satisfies them. Second, in the argument, much is made of individuals committing murders who have previous arrests for murder. It must be pointed out that there is a difference between someone *arrested* for a crime and the person being *convicted* for a crime. If the evidence could support the statement that individuals with previous convictions will murder again, as in premise 3, then premises 4 and 5 would be much stronger. These are problems, but I believe the argument is still strong because of the weakness of its conclusion. Notice that it simply claims that if we do not have capital punishment, then an innocent person might be killed. This statement is extremely weak and is well supported by the evidence.

****

The foregoing evaluation of Koch's article illustrates how the critical-reasoning process works. In the first place, the process ought to stimulate research. In our example, we noted that numerous questions could be raised concerning Koch's argument. These questions can serve as a guide for further research. Regardless of whether we agree with Koch, if we follow the proper procedure and carry out the research suggested by the questions raised, we will end up with a better understanding of the issue of capital punishment.

STUDENT EXAMPLE

NEW URBANISM: DOES IT CREATE A SENSE OF COMMUNITY?[24]

In Part I of this project, I identified several arguments contained in the article by Emily Talen on the new urbanism.[25] In this section, I will evaluate several of those arguments.

Overall Argument

> The promoters of new urbanism claim that the built environment creates a sense of community.
> Some research supports the relationship between environmental factors and social interaction via an intermediate variable.
> It has not been disproven that another urban design creed could produce the same result through a different design philosophy.
> ∴   Further research is needed.

This overall argument is an inductive generalization; however, analyzing it would be premature, since each premise is the conclusion of an internal argument. If any or all of those arguments are weak, then the overall argument must be considered weak.

　　　　1.   Talen claims that promoters of the new urbanism maintain that the built environment creates a sense of community and that they have translated the building of a sense of community into a specific design manifesto. To support her claim, she offers the following arguments as evidence:

> New urbanists attempt to build a sense of community via two avenues: integrating private residential space with surrounding public space; and careful design and placement of public space.
> There are studies which substantiate the idea that physical factors can act as a mechanism to promote interaction among residents of a community. To new urbanists, the physical design characteristics they create improve social interaction.
> ∴   To new urbanists, a sense of community is indisputable.

(and)

The social prescription of new urbanism is based on spatial determinism—the
notion that interaction among residents and a sense of community are
cultivated via the organizing power of space.
New urbanists also align themselves with the sociological tradition which asserts
that a sense of community is vital to human functioning.
Studies by Glynn and by Goudy have found that the concept of new urbanism
has a universal definition and appeal and that community attachment is
associated with mental health.
∴   A theoretical basis for the social doctrine of new urbanism exists.

Analysis:

The first argument is a simple enumeration; the movement is from particular to
particular.

Criteria:

Total Evidence: As critical reasoners, we find that several questions come to
mind. First of all, does providing the mechanism for social interaction to occur guarantee that it will? If residents do not have common interests, will living in the same
neighborhood and sitting in the same park create a sense of community? Is there evidence that people will feel connected merely by proximity? Although the theoretical
basis for new urbanism may exist, does the empirical evidence exist to support it?

Diverse Sample: New urbanist communities are still relatively few. Can these
samples speak for the rest of the nation? What type of residents are drawn to new
urbanist communities, and do they represent a diverse cross section of our population?

Fallacy: Although the foregoing questions may be problematic for the argument, they do not constitute any clear violation of the criteria. Therefore, there are
no identifiable fallacies.

Although the premises of the argument raise questions, there are no violations
present. If further research substantiates the total evidence, and if there are no fallacies with regard to the diversity of the sample, I will change my evaluation to strong,
but for the present, I can say only that the argument is moderate.

The second argument is an appeal to authority. That is, Talen appeals to the
authority of Glynn and Goudy as experts.

Criteria:

The first criterion for appeals to authority is that the person cited must be an
expert in the area for which he is cited. W. J. Goudy has been published in a professional journal, establishing his credentials. I have not yet done research on Glynn to
determine his strength as an expert, but, at least on the basis of Goudy's expertise, it
appears that this criterion has been met.

The second criterion is that there must be some consensus amongst experts
that the position stated by Glynn and Goudy is correct. On the surface, it appears that

this criterion is met, as the two studies corroborate each other. Further research may prove otherwise, but for the present, this criterion appears to be met.

Fallacy: Assuming that further research will support the credentials of Glynn and Goudy and their studies, it appears that this argument does not violate the required conditions. Therefore, no fallacies exist.

The corroboration of the two experts cited makes the argument strong.

2.   Talen claims that much research on communities ties in with the non-spatial sense of a community paradigm and that existing research has been scant in linking environmental variables such as the design or architecture of a town more directly to a sense of community.

Campbell and Lee found a complex picture of social interaction and maintained that socioeconomic status, age, and gender were the most important factors in determining interaction among residents.
Gans suggested early on that community is formed on the basis of social class and a commonality of values, not propinquity.
The differentiating element to be used in understanding the potential (i.e., hypothetical) relationship between new urbanism and the various dimensions of neighborhood social life is new urbanism's emphasis on public space.
The exact nature of the connection between public space, interaction among residents, and a sense of community is theoretically deficient.

∴   If the new urbanist design philosophy creates other conditions that in turn create a sense of community, then the same results could be achieved from any number of other town design principles.

Analysis:

This argument is an appeal to authority. That is, Talen appeals to the authority of K. E. Campbell and B. A. Lee, as well as the authority of H. J. Gans.

Criteria:

The first criterion for appeals to authority is that the individual must be an expert in the area for which he or she is cited. All three individuals are published in the area of social integration and sense of community. I believe that the credentials of the three individuals cited support Talen's appeal to them as experts.

The second criterion is that there must be some consensus among experts that the positions stated by Campbell and Lee, on the one hand, and Gans, on the other, is correct. This does not, of course, require unanimity, but merely that the position advocated be viewed as a viable position by other experts. The fact that each of the studies conducted corroborates the other provides the necessary consenses.

Fallacy: Assuming that further research will support the credentials of all three experts, it appears that this argument does not violate any criterion. Therefore, no fallacies appear in the argument.

On the basis of the corroboration by the two studies, there is a strong possibility that further research will strengthen the argument. The fact that the three experts cited have been published (although Gans has published more extensively) gives credibility to the argument.

3.   Talen's conclusion is that the success of the new urbanism could rest on the basis of the quality of its design and not on its social goals. However, further empirical investigation is necessary to bring the relationship between the design of towns and a sense of community into a clearer light. To support her position, Talen offers the following arguments:

The new urbanism increases interaction among residents, which in turn creates at least weak social ties.
Moving beyond this position implies assumptions about the quality of the interaction involved—mainly that public and private space exhibit a deeper relationship, a claim that is currently without basis.
New urbanists must concede the possibility that new urbanism does not create a sense of community, but rather attracts individuals with a certain predisposition for social interaction and the need for local community attachment.
There must be a better understanding of what it takes for the new urbanist vision of sense of community to be fulfilled.
∴ Further empirical investigation will bring the relationship between town design and sense of community into clearer light.

Analysis:

Simple enumeration (particular to particular)

Criteria:

Total Evidence: The argument raises numerous questions regarding what generates a sense of community and how one measures the quality of the social interactions that occur. Is it possible that new urbanism attracts a homogenous population, in direct contradiction to its claims? While such questions could be problematic for the argument, in themselves they do not constitute a violation of the criteria.

Diverse Sample: The premises address several of the claims of new urbanism and the conflicts posed by those claims. Do weak social ties generate a sense of community? Does the use of public and private space generate "quality" social interaction? Could it be that the new urbanism attracts like residents to a community? While only research can answer the questions, they do not violate the criteria.

Fallacy: There are no clear violations of the criteria; therefore, there are no fallacies present.

With as many questions that are raised and no clear answers as yet, I would have to agree that more research would definitely help clarify the issue, so Talen's argument is strong.

This initial evaluation of Talen's argument clearly demonstrates the critical-reasoning process and its value. Most of all, the process has raised questions about what I've read. These questions are stimulating further research, and if the procedures of evaluation set forth in this chapter are followed, I will definitely gain a better understanding of new urbanism.

Notes for Part II

[1]David Hume, *A Treatise of Human Nature*, 2d ed., ed. L. A. Selby-Bigge and corrected by P. H. Nidditch (Oxford, U.K.: Clarendon Press, 1978) (Book I, Part III, section VI), p. 89.

[2]David Hume, *An Enquiry Concerning Human Understanding* (La Salle, IL: Open Court Publishing Company, 1938) (Section IV, part II), pp. 34–37.

[3]Contrary to popular approaches to critical reasoning, we need a fairly sophisticated system for both induction and deduction if we are to develop strong and influential habits of reasoning. The weak-minded approaches of popularized critical reasoning do have some value: They inform us that not everything in print is true and that advertisments may be deceptive.

[4]John S. Mill, *Autobiography*, ed. Jack Stillinger (Boston: Houghton Mifflin Co., 1969), p. 96.

[5]Max Black, *Margins of Precision* (Ithaca, NY: Cornell University Press, 1970), p. 70.

[6]*Ibid.*, p. 70.

[7]Carl Hempel, *Philosophy of Natural Science* (Englewood Cliffs, NJ: Prentice Hall, 1966) 52. (Also see, J. Hintikka and J. Bachman, *What If . . . ?: Toward Excellence in Reasoning* (Mountain View, CA: Mayfield Publishing Co., 1991).

[8]Karl Popper, *The Logic of Scientific Discovery* (New York: Harper Torchbooks, 1968, p. 27. (The parentheses are Popper's.)

[9]Wesley Salmon, *The Foundations of Scientific Inference* (Pittsburgh: University of Pittsburgh Press, 1967), p. 52.

[10]*Ibid.*, p. 53.

[11]The terms *plausible reasoning* and *demonstrative reasoning* are taken from G. Polya's fine work, *Induction and Analogy in Mathematics* (Princeton, NJ: Princeton University Press, 1973).

[12]Subjectivist probability contrasts with objective probability as maintained by John Pollock, *Nomic Probability and the Foundations of Induction* (New York: Oxford University Press, 1990).

[13]Bruno de Finetti, *Probability, Induction, and Statistics: The Art of Guessing* (New York: John Wiley & Sons, 1972), p. 9. (Italics and parentheses are de Finetti's.)

[14]William Kneale, *Probability and Induction* (Oxford, U.K.: Clarendon Press, 1949), p. 9.

[15]For excellent discussions of probability theories that are eminently readable, see Davis Baird, *Inductive Logic: Probability and Statistics* (Englewood Cliffs, NJ: Prentice Hall, 1992; William Gustason, *Reasoning from Evidence* (New York: Macmillan College Publishing Company, 1994); and Brian Skyrms, *Choice and Chance* (Belmont, CA: Wadsworth Publishing Company, 1986).

[16]*The Philosophical Works of Descartes*, I, translated by Elizabeth S. Haldane and G. R. T. Ross (Cambridge, U. K.: Cambridge University Press, 1984), p. 192.

[17]Following the hints of P. F. Strawson, we are placing together several kinds of inductive reasoning under the umbrella of enumerative induction. See R. Boyd, "Strawson on Induction," *The Philosophy of P. F. Strawson*, ed. Lewis Hahn (Chicago: Open Court, 1998), pp. 263–271.

[18]Justification for the list is based on two studies, one by Ray Simpson (1944) and the other by Milton Hakel (1968), as presented in Daniel McNeill and Paul Freiberger, *Fuzzy Logic* (New York: Touchstone Books, 1993), p. 68. See also George Lakoff, "Hedges: A Study in Meaning Criteria and the Logic of Fuzzy Concepts," *Journal of Philosophical Logic* 2 (1973):458–508.

[19]John Stuart Mill, *A System of Logic*, 8th ed. (New York: Harper and Brothers Co., 1874), p. 280.

[20]*Ibid.*

[21]*Ibid.*, p. 284.

[22]*Ibid.*, p. 285.

[23]*Ibid.*, p. 287.

[24]Linda Calandra, "New Urbanism: Does it Create a Sense of Community?" an essay submitted in partial fulfillment of the course requirements for Critical Reasoning (English 3), November 1999. Used by permission of Linda Calandra.

[25]Emily Talen. "Can Sense of Community be Built? An Assessment of the Social Doctrine of New Urbanism." *Urban Studies* 36, 8 (1999): 1361–1379.

PART THREE

Deductive Reasoning

Preface to Deduction

Earlier, we noted that in deductive reasoning the conclusion must be true if the premises are true and the argument has a proper form. We therefore can guarantee that the conclusion can be derived from the evidence, provided that the premises are true and the argument employs good deductive reasoning.

Unlike the situation in inductive reasoning, in deductive reasoning there is a clear line of demarcation between good and bad reasoning. Moreover, whereas we evaluate inductive reasoning in light of its content, we evaluate deductive reasoning according to its form or structure. As a result, if an argument that displays deductive reasoning has an acceptable form, we call it a **valid** argument. If it has an unacceptable form, we call it an **invalid** argument.

Because the characteristics of good deductive reasoning are different from those of good inductive reasoning, different methods are used to evaluate deductive reasoning. These methods test the form of the argument; they tell us nothing about its content.

Because of the power of deductive reasoning and its ability to provide clear, definite responses to the question "Is this argument a good one?" there is a temptation to assume that if an argument is deductively valid its conclusion must be true. However, we cannot

By permission of Johnny Hart and Creators Syndicate, Inc.

state that a conclusion is true unless we establish the truth of the premises, and that frequently depends upon the context in which they are found. This means that, ultimately, any valid argument that purports to present truth is dependent on some inductive reasoning, since induction is the logic of content.

Generally, however, when we use deduction we simply *assume* that the premises are true. Thus, in the chapters that follow, we will not be concerned with the truthfulness of premises; we will focus instead on the validity of arguments.

CHAPTER SEVEN

Conditional Logic

The introduction to Part III emphasized that deduction is a logic of *form*, not of *content*. If a deductive argument is good, it is because of its form. An argument is valid if its form is correct. If the form is incorrect, the argument is invalid.

This chapter focuses on **conditional logic**, or reasoning in which at least one premise is a conditional statement. We will find that a conditional argument is valid if it has a proper form or structure. It is invalid if it does not.

7.1 CONDITIONAL STATEMENTS

The clearest example of a conditional statement is a sentence that has the following pattern:

7.1a

If . . . , then . . .

In this pattern, two statements are connected; the connection is represented by the ellipsis (. . .). The statement that immediately follows the word *if* is called the **antecedent**, and the statement that follows the word *then* is called the **consequent**. In writing a conditional statement in standard form, it is important to follow the pattern presented in Example 7.1a.

Since variety is a key feature of good writing, writers often vary the "if . . . , then . . . " pattern. For example, instead of saying, "If it is raining, then I will carry my umbrella," they might say, "I will carry my umbrella if it is raining." Such a variation is logically proper. However, for the sake of analysis, when a conditional argument is written in standard form, it must follow the "if . . . , then . . . " pattern, which emphasizes its structure. (*Beware*: The word *then* is often used as a transition word indicating a temporal sequence. In such cases, it is not part of a conditional statement.)

A rule of thumb for finding the antecedent and consequent of a statement that is not written in the form shown in Example 7.1a is as follows:

7.1b

Whatever follows "if" is the antecedent, unless "if" is preceded by "only."

However, this rule does not apply to all sentence structures. The chart in Example 7.1c provides a guide for rewriting conditional sentences in standard form. It can also serve as a guide for providing variety in writing conditional statements. (The symbols **P** and **Q** are used as placeholders, much like variables in algebra. Sometimes logicians use them to abbreviate long statements in English. In the next chapter, we will learn more about **P** and **Q**. If your parents ever told you to mind your **P**'s and **Q**'s, this is probably not what they were referring to.)

7.1c

Equivalent Translations

Ordinary English Usage	*Proper Conditional Form*
If **P**, then **Q**.	If **P**, then **Q**.
Assuming **P, Q**.	If **P**, then **Q**.
Whenever **P, Q**.	If **P**, then **Q**.
Given **P, Q**.	If **P**, then **Q**.
Provided **P, Q**.	If **P** then **Q**.
Only if **Q, P**. (**P** only if **Q**).	If **P**, then **Q**.
A necessary condition of **P** is **Q**.	If **P**, then **Q**.
P if **Q**.	If **Q**, then **P**.
P when **Q**.	If **Q**, then **P**.
P since **Q**.	If **Q**, then **P**.
P in case **Q**.	If **Q**, then **P**.
P so long as **Q**.	If **Q**, then **P**.
A sufficient condition of **P** is **Q**.	If **Q**, then **P**.
P unless **Q**.	If not **Q**, then **P**.
	(or)
	If not **P**, then **Q**.

Referring to this chart, we would rewrite the sentence "I will carry my umbrella if it is not raining" as "If it is not raining, then I will carry my umbrella." Moreover, "Whenever it is raining, I will carry my umbrella" would be rewritten as "If it is raining, then I will carry my umbrella." As the chart indicates, statements that contain the word *unless* can be translated in two ways. Both are technically correct and will not affect the evaluation of an argument. However, sometimes one approach may be preferable, depending on the context.

7.1A EXERCISE: CONDITIONAL STATEMENTS

Rewrite the following conditional statements in the proper "if . . . , then . . . " form. If an item does not contain a conditional statement, briefly state why it does not.

1. When you finish the exam, you may leave the room.

2. When Joan attends her classes, she always gets A's.

3. Given that Donna takes critical reasoning this semester, she will graduate in May.

*4. A sufficient condition of passing this course is turning in all of the assignments.

5. Spencer will teach critical reasoning only if Gregg will not teach it.

6. Mary will not take history of philosophy unless Richard teaches it.

7. A necessary condition of Ted teaching a course on medical ethics is that a sufficient number of students register for the class.

8. If Donna types this paper, I will be able to finish my other papers.

*9. A tree falling in the forest will make a sound only if someone is there to hear it.

10. Unless Peter attends class today, he will fail the course.

11. Whenever Joe finishes his lunch, he will take a nap.

12. Given that you finish this assignment, you might pass the course.

13. A sufficient condition for passing critical reasoning is the completion of this assignment.

14. Only if you finish this assignment will you pass this course.

15. A necessary condition of passing critical reasoning is the completion of this assignment.

The following are from Plato's *Apology*:[1]

16. "When it becomes obvious that I have not the slightest skill as a speaker—unless, of course, by a skillful speaker they mean one who speaks the truth." (4)

17. "I felt that Evenus was to be congratulated if he really was a master of this art and taught it at such a moderate fee." (6)

18. "But if I believe in supernatural activities, it follows inevitably that I also believe in supernatural beings." (13)

19. "And the most fantastic thing of all is that it is impossible for me to know and tell you their names, unless one of them happens to be a playwright." (15)

20. "Please do not be offended if I tell you the truth." (17)

The following are from Aristotle's *On Interpretation*:[2]

*21. "First we must define the terms 'noun' and 'verb,' then the terms 'denial' and 'affirmation,' then 'proposition' and 'sentence.' " (16)

22. "... there is no truth or falsity about it, unless 'is' or 'is not' is added ... " (16)

23. "But if we separate one syllable of the word 'human' from the other, it has no meaning ... " (16)

24. "If, then, a man states a positive and a negative proposition of universal character with regard to a universal, these two propositions are 'contrary.' " (17)

25. "... when the subject is universal, but the propositions are not of a universal character, there is no such necessity." (18)

The following are from Aristotle's *Prior Analytics*:[3]

26. "Whenever three terms are so related to one another that the last is contained in the middle as in a whole, and the middle is either contained in, or excluded from, the first as in or from a whole, the extremes must be related by a perfect syllogism." (25)

*27. "Nor can there in any way be a syllogism if both the relations of the subject and predicate are particular ... " (26)

28. "Whenever the same thing belongs to all of one subject, and to none of another, or to all of each subject or to none of either, I call such a figure the second... " (26)

29. "If then the terms are related universally a syllogism will be possible, whenever the middle belongs to all of one subject and to none of another." (27)

30. "If one term is related universally to the middle, the other in part only, when both are affirmative there must be a syllogism, no matter which of the premises is universal." (28)

The following are from Aristotle's *Metaphysics*:[4]

31. "As regards Anaxagoras, if one were to suppose that he said there were two elements, the supposition would accord thoroughly with an argument which Anaxagoras himself did not state articulately, but which he must have accepted if anyone had led him on to it." (989)

*32. "Therefore there is no other cause here unless there is something which caused the movement from potency unto actuality." (845)

33. "Things are like if, not being absolutely the same, nor without difference in respect of their concrete substance, they are the same in form... " (854)

34. "But if the principles are universal, either the substances composed of them are also universal, or non-substance will be prior to substance... " (887)

35. "The theologians seem to agree with some thinkers of the present day ... and say that both the good and the beautiful appear in the nature of things only when that nature has made some progress." (890)

The following are from Plotinus' *The Descent of the Soul*:[5]

36. "No being would exist, if The One remained shut up in itself." (#6)

37. "Of necessity, then, by the very law of its nature, it proceeds to the level of The Soul." (#7)

38. "But if the part that is in the realm of sense dominates, or rather becomes dominated and disturbed, it keeps us unaware of what the higher part of the soul contemplates." (#8)

39. "The One must not be solely the solitary. If it were, reality would remain buried and shapeless. . . " (#6)

40. ". . . if the realm of sense is to be completed, it is necessary that it contain as many kinds of living beings as does the intelligible realm." (#1)

The following are from Ockham's *Epistemological Problems*:[6]

41. "For our intellect does not assent to anything unless we believe it to be true, nor does it dissent from anything unless we believe it to be false." (21)

42. ". . . Since the causes existing in the intellective part can be sufficient, the assumption of the other causes is superfluous." (23)

*43. "Given these premises I shall prove the main conclusion as follows." (23)

44. ". . . any non-complex cognition of one or more terms or things, is an intuitive cognition, if it enables us to know a contingent truth. . . " (26)

45. "However, we always get an impression of the concept 'existent,' because if the object is sufficiently close, a concept of the species and the concept 'existent' are simultaneously caused by the extra-mental singular thing." (35)

The following are from James's *Pragmatism and Other Essays*:[7]

46. "Whenever such an extra truth becomes practically relevant to one of our emergencies, it passes from cold-storage to do work in the world and our belief in it grows active." (90)

47. "If truths mean verification-process essentially, ought we then to call such unverified truths as this abortive?" (91)

48. "I try to imagine myself as the sole reality in the world, and then to imagine what more I would 'claim' if I were allowed to." (83)

*49. "You see that pragmatism can be called religious, if you allow that religion can be pluralistic or merely melioristic in type." (132)

50. "Whenever he finds that the feeling he is studying contemplates what he himself regards as a reality, he must of course admit the feeling itself to be truly cognitive." (145)

7.1B EXERCISE: WRITING CONDITIONAL STATEMENTS

Write five conditional statements in the "if . . . , then . . . " form. Then rewrite each statement in an equivalent translation, using a different pattern for each.

7.2 CONDITIONAL ARGUMENTS

In a conditional argument, one premise consists of a conditional statement and the other premise either affirms or denies the antecedent or affirms or denies the consequent. Thus, a conditional arguments conform to one of four possible forms.[8] The following arguments illustrate these four possibilities:

7.2a

Affirming the Antecedent

If it rains, then I will carry my umbrella.
It is raining.
∴   I will carry my umbrella.

7.2b

Denying the Antecedent

If it rains, then I will carry my umbrella.
It is not raining.
∴   I will not carry my umbrella.

7.2c

Affirming the Consequent

If it rains, then I will carry my umbrella.
I am carrying my umbrella.
∴   It is raining.

7.2d

Denying the Consequent

If it rains, then I will carry my umbrella.
I am not carrying my umbrella.
∴   It is not raining.

While in each of these examples the conditional statement is listed first, this is not a necessary feature of conditional arguments. Example 7.2d could have been presented as follows:

7.2e

> I am not carrying my umbrella.
> <u>If it rains, then I will carry my umbrella.</u>
> ∴   It is not raining.

Notice how, as we pass among the four forms, the conclusion changes. This must be if the structure of the argument is to be preserved. For example, if the premises include a denial of the consequent, the conclusion *must* be a denial of the antecedent.

The next chart summarizes the four types of conditional arguments. Two of these argument forms are valid and two are invalid. The two valid forms have historically been known by the Latin names **modus ponens** and **modus tollens**.

7.2f

Valid Forms

1.   Affirming the Antecedent (*Modus Ponens*)

> If **P**, then **Q**.
> <u>**P**.</u>
> ∴   **Q**.

2.   Denying the Consequent (*Modus Tollens*)

> If **P**, then **Q**.
> <u>not **Q**.</u>
> ∴   not **P**.

Invalid Forms

1.   Affirming the Consequent (Modus Moron)

> If **P**, then **Q**.
> <u>**Q**.</u>
> ∴   **P**.

2.   Denying the Antecedent (Modus Ignoramus)

> If **P**, then **Q**.
> <u>not **P**.</u>
> ∴   not **Q**

7.2A EXERCISE: CONDITIONAL ARGUMENTS

Write the conditional arguments that follow in standard form, properly rewriting the conditional statements. Next, indicate the type of conditional argument. Finally, state whether the argument is valid or invalid. If necessary, supply implied premises or conclusions.

1.   If Peter finishes his dissertation, then he will have a teaching position. Peter does finish his dissertation. Thus, Peter has a teaching position.

*2.   If Peter finishes his dissertation, then he will have a teaching position. Peter has a teaching position. Hence, Peter finished his dissertation.

3.   If Peter finishes his dissertation, then he will have a teaching position. Peter does not finish his dissertation. Therefore, Peter does not have a teaching position.

4.   If Peter finishes his dissertation, then he will have a teaching position. Peter does not have a teaching position. Thus, Peter did not finish his dissertation.

5.   Whenever Peter finishes his dissertation, he will have a teaching position. Peter does not have a teaching position. Therefore, Peter has not finished his dissertation.

6.   Given that Peter finishes his dissertation, he will have a teaching position. Peter has a teaching position. Hence, Peter has finished his dissertation.

7.   A sufficient condition for Peter having a teaching position is finishing his dissertation. Peter does not finish his dissertation. Consequently, Peter does not have a teaching position.

8.   Peter does not get a teaching position unless he finishes his dissertation. Peter does get a teaching position. Hence, Peter has finished his dissertation.

9.   Peter will get a teaching position only if he finishes his dissertation. Peter does not finish his dissertation. Thus, Peter does not have a teaching position.

10.   A necessary condition of Peter having a teaching position is finishing his dissertation. Peter does not finish his dissertation. Consequently, Peter does not have a teaching position.

*11.   If Peter and Joan attend the party and dress in their normal way, then the party will be extremely successful. However, the party was not extremely successful. We may conclude that Peter and Joan either did not attend the party or did not dress in their normal fashion.

12.   This class will be exciting and challenging only if all the students do what is expected of them. Not of the students did what was expected of them. Therefore, the class was not exciting and challenging.

13.   If it rains Thursday, then logic class is canceled. If logic class is canceled, then I will not understand the material. If I do not understand the material, I will fail the course. My scholarship will not be taken away only if I do not fail this course. It rained Thursday. As a result, I lost my scholarship.

14.   If Petersburg falls into the hands of the Germans, then a revolt will take place. A revolt did take place. Thus, Petersburg fell into the hands of the Germans.

15.   A tree falling in a forest will make a sound only if someone is there to hear it fall. Spencer was there. Hence, the falling tree made a sound.

16. A necessary condition for receiving a scholarship from TCU is the recommendation by a department head of the university. Dr. Smith, the philosophy department head, has recommended Stacey Jones for a scholarship. Therefore, Stacey will receive the scholarship.

17. Spencer will write a book on the philosophy of art only if he receives a grant from the National Humanities Endowment. He does not receive the grant. Therefore, Spencer will not write the book.

*18. Unless Ted is allowed to chair the committee, the findings of that committee will be significant. Ted is not to chair the committee, so we may conclude that the findings will not be significant.

19. A sufficient condition for Richard publishing his current article in *Mind* is his mailing it to Magdalen College, Oxford. Richard's article is not published. It is obvious that he did not send it to Magdalen College.

20. Whenever Gregg finishes his book, it will be published by Colonial Press. Gregg has not finished writing the book. Therefore, it will not be published by Colonial Press.

21. If truth is not a property of an object and its relation to the universe, we could never properly claim to possess truth. However, there are some truths that we do properly claim.

22. If truth is a property of an object and its relation to the universe, then the pursuit of truth is possible. The pursuit of truth is possible.

23. The pursuit of truth is possible so long as the property of an object and its relation to the universe is not limited to the empirical arena. While the empirical arena is important in the study of an object, it is not always adequate.

24. If truth deals with the property of an object and its relation to the universe, then relativism must be rejected. For if truth is so defined, then truth will have a universal nature. But relativism denies that truth has a universal nature.

25. If, by *truth*, we simply mean "What I hold to be true," then a form of subjectivism is being claimed. However, usually truth is not assigned to things that are held only by an individual. Therefore, we must reject subjectivism.

26. Given the transparent nature of truth, it is impossible to find any agreement concerning what might be truth. Truth must not be totally transparent, for we do find some agreement concerning truth.

*27. If this argument preserves truth, then it is valid. This argument is not valid, for it does not preserve truth.

28. If truth is a property of an object, and a given proposition is an accurate account of its object, then such a proposition contains truth. Truth is not something presented by the proposition, but the proposition has the property of truth. However, it is often thought that while propositions present truth, propositions do not have the property of truth. Therefore, either truth is not a property of an object or propositions cannot give an accurate account of their objects.

29. If there were no truths, this statement could not be made. Obviously, some truths must exist, for the preceding statement was made.

*30.   "If the universe is quasi-Euclidean, and its radius of curvature therefore infinite, then σ would vanish. But it is improbable that the mean density of matter in the universe is actually zero." (Albert Einstein, *The Meaning of Relativity*, p. 107)

The following are from Aquinas's essay "Truth":[9]

31.   "If the truth is not the same as being, it must be a state of being. But it cannot be a state of being." (Art. I, dif. 4)

32.   "If they were not entirely the same, the true would add something to being. But the true adds nothing to being, even though it has greater extension than being. . . . Consequently, . . . it seems to be entirely the same as being." (Art. II, dif. 7)

33.   "If truth is principally in the intellect, anything which pertains to the intellect should be included in the definition of truth. Augustine, however, sharply criticizes such definitions. . . . Truth, therefore, is not principally in the intellect." (Art. II, dif. 4)

34.   "If the true were the same as being, it would be meaningless to say: 'Being is true.' This, however, is hardly correct. Therefore, they are not the same." (Art. I, con. 1)

35.   "Anselm argues as follows: If there are as many truths as there are true things, then truths should change as true things change. But truths do not change with the changes of true things. . . . There is, therefore, only one truth." (Art. IV, dif. 3)

36.   "As Augustine says, only God is greater than the human mind. But, as he proves elsewhere, truth is greater than the human mind. . . . If this were so, it would be within the competence of the mind to pass judgment on truth. This, of course, is false. . . . Truth, therefore, must be God alone, and so there is only one truth." (Art. IV, dif. 5)

37.   "Now, a consequence of the destruction of truth is that truth is; for, if truth is not, the fact that truth is not is true, and nothing can be true except by truth. Therefore, truth is eternal. (Art. V, dif. 2)

38.   "If the truth of propositions is not eternal, then a time must be assigned when their truth was not. But at that time it was true to say: 'There is no truth of propositions.' . . . Therefore, one cannot say that the truth of propositions is not eternal." (Art. V, dif. 3)

39.   "If the truth of a proposition changes, it changes especially when a thing changes. But when a thing has been changed, the truth of the proposition remains. Therefore, the truth of the proposition is immutable." (Art. VI, dif. 2)

40.   "If truth is changed, this can be only because the subject in which truth inheres has previously been changed—just as certain forms cannot be said to be changed unless their subjects have changed. But truth is not changed with the change of true things. . . . Therefore, truth is entirely immutable." (Art. VI, dif. 3)

7.2B EXERCISE: WRITING CONDITIONAL ARGUMENTS

Write ten conditional arguments, using a variety of conditional sentence forms. In each case, indicate the type of conditional argument and whether it is valid or invalid.

7.3 USING CONDITIONAL REASONING TO WRITE

Conditional reasoning is a valuable aid in writing essays. The example that follows, on the topic of welfare programs, illustrates the procedure for using conditional reasoning in the writing process. We assume that the topic has been presented in a text of some kind and that, on the basis of an examination of that text, some research has been done. As a result of our research, we conclude that welfare programs should not be eliminated. Moreover, our research has motivated us to write an essay expressing our view. Our thesis is "Welfare programs should not be cut."

As part of our **prewriting**, we must decide on the most effective approach for presenting our position. Conditional reasoning offers two options: affirming the antecedent or denying the consequent.[10] At this point, both options should be written in standard form, as follows:

7.3a Affirming the Antecedent

If we have citizens with basic needs, then welfare programs should not be cut.
We have citizens with basic needs.
∴   Welfare programs should not be cut.

7.3b Denying the Consequent

If welfare programs should be cut, then there is no longer a need for such programs.
There is still a need for such programs.
∴   Welfare programs should not be cut.

On the basis of our research, we decide that it will be easier to support the statement "We have citizens with basic needs" than the statement "There is still a need for such programs." As a result, we choose affirming the antecedent as the model for our essay.

Our introductory paragraph will include the thesis "Welfare programs should not be cut." It will also include the "road map"—that is, the two points supporting our claim ("If we have citizens with basic needs, then welfare programs should not be cut" and "We have citizens with basic needs"). The second paragraph will have the topic sentence "If we have citizens with basic needs, then welfare programs should not be cut." In this paragraph, we will support this claim by using some form of inductive reasoning, probably an inductive generalization. Remember, the goal of the paragraph is not to show that needs exist. Rather, it is to support the relationship between the antecedent and the consequent.

In the third paragraph, the topic sentence is "We have citizens with basic needs." The goal of this paragraph is to support that claim. We might do so by using a conditional argument, or we might use some form of induction. (Notice that the purpose of paragraph two is to increase the likelihood that a reader will accept the claim "If . . . , then. . . . " The purpose of paragraph three is to persuade the reader that the need does currently exist.) The concluding paragraph pulls everything together and makes the reasoning explicit. It shows that if the reader accepts the topic sentences of paragraphs two and three, he or she must accept the thesis of the essay.

7.3 EXERCISE: WRITING AN ESSAY USING CONDITIONAL REASONING

Write a three- to four-page essay on a topic other than welfare programs. The structure of the essay should be controlled by conditional reasoning. (See Gail Mayberry's example in "Part III: Application.")

CHAPTER EIGHT

Propositional Logic

Deductive reasoning is not limited to conditional reasoning, useful though that is. Consider the following argument:

> John or Mary attended the meeting.
> John did not attend the meeting.
> ∴   Mary attended the meeting.

Notice that the premises provide conclusive support for the conclusion. The argument illustrates deductive reasoning, but not conditional reasoning, as as discussed in the previous chapter. Accordingly, our system of deductive reasoning must be enhanced.

For centuries, scholars dreamed of a system of logic that could be used to analyze all forms of deductive reasoning. Then, in the late nineteenth century, such a system began to take shape. The American philosopher Charles S. Peirce (1839–1914) was instrumental in developing it, although numerous other renowned thinkers—Bertrand Russell and Alfred North Whitehead, to mention just two[11]—played key roles as well. The system they created has at its foundation the examination of *statements* or *propositions*, the most basic components of deductive reasoning.

In this chapter, we study the logic that dominated the twentieth century. It is the foundation of the logic that will emerge in the twenty-first century. Our approach begins with the presentation of several key concepts. Then we develop a formal language that we use to present propositional logic. Finally, we examine three distinct, mutually consistent, ways of applying propositional logic.

8.1 KEY CONCEPTS

In Chapter 3, we defined a **statement** as a simple sentence that can be judged to be true or false and a **proposition** as the meaning of a statement. We can judge a statement as true or false because it has a **truth-value**.

Some statements are "simple," or "atomic," in that they make a single claim. No other claims are embedded within them. Here are a few examples:

8.1a

1.   Antique Early American furniture is not a wise choice for a contemporary styled home.
2.   Institutional green is a drab color.
3.   Columbus sailed the ocean blue.

As we saw in Chapter 3, however, not all statements are simple. Some, like the following, are **compound statements**:

8.1b

1.   Ms. Fulkerson thinks that the United States will invade Haiti.
2.   This coffee, which contains a variety of rare beans and spices, is very expensive.
3.   Rhonda and Erica were class officers during their senior year.

The statements in 8.1b cannot be classified as simple statements. Sentence 1 contains the statement "the United States will invade Haiti" embedded within the statement "Ms. Fulkerson thinks that the stated invasion will occur." There are also two claims in sentence 2: "This coffee contains a variety of rare beans and spices" and "This coffee is very expensive." Likewise, sentence 3 can be divided into the two statements "Rhonda was a class officer during her senior year" and "Erica was a class officer during her senior year."

Some compound sentences are true—or false—regardless of the truth of their component statements. The sentence "Ms. Fulkerson thinks that the United States will invade Haiti" will be true if it accurately reflects what Ms. Fulkerson thinks. It will be true regardless of the truth or falsity the statement "the United States will invade Haiti." Such compound statements are **non-truth-functional compound sentences**. Their truth is not determined by the truth-value of their component statements.

Other compound statements are **truth-functional compound sentences.** Contrast the statement about Ms. Fulkerson with the one about coffee. The latter sentence is truth functional. That is, its truth is determined by the truth-value of its component statements. To illustrate this, the compound sentence could be rewritten as follows:

8.1c

This coffee contains a variety of rare beans and spices, and this coffee is very expensive.

If either or both of the component statements is false, the entire sentence will be false.

In addition, Chapter 3 suggested that simple statements can be turned into compound statements by means of several logical connectors—the **truth-functional connectors**. In the sentence dealing with coffee, the truth-functional connective is the word *and*. The following are five truth-functional connectives:

8.1d

and
not
or
if . . . , then . . .
. . . if and only if . . .

8.1e

John attended the party *and* Mary attended the party.
Humphrey took a plane *or* a train to Seattle.
Jim was *not* happy with the car his wife bought.
If it rains, *then* I will carry my umbrella.
Peter will pass American History *if and only if* Professor Smith feels sorry for him.

Early pioneers in propositional logic recognized that, since deductive reasoning is a logic of structure, ordinary or natural language distracts from our understanding of such reasoning. That is, the language used in daily life acts as a barrier to a full understanding of propositional logic. Ordinary language often clouds the reasoning process, and when the emphasis is on structure, such cloudiness must be avoided at all costs. These concerns led to the development of an artificial or formal language that could be used to highlight the structure of deductive reasoning. In the next section, we will present this language, along with procedures for evaluating statements and arguments formulated in it. We will also discuss the connection between the formal language and ordinary language. We will see that the formal language is not really so artificial. Before proceeding, however, we must introduce several key ideas that are central to deductive reasoning.

Consistency

A set of statements is **consistent** if and only if there is at least one situation in which all of its members are true. A set of statements is **inconsistent** if and only if there is no situation in which all of its members are true. For example, the set of statements:

8.1f

{Today is December 24. Today is Monday. Today it is cold. Today the sun is shining.}

is consistent if and only if all of its statements can simultaneously be true (which they in fact can).

A set may also be empty, in which case it is called the **null set**, symbolized {∅}. The null set is consistent set. (Since it has no statements, all of its statements—namely, none—can simultaneously be true—or false, or whatever.) However, the following set is inconsistent because both of its members cannot be true at the same time.

8.1g

{It is raining; It is not raining}

Equivalence

A second concept that is very important in propositional logic is the notion of **equivalence**. Two propositions are **equivalent** if and only if there is no situation in which they have different truth-values. For example, let **P** and **Q** stand for different statements. If, in every situation in which both **P** and **Q** exist, they have the same truth-value, then **P** and **Q** are equivalent. That is, if **P** is true, **Q** is true, and if **P** is false, **Q** is false.

Types of Statements

In propositional logic, we can categorize a statement into one of three types: a tautology, a contradiction, or a contingent statement. A statement is a **tautology** if and only if it is always true. This means, of course, that if a statement is a tautology, it is never false. For example, the statement "All bachelors are unmarried men" has a constant truth-value. It is true, and it is *always* true. Therefore, it is a tautology.

  A statement is a **contradiction** if and only if it is always false. So if a statement is a contradiction, it is never true. The statement "It is snowing and not snowing (here and now)" is a contradiction, for it will always be false.

  Most statements are neither tautologies nor contradictions. Instead, they are **contingent**: Their truth-value depends on the situation. Consider the statement "It is raining." There are times when this statement is true, and times when it is false. Since the truth-value of the statement is dependent on the situation in which it is uttered or written it is a contingent statement.

Validity

As with conditional reasoning, in propositional reasoning an argument is **valid** if it conforms to an acceptable form.

8.1h

An argument is valid if and only if it is not possible to have all the premises be true and the conclusion be false.

A valid argument may be presented in three different forms. Ideally, a valid argument has true premises and a true conclusion. But valid arguments can also have false premises and a true conclusion or false premises and a false conclusion.

8.1i

If cows jump over the moon, then I am a millionaire.
Cows do jump over the moon.
∴ I am a millionaire.

Trust me, at least one of the premises is false and the conclusion is false. Yet argument 8.1i is valid.

A propositional argument is **invalid** if it has a **counterexample**—that is, if there is a situation in which the premises are true, but the conclusion is false.

8.1j

> The sun will set this evening or the moon is made of green cheese.
> The sun will set this evening.
> ∴   The moon is made of green cheese.

The premises are true, but the conclusion is false.

A valid argument does not tell us anything about truth. It tells us only that if the premises are true, the conclusion must also be true. Truth becomes a property of a statement only when the statement is an accurate depiction of the world. Truth is a property of the world, and a proposition may inherit that property if it presents the world accurately.

We can say that a propositional argument is valid if and only if it is not invalid, but often we cannot say anything more about it. While it is tempting to conclude that any deductive reasoning which is valid presents truth, this is not necessarily so.

8.1k

> Either God exists or God does not exist.
> It is not the case that God does not exist.
> ∴   God exists.

While this argument is valid, does it really prove its conclusion true? If you think it does, then just observe that a similar argument whose second premise is "It is not the case that God exists" would prove the conclusion "God does not exist."

Logicians often refer to arguments as sound or unsound. To be **sound**, an argument must satisfy two conditions: (1) It must be valid, and (2) all of its premises must be true. Propositional logic will aid in determining whether the first condition has been satisfied, but propositional logic alone cannot aid in determining whether the second condition has been met. When we say that a statement is true, we are making a claim about the world, albeit perhaps a hypothetical claim that is dependent on inductive reasoning.

8.2 CREATING A FORMAL LANGUAGE

Like all languages, the formal language of propositional logic must have a syntax and a semantics. The **syntax** of a language consists of all the grammatical rules for combining the elements of the language. The syntax of propositional logic consists of (1) simple or *atomic* statements, (2) grouping symbols, (3) truth-functional connectors, and (4) grammatical rules. **Semantics** gives meaning to the sentences or symbols established by a language's syntax. The semantics of our formal language will be determined by means of **truth tables**. In this section, we will discuss each of these components in turn.

A **truth table** is a table that presents all possible combinations of truth-values that can be assigned to a statement. Truth tables are designed to show logical relationships, and they are used primarily in computer science, electrical engineering, logic, and mathematics.

Later in the chapter, we will learn how to translate sentences in English into our formal language. For now, however, we will focus on the formal language itself.

8.2a

An atomic proposition is represented by a lowercase Roman letter from p through v. These are the *variables* of the language. p, q, r, s, t, u, and v. They are also known as 'sentence members.'

8.2b

There are three pairs of grouping symbols: (and); [and]; and {and}. These are the left and right parentheses, the left and right brackets, and the left and right braces, respectively.

8.2c

There are five truth-functional connectives:

$$\&, \sim, \lor, \supset, \text{ and } \equiv$$

Before we introduce the grammatical rules, we must define two additional terms. The **object language** is the language we are discussing. The variables p through v are members of the object language we are discussing in this section, namely, the language of propositional logic. When we discuss an object language, however, we often use another language or symbols that are not part of the object language. These are known as a **metasymbols**. For example, if we were studying French, the object language would be French, but there would be times when we would talk about that language in English; in that case, English would be a metalanguage.

In presenting the grammatical rules of our formal language, we will use two members of a metalanguage: "**P**" and "**Q**". These will represent any statement that conforms to the following grammatical rules:

8.2d

> If **P** is an atomic statement of the language, then **P** is a well-formed formula (a complete and proper sentence within the language—**WFF** for short).
> If **P** is a WFF, then ~**P** is a WFF.
> If **P** and **Q** are WFFs, then (**P** & **Q**) is a WFF.
> If **P** and **Q** are WFFs, then (**P** ∨ **Q**) is a WFF.
> If **P** and **Q** are WFFs, then (**P** ⊃ **Q**) is a WFF.
> If **P** and **Q** are WFFs, then (**P** ≡ **Q**) is a WFF.

As noted earlier, the semantics of a language provide the meaning of statements within that language. Without semantics, meaning is impossible. Thus, at this point it is impossible to say what (**P** ⊃ **Q**) means. We will determine the truth-functional meaning of (**P** ⊃ **Q**) and other formulas in our formal language by using truth tables. The logical relationship between **P** and **Q** when connected by the connective ⊃ is what is meant by "truth-functional meaning." Truth functions boast a long history, even having been used by ancient as well as medieval logicians.[12]

In setting up a truth table, the following pattern is employed:

8.2e

list the individual variable(s) alphabetically	list the statement(s) to be tested

The individual variables, listed in the upper left quadrant, are the atomic statements contained in the statements we want to test. These variables are listed in alphabetical order. The number of rows in the table will be determined by the number of variables listed on the left-hand side of the vertical line. The formula for finding the number of rows is 2^n, where n is the number of variables. Given this formula, we can develop the following table:

8.2f

#of variables = rows down

1	2
2	4

3	8
4	16
5	32
6	64

Each row of the table is best understood as a possible world, or a way in which things could be arranged.[13] We assign a truth-value to each variable listed in the upper left quadrant. These values are listed in the lower left quadrant; again, the number of rows is dependent on the number of variables. Once it has been completed, the left-hand side of the table serves as a key or guide that can be used in reading the remainder of the table.

8.2g

p q r s	
T T T T	
T T T F	
T T F T	
T T F F	
T F T T	
T F T F	
T F F T	
T F F F	
F T T T	
F T T F	
F T F T	
F T F F	
F F T T	
F F T F	
F F F T	
F F F F	

The column nearest to the vertical line will always alternate between T and F, with T standing for true and F for false. The next column will consist of alternating *pairs* of T's and F's and the third column will consist of alternating sets of four. If the table had five variables, the fifth column would consist of alternating sets of sixteen and would have thirty-two rows.

Earlier, we introduced the idea of possible worlds. The table in 8.2g illustrates sixteen possible worlds; each row represents a different world, with a different relationship among its members. For example, in the first world, the peculiar relationship among the four members arises because all four are true in that world. In the final world, their relationship is different from that in the first world because all the members are false.

Now that we have seen how truth tables are constructed, we can present the semantics of our formal language. The syntax permits six kinds of statements: **P**, ~**P**, (**P** & **Q**), (**P** ∨ **Q**), (**P** ⊃ **Q**), and (**P** ≡ **Q**). The semantics, using truth tables, provides the truth-functional meaning of each type of statement. The most obvious of these is the following:

8.2h

P

P	P
T	T
F	F

This statement simply claims that in the world in which **P** is true, **P** is true, and that in the world in which **P** is false, **P** is false.

8.2i

~P

P	~P
T	F
F	T

This table defines ~**P** such that its truth-value in a given world is the opposite of that of **P** in that world. That is, if, in a given world, **P** is true, then ~**P** is false in that world. If **P** is false in a given world then ~**P** is true in that world.

8.2j

(P & Q)

P Q	(P & Q)
T T	T
T F	F
F T	F
F F	F

This truth table shows that (**P & Q**) is true only in that world in which both **P** and **Q** are true. All other possible worlds find (**P & Q**) to be false.

8.2k

(P ∨ Q)

P Q	(P ∨ Q)
T T	T
T F	T
F T	T
F F	F

According to this truth table, (**P** ∨ **Q**) means that whenever at least one component proposition is true, then the statement is true. Only in the world in which both **P** and **Q** are false is (**P** ∨ **Q**) false.

8.2l

(P ⊃ Q)

P Q	(P ⊃ Q)
T T	T
T F	F
F T	T
F F	T

In this construction (**P** ⊃ **Q**) will be true in every possible world, except that world in which **P**, the antecedent, is true and **Q**, the consequent, is false.

8.2m

(P ≡ Q)

P Q	(P ≡ Q)
T T	T
T F	F
F T	F
F F	T

This table indicates that the meaning of (**P** ≡ **Q**) is such that, whenever both **P** and **Q** have the same truth-value, (**P** ≡ **Q**) is true, and whenever they have different truth-values, (**P** ≡ **Q**) is false.

Given these tables, the various truth-functional connectives operate in a manner similar to the way certain English words operate. The "~" operates like the English word "not." "~p" will thus be read as "not p." The "&" is like the English "and," so that "(p & q)" will be read as "p and q." The wedge, or "∨," operates like the inclusive "or" of English, so statements like "(p ∨ q)" will be read as "p or q." The horseshoe denotes the material conditional, and "(p ⊃ q)" will be read as either "p implies q" or "if p, then q." The triple bar is a biconditional, and "(p ≡ q)" is to be read as "p if and only if q."[14]

In developing a truth table, we must always keep in mind how the symbols are grouped in the statement we are examining. For example, ~p & q is not saying the same thing[15] as ~(p & q). The main connector in the first statement is &, while in the second statement it is ~. The main connector in a statement is the connector that has the greatest range. Notice in the first statement that the ~ ranges only over the p, whereas the & ranges over the entire statement. By contrast, in the second statement the range of the & is limited to what is within the parentheses, and it is the ~ that governs the entire statement. The main connector is always the last connector interpreted in setting up a truth table. In Example 8.2n, the ∨ is the main connector, since it links (p & q) with ~(r & q); accordingly, it will be the last connective interpreted in establishing a truth table. The ~ just negates the ampersand within the parentheses that contain r & q. The sequence used to identify and understand the logical relationships within a statement is known as the **order of interpretation**.

8.2n

(p & q) ∨ ~(r & q)
1   4 3   2

The order of interpretation for this statement requires the first **&** and the ~ to be understood before the ∨, and the second **&** must be understood before the ~.

8.2A EXERCISE: ORDER OF INTERPRETATION

For each of the following statements, give its order of interpretation:

    1.   ~(p ≡ q)
*2.   ~(p & ~q) ⊃ (p ⊃ q)
    3.   (p ∨ q) & (p ⊃ q) ∨ s
*4.   [(p & q) & ~r] ∨ [(~p & q) & r]
    5.   (r ∨ q) ⊃ [p ⊃ (s ≡ t)]
    6.   ~(~p & ~q)
*7.   ~~(~p & ~q) ∨ (s ⊃ ~t)
    8.   {[~ p ⊃ (p & q)] ∨ t} ≡ (s ∨ ~t)
*9.   ~~(r & ~s)
    10.   ~p ⊃ (r ≡ ~t)

8.2B EXERCISE: WRITING WFFs

Write ten WFFs (well-formed formulas) in the formal language of propositional logic. Circle the main connector in each.

8.3 CONSISTENCY AND TRUTH TABLES

Since achieving consistency is a major purpose of using an artificial language, it is important to learn how to test a set of statements for consistency. We will test the set {~q ⊃ p; p ⊃ q. Remember that a set is consistent if there is at least one situation (i.e., possible world) in which all members of that set are true. (This world does not have to be the actual world; *any* logically possible world will do.) In the given set, there are two variables; hence, there will be four possible worlds, or rows in the truth table. The table should be constructed in the following fashion:

8.3a

p q	~q ⊃ p: p ⊃ q
T T	
T F	
F T	
F F	

To determine the truth-value of the first statement, (~q ⊃ p), we must determine the truth-value of the ~ in order to understand the antecedent properly. Hence, the next step is as follows:

8.3b

p q	~q ⊃ p; p ⊃ q
T T	F
T F	T
F T	F
F F	T

The conditional in world 1 is read as "F implies T," and so forth, according to the semantics for the horseshoe:

8.3c

p q	~q ⊃ p; p ⊃ q
T T	F T
T F	T T
F T	F T
F F	T F

Employing the same procedure, we complete the table as follows:

8.3d

p q	~q ⊃ p; p ⊃ q	
T T	F T	T
T F	T T	F
F T	F T	T
F F	T F	T

Since there exists at least one world in which both statements in the set are true (there are actually two such worlds), the set is consistent. If there were no worlds in which both statements were true, the set would be inconsistent.

8.3A EXERCISE: TRUTH TABLES AND CONSISTENCY

Using truth tables, test each of the following sets of sentences for consistency, and state whether the set is consistent or inconsistent:

*1.   {p ⊃ (q ∨ r); ~(~p ∨ r); ~q; r}
*2.   {p ∨ q; q & s; q ⊃ r}
3.   {~p ⊃ ~q; r & s; s ⊃ ~t; (p & r) ⊃ (q ⊃ t)}
4.   {~(p ⊃ q); q ⊃ r; p ⊃ r}
5.   {p ⊃ (q & ~r); p ≡ s; (q & r) & ~s; p ∨ r; q ⊃ s}
6.   {~p; q ∨ p; q & r; r}
7.   {p ≡ q; p; q ∨ r; s & ~t}
8.   {q ⊃ ~p; ~~(q & p)}
9.   {p ⊃ q; s ∨ ~q; ~s; t ≡ u; ~p}
10.   {~p; r ⊃ ~q; (q ∨ ~r) ⊃ ~(r & p)}
11.   {p ⊃ ~(q & r); s ⊃ ~(p & t); p & s; ~q; ~r & ~t}
12.   {p ⊃ q; ~q ⊃ p}
13.   {(p ∨ q) ∨ s; p ⊃ r; q ⊃ t; s ⊃ u; ~p & ~q; u}
14.   {p ⊃ q; q ⊃ r; ~r ⊃ ~p}
15.   {p ⊃ q; q ⊃ p}
16.   {p & q; p; q; ~[(t & s) ≡ (u & v)]}
17.   {p & q; r ∨ p; (~r & t) ⊃ q}
*18. {~s; p ⊃ ~q; ~p ⊃ (r ⊃ ~q); (~s ∨ ~r) ⊃ q; ~r}
19.   {p ≡ (q ≡ p); ~q}
20.   {r ∨ q; ~q ∨ r; r & s; s}
21.   {~p; p ∨ q; q ⊃ r; s ≡ r; ~s}
22.   {p ∨ ~p; p & q; ~q}
23.   {p ≡ q; q ⊃ r; r ⊃ p}
24.   {~p; r ⊃ q; (q ∨ ~r) ⊃ ~(r & p)}

All of the preceding problems consist of sets that contain more than one statement. However, a set, of course, can consist of a single statement. There are times when we want to test the consistency of a particular statement. For example, the following statement is inconsistent because its truth table shows that there is no world in which the statement is true:

8.3e

{p & ~p}

p	p & ~p
T	F F
F	F T

8.3B EXERCISE: CONSISTENCY OF A SINGLE STATEMENT

Using truth tables, test each of the following statements for consistency, and state whether it is consistent or inconsistent:

1.   {[(p ⊃ q) & p] & q}
*2. {[(p ⊃ q) & ~q] & ~p}
3.   {[(p ∨ q) & p] & q}
4.   {~(p & q) ≡ (~p ∨ ~q)}
5.   {[p & (q ∨ r)] ≡ [(p & q) ∨ (p & r)]}
6.   {p & (p ∨ q)}
7.   {[p ∨ (q ∨ r)] ≡ [(p ∨ q) ∨ r]}
8.   {p ≡ (p ∨ ~p)}
9.   {(p ≡ ~q) ≡ [(p & q) ∨ (~p & ~q)]}
10. {(p & ~q) & p}
11. {(p ⊃ q) ≡ (~p ⊃ ~q)}
12. {(p ∨ q) ≡ (q ∨ p)}
13. {~(p ∨ q) ≡ (~p & ~q)}
14. {(p ⊃ q) & [p ⊃ (p & q)]}
15. {[p ∨ (q & r)] ≡ [(p ∨ q) & (p ∨ r)]}
16. {(p & q) ≡ (q & p)}

8.3C EXERCISE: WRITING SETS OF WFFS AND TESTING THEM

Write ten sets of WFFs and test each set for consistency.

8.4 LOGICAL EQUIVALENCE AND TRUTH TABLES

Truth tables can be used to determine whether two statements are equivalent. Earlier, we defined equivalence as a property of two statements that always have the same truth-value. That is, in any given world, if one statement is true, then the other statement also is true, and if one is false, then the other is false. If this sameness of truth-values exists in all worlds, the two statements are equivalent. The best way to test for equivalence by using truth tables is to put the statements into a biconditional relationship—that is, connect them together with a ≡. If the ≡ relationship is true in all possible worlds, then the two statements are equivalent. Otherwise the statements are not equivalent. For example, is ~q ⊃ p equivalent to q ∨ p? To find out, we use the following truth table:

8.4a

p q	(~q ⊃ p) ≡ (q ∨ p)
T T	F	T	T	T
T F	T	T	T	T
F T	F	T	T	T
F F	T	F	T	F

This table shows that the two statements are equivalent.

8.4A EXERCISE: LOGICAL EQUIVALENCE AND TRUTH TABLES

Test each of the following pairs of statements for equivalence by putting the two statements into a biconditional relationship, and state whether they are equivalent:

1.   p; ~~p
2.   ~(p & q); (~p ∨ ~q)
3.   ~(p ∨ q); (~p & ~q)
4.   (p ∨ q); (q ∨ p)
5.   [p ∨ (q ∨ r)]; [(p ∨ q) ∨ r]
*6. (p ⊃ q); (~p ∨ q)
7.   [p & (q ∨ r)]; [(p & q) ∨ (p & r)]
8.   (p ⊃ q); (~q ⊃ ~p)
9.   [(p & q) ⊃ r]; [p & (q ⊃ r)]
*10. ~(p ⊃ q); (~p ⊃ ~q)
11. (p ≡ q); [(p & q) ∨ (~p & ~q)]
12. ~(p ∨ q); (~p ∨ ~q)
13. [p ⊃ (q ⊃ r)]; [(p ⊃ q) ⊃ r]
14. (p ⊃ q); ~(p & ~q)
15. [(p & q) ⊃ r]; [p ⊃ (q ⊃ r)]
16. ~~~~~p; ~~~~~~~p

8.4B EXERCISE: WRITING PAIRS OF WFFs AND TESTING FOR EQUIVALENCE

Write five pairs of WFFs, and use truth tables to test each pair for equivalence.

8.5 STATEMENTS AND TRUTH TABLES

Propositional logic can tell us something about the nature of individual propositions. Truth tables can be used to determine whether a proposition is a tautology, a contradiction, or a contingent statement. A proposition is a **tautology** if it is true in every possible world. If it is false in every possible world, it is a **contradiction**. If it is true in some worlds, but false in others, it is a **contingent statement**. The following examples illustrate these three types of propositions:

8.5a

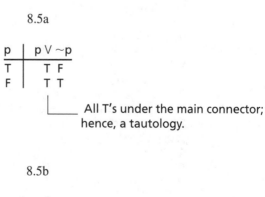

p	p ∨ ~p
T	T F
F	T T

All T's under the main connector; hence, a tautology.

8.5b

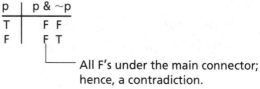

p	p & ~p
T	F F
F	F T

All F's under the main connector; hence, a contradiction.

8.5c

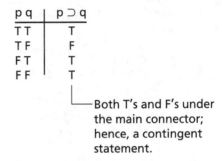

└─ Both T's and F's under
the main connector;
hence, a contingent
statement.

8.5A EXERCISE: STATEMENTS AND TRUTH TABLES

Determine whether each of the following statements is a tautology, a contradiction, or a contingent statement:

1. $(p \,\&\, q) \supset p$
*2. $(\sim p \supset p) \,\&\, (p \supset \sim p)$
3. $(p \,\&\, q) \supset (p \lor q)$
*4. $p \,\&\, (p \lor q)$
5. $(p \supset q) \equiv (\sim p \lor q)$
6. $\sim p \lor (\sim p \,\&\, \sim q)$
7. $\sim(\sim p \equiv q) \supset (q \lor \sim r)$
*8. $p \supset (q \supset p)$
9. $(p \lor q) \supset (p \,\&\, q)$
10. $[(p \supset q) \,\&\, p] \,\&\, q$
11. $\sim p \lor [(p \,\&\, q) \lor (\sim p \,\&\, \sim q)]$
12. $p \supset (q \lor p)$
13. $\sim(p \supset q) \,\&\, (\sim q \supset \sim p)$
14. $(q \,\&\, r) \supset [(q \lor p) \,\&\, (r \lor p)]$
15. $(p \supset q) \supset [\sim(q \lor r) \supset \sim(p \,\&\, r)]$
16. $[(p \supset q) \,\&\, p] \supset q$
17. $[(p \supset q) \,\&\, (p \supset r)] \supset (q \supset r)$
18. $\sim(p \lor \sim p)$
19. $[\sim p \lor (q \,\&\, r)] \,\&\, (q \,\&\, \sim r)$
20. $[(p \,\&\, r) \supset (q \,\&\, s)] \equiv (r \,\&\, s)$
21. $\{[(q \supset r) \,\&\, (p \supset s)] \,\&\, (q \lor p)\} \supset (r \lor s)$
22. $p \equiv \sim\sim p$
23. $[p \,\&\, (q \lor r)] \equiv [(p \,\&\, q) \lor (p \,\&\, r)]$
24. $p \equiv [(r \,\&\, s) \lor p]$
25. $\{(p \,\&\, q) \equiv [(q \,\&\, p) \lor (s \equiv \sim t)]\} \equiv [(p \,\&\, q) \lor (\sim p \,\&\, \sim q)]$

8.5B EXERCISE: WRITING WFFS AND TESTING STATEMENTS

Write ten WFFs, and test each to determine whether it is a tautology, a contradiction, or a contingent statement.

8.6 ARGUMENTS AND TRUTH TABLES

To test the validity of an argument by means of truth tables, we list all of the argument's premises and its conclusion in the upper right quadrant of the table and find the truth-value of each statement. Then we read the table to determine whether the argument form is valid. Remember that if there is one row of the truth table in which all of the premises are true and the conclusion is false (i.e., if there is a counterexample to the argument), the argument is invalid. A valid argument does not have a counterexample.

In the section on conditional reasoning, we found that the following argument form was invalid:

$$\begin{array}{l} \text{If P, then Q} \\ \underline{\sim P} \\ \therefore \qquad \sim Q \end{array}$$

We can show it to be invalid by converting the argument into propositional language:

$$\begin{array}{l} p \supset q \\ \underline{\sim p} \\ \therefore \qquad \sim q \end{array}$$

p q	p ⊃ q	~p	~q
T T	T	F	F
T F	F	F	T
F T	T	T	F
F F	T	T	T

In worlds one and two of this argument, not all of the premises are true. (One premise is true in world one, and neither premise is true in world two.) Hence, we are not concerned with the truth-value of the conclusion in those worlds. However, in worlds three and four both premises are true; therefore, we must be concerned with the conclusion. Notice that in world four the conclusion is also true, but in the third world we have true premises and a false conclusion. This world, then, represents a counterexample, and an argument that contains at least one counterexample is invalid. Moreover, the world in which the counterexample appears can be identified by the truth-value assignments made to the atomic propositions in that world. Here, the world that contains the counterexample is the world in which p is false and q is true.

In the preceding chapter, we saw that the argument "If P, then Q; Q; therefore, P" is invalid. We can set up a truth table for this argument as follows:

p q	p ⊃ q	q	p
T T	T	T T	
T F	F	F T	
F T	T	T F	
F F	T	F F	

In this argument, both premises are true in worlds one and three; however, in world three, the conclusion is false. Therefore, we have a counterexample, and it appears in the world in which p is false and q is true. Because we have a counterexample, the argument form is invalid. We will document this counterexample with the following notation:

$$\frac{p \; q}{F \; T}$$

8.6A EXERCISE: ARGUMENTS AND TRUTH TABLES

Test the validity of each of the following arguments, indicating the counterexample for arguments that are invalid:

1. p ⊃ q
    p
    ∴   q

2. p ∨ q
    ~p
    ∴   q

3. ~(p & q)
    ~p
    ∴   q

*4. p & q
     ~p
     ∴   ~q

5. ~(p ⊃ q)
    p
    ∴   ~q

6. ~(p ∨ q)
    ~p
    ∴   ~q

7. p ≡ q
    p
    ∴   q

8. ~(p ≡ q)
    p
    ∴   ~q

9. ~q ⊃ r
    ~p ⊃ t
    t ⊃ ~r
    ∴   q ∨ p

*10. p ⊃ q
      q ⊃ r
      ∴   r ⊃ p

11. (p & q) ⊃ r
     (r ∨ s) ⊃ t
     ∴   (p & q) ⊃ t

*12. ~(p ⊃ t) & q
      ~(q ∨ p) ⊃ t
      ~(p & q) ∨ s
      ∴   ~t

13. ~[(p & q) ≡ (r & s)]
     p ≡ r
     ∴   ~(q ≡ s)

14. q
     q ⊃ p
     p ∨ r
     r ⊃ s
     ∴   p & s

15. ~[(p ⊃ q) & (q ≡ s)] & t
     t ≡ r
     ∴   (r ∨ p) ∨ [(p ⊃ s) & (s ⊃ q)]

16. ~(p ≡ r)
     ~(r ≡ q)
     ∴   ~(p ⊃ q)

17. p ⊃ ~(q & r)
     s ⊃ ~(p & t)
     p & s
     ~~~q
     ∴   ~r & ~t

18. [(p ≡ q) ≡ (r ≡ s)]
     p ∨ ~t
     s
     ∴   p

19. ~[(t & p) ≡ (s & q)]
     t ≡ s
     ∴   p ≡ q

20. p ⊃ q
     s ∨ ~q
     ~s
     ∴   ~p

*21. ~[(s & t) ⊃ (r ∨ ~p)]
      p ⊃ s
      q ⊃ t
      ∴   ~[(p & q) ⊃ r]

22. p ⊃ q
     p
     ∴   q

23. (p ⊃ q) & [(p ⊃ r) & (s ⊃ p)]
     p & t
     ∴   s

24. p ⊃ (q ⊃ ~p)
     ∴   q ⊃ ~p

25. r ∨ s
     (r ⊃ p) & (~p ⊃ s)
     ∴   p

26. p
     q & r
     (q & p) ⊃ s
     ∴   s ∨ t

27. (p ⊃ q) & (r ∨ p)
     (r ⊃ p) & (r ⊃ ~p)
     ∴   ~(p & ~q)

28. p ⊃ q
     p ⊃ r
     ∴   q ∨ r

29. (p ⊃ q) & (r ⊃ s)
     p ∨ r
     ∴   q ∨ s

30. (p & q) ⊃ (r & s)
     ∴   (p & q) ⊃ [(p & q) & (r & s)]

31. [p ⊃ (p & q)] & [q ⊃ (q & p)]
     ∴   p ⊃ (p & q)

32. p ⊃ (q ∨ r)
     (q ∨ r) ⊃ ~p
     ∴   ~p

33. (p ∨ q) ⊃ r
     r ⊃ (p & q)
     ∴   (p ∨ q) ⊃ (p & q)

34. (p ⊃ q) & [(p & q) ⊃ r]
     p ⊃ (r ⊃ s)
     ∴   p ⊃ s

35. (p ∨ q) ⊃ (p & q)
     ~(p & q)
     ∴   ~(p ∨ q)

36. (p ∨ q) ⊃ (p & q)
     ~(p ∨ q)
     ∴   ~(p & q)

37. p ∨ (q & ~q)
     p
     ∴   ~(p & ~p)

38. p ⊃ q
     q ⊃ r
     s ⊃ t
     p ∨ s
     ∴   r ∨ t

39. $p \equiv q$
    $\sim p$
    $\therefore \quad \sim q$

40. $(p \lor q) \supset r$
    $r \supset (p \And q)$
    $\therefore \quad (p \And q) \supset (p \lor q)$

41. $r \supset (p \lor q)$
    $(p \And q) \supset \sim r$
    $\therefore \quad \sim r$

42. $(p \lor q) \supset \sim(r \And \sim s)$
    $\sim\sim(r \And \sim s)$
    $\therefore \quad \sim(p \lor q)$

43. $\sim(\sim p \And q)$
    $\sim(q \lor r)$
    $\therefore \quad p$

44. $[p \supset (q \And r)] \And [s \supset (p \And t)]$
    $p \lor s$
    $\therefore \quad (q \And r) \lor (p \And t)$

45. $(p \equiv q) \lor [(s \And t) \lor (s \And r)]$
    $\sim(p \equiv q)$
    $\therefore \quad (s \And t) \lor (s \And r)$

46. $\sim p \lor q$
    q
    $\therefore \quad p$

47. $\sim(p \And \sim q) \supset (p \supset q)$
    $(p \equiv q) \supset \sim(p \And \sim q)$
    $\therefore \quad (p \equiv q) \supset (p \supset q)$

48. $\sim s$
    $p \supset \sim q$
    $\sim p \supset (r \supset \sim q)$
    $(\sim s \lor \sim r) \supset \sim\sim q$
    $\therefore \quad \sim r$

49. $(p \lor q) \supset \sim(r \lor s)$
    $q \And \sim u$
    $\sim t \supset u$
    $\therefore \quad r \And \sim s$

50. $(q \supset p) \And (p \equiv \sim r)$
    r
    $\therefore \quad q$

51. $(p \supset q) \lor (q \supset r)$
    $(r \lor p) \equiv p$
    $\sim s \supset q$
    $\therefore \quad s$

52. $p \supset q$
    $q \supset r$
    p
    $\therefore \quad p \supset \sim r$

53. $p \supset (q \lor r)$
    $(q \And s) \supset t$
    p
    $\sim t$
    $\therefore \quad (q \And s) \lor r$

54. $p \lor q \lor s$
    $p \supset r$
    $q \supset t$
    $s \supset u$
    $\sim p \And \sim q$
    $\therefore \quad u$

55. $\sim p$
    $\therefore \quad p \supset q$

56. $p \lor (q \And r)$
    $\therefore \quad (p \lor q) \And (p \lor r)$

57. $p \supset (q \And r)$
    $\therefore \quad (p \supset q) \And (p \supset r)$

58. $p \equiv q$
    $q \equiv r$
    $\therefore \quad [(p \And q) \And \sim r] \lor [(\sim p \And q) \And r]$

59. $(p \lor q) \supset r$
    $(r \lor q) \supset p \supset (s \equiv t)$
    $p \And q$
    $\therefore \quad s \equiv t$

60. $(\sim p \lor q) \supset [p \lor (q \And r)]$
    $\sim p$
    $\therefore \quad (q \And r)$

61. (p ∨ q) ⊃ t
    ~t & ~p
    ∴   ~(p ∨ q)

62. p ≡ (q ≡ r)
    ∴   (p ≡ q) ≡ r

63. {p & [r ⊃ (q ∨ p)]}
    ~r & ~q
    ∴   p

64. p ⊃ q
    q ⊃ r
    r ⊃ s
    ∴   p ⊃ s

65. p ∨ (~~r & ~~q)
    p ⊃ q
    s ⊃ ~r
    ~(p & q)
    ∴   ~s ∨ ~q

66. [p ⊃ (q & ~r)] & [q ⊃ (p ⊃ r)]
    (p & q) & ~s
    s ≡ ~(q & ~r)
    s ∨ ~s
    ∴   r & s

67. (p ⊃ q) & (q ⊃ p)
    (r & q) ∨ (~q & ~r)
    (r ∨ s) ∨ (p ∨ q)
    ~r ⊃ (t & u)
    (s ⊃ ~p) & (~s ⊃ ~v)
    t ⊃ (~v ⊃ ~t)
    (r ∨ p) & (s ∨ v)
    ∴   ~t & v

68. p ⊃ (q & r)
    (q ⊃ s) ∨ ~p
    t ⊃ (u ∨ ~s)
    (~u ∨ v) & ~v
    (p ∨ ~u) ∨ ~r
    ∴   p ⊃ q

69. (p ∨ q) ⊃ [[(r & s) ∨ t] ⊃ u]
    q & ~p
    p & ~q
    [(s ⊃ u) ⊃ ~v] ⊃ q
    ∴   r ⊃ v

70. (p & q) ⊃ (r & s)
    r ∨ t
    t ∨ s
    (p & t) ∨ (p & s)
    ∴   ~~~q

8.6B EXERCISE: WRITING ARGUMENTS

Write five arguments and test each for validity.

8.7 TRANSLATING FROM ENGLISH INTO FORMAL LANGUAGE

Mastery of truth tables is important. However, unless they can be applied to the everyday world, their use is limited. Fortunately, since ordinary language can be translated into formal language, truth-functional statements made in English can be tested by using truth tables. The following charts (which are not exhaustive) will aid in making such translations. Uppercase boldface letters stand for any statement made in English or any other natural language. Following each statement is its translation into formal language.

Negations:
    It is false that **P**.   ~p
    It is not the case that **P**.   ~p
    It is not true that **P**.   ~p
    Not **P**.   ~p

Conditionals (including translations from chapter seven):
  If **P**, then **Q**. p ⊃ q
  P if **Q**. q ⊃ p
  P only if **Q**. p ⊃ q
  P since **Q**. q ⊃ p

Biconditionals:
  P if and only if **Q**. p ≡ q
  P just in case **Q**. p ≡ q

Conjunctions:
  P and **Q**. p & q
  P, but **Q**. p & q
  P despite the fact that **Q**. p & q
  P, while **Q**. p & q

Disjunctions:
  P or **Q** or both. p ∨ q
  P or **Q** (inclusive). p ∨ q
  P, or, alternatively, **Q**. p ∨ q
  Either **P** or **Q** (inclusive). p ∨ q

Complex Connecting Words:
  Neither **P** nor **Q**. ~(p ∨ q) or ~p & ~q
  P except if **Q** (inclusive). ~q ⊃ p
  Either **P** or **Q** (exclusive). (p ∨ q) & ~(p & q)
  P unless **Q** (exclusive). (p v q) & ~(p & q)
  P unless **Q** (inclusive). ~q ⊃ p *or* q ∨ p *or* ~p ⊃ q

8.7A EXERCISE: TRANSLATING SENTENCES

Translate the following sentences into formal language:

1. Brian will pass critical reasoning, but Mary will not.
*2. Joan will take philosophy of science despite the fact that she does not like science.
3. Not only will Jamie take symbolic logic next semester, but she will also take advanced epistemology.
*4. It is false that Mandie has taken art classes.
5. It is absurd that Jonie earned an A in European history.
*6. I will teach either symbolic logic or philosophy of science next semester.
7. John will take contemporary metaphysics or advanced epistemology, or, possibly, both.
*8. On the condition that Professor Peters teaches critical reasoning, I will take it next semester.
9. I will do well in critical reasoning only if the professor simply gives me an A just for showing up.

*10.   I will do well in critical reasoning if the professor simply gives me an A just for showing up.

11.   The truth will set you free if and only if you are in bondage to falsehood.

*12.   Jamison will play tight end next week if Brown is still sick; otherwise Jamison will not.

13.   I will teach critical reasoning next semester regardess of whether Brown is back by then.

*14.   You will benefit from this course even if you fail the course.

15.   Neither Smith nor Wertz were at the awards banquet.

*16.   We will go to Iowa, unless we go to Illinois first. (Interpret as inclusive.)

17.   Brown will be on time, except if he flies with the American Flyers. (Interpret as inclusive.)

*18.   Peter will attend the meeting, or Mary will. (Interpret as exclusive.)

19.   Wertz will read his paper on Hume, or Richard will read his on moral theory, but not both papers will be read.

20.   It will be hot on the beach, unless the clouds are hiding the sun. (Interpret as exclusive.)

21.   Peter will present the award if Mary is to receive it; otherwise Gregg will present the award.

22.   Mary will get the position, unless she does not want it, in which case Peter will take it.

23.   I received a B in her class, rather than an A.

24.   Ted's paper will be accepted if he can make the necessary corrections; otherwise it will not be accepted.

25.   Peter will attend the party without Mary.

8.7B EXERCISE: TRANSLATING ARGUMENTS
Translate each of the following arguments into formal language, and then test it for validity:

1.   It will snow at Christmas time only if my kids want it to. My kids wanted it to snow, since it snowed at Christmas time.

*2.   Either it will rain today, or it will not rain and the sun will shine. It is not the case that it will rain. Thus, the sun will shine.

3.   It is not the case that Peter and Joan attended the party. We know that Peter did not attend. Therefore, Joan must have attended the party.

*4.   Since passing a class and enjoying the class go together, and you did not pass Biology 101, we must conclude that you did not enjoy biology.

5.   It is not the case that Mary passes a course whenever she wants. Mary passed critical reasoning; therefore, she did not want to pass.

*6.   It is not the case that either John or Mary enjoyed the musical. John did not enjoy it. Hence, Mary did not enjoy the musical either.

7.   Brian will enjoy the computer program if and only if Mandie does. Since Brian enjoyed the program, we can conclude that Mandie did also.

*8.   It is not the case that the earth is round when and only when the moon is out. Since the earth is round, it follows that the moon is not out.

9.   Our perception of the world is accurate, unless an evil demon exists. We always hallucinate, unless God exists. But if God exists, then an evil demon does not exist. Hence, either our perception of the world is accurate or we always hallucinate.

*10.   A necessary condition for truth is our ability to recognize it. A sufficient condition for error is our ability to recognize it. Therefore, error implies truth.

11.   If I am perceiving the desk despite the fact that the light is poor, then the desk is in the corner. If it is in the corner or in the house, then I will use the phone. Therefore, if I am perceiving the desk and the light is poor, then I will use the phone.

*12.   It is not the case that my perceiving the desk implies that I have good vision, but I am wearing my glasses. If it is not the case that either I am wearing my glasses or I am perceiving the desk, then I have good vision. But either it is not the case that I am perceiving the desk and I am wearing my glasses, or I am hallucinating. From all this, I can conclude that I do not have good vision.

13.   It is not the case that your understanding of this problem and your correct translation of it is both the necessary and sufficient condition of passing this course and receiving an A. You will pass this course if and only if you understand this problem. Therefore, it is not the case that you will correctly translate the problem if and only if you receive an A.

*14.   Accordingly, truth is a liberation from falsehood and we are never free. This may be deduced from the fact that freedom is the essence of truth. And if freedom is the essence of truth, then truth is a liberation from falsehood. Furthermore, either truth is a liberation from falsehood or truth is an illusion. And if truth is an illusion, then we are never free.

15.   It is not the case that, if I am correct, then I know the truth, and I know the truth if and only if my perception is accurate. My perception is not accurate. Therefore, I know that I am not correct.

{The next five problems are from Richard Purtill, *Logic for Philosophers*.[16] Professor Purtill based these problems on Plato's *Crito* and *Apology*.}

16.   "Socrates will not do what is wrong. If he returns evil for evil, he will do wrong. If he breaks an agreement with the state because he has been unjustly condemned, he will return evil for evil. Therefore, if by making his escape he will be breaking an agreement because he has been unjustly condemned, he will not make his escape."

17.   "If Socrates did not approve of the Laws of Athens, he could have either emigrated from Athens or tried to have the Laws changed. If he neither emigrated nor tried to have the Laws changed, then Socrates agreed to obey the Laws. It is not true that Socrates emigrated from Athens. Therefore, if he did not try to have the Laws changed, then he approved of the Laws and agreed to obey them."

18.   "If Socrates avoids well-governed cities, his life will not be worth living. If he goes to Thessaly, he will become a laughingstock and will not be able to bring up his children well. Therefore, if escaping means that Socrates will go to

Pluggers

To understand the meaning of life we need
to start with a good cup of coffee.

Thessaly or will avoid well-governed cities, then, if his life is worth living, his children will not be well educated."

19. "If Socrates escapes, then things will not be better for him in this world and when he comes to the next world, he will come as a lawbreaker. If Socrates is persuaded by Crito, he will escape. If things will not be better for him in this world, he will not be happy in this world, and, if he comes to the next world as a lawbreaker, he will not be happy in the next world. Therefore, if Socrates is persuaded by Crito, he will be unhappy both in this world and in the next."

20. "Either death is a complete extinction and the dead man feels nothing, or death is a change and migration for the soul from this place to another place. If the dead man feels nothing, then eternity is like a night of dreamless sleep, and death is a blessing. If death is a change and migration from this place to another and if, as they say, all the dead are in that place, then we shall be with the great men of the past, and death is a blessing. Thus, if, as they say, all the dead are in that place, then death is a blessing."

8.7C EXERCISE: WRITING AND TRANSLATING ARGUMENTS

Write three arguments in English and translate each into formal language. Use as many truth-functional connectives as possible.

8.8 TRUTH TREES

Truth tables are extremely important to the development of a formal language. However, they have some major limitations. Consider an argument that contains five or more variables. Few people would attempt to create a truth table for such an argument (unless it was part of a homework assignment). Truth tables become impractical when they require sixty-four or more possible worlds. We need a methodology that accomplishes everything that truth tables do and yields the same results, but without the bulk of truth tables. Such a methodology exists: It is known as the **truth tree method** or as **semantic tableaux**. While trees can be developed in several ways, the procedures described here were popularized by Richard C. Jeffrey.[17]

The tree method produces a graph with the use of eight rules of inference.[18] The syntax and semantics are the same as those for truth tables. Although there are no rules governing which major connectives to unpack first, it is best to begin with rules of inference that do not branch. The value of this suggestion will become evident as we proceed.

The rules of inference can be divided into three categories:

8.8a

those which stack:

P & Q	~(P ⊃ Q)	~(P ∨ Q)
P	P	~P
Q	~Q	~Q

those which branch:

~(P & Q)
      /\
   ~P   ~Q

P ⊃ Q
    /\
  ~P   Q

P ∨ Q
    /\
   P   Q

and those which branch and stack:

P ≡ Q
    /\
  P   ~P
  Q   ~Q

~(P ≡ Q)
      /\
   ~P   P
   Q   ~Q

Before we can use these rules, we need several operational rules that deal with specific concerns in formal logic: validity, denials, consistency, tautology, contradiction, and contingency.

Validity and Denials

8.8b

Validity

If, at the end of applying a procedure, every path closes, then the argument in question is valid. If one or more paths are still open, the argument is invalid. A path is closed if both a statement and its denial appear (e.g., **P** and ~**P**).

Denials

Whenever a statement includes a double denial (e.g., ~~**P**), rewrite the statement without any denial (e.g., **P**).

In setting up a truth tree for a given argument, two steps are involved. First we list the premises, and then we list the denial of the conclusion. (This procedure stems from the fact that truth trees are tested for validity by attempting to develop a counterexample.) With this construction and the rules just presented, we produce a graphlike structure that tests whether an argument is valid. The following examples demonstrate the use of this method:

8.8c

$$p \supset q$$
$$\underline{p}$$
$$\therefore \quad q$$

1.	$p \supset q$	set member; hereafter written as sm
2.	p	sm
3.	~q	denial of conclusion; hereafter written as ~sm

4. ~p   q   from line 1; using the inference
    *   *   rule for $\supset$; hereafter written as
  (2,4)   (3,4)   1; $\supset$

Since, in each path, we have a sentence and its denial, each path closes. We show this by placing an asterisk at the bottom of each closed path. (Note that the lines in virtue of which we close the paths are given below the asterisk.) Since each path is closed, the argument is valid.

8.8d

$$r \supset s$$
$$\underline{p \supset q}$$
$$\therefore \quad (r \lor p) \supset (s \lor q)$$

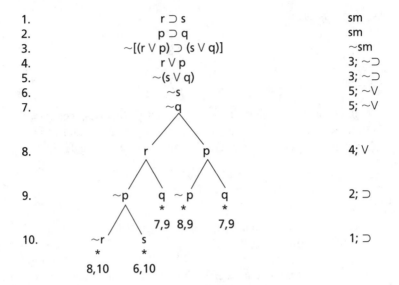

1.	$r \supset s$	sm
2.	$p \supset q$	sm
3.	$\sim[(r \lor p) \supset (s \lor q)]$	$\sim$sm
4.	$r \lor p$	3; $\sim\supset$
5.	$\sim(s \lor q)$	3; $\sim\supset$
6.	$\sim s$	5; $\sim\lor$
7.	$\sim q$	5; $\sim\lor$
8.	r p	4; $\lor$
9.	$\sim$p q $\sim$p q	2; $\supset$
	* * *	
	7,9 8,9 7,9	
10.	$\sim$r s	1; $\supset$
	* *	
	8,10 6,10	

Since all paths close, the argument form is valid.

8.8e

$$p \supset q$$
$$\underline{\sim p}$$
$$\therefore \quad q$$

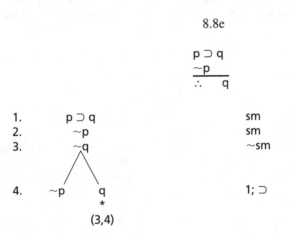

1.	$p \supset q$	sm
2.	$\sim p$	sm
3.	$\sim q$	$\sim$sm
4.	$\sim$p q	1; $\supset$
	*	
	(3,4)	

The path containing q closes, but since the path containing $\sim$p does not contain p, that path remains open. Thus, this argument is invalid.

The procedure for testing validity with truth trees assumes that the premises are all true. This is why we list the premises as given. The procedure assumes the conclusion to be false; we therefore list the denial of the conclusion. The tree then proceeds to test whether the set of true premises and false conclusion involves a contradiction in all possible interpretations. If a contradiction (e.g., p and $\sim$p) occurs in all paths, it is impossible to have the premises of the argument be true and the conclusion false. Therefore, it must be the case that whenever the premises are true the conclusion must also be true. In short, no counterexample to the argument exists.

8.8A EXERCISE: TRUTH TREES AND VALIDITY

Use truth trees to test whether each of the following arguments is valid or invalid:

*1. p ⊃ q
     p
     ∴   q

2.   p ∨ q
     ~p
     ∴   q

*3. ~(p & q)
     ~p
     ∴   q

4.   p & q
     ~p
     ∴   ~q

*5. ~(p ⊃ q)
     p
     ∴   ~q

6.   ~(p ∨ q)
     ~p
     ∴   ~q

*7. p ≡ q
     p
     ∴   q

8.   ~(p ≡ q)
     p
     ∴   ~q

*9. ~q ⊃ r
     ~p ⊃ t
     t ⊃ ~r
     ∴   q ∨ p

10. p ⊃ q
     q ⊃ r
     ∴   r ⊃ p

*11. (p & q) ⊃ r
     (r ∨ s) ⊃ t
     ∴   (p & q) ⊃ t

12. ~(p ⊃ t) & q
     ~(q ∨ p) ⊃ t
     ~(p & q) ∨ s
     ∴   ~t

13. ~[(p & q) ≡ (r & s)]
     p ≡ r
     ∴   ~(q ≡ s)

14. q
     q ⊃ p
     p ∨ r
     r ⊃ s
     ∴   p & s

*15. ~[(p ⊃ q) & (q ≡ s)] & t
     t ≡ r
     ∴   (r ∨ p) ∨ [(p ⊃ s) & (s ⊃ q)]

16. ~(p ≡ r)
     ~(r ≡ q)
     ∴   ~(p ⊃ q)

17. p ⊃ ~(q & r)
     s ⊃ ~(p & t)
     p & s
     ~~~q
     ∴   ~r & ~t

18. [(p ≡ q) ≡ (r ≡ s)]
     p ∨ ~t
     s
     ∴   p

19. ~[(t & p) ≡ (s & q)]
     t ≡ s
     ∴   p ≡ q

20. p ⊃ q
     s ∨ ~q
     ~s
     ∴   ~p

21. $\sim[(s \,\&\, t) \supset (r \vee \sim p)]$
     $p \supset s$
     $q \supset t$
     $\therefore \quad \sim[(p \,\&\, q) \supset r]$

22. $p \supset q$
     p
     $\therefore \quad q$

23. $(p \supset q) \,\&\, [(p \supset r) \,\&\, (s \supset p)]$
     $p \,\&\, t$
     $\therefore \quad s$

24. $p \supset (q \supset \sim p)$
     $\therefore \quad q \supset \sim p$

25. $r \vee s$
     $(r \supset p) \,\&\, (\sim p \supset s)$
     $\therefore \quad p$

26. p
     $q \,\&\, r$
     $(q \,\&\, p) \supset s$
     $\therefore \quad s \vee t$

27. $(p \supset q) \,\&\, (r \vee p)$
     $(r \supset p) \,\&\, (r \supset \sim p)$
     $\therefore \quad \sim(p \,\&\, \sim q)$

28. $p \supset q$
     $p \supset r$
     $\therefore \quad q \vee r$

29. $(p \supset q) \,\&\, (r \supset s)$
     $p \vee r$
     $\therefore \quad q \vee s$

30. $(p \,\&\, q) \supset (r \,\&\, s)$
     $\therefore \quad (p \,\&\, q) \supset [(p \,\&\, q) \,\&\, (r \,\&\, s)]$

31. $[p \supset (p \,\&\, q)] \,\&\, [q \supset (q \,\&\, p)]$
     $\therefore \quad p \supset (p \,\&\, q)$

32. $p \supset (q \vee r)$
     $(q \vee r) \supset \sim p$
     $\therefore \quad \sim p$

33. $(p \vee q) \supset r$
     $r \supset (p \,\&\, q)$
     $\therefore \quad (p \vee q) \supset (p \,\&\, q)$

34. $(p \supset q) \,\&\, [(p \,\&\, q) \supset r]$
     $p \supset (r \supset s)$
     $\therefore \quad p \supset s$

35. $(p \vee q) \supset (p \,\&\, q)$
     $\sim(p \,\&\, q)$
     $\therefore \quad \sim(p \vee q)$

36. $(p \vee q) \supset (p \,\&\, q)$
     $\sim(p \vee q)$
     $\therefore \quad \sim(p \,\&\, q)$

37. $p \vee (q \,\&\, \sim q)$
     p
     $\therefore \quad \sim(p \,\&\, \sim p)$

38. $p \supset q$
     $q \supset r$
     $s \supset t$
     $p \vee s$
     $\therefore \quad r \vee t$

39. $p \equiv q$
     $\sim p$
     $\therefore \quad \sim q$

40. $(p \vee q) \supset r$
     $r \supset (p \,\&\, q)$
     $\therefore \quad (p \,\&\, q) \supset (p \vee q)$

41. $r \supset (p \vee q)$
     $(p \,\&\, q) \supset \sim r$
     $\therefore \quad \sim r$

42. $(p \vee q) \supset \sim(r \,\&\, \sim s)$
     $\sim\sim(r \,\&\, \sim s)$
     $\therefore \quad \sim(p \vee q)$

43. $\sim(\sim p \,\&\, q)$
     $\sim(q \vee r)$
     $\therefore \quad p$

44. $[p \supset (q \,\&\, r)] \,\&\, [s \supset (p \,\&\, t)]$
     $p \vee s$
     $\therefore \quad (q \,\&\, r) \vee (p \,\&\, t)$

45. $(p \equiv q) \vee [(s \& t) \vee (s \& r)]$
    $\sim(p \equiv q)$
    _____
    ∴ $(s \& t) \vee (s \& r)$

46. $\sim p \vee q$
    q
    _____
    ∴ p

47. $\sim(p \& \sim q) \supset (p \supset q)$
    $(p \equiv q) \supset \sim(p \& \sim q)$
    _____
    ∴ $(p \equiv q) \supset (p \supset q)$

48. $\sim s$
    $p \supset \sim q$
    $\sim p \supset (r \supset \sim q)$
    $(\sim s \vee \sim r) \supset \sim \sim q$
    _____
    ∴ $\sim r$

49. $(p \vee q) \supset \sim(r \vee s)$
    $q \& \sim u$
    $\sim t \supset u$
    _____
    ∴ $r \& \sim s$

50. $(q \supset p) \& (p \equiv \sim r)$
    r
    _____
    ∴ q

51. $(p \supset q) \vee (q \supset r)$
    $(r \vee p) \equiv p$
    $\sim s \supset q$
    _____
    ∴ s

52. $p \supset q$
    $q \supset r$
    p
    _____
    ∴ $p \supset \sim r$

53. $p \supset (q \vee r)$
    $(q \& s) \supset t$
    p
    $\sim t$
    _____
    ∴ $(q \& s) \vee r$

54. $p \vee q \vee s$
    $p \supset r$
    $q \supset t$
    $s \supset u$
    $\sim p \& \sim q$
    _____
    ∴ u

55. $\sim p$
    _____
    ∴ $p \supset q$

56. $p \vee (q \& r)$
    _____
    ∴ $(p \vee q) \& (p \vee r)$

57. $p \supset (q \& r)$
    _____
    ∴ $(p \supset q) \& (p \supset r)$

58. $p \equiv q$
    $q \equiv r$
    _____
    ∴ $[(p \& q) \& \sim r] \vee [(\sim p \& q) \& r]$

59. $(p \vee q) \supset r$
    $(r \vee q) \supset p \supset (s \equiv t)$
    $p \& q$
    _____
    ∴ $s \equiv t$

60. $(\sim p \vee q) \supset [p \vee (q \& r)]$
    $\sim p$
    _____
    ∴ $(q \& r)$

61. $(p \vee q) \supset t$
    $\sim t \& \sim p$
    _____
    ∴ $\sim(p \vee q)$

62. $p \equiv (q \equiv r)$
    _____
    ∴ $(p \equiv q) \equiv r$

63. $\{p \& [r \supset (q \vee p)]\}$
    $\sim r \& \sim q$
    _____
    ∴ p

64. $p \supset q$
    $q \supset r$
    $r \supset s$
    _____
    ∴ $p \supset s$

65. $p \vee (\sim\sim r \& \sim\sim q)$
    $p \supset q$
    $s \supset \sim r$
    $\sim(p \& q)$
    _____
    ∴ $\sim s \vee \sim q$

66. $[p \supset (q \& \sim r)] \& [q \supset (p \supset r)]$
    $(p \& q) \& \sim s$
    $s \equiv \sim(q \& \sim r)$
    $s \vee \sim s$
    _____
    ∴ $r \& s$

67. (p ⊃ q) & (q ⊃ p)
     (r & q) V (~q & ~r)
     (r V s) V (p V q)
     ~r ⊃ (t & u)
     (s ⊃ ~p) & (~s ⊃ ~v)
     t ⊃ (~v ⊃ ~t)
     (r V p) & (s V v)
     ∴   ~t & v

68. p ⊃ (q & r)
     (q ⊃ s) V ~p
     t ⊃ (u V ~s)
     (~u V v) & ~v
     (p V ~u) V ~r
     ∴   p ⊃ q

69. (p V q) ⊃ [[(r & s) V t] ⊃ u]
     q & ~p
     p & ~q
     [(s ⊃ u) ⊃ ~v] ⊃ q
     ∴   r ⊃ v

70. (p & q) ⊃ (r & s)
     r V t
     t V s
     (p & t) V (p & s)
     ∴   ~~~q

Consistency

Truth trees can be used not only to test the validity of arguments, but also to test the consistency of a set of statements. To do so, we list the statements in the set and construct a tree. We do not list the denial of any of the statements.

8.8f

Consistency

After the tree has been constructed, if there is at least one open path, the set is consistent. If all paths are closed, the set is inconsistent. Consider the following set of statements:

8.8g

{(p ⊃ q), (p & r), (r V s)}

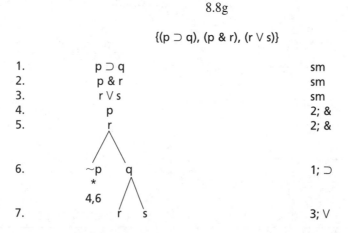

Since we have at least one open path, the set is consistent.

8.8B EXERCISE: TRUTH TREES AND CONSISTENCY

Use truth trees to test the following sets of statements for consistency:

*1. {p ⊃ (q ∨ r); ~(~p ∨ r); ~q; r}
 2. {p ∨ q; q & s; q ⊃ r}
*3. {~p ⊃ ~q; r & s; s ⊃ ~t; (p & r) ⊃ (q ⊃ t)}
 4. {~(p ⊃ q); q ⊃ r; p ⊃ r}
*5. {p ⊃ (q & ~r); p ≡ s; (q & r) & ~s; p ∨ r; q ⊃ s}
 6. {~p; q ∨ p; q & r; r}
 7. {p ≡ q; p; q ∨ r; s & ~t}
 8. {q ⊃ ~p; ~~(q & p)}
 9. {p ⊃ q; s ∨ ~q; ~s; t ≡ u; ~p}
10. {~p; r ⊃ ~q; (q ∨ ~r) ⊃ ~(r & p)}
11. {p ⊃ ~(q & r); s ⊃ ~(p & t); p & s; ~q; ~r & ~t}
12. {p ⊃ q; ~q ⊃ p}
13. {(p ∨ q) ∨ s; p ⊃ r; q ⊃ t; s ⊃ u; ~p & ~q; u}
14. {p ⊃ q; q ⊃ r; ~r ⊃ ~p}
15. {p ⊃ q; q ⊃ p}
16. {p & q; p; q; ~[(t & s) ≡ (u & v)]}
17. {p & q; r ∨ p; (~r & t) ⊃ q}
18. {~s; p ⊃ ~q; ~p ⊃ (r ⊃ ~q); (~s ∨ ~r) ⊃ q; ~r}
19. {p ≡ (q ≡ p); ~q}
20. {r ∨ q; ~q ∨ r; r & s; s}
21. {~p; p ∨ q; q ⊃ r; s ≡ r; ~s}
22. {p ∨ ~p; p & q; ~q}
23. {p ≡ q; q ⊃ r; r ⊃ p}
24. {~p; r ⊃ q; (q ∨ ~r) ⊃ ~(r & p)}
25. {[(p ⊃ q) & p] & q}
26. {[(p ⊃ q) & ~q] & ~p}
27. {[(p ∨ q) & p] & q}
28. {~(p & q) ≡ (~p ∨ ~q)}
29. {[p & (q ∨ r)] ≡ [(p & q) ∨ (p & r)]}
30. {p & (p ∨ q)}
31. {[p ∨ (q ∨ r) ≡ [(p ∨ q) ∨ r]}
32. {p ≡ (p ∨ ~p)}
33. {(p ≡ ~q) ≡ [(p & q) ∨ (~p & ~q)]}
34. {(p & ~q) & p}
35. {(p ⊃ q) ≡ (~p ⊃ ~q)}
36. {(p ∨ q) ≡ (q ∨ p)}
37. {~(p ∨ q) ≡ (~p & ~q)}
38. {(p ⊃ q) & [p ⊃ (p & q)]}
39. {[p ∨ (q & r)] ≡ [(p ∨ q) & (p ∨ r)]}
40. {(p & q) ≡ (q & p)}

Tautology, Contradiction, and Contingency

8.8h

Tautology

To decide whether a statement is a tautology, test the denial of the statement. If all branches are closed it is a tautology.

8.8i

Contradiction

To decide whether a statement is a contradiction, test the statement itself (not its denial). If all branches are closed, it is a contradiction.

8.8j

Contingency

To decide whether a statement is contingent, test the statement to determine whether it is either a tautology or a contradiction. If it is neither, it is contingent.

8.8C EXERCISE: TRUTH TREES AND STATEMENTS

Use truth trees to test whether each of the following statements is a tautology, a contradiction, or a contingent statement:

1. $(p \;\&\; q) \supset p$
*2. $(\sim p \supset p) \;\&\; (p \supset \sim p)$
3. $(p \;\&\; q) \supset (p \lor q)$
4. $p \;\&\; (p \lor q)$
5. $(p \supset q) \equiv (\sim p \lor q)$
*6. $\sim p \lor (\sim p \;\&\; \sim q)$
7. $\sim(\sim p \equiv q) \supset (q \lor \sim r)$
8. $p \supset (q \supset p)$
9. $(p \lor q) \supset (p \;\&\; q)$
10. $[(p \supset q) \;\&\; p] \;\&\; q$
11. $\sim p \lor [(p \;\&\; q) \lor (\sim p \;\&\; \sim q)]$
12. $p \supset (q \lor p)$
13. $\sim(p \supset q) \;\&\; (\sim q \supset \sim p)$
14. $(q \;\&\; r) \supset [(q \lor p) \;\&\; (r \lor p)]$
15. $(p \supset q) \supset [\sim(q \lor r) \supset \sim(p \;\&\; r)]$

16.   [(p ⊃ q) & p] ⊃ q
17.   [(p ⊃ q) & (p ⊃ r)] ⊃ (q ⊃ r)
18.   ~(p ∨ ~p)
19.   [~p ∨ (q & r)] & (q & ~r)
20.   [(p & r) ⊃ (q & s)] ≡ (r & s)
21.   {[(q ⊃ r) & (p ⊃ s)] & (q ∨ p)} ⊃ (r ∨ s)
22.   p ≡ ~~p
23.   [p & (q ∨ r)] ≡ [(p & q) ∨ (p & r)]
24.   p ≡ (r & s) ∨ p
25.   {(p & q) ≡ [(q & p) ∨ (s ≡ ~t)} ≡ (p & q) ∨ (~p & ~q)]

Logical Equivalence

8.8k

Logical Equivalence

To determine whether two statements are equivalent, join them with a biconditional and test its denial. If every branch is closed, the statements are logically equivalent.

8.8D EXERCISE: TRUTH TREES AND EQUIVALENCE
Use truth trees to test the following pairs of statements for equivalence:

1.   p ; ~~p
*2.   ~(p & q) ; (~p ∨ ~q)
3.   ~(p ∨ q) ; (~p & ~q)
4.   (p ∨ q) ; (q ∨ p)
5.   [p ∨ (q ∨ r)]; [(p ∨ q) ∨ r]
6.   (p ⊃ q) ; (~p ∨ q)
7.   [p & (q ∨ r)] ; [(p & q) ∨ (p & r)]
8.   (p ⊃ q) ; (~q ⊃ ~p)
9.   [(p & q) ⊃ r] ; [p & (q ⊃ r)]
*10. ~(p ⊃ q) ; (~p ⊃ ~q)
11.   (p ≡ q); [(p & q) ∨ (~p & ~q)]
12.   ~(p ∨ q) ; (~p ∨ ~q)
13.   [p ⊃ (q ⊃ r)] ; [(p ⊃ q) ⊃ r]
14.   (p ⊃ q) ; ~(p & ~q)
15.   [(p & q) ⊃ r] ; [p ⊃ (q ⊃ r)]
16.   ~~~~~p; ~~~~~~~p

As should be clear by now, the truth tree construction performs all the tasks that truth tables perform. In addition, we can modify trees for areas of formal logic that truth tables cannot handle, such as many-valued logics, modal logics, and predicate logic. Moreover, insight gained from the use of truth trees to decompose compound truth-functional propositions provides direction for the next topic in deductive reasoning.

8.9 NATURAL DEDUCTION

Truth tables and truth trees are valuable tools, but developing them is a time-consuming process. In some situations, such as listening to a debate or writing a paper, natural deduction may be preferable. **Natural deduction** is the process of mentally working through an argument in accordance with certain rules to see whether the argument is valid.[19]

The system of natural deduction set forth here is based on information presented earlier in connection with truth tables and truth trees. It is not the most elegant or powerful such system; it is simply a practical approach to using propositional logic in everyday reasoning.

We can identify two types of relational inferences: replacement and derivation. **Replacement** refers to replacing a statement with an equivalent one. That is, the rules for replacement allow one statement to be rewritten as another statement that is equivalent to it. In the formal presentation of these rules, the symbol "::" means "is interchangeable with." This operation is like defining a word by giving a synonym, as in "poverty" :: "destitution."

In a **derivation**, a new statement is derived from another set of statements. In the formal presentation of the rules for derivation, the symbol "⊢" means "implies" or "entails." Consider a situation in which a friend makes the following statements: (1) "If I get the job next week, my income will triple." (2) "If my income triples, I am going to buy a new car." These two statements together imply or entail the statement "if he gets the job next week, he will buy a new car."

8.9A REPLACEMENT RULES

Associativity. The first replacement rule is **associativity**. In the truth tree method, when a truth-functional statement of the type **P & (Q & R)** is unpacked, each conjunct is listed in a single path. The same path would result if the statement were (**P & Q**) & **R**. Moreover, if the connectives were ∨, the placement of the parentheses would still not affect the resulting branches. Therefore, by associativity, in each of the following pairs of statements, the left and right members can replace each other:

8.9a

P & (Q & R) :: (P & Q) & R
P ∨ (Q ∨ R) :: (P ∨ Q) ∨ R

Biconditionality. The **biconditionality** replacement rule simply says that (**P ⊃ Q**) & (**Q ⊃ P**) is equivalent to **P ≡ Q**. Furthermore, semantic tableaux equally support the two replacements listed underneath this rule.

8.9b

$$(P \supset Q) \& (Q \supset P) :: P \equiv Q$$
$$(P \& Q) \lor (\sim P \& \sim Q) :: P \equiv Q$$
$$(P \& \sim Q) \lor (\sim P \& Q) :: \sim (P \equiv Q)$$

Commutativity. The **commutativity** rule of replacement states that the order in which the same statements are placed around an & or a ∨ does not affect the decomposition of those connectives. Hence,

8.9c

$$P \& Q :: Q \& P$$
$$P \lor Q :: Q \lor P$$

DeMorgan's Rule. We may remember the fourth replacement rule from mathematics. It comes into play in decomposing two types of statements. In decomposing ∼(P & Q), we list the denial of each member of the conjunct at the end of a branch. Because branching represents alternatives, the decomposition of ∼(P & Q) could be read as "∼P or ∼Q." The second type of statement that illustrates this rule is ∼(P ∨ Q). Here, the denial of each member of the disjunction is placed in the same path, and the decomposition could be read as "∼P and ∼Q." This rule, known as **DeMorgan's rule**, provides the following equivalent patterns:

8.9d

$$\sim(P \& Q) :: \sim P \lor \sim Q$$
$$\sim(P \lor Q) :: \sim P \& \sim Q$$

Distributivity. The **distributivity** rule of replacement is supported by the semantic tableau deconstruction of statements like P & (Q ∨ R) and (P & Q) ∨ (P & R). In both cases, two paths result. We obtain the same results for P ∨ (Q & R) and (P ∨ Q) & (P ∨ R). Hence, the distributivity rule encompasses the following two constructions:

8.9e

$$P \& (Q \lor R) :: (P \& Q) \lor (P \& R)$$
$$P \lor (Q \& R) :: (P \lor Q) \& (P \lor R)$$

Double Negation. The rule of **double negation** was introduced in the discussion of truth tables and reinforced in that of tableaux. It is as follows:

8.9f

$$\sim\sim P :: P$$

Exportation. The rule of **exportation** says that $P \supset (Q \supset R)$ is equivalent to $(P \& Q) \supset R$. Truth trees for these statements both result in three separate paths, one containing $\sim P$, another $\sim Q$, and the third R. Hence,

8.9g

$$P \supset (Q \supset R) \; :: \; (P \& Q) \supset R$$

Implication. The eighth replacement rule is the rule of **implication**. When we decomposed $P \supset Q$ in a tableau, we listed the denial of the antecedent on one path and the consequent, as given, on the other. As indicated before, such branching illustrates alternatives; we understand it as indicating "or." Thus, $P \supset Q$ is equivalent to $\sim P \vee Q$. Decomposing $\sim(P \supset Q)$ results in listing a denial of its consequent in the same path as the antecedent. Therefore, $\sim(P \supset Q)$ is equivalent to $P \& \sim Q$.

8.9h

$$P \supset Q \; :: \; \sim P \vee Q$$
$$\sim(P \supset Q) \; :: \; P \& \sim Q$$

Transposition. When we tested pairs of statements for equivalence, we determined that $P \supset Q$ is equivalent to $\sim Q \supset \sim P$. This equivalence is known as **transposition**.

8.9i

$$P \supset Q \; :: \; \sim Q \supset \sim P$$

Following is a list of all the replacement rules we have discussed:

8.9j

Replacement Rules

Associativity:
    $P \& (Q \& R) \; :: \; (P \& Q) \& R$
    $P \vee (Q \vee R) \; :: \; (P \vee Q) \vee R$

Biconditionality:
    $(P \supset Q) \& (Q \supset P) \; :: \; P \equiv Q$
    $(P \& Q) \vee (\sim P \& \sim Q) \; :: \; P \equiv Q$
    $(P \& \sim Q) \vee (\sim P \& Q) \; :: \; \sim(P \equiv Q)$

Commutativity:
    $P \& Q \; :: \; Q \& P$
    $P \vee Q \; :: \; Q \vee P$

DeMorgan's Rule:
   ~(P & Q) :: ~P ∨ ~Q
   ~(P ∨ Q) :: ~P & ~Q

Distributivity:
   P & (Q ∨ R) :: (P & Q) ∨ (P & R)
   P ∨ (Q & R) :: (P ∨ Q) & (P ∨ R)

Double Negation:
   ~~P :: P

Exportation:
   P ⊃ (Q ⊃ R) :: (P & Q) ⊃ R

Implication:
   P ⊃ Q :: ~P ∨ Q
   ~(P ⊃ Q) :: P & ~Q

Transposition:
   P ⊃ Q :: ~Q ⊃ ~P

8.9A EXERCISE: NATURAL DEDUCTION AND REPLACEMENT RULES

Use the rules of replacement to rewrite each of the statements that follow. Cite the rule employed in each case. Note that more than one rule may be relevant.

   1.   p & q
   2.   p & (q & r)
   3.   p ≡ q
  *4.   ~[(p & q) ∨ (t ≡ s)]
   5.   (p & q) ⊃ (s ∨ ~t)
   6.   (t & q) ⊃ ~p
   7.    ~~~p
  *8.   (p ⊃ q) & [(p & q) ⊃ r]
   9.   (p & q) ∨ (~p & ~q)
  10.   ~(p & t) ∨ ~(s ⊃ r)
  11.   p ⊃ (q ⊃ r)
  12.   ~(p ∨ t) ⊃ ~(q & r)
 *13.   (p ≡ r) ⊃ [(s & t) ⊃ (~s ∨ ~r)]
  14.   (~p & q) ∨ (p & ~q)
  15.   [p ⊃ (t & r)] ∨ [(s ≡ q) & p]
  16.   (p ∨ q) & (p ∨ t)
  17.   [(q ∨ t) & s] ⊃ [(s ∨ w) ⊃ p]
  18.   p & (q & r)
  19.   ~~[q ∨ (s & t)]
  20.   (p & r) ∨ (~p & ~r)

8.9A-2 EXERCISE: NATURAL DEDUCTION AND ORDINARY LANGUAGE

Use the rules of replacement to rewrite each of the following sentences in an equivalent English form:

1. Neither Mary nor Jane attended class today.
2. If you pass critical reasoning, you will be prepared for my class next semester.
*3. It is not true that doing well on this assignment implies that you have done well all semester.
4. If you don't take next week's exam, then you won't pass the course.
5. You will take principles of biology next semester and human physiology the following semester, or you will take neither the biology course nor the course in physiology.

8.9B EXERCISE: DERIVATION RULES

When we tested arguments for validity, several common valid patterns of reasoning emerged. These patterns are highlighted in the rules of derivation.

Addition. The first derivation rule is based on the nature of a disjunction and is known as the rule of **addition**. Let **P** be a true statement. Then what else must be true? Because of the nature of a disjunction, if **P** is true, then the disjunction of **P** with any other statement must also be true. Hence,

8.9k

$$\mathbf{P} \, / \vdash \mathbf{P} \vee \mathbf{Q}$$

Biconditional Elimination. If $\mathbf{P} \equiv \mathbf{Q}$ is true and if either member of the biconditional is true, then the other member must also be true. Also, if either member of the biconditional is false, then the other member must be false as well.

8.9l

$$\mathbf{P} \equiv \mathbf{Q}, \mathbf{P} \, / \vdash \mathbf{Q}$$
$$\mathbf{P} \equiv \mathbf{Q}, \sim\!\mathbf{P} \, / \vdash \sim\!\mathbf{Q}$$

Conjunction. The rule of **conjunction** specifies that two or more statements that are assumed to be true may be connected by an ampersand. That is, if **P** is true and **Q** is true, then **P** & **Q** must also be true.

8.9m

$$\mathbf{P}, \mathbf{Q} \, / \vdash \mathbf{P} \, \& \, \mathbf{Q}$$

Constructive Dilemma. A fourth derivation rule is the **constructive dilemma**. If **P** ∨ **Q**, **P** ⊃ **S** and **Q** ⊃ **T** are each true, then so is **S** ∨ **T**.

8.9n

P ∨ Q, P ⊃ S, Q ⊃ T / ⊢ S ∨ T

Disjunctive Syllogism. The rule of **disjunctive syllogism** states that if **P** ∨ **Q** is true and if one member of the disjunction is false, then the remaining member of the disjunction is assumed to be true.

8.9o

P ∨ Q, ~P / ⊢ Q

Hypothetical Syllogism. The rule of **hypothetical syllogism** claims that if **P** implies **Q** and **Q** implies **R**, then **P** implies **R**.

8.9p

P ⊃ Q, Q ⊃ R / ⊢ P ⊃ R

Modus Ponens. In discussing conditional reasoning in chapter 7, we noted that affirming the antecedent is a valid pattern of reasoning. This claim is supported by both truth tables and semantic tableaux. As a rule of derivation, rule it is known as **modus ponens**.

8.9q

P ⊃ Q, P / ⊢ Q

We also discussed the validity of denying the consequent. As a derivation rule, this is known as **modus tollens**.

8.9r

P ⊃ Q, ~Q / ⊢ ~P

Simplification. If **P** & **Q** is true, both conjuncts of the conjunction must be true. The **simplification** rule allows for individual conjuncts to be derived.

8.9s

P & Q / ⊢ P

Following is a list of all the derivation rules we have discussed:

8.9t

Derivation Rules

Addition
  P / ⊢ P ∨ Q

Biconditional Elimination
  P ≡ Q, P / ⊢ Q
  P ≡ Q, ~P / ⊢ ~Q

Conjunction
  P, Q / ⊢ P & Q

Constructive Dilemma
  P ∨ Q, P ⊃ S, Q ⊃ T / ⊢ S ∨ T

Disjunctive Syllogism
  P ∨ Q, ~P / ⊢ Q

Hypothetical Syllogism
  P ⊃ Q, Q ⊃ R / ⊢ P ⊃ R

Modus Ponens
  P ⊃ Q, P / ⊢ Q

Modus Tollens
  P ⊃ Q, ~Q / ⊢ ~P

Simplification
  P & Q / ⊢ P

8.9C USING REPLACEMENT AND DERIVATION RULES TO TEST FOR VALIDITY

We can use the rules of replacement and derivation to test for the validity of an argument. To construct a natural-deduction proof, we list the premises of the argument on separate lines. Then we list the conclusion on the same line as the final premise, separating them by a slash (/), followed by the turnstile (⊢)—that is, the symbol for "implies" or "entails." For example,

8.9u

p ∨ q
~p
∴   q

| 1. | p ∨ q | given |
| 2. | ~p / ⊢ q | given |

Constructing the proof requires three columns: The first for the line number, the second for the work presented, and the third for the justification for that step. (The work presented below Argument 8.9u, in standard form, is the set-up for à natural-deduction proof.) We then show how, using the rules for natural deduction, we can obtain the conclusion, in this case q:

1.	p ∨ q	given
2.	~p / ⊢ q	given
3.	q	1,2; disjunctive syllogism

Our proof is complete, for we have shown that, by using just the rules of natural deduction, we can infer the conclusion from the premises. Remember, natural deduction can only show an argument to be valid (if it is). We cannot prove an invalid argument to be invalid using natural deduction.

A more complicated problem is handled in the same way:

8.9v

p
q & r
(q & p) ⊃ s
∴   s ∨ t

1.	p	given
2.	q & r	given
3.	(q & p) ⊃ s / ⊢ s ∨ t	given
4.	q	2; simplification
5.	q & p	1,4; conjunction
6.	s	3,5; modus ponens
7.	s ∨ t	6; addition

8.9C EXERCISE: NATURAL DEDUCTION AND JUSTIFICATION

Provide the missing justifications in each of the following proofs:

1.

1.	~p ∨ ~(r ∨ q)	given
2.	v ⊃ p	given
3.	s ∨ v	given
4.	~s	given
5.	~(r ∨ q) ⊃ u / ⊢ u	given
6.	v	_____
7.	p	_____
8.	~(r ∨ q)	_____
9.	u	_____

*2.

1.	(p ⊃ r) & (q ⊃ v)	given
2.	p ∨ q	given
3.	(r ⊃ q) & (v ⊃ t)	given
4.	~(q ∨ t) ∨ s / ⊢ s	given
5.	r ⊃ q	_____
6.	v ⊃ t	_____
7.	p ⊃ r	_____
8.	q ⊃ v	_____
9.	r ∨ v	_____
10.	q ∨ t	_____
11.	s	_____

3.

1.	(p & r) ⊃ q	given
2.	p ∨ r	given
3.	q ∨ r	given
4.	~(r ⊃ q) / ⊢ ~p ∨ r	given
5.	p ⊃ (r ⊃ q)	_____
6.	~p	_____
7.	r	_____
8.	~p ∨ r	_____

4.

1.	(p ⊃ r) & (q ⊃ v)	given
2.	p ∨ q	given
3.	~v & q	given
4.	~(~p ∨ ~r) / ⊢ v ∨ u	given
5.	~~p & ~~r	_____
6.	p & r	_____
7.	p	_____
8.	r	_____
9.	p ⊃ r	_____
10.	q ⊃ v	_____
11.	r ∨ v	_____
12.	q	_____
13.	v	_____
14.	v ∨ u	_____

5.

1.	~[(r ⊃ s) & (s ⊃ r)]	given
2.	(p & t) ⊃ (r ≡ s)	given
3.	[(s ⊃ r) ⊃ p] & p / ⊢ ~t ∨ r	given
4.	~(r ≡ s)	_____
5.	~(p & t)	_____
6.	~p ∨ ~t	_____
7.	p	_____
8.	~t	_____
9.	~t ∨ r	_____

6.

1.	p	given
2.	~r ∨ p	given
3.	q ⊃ (p ⊃ r)	given
4.	v ∨ q	given
5.	p ∨ (r & q)	given
6.	~v / ⊢ (p ≡ r) & (p & r)	given
7.	q	_____
8.	p ⊃ r	_____
9.	r ⊃ p	_____
10.	(p ⊃ r) & (r ⊃ p)	_____
11.	p ≡ r	_____
12.	r	_____
13.	p & r	_____
14.	(p ≡ r) & (p & r)	_____

Complete the following proofs as necessary, and provide the justifications:

*7.

1.	~p & q	given
2.	(r ⊃ p) & (s & t)	given
3.	r ∨ u	given
4.	~u ∨ v / ⊢ v	given
5.	u ⊃ v	_____
6.	r ⊃ p	_____
7.	v ∨ p	_____
8.	~v ⊃ p	_____
9.	_____	_____
10.	_____	_____

8.

1.	(p ⊃ q) & (r ⊃ s)	given
2.	(p ∨ r)	given
3.	(q ⊃ r) & (s ⊃ t)	given
4.	~(r ∨ t) ∨ u / ⊢ u	given
5.	p ⊃ q	_____
6.	r ⊃ s	_____
7.	q ⊃ r	_____
8.	_____	_____
9.	_____	_____
10.	_____	_____
11.	_____	_____
12.	_____	_____

9.

1.	(p ∨ q) & (p ∨ r)	given
2.	~(p ∨ q)	given
3.	r ⊃ s	given
4.	t / ⊢ t & s	given
5.	p ∨ (q & r)	_____

6.	~p & ~q	_____
7.	~p	_____
8.	_____	_____
9.	_____	_____
10.	_____	_____
11.	_____	_____

10.

1.	p	given
2.	(p & r) ⊃ s	given
3.	p ⊃ q / ⊢ q ∨ s	given
4.	p ⊃ (r ⊃ s)	
5.	_____	_____
6.	_____	_____
7.	_____	_____

Finish each of the following proofs (they can be done in different ways):

11.

1.	(p ∨ q) & (p ∨ r)	given
2.	~q ∨ ~r	given
3.	p ⊃ [~(t ∨ u) ∨ s]	given
4.	~(s ∨ t) / ⊢ ~u	given

Pepper...and Salt

"Evolution, maybe, but algebra is *not* just a theory!"

*12.

1.	$\sim p \vee r$	given
2.	$r \supset q$	given
3.	$\sim q / \vdash p \equiv q$	given

13.

1.	$p \supset q$	given
2.	$p \vee p$	given
3.	$p \supset s / \vdash \sim[\sim(p \vee p) \vee \sim(s \vee q)]$	given

14.

1.	$(p \supset q) \& (p \vee r)$	given
2.	$\sim r \vee s$	given
3.	$\sim(q \vee s) \vee t$	given
4.	$t \supset \sim(u \vee v) / \vdash \sim v$	given

15.

1.	$(\sim p \vee r) \& (p \vee s)$	given
2.	$(p \supset r) \supset (s \supset q)$	given
3.	$(r \vee q) \supset (t \vee u)$	given
4.	$\sim(\sim t \& \sim u) \supset v / \vdash v \& (\sim s \vee q)$	given

16.

1.	$\sim p$	given
2.	$s \supset r$	given
3.	$(\sim s \vee r) \supset t$	given
4.	$u \supset \sim t$	given
5.	$\sim u \supset v$	given
6.	$m \vee v$	given
7.	$v \supset w / \vdash w$	given

*17.

1.	$(s \vee p) \supset q$	given
2.	$(t \vee r) \supset u$	given
3.	$v \supset \sim(q \& u)$	given
4.	$s \& t / \vdash \sim v$	given

18.

1.	$\sim[\sim p \& (u \& q)] \vee \sim u$	given
2.	$(r \equiv v) \supset \sim(\sim t \vee \sim u)$	given
3.	$(p \& \sim q) \supset \sim(t \vee w)$	given
4.	$(s \vee w) \supset (r \equiv v)$	given
5.	$s / \vdash p \equiv q$	given

*19.

1.	$\sim(v \& \sim v) \supset \sim(w \supset v)$	given
2.	$(u \supset p_1) \vee (w \supset v)$	given
3.	$[u \vee (t \& q_1)] \vee v$	given
4.	$(u \supset p_1) \supset (t \supset x)$	given
5.	$\sim p \supset \sim(p_1 \vee x)$	given
6.	$v \equiv w / \vdash (\sim q_1 \supset u) \& p$	given

20.
  1. ~q   given
  2. p ≡ r   given
  3. ~(p & r) / ⊢ ~p ⊃ (q ⊃ ~r)   given

21.
  1. p ∨ ~q   given
  2. ~(q ⊃ r) ∨ r   given
  3. (q ⊃ p) ⊃ ~r / ⊢ q & ~r   given

22.
  1. (p ∨ q) ⊃ (r ∨ s)   given
  2. r ⊃ t   given
  3. s ⊃ u   given
  4. p / ⊢ t ∨ u   given

23.
  1. p ∨ (q & r)   given
  2. ~s ⊃ ~p   given
  3. s ⊃ t   given
  4. ~t / ⊢ q & r   given

24.
  1. p ∨ (q & r)   given
  2. ~(p ∨ q) / ⊢ q   given

25.
  1. ~[p & (q & ~r)]   given
  2. (q ⊃ r) ⊃ ~p / ⊢ ~p   given

8.9D REDUCTIO AD ABSURDUM

The truth tree illustrates another proof procedure used in natural deduction. When we construct a tree, we assume the premises and deny the conclusion. If this construction produces a contradiction in all paths, the argument has no counterexamples and hence is valid. This procedure illustrates our final rule of derivation. **Reductio ad absurdum** is the Latin phrase meaning "reduction to absurdity" and, as used here, involves making an assumption. The procedure presented entails assuming the denial of the conclusion. If a contradiction appears as a direct result of this assumption, the assumption must be wrong. This procedure is also known as **indirect proof**. The derivation rule can be formulated as follows:

8.9w

assume **P, P ⊃ Q, ~Q / ⊢ ~P**

Whenever we make an assumption, we can apply the reductio ad absurdum procedure. For example, if a disjunct appears in a line of proof, one member of that disjunct could be assumed. If a contradiction appears within the assumption, the denial of the assumption is true. Hence, 8.9s can be expanded to include the following:

8.9x

P ∨ **Q**, assume **P**, ~**P** / ⊢ ~**P**

The introduction of assumptions requires two additional rules. First, whenever we introduce an assumption, it must be set apart from the rest of the proof. Two types of marking are used: (1) A series of horizontal dashes (the opening) is placed immediately before the assumption. (2) A line of reasoning that involves an assumption is followed by a solid line (the closing), A completed assumption must have both an opening and a closing, resulting in a pair of **assumption bars**. Any statement located outside a pair of assumption bars may be brought into an assumption set by means of the **reiteration rule**, which simply allows us to restate any statement we already know to be true.

As an example of proof by reductio ad absurdum, consider the following argument:

8.9y

p ∨ q
~p
∴   q

The proof procedure for this argument requires that the premises and the conclusion be listed in the following manner:

1.   p ∨ q   given
2.   ~p / ⊢ q   given

Next, the denial of the conclusion is assumed, resulting in the following steps:

1.   p ∨ q   given
2.   ~p / ⊢ q   given
----
3.   ~q   assume denial of conclusion

Notice that a dashed line is placed between lines 2 and 3 to indicate the opening of an assumption. Moreover, we place a justification to the right of each line. Line 1 will now be reiterated or restated within the scope of the assumption to complete the proof as follows:

1.   p ∨ q   given
2.   ~p / ⊢g   given
----
3.   ~q   assume denial of conclusion
4.   p ∨ q   1; reiteration
5.   p   3,4; disjunctive syllogism
6.   ~p   2; reiteration
7.   q   3–6; reductio ad absurdum

Other proofs may involve more than one assumption and may be more complicated. Following is an example:

8.9z

$$\sim[(p \& q) \equiv (r \& s)]$$
$$\underline{p \equiv r}$$
$$\therefore \quad \sim(q \equiv s)$$

1.	$\sim[(p \& q) \equiv (r \& s)]$	given
2.	$p \equiv r / \vdash \sim(q \equiv s)$	given

3.	$\sim\sim(q \equiv s)$	assume denial of conclusion
4.	$q \equiv s$	3; double negation
5.	$\sim[(p \& q) \equiv (r \& s)]$	1; reiteration
6.	$[(p \& q) \& \sim(r \& s)] \lor [\sim(p \& q) \& (r \& s)]$	5; implication
-------------------------		
7.	$(p \& q) \& \sim(r \& s)$	assumption
8.	$p \& q$	7; simplification
9.	p	8; simplification
10.	$p \equiv r$	2; reiteration
11.	r	9,10; biconditional elimination
12.	$\sim(r \& s)$	7; simplification
13.	$\sim r \lor \sim s$	12; DeMorgan's rule
14.	$\sim s$	11,13; disjunctive syllogism
15.	$q \equiv s$	4; reiteration
16.	$\sim q$	14,15; biconditional elimination
17.	$\underline{q}$	8; simplification
18.	$\sim(p \& q) \& (r \& s)$	6,7–17; disjunctive syllogism
19.	$r \& s$	18; simplification
20.	s	19; simplification
21.	$q \equiv s$	4; reiteration
22.	q	20,21; biconditional elimination
23.	$\sim(p \& q)$	18; simplification
24.	$\sim p \lor \sim q$	23; DeMorgan's rule
25.	$\sim p$	22,24; disjunctive syllogism
26.	$p \equiv r$	2; reiteration
27.	$\sim r$	25,26; biconditional elimination
28.	$\underline{r}$	19; simplification
29.	$\sim(q \equiv s)$	3–28; reductio ad absurdum

8.9D EXERCISE: NATURAL DEDUCTION AND REDUCTIO AD ABSURDUM

Finish each of the following proofs:

1.

1.	$(p \supset p) \supset q$	given
2.	$(q \lor r) \supset s / \vdash s$	given
-------------------------		

 3.   ~s   assume
 4.   (q ∨ r) ⊃ s   _____
 5.   ~(q ∨ r)   _____
 6.   ~q & ~r   _____
 7.   _____   6; simplification
 8.   _____   1; reiteration
 9.   ~(p ⊃ p)   _____
 10.   _____   9; implication
 11.   _____   _____
 12.   _____   _____
 13.   s   3–12; reductio ad absurdum

2.

 1.   t ⊃ [(~r ⊃ (p & q)]   given
 2.   (t ⊃ r) ⊃ (p & q) / ⊢ p & q   given
 ----
 3.   ~(p & q)   assume
 4.   (t ⊃ r) ⊃ (p & q)   2; reiteration
 5.   _____   _____
 6.   t & ~r   _____
 7.   _____   _____
 8.   t ⊃ [(~r ⊃ (p & q)]   _____
 9.   ~r ⊃ (p & q)   _____
 10.   _____   _____
 11.   p & q   9, 10; modus ponens
 12.   p & q   3–11; reductio ad absurdum

3.

 1.   p ⊃ q   given
 2.   (q ⊃ r) & p / ⊢ q ⊃ (r ⊃ p)   given
 ----
 3.   ~[q ⊃ (r ⊃ p)]   assume
 4.   _____   3; implication
 5.   _____   4; simplification
 6.   _____   _____
 7.   ~p   6; simplification
 8.   _____   2; reiteration
 9.   p   8; simplification
 10.   q ⊃ (r ⊃ p)   3–9; reductio ad absurdum

4.

 1.   p ∨ (s & r)   given
 2.   ~p ⊃ (r ⊃ q)   given
 3.   q ⊃ p / p   given
 ----
 4.   ~p   assume
 5.   p ∨ (s & r)   _____
 6.   s & r   _____
 7.   ~p ⊃ (r ⊃ q)   _____

    8.   r ⊃ q   _____

    9.   r   _____

   10.   q   _____

   11.   q ⊃ p   _____

   12.   p   _____

   13.   p   _____

5.

1.	(r & s) ⊃ p	given
2.	~(r ∨ p) ∨ (p & ~r) / ⊢ ~(r & s)	given

3.   r & s   assume

4.   _____   3; simplification

5.   _____   4; addition

6.   _____   2; reiteration

7.   _____   5,6; disjunctive syllogism

8.   _____   7; simplification

9.   _____   4–8; reductio ad absurdum

6.

1.	p ⊃ (q ⊃ r)	given
2.	~r	given
3.	(~p ∨ ~q) ⊃ s	given
4.	s ⊃ ~t / ⊢ ~t	given

5.   t   assume

7.

1.	s ∨ (q & p)	given
2.	s ⊃ p / ⊢ p	given

3.   ~p   assume

*8.

1.	(t ∨ q) ⊃ (u & r)	given
2.	(r ∨ p) ⊃ s	given
3.	t ∨ p /20⊢ s	given

4.   ~s   assume

9.

1.	(p & q) ∨ (s & r)	given
2.	(p & q) ⊃ r / ⊢ r	given

3.   ~r   assume

*10.

1.	~p ⊃ ~(q & ~r)	given
2.	(q & ~r) ∨ r / ⊢ ~r ⊃ p	given

3.   ~(~r ⊃ p)   assume

8.9E CONDITIONAL PROOFS

When we use natural deduction to prove the validity of an argument, several strategies or tools are available to us. We can use the replacement rules to rewrite some statements. The rules of derivation enable us to use certain combinations of statements to derive another statement. We can assume a statement, and if this statement produces a contradiction when it is combined with already given statements, then our assumed statement is false and its opposite is true. This strategy is known as reductio ad absurdum, or indirect proof.

In this section, we focus on another strategy that can be used in natural deduction. In a **conditional proof**, we assume a statement, and if the assumption leads to another statement, then we are justified in claiming that the assumed statement implies the second statement. This strategy is extremely helpful if our conclusion is a conditional statement or if, within a proof, we need a conditional statement to advance further. To illustrate the strategy, we begin with an obviously valid argument and pretend that we do not have the rule of hypothetical syllogism.

8.9aa

1.	$p \supset q$	given
2.	$q \supset r / \vdash p \supset r$	given

Since our conclusion is a conditional, we start by assuming its antecedent, p:

3.	p	assume
4.	$p \supset q$	1; reiteration
5.	q	3,4; modus ponens
6.	$q \supset r$	2; reiteration
7.	r	5,6; modus ponens

Next, we close the line of reasoning that began with the assumption and claim that p implies r:

_____

8.	$p \supset r$	3–7; conditional proof

Consider the following proofs:

8.9bb

1.	(p & q) $\supset$ (r & s) / $\vdash$ (p & q) $\supset$ [(p & q) & (r & s)]	

2.	p & q	assume
3.	(p & q) $\supset$ (r & s)	1; reiteration

4.	(r & s)	2,3; modus ponens
5.	(p & q) & (r & s)	3,4; conjunction
6.	(p & q) ⊃ [(p & q) & (r & s)]	2–5; conditional proof

and

1.	(p ∨ q) ⊃ [[(r & s) ∨ t] ⊃ u]	given
2.	q & ~p	given
3.	p & ~q	given
4.	[(s ⊃ u) ⊃ ~w] ⊃ q / ⊢ r ⊃ w	given
5.	r	assume
6.	p & ~q	3; reiteration
7.	p	6; simplification
8.	p ∨ q	7; addition
9.	(p ∨ q) ⊃ [[(r & s) ∨ t] ⊃ u]	1; reiteration
10.	[[(r & s) ∨ t] ⊃ u]	8,9; modus ponens
11.	~q	6; simplification
12.	[(s ⊃ u) ⊃ ~w] ⊃ q	4; reiteration
13.	~[(s ⊃ u) ⊃ ~w]	11, 12; modus tollens
14.	(s ⊃ u) & ~~w	13; implication
15.	~~w	14; implication
16.	w	15; double negation
17.	r ⊃ w	5–16; conditional proof

8.9E EXERCISE: NATURAL DEDUCTION AND CONDITIONAL PROOFS

Finish each of the following conditional proofs:

1.

1.	~(~p & ~r)	given
2.	q ⊃ (p ≡ r) / ⊢ q ⊃ r	given
3.	q	assume
4.	q ⊃ (p ≡ r)	_____
5.	p ≡ r	_____
6.	(p & r) ∨ (~p & ~r)	_____
7.	~(~p & ~r)	_____
8.	p & r	_____
9.	r	_____
10.	q ⊃ r	_____

2.

| 1. | p ⊃ (q & r) / ⊢ (s ⊃ p) ⊃ (s ⊃ r) | given |
| 2. | s ⊃ p | assume |

3. $p \supset (q \& r)$ _____
4. $s \supset (q \& r)$ _____

----

5. s assume
6. $s \supset (q \& r)$ _____
7. $q \& r$ _____
8. r _____
9. $s \supset r$ _____
10. $(s \supset p) \supset (s \supset r)$ _____

3.

1. $p \equiv q$ given
2. r given
3. $s \supset (p \& r) / \vdash s \supset (r \& q)$ given

----

4. s assume
5.   _____   3; reiteration
6.   _____   4,5; modus ponens
7.   _____   6; simplification
8.   _____   1; reiteration
9.   _____   7,8; equivalence
10. _____   6; simplification
11. $r \& q$ 9,10; conjunction
12. $s \supset (r \& q)$ 4–11; conditional proof

4.

1. $(p \lor q) \lor s$ given
2. $(s \supset r) \& \sim p$ given
3. $\sim(p \& s) / \vdash p \supset r$ given

----

4. p assume
5.   _____   1; reiteration
6. $p \lor (q \lor s)$ _____
7. $(s \supset r) \& \sim p$ _____
8.   _____
9. $q \lor s$ _____
10. _____   7; simplification
11. $p \lor r$ _____
12. $r \lor p$
13. _____   12; implication
14. _____   8,13; modus tollens
15. r 14; double negation
16. $p \supset r$ _____

5.

1. $\sim(r \& p) \supset [\sim(u \lor t) \lor \sim(q \lor t)]$ given
2. $s \lor (u \& q)$ given
3. $p \supset \sim(u \& q)$ given
4. $\sim(r \& p) \lor \sim s / \vdash (u \lor t) \supset \sim(q \lor t)$ given

----

5.	u ∨ t	assume

6.	~s	assume
7.	s ∨ (u & q)	_____
8.	_____	_____
9.	p ⊃ ~(u & q)	_____
10.	~p	_____
11.	~r ∨ ~p	_____
12.	_____	11; DeMorgan's rule
13.	~(r & p) ⊃ [~(u ∨ t) ∨ ~(q ∨ t)]	_____
14.	~(u ∨ t) ∨ ~(q ∨ t)	_____
15.	u	8; simplification
16.	u ∨ t	_____
17.	~(q ∨ t)	_____
18.	_____	17; DeMorgan's rule
19.	_____	18; simplification
20.	q	_____
21.	s	_____
22.	~(r & p) ∨ ~s	_____
23.	_____	_____
24.	_____	1; reiteration
25.	_____	_____
26.	_____	5; reiteration
27.	~(q ∨ t)	_____
28.	_____	_____

6.

1.	r ⊃ (p ⊃ t)	given
2.	~t & p	given
3.	r ⊃ (p ⊃ ~q) / ⊢ r ⊃ (~p & ~q)	given

4.	r	assume

*7.

1.	[(p ∨ r) & (s & ~q)] ⊃ t	given
2.	~(u & v) ⊃ ~(s ⊃ q)	given
3.	(s & ~q) ⊃ (~p ⊃ r)	given
4.	~t ∨ q / ⊢ ~v ⊃ t	given

8.

1.	[(p ∨ r) ⊃ (~r ∨ s)] & ~t	given
2.	t ∨ (p ⊃ q)	given
3.	[(q ⊃ s) ⊃ ~(p ⊃ q)] ∨ ~(q ∨ s)	given
4.	~(q ⊃ s) ⊃ u / ⊢ (p ∨ r) ⊃ u	given

*9.

1.	(p ∨ q) ⊃ (r & s)	given
2.	(s ∨ t) ⊃ (u & v)	given
3.	q₁ ≡ p₁ / ⊢ (p ⊃ u) & (~q₁ ∨ p₁)	given

*10.

  1. (q ⊃ p) & s   given
  2. (q & p) ⊃ r   given
  3. (t & r) ⊃ ~u / ⊢ q ⊃ (t ⊃ ~u)   given

8.9F EXERCISE: NATURAL DEDUCTION AND VALIDITY

Show that each of the arguments that follow is valid. Usually, more than one proof is possible. Try to mix your proof strategies and not use only one approach.

1. p ⊃ q
    p
    ∴   q

2. ~(p ∨ q)
    ~p
    ∴   ~q

3. p & q
    ~p
    ∴   ~q

4. ~(p ≡ q)
    p
    ∴   ~q

5. ~(p ⊃ q)
    p
    ∴   ~q

*6. ~(p ⊃ t) & q
     ~(q ∨ p) ⊃ t
     ~(p & q) ∨ s
     ∴   ~t

7. p ≡ q
    p
    ∴   q

8. (p ⊃ q) & (r ⊃ s)
    p ∨ r
    ∴   q ∨ s

9. ~q ⊃ r
    ~p ⊃ t
    t ⊃ ~r
    ∴   q ∨ p

10. p ⊃ (q ∨ r)
    (q ∨ r) ⊃ ~p
    ∴   ~p

11. (p & q) ⊃ r
    (r ∨ s) ⊃ t
    ∴   (p & q) ⊃ t

12. (p ⊃ q) & [(p & q) ⊃ r]
    p ⊃ (r ⊃ s)
    ∴   p ⊃ s

*13. ~[(p & q) ≡ (r & s)]
     p ≡ r
     ∴   ~(q ≡ s)

14. (p ⊃ q) & (r ∨ p)
    (r ⊃ p) & (r ⊃ ~p)
    ∴   ~(p & ~q)

15. ~[(p ⊃ q) & (q ≡ s)] & t
    t ≡ r
    ∴   (r ∨ p) ∨ [(p ⊃ s) & (s ⊃ q)]

16. p ⊃ q
    s ∨ ~q
    ~s
    ∴   ~p

17. p ⊃ q
    p
    ∴   q

18. [p ⊃ (p & q)] & [q ⊃ (q & p)]
    ∴   p ⊃ (p & q)

19. $p \supset (q \supset {\sim}p)$
∴ $q \supset {\sim}p$

20. $(p \& q) \supset (r \& s)$
∴ $(p \& q) \supset [(p \& q) \& (r \& s)]$

21. $(p \lor q) \supset r$
$r \supset (p \& q)$
∴ $(p \lor q) \supset (p \& q)$

22. $p \lor q \lor s$
$p \supset r$
$q \supset t$
$s \supset u$
${\sim}p \& {\sim}q$
∴ u

23. $(p \lor q) \supset (p \& q)$
${\sim}(p \& q)$
∴ ${\sim}(p \lor q)$

24. $(p \lor q) \supset (p \& q)$
${\sim}(p \lor q)$
∴ ${\sim}(p \& q)$

25. $p \lor (q \& {\sim}q)$
p
∴ ${\sim}(p \& {\sim}p)$

26. $p \supset q$
$q \supset r$
$s \supset t$
$p \lor s$
∴ $r \lor t$

27. $p \equiv q$
${\sim}p$
∴ ${\sim}q$

*28. $(p \lor q) \supset r$
$r \supset (p \& q)$
∴ $(p \& q) \supset (p \lor q)$

29. $(p \lor q) \supset {\sim}(r \& {\sim}s)$
${\sim}{\sim}(r \& {\sim}s)$
∴ ${\sim}(p \lor q)$

30. $[p \supset (q \& r)] \& [s \supset (p \& t)]$
$p \lor s$
∴ $(q \& r) \lor (p \& t)$

31. $(p \equiv q) \lor [(s \& t) \lor (s \& r)]$
${\sim}(p \equiv q)$
∴ $(s \& t) \lor (s \& r)$

32. $(p \lor q) \supset {\sim}(r \lor s)$
$q \& {\sim}u$
${\sim}t \supset u$
∴ ${\sim}r \& {\sim}s$

33. ${\sim}(p \& {\sim}q) \supset (p \supset q)$
$(p \equiv q) \supset {\sim}(p \& {\sim}q)$
∴ $(p \equiv q) \supset (p \supset q)$

34. ${\sim}s$
$p \supset {\sim}q$
${\sim}p \supset (r \supset {\sim}q)$
$({\sim}s \lor {\sim}r) \supset {\sim}{\sim}q$
∴ ${\sim}r$

35. ${\sim}p$
∴ $p \supset q$

36. $p \lor (q \& r)$
∴ $(p \lor q) \& (p \lor r)$

37. $p \supset (p \& r)$
∴ $(p \supset q) \& (p \supset r)$

*38. $p \equiv q$
$q \equiv r$
∴ $[(p \& q) \& {\sim}r] \lor [({\sim}p \& q) \& r]$

39. $(p \lor q) \supset r$
$(r \lor q) \supset [p \supset (s \equiv t)]$
$p \& q$
∴ $s \equiv t$

40. $({\sim}p \lor q) \supset [p \lor (q \& r)]$
${\sim}p$
∴ $(q \& r)$

41. $(p \lor q) \supset t$
     $\sim t \,\&\, \sim p$
     $\overline{\therefore \qquad \sim(p \lor q)}$

42. $p \equiv (q \equiv r)$
     $\overline{\therefore \qquad (p \equiv q) \equiv r}$

43. $\{p \,\&\, [r \supset (q \lor p)]\}$
     $\sim r \,\&\, \sim q$
     $\overline{\therefore \qquad p}$

44. $p \supset q$
     $q \supset r$
     $r \supset s$
     $\overline{\therefore \qquad p \supset s}$

45. $p \lor (\sim\sim r \,\&\, \sim\sim q)$
     $p \supset q$
     $s \supset \sim r$
     $\sim(p \,\&\, q)$
     $\overline{\therefore \qquad \sim s \lor \sim q}$

46. $[p \supset (q \,\&\, \sim r)] \,\&\, [q \supset (p \supset r)]$
     $(p \,\&\, q) \,\&\, \sim s$
     $s \equiv \sim(q \,\&\, \sim r)$
     $s \lor \sim s$
     $\overline{\therefore \qquad r \,\&\, \sim s}$

47. $(p \lor q) \supset [[(r \,\&\, s) \lor t] \supset u]$
     $q \,\&\, \sim p$
     $p \,\&\, \sim q$
     $[(s \supset u) \supset \sim w] \supset q$
     $\overline{\therefore \qquad r \supset w}$

8.9G NATURAL DEDUCTION AND WRITING

Natural deduction can be used to facilitate writing in natural languages. First, we construct a topic sentence that is a well-formed formula in formal language. Next, using the rules of natural deduction, we work backward to a set of premises.

Consider the following example:

8.9cc

Topic sentence: While some types of literature are detrimental and possibly should not be promoted, censorship of any type of literature should not be tolerated.

This topic sentence has two basic parts: (1) Some types of literature are detrimental and possibly should not be promoted, and (2) censorship of any type of literature should not be tolerated. One strategy would be to develop both points separately and then bring them together in the topic sentence by conjunction. The topic sentence could then be written as $[(p \,\&\, \sim q) \,\&\, \sim r]$, where p = some types of literature are detrimental, q = all literature should be promoted, and r = censorship should be tolerated.

$\qquad$ $p \,\&\, \sim q$ might be developed by showing that some types of literature are detrimental and that not all literature should be promoted. If each of these statements can be supported, we can deduce $p \,\&\, \sim q$ by conjunction. Using inductive reasoning, we might develop arguments for each statement. The formula $\sim r$ could be derived from "censorship should be tolerated if and only if one can easily tell the difference between good and bad literature, but the distinction is not always clear." Again, induction will be used to support this claim. From the structure provided by deduction and supported by inductive reasoning, we might write the following paragraph:

8.9dd

While some types of literature are detrimental and possibly should not be promoted, censorship of any type of literature should not be tolerated. Psychological and sociological evidence suggests that some types of literature promote violent responses from readers. Furthermore, any literature that promotes such responses is detrimental and possibly should not be promoted. However, censorship of any type of literature can be permitted if and only if there is always a clear distinction between good and bad literature. Unfortunately, that distinction does not always exist, for several works, such as James Joyce's *Ulysses*, have been judged differently at different times. In spite of some literary works being detrimental and not worthy of our support, censorship cannot be tolerated.

8.9H EXERCISE: USING NATURAL DEDUCTION TO WRITE

Write a five-paragraph essay supporting a claim of your choice. Make sure that your process of deductive reasoning is evident.

CHAPTER NINE

Categorical and Predicate Logics

While propositional logic provides greater clarity and precision than enumerative induction, it is not always adequate. Consider the sentence "Snoopers are dogs." If we translated this sentence into propositional logic, we might simply rewrite it as p. For much reasoning—for example,

> If cows jump over the moon, then snoopers are dogs.
> Cows do jump over the moon.
> Therefore, snoopers are dogs.

such a translation is adequate. However, the sentence "Snoopers are dogs" can be more complex than p indicates. The sentence posits a relationship between two classes of things—the class of snoopers and the class of dogs—and sometimes this relationship may be crucial. Moreover, once we see this relationship, we might note that the sentence is ambiguous: Does it mean "All snoopers are dogs" or "Some snoopers are dogs"?

This chapter has two main purposes, the first of which lays the foundation for the second. First we introduce the logic of the relational terms *all*, *no*, and *some*. In this introduction, we do not develop a complete categorical logic (the logic that deals with these terms). Rather, we present a basic introduction that will enable us to make appropriate inferences from statements such as "All drug dealers are criminals" or "Some world leaders are not worthy of their positions." This basis provides a foundation for extending propositional logic to deal with these relational terms. The extension is known as *predicate logic*, and presenting it is the primary purpose of this chapter.

9.1 INTRODUCTION TO CATEGORICAL LOGIC

Categorical logic is a form of deductive logic that deals with the relational terms *all*, *no*, and *some*. It is a form of reasoning that places things in categories or classes and then stands them in certain relationships to other categories or classes. Consider the following examples:

"WHAT IT IS IS JUST A GROUP OF VENN DIAGRAMS."

© 1998 by Sidney Harris

1. All students are intelligent persons.
2. No administrators are capable of being trusted.
3. Some professors are narrow minded.
4. Some students will not pass their course in critical reasoning.

In each of these sentences, there is a **subject term** and a **predicate term**. In the first one, the subject term is "students" and the predicate term is "intelligent persons." We have two classes of things: students and persons who are intelligent. Categorical reasoning deals with the relationship between these two classes. In the first sentence, all members of the subject class are members of the predicate class. (We are not told how many members of the predicate class are members of the subject class.) The second sentence claims that no members of the subject class are members of the predicate class. Both sentences are **universal statements**, since either all or none of the members of the subject class are members of the predicate class.

Sentences 3 and 4 are **particular statements**. They claim that some—that is, at least one—members of the subject class are or are not members of the predicate class.

Another distinction is between **negative statements** and **affirmative statements**. Sentences 2 and 4 are negative statements, whereas sentences 1 and 3 are affirmative statements. All of the sentences are **categorical statements**, because they assert that all or some of the class of things identified by the subject term are included in or excluded from the class of things identified by the predicate term.

Frequently, **Venn diagrams** are used to make the relationship between subject class and predicate class more visual. A Venn diagram may simply involve two overlapping circles:

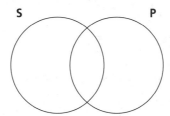

The first circle, labeled 'S', represents the subject class, and the second circle, labeled 'P', represents the predicate class. Notice that these two overlapping circles present three areas: an area containing just **S**, an area containing both **S** and **P**, and an area containing just **P**. In the case of a universal statement, such as "All students enjoy Venn diagrams," we will shade the area of just **S**, to indicate that that area represents an empty set:

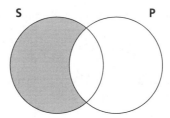

This diagram tells us that all members of the class **S** (students) are members of the class **P** (things that enjoy Venn diagrams). What does the following diagram tell us?

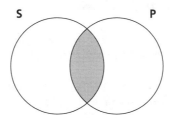

Notice that the shaded area, the empty set, is in the overlapping section. It tell us that no member of the class **S** is a member of the class **P**, or "No students enjoy Venn diagrams."

Diagraming particular statements does not involve shading an area, but rather, requires placing an '**x**' in the appropriate area. The '**x**' designates a class that contains at least one member. Consider the sentence "Some students like Venn diagrams." This sentence asserts that at least one member of the subject class is a member of the predicate class.

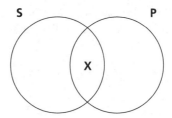

If the sentence were "Some students do not like Venn diagrams," then our diagram would be

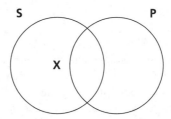

This depiction tells us that at least one student is not a member of the class that likes Venn diagrams.

The distinctions just discussed result in four types of categorical statements:

1. A **universal affirmative (UA)** statement asserts that all members of the subject class are included in the predicate class.

   All of our high school seniors are going to college.
   Everyone in the room felt the earthquake.

2. A **universal negative (UN)** statement asserts that all members of the subject class are excluded from the predicate class.

   No foreign films are shown at the local theater.
   None of the presidential candidates addressed the issues.

3. A **particular affirmative (PA)** statement asserts that at least one member of the subject class is included in the predicate class.

   Some brands of coffee are packaged in red cans.
   Most students at this college live at home with their parents.

4. A **particular negative (PN)** statement asserts that at least one member of the subject class is excluded from the predicate class.

   Some sentences are not complex sentences.
   Some students are not married students.

In a categorical statement, a term is **distributed** if the statement claims something about all the members of the class represented by the term. In a universal statement, the statement claims something about all members of its subject class. For example, in the statement "All of our high school seniors are going to college," we are told something about all of our high school seniors. Thus, "our high school seniors" is distributed. In a negative statement, the statement claims something about all members of its predicate class. For example, in "Some vegetarians will not eat cheese" we are told something about all non–cheese eaters. Hence "cheese eaters" is distributed.

Since whether terms are distributed is critical to the analysis of a categorical argument, we must formalize the process of identifying when they are. The test used to identify a term that is distributed is performed on each sentence of the argument and involves two simple steps. First, if the sentence is a universal statement, it distributes its subject term. Second, if the sentence is a negative statement, it distributes its predicate term. We will identify distributed terms by placing an asterisk after them, as shown in the following examples:

9.1a

All S* are P*.
No S* are P*.
Some S are P.
Some S are not P*.

9.1A EXERCISE: CATEGORICAL STATEMENTS

Examine each of the statements that follow, and rewrite it, using S to stand for the subject term and P for the predicate term. Identify the term or terms that are distributed by the statement. Indicate whether the statement is a UA, UN, PA, or PN. Finally, draw a Venn diagram for each of the statements.

*1. All college freshmen take English composition.
2. Some students who take English composition are not in world literature.
3. No students in English composition write a perfect essay.
4. No college freshmen write a perfect essay.
5. All students in world literature read Huxley's *Brave New World*.
6. Some students prefer IBM compatibles.
7. Some students who prefer IBM compatibles are using WordPerfect.
8. Some who use WordPerfect knows what happens when they strike Cntl, F7.
9. No students use slide rulers in calculus today.
10. All computer science students must take symbolic logic.

Nonstandard Categorical Statements

Categorical statements are often written in forms that are not obviously related to one of the four basic types. Consider "No race cars are not safe" or "All nonsafe cars are nonrace cars." The following chart provides equivalent translations for nonstandard types of statement.[20]

9.1b

No S are non-P. :: All S are P.
All S are non-P. :: No S are P.
No P are S. :: No S are P.
Some P are S. :: Some S are P.
All non-P are non-S. :: All S are P.
Some non-P are not non-S. :: Some S are not P.

9.1B EXERCISE: NONSTANDARD CATEGORICAL STATEMENTS

Translate each of the following nonstandard categorical statements into an equivalent English statement:

    *1.   All nonseniors are expected not to attend the lecture.

    2.   All of tonight's speakers are noncitizens.

    *3.   Some nonpolitical types are not nonpacifists.

    4.   No administrators are nonfaculty.

    5.   Some classical music was barroom music.

    6.   No student fails underwater basket weaving.

Categorical Syllogisms

The major form of argumentation using categorical reasoning is the categorical syllogism. A **categorical syllogism** is an argument that has only two premises and consists entirely of categorical statements. An example is

9.1c

All cold things are blue.
All tall things are cold.
∴   All tall things are blue.

In this example, we notice several characteristics of categorical syllogisms. First, three classes or categories of things are identified in the argument: cold things, blue things, and tall things. While each sentence contains subject and predicate terms, the argument as a whole contains three terms. This is true of any categorical syllogism. There will always be the **subject term of the argument**, the **predicate term of the argument**, and the **middle term of the argument**.

    To identify these terms, we examine the conclusion of the argument. Whatever is the subject term in the conclusion will be the subject term of the argument; whatever is the predicate term in the conclusion will be the predicate term of the argument. The middle term *never* appears in the conclusion, and *always* appears in both premises. Thus, in the previous example, "tall things" is the subject term of the argument and "blue things" is the predicate term; "cold things" is the middle term.

We also notice that the subject term of the argument occurs in exactly one of the premises and the predicate term also occurs in exactly one of the premises. The subject term of the argument *never* appears in the same premise as the predicate term.

There are several methods for testing the validity of a categorical argument. Here, we consider only testing by rules. This approach is efficient and accurate. Moreover, once we become proficient with the rules, the test for validity can be performed mentally and does not require drawing diagrams. (This is especially important in taking standardized tests that are timed.)

9.2 TESTING BY RULES

The first step in analyzing a categorical syllogism is to rewrite the argument in such a way as to highlight the various terms. We replace the English phrases that identify the categories of things discussed with either S, P, or M, depending on whether the phrase identifies the subject, the predicate, or the middle term. Thus, 9.1c would look like this:

9.2a

All M are P.
All S are M.
∴   All S are P.

When we apply the distribution rules to this argument, the result is as follows:

9.2b

All M* are P.
All S* are M.
∴   All S* are P.

The third step is to compare the argument with the following criteria that must be satisfied by a valid categorical syllogism:

1. The middle term must be distributed at least once.
2. These must be the same number of negatives in the premises as in the conclusion.
3. If a term is distributed in the conclusion, it must be distributed in the premises.
4. If the conclusion is particular, exactly one of the premises must also be particular.
5. If the conclusion is universal, both premises must be universal.

If the argument meets all five of these criteria, it is valid. If it violates any of them, it is invalid. Since 9.1c satisfies all of the criteria, it is valid.

9.2A EXERCISE: CATEGORICAL ARGUMENTS

Test the following categorical arguments for validity:

*1.   Since no professors attended the party and all of the students did attend, it is safe to conclude that no students are professors.

2.   Some sports cars are not American made, for no Italian cars are American made and all Italian cars are sports cars.

*3.   Since no gillygongs are visible, we can conclude that no dogs are gillygongs for all dogs are visible.

4.   Some students do not take the LSAT, for no one who takes the LSAT fails, but some students do fail.

5.   Since all computers are helpful and some typewriters are not helpful, no typewriters are computers.

6.   No students at DBU are heavy drinkers, for some heavy drinkers are teetotalers and some students at DBU are teetotalers.

7.   Since all homes in Texas are air conditioned and some homes in Indiana are not air conditioned, some homes in Texas are not homes in Indiana.

8.   All players on our basketball team are over 6 feet tall. No baseball player is over 6 feet tall. Hence, no baseball player plays on our basketball team.

9.   Some students are not female, but some males are not students; thus, some males are not females.

10.   All those who do well in categorical reasoning will enjoy reading Aristotle. No contemporary logician enjoys reading Aristotle. Hence, no contemporary logician will do well in categorical reasoning.

9.2B EXERCISE: CATEGORICAL ARGUMENTS

In each of the arguments that follow, either the conclusion is omitted or a premise is missing. Supply the missing component, and then show that the argument is valid.

1.   All bad things are unpleasant. No fun things are unpleasant.

*2.   Some fun things are dangerous. Some fun things are free.

3.   Some moral issues are not clear cut. No clear-cut issue is problematic.

*4.   All perfect trees are evergreen. All evergreens are hardwood.

5.   No discussion of metaphysics is without controversy. Some controversial issues should be avoided.

*6.   All non-English sentences should be removed from this book. No Spanish is English.

7.   All logic problems are not difficult. Some mathematics is not logic.

8.   No formal logic is without value. No mathematics is not formal logic.

9.   No scientific theory is absolute. All scientific theories are nonobjective.

10.   No history course is uninformative. Some nonhistory courses are not non-theoretical studies.

9.3 INTRODUCTION TO PREDICATE LOGIC

We have seen that propositional logic is inadequate for the analysis of certain kinds of sentences, such as "All happy people lead productive lives." Categorical logic may also be inadequate in some cases. Not all English sentences that depend on relationships within the sentence can easily be translated into any of the four basic types of sentence:

9.3a

All S are P.
No S are P.
Some S are P.
Some S are not P.

Consider the following sentences:

9.3b

Anyone who takes the advanced-placement exam in history and passes will receive credit for History 101.
Some who take the advanced placement exam in history and pass will receive credit for History 101.
If Brian takes the advanced-placement exam in history and passes, he will receive credit for History 101.

The first two sentences appear to follow patterns of categorical logic; we could translate them as "All S are P" and "Some S are P," respectively. However, these translations lose the complexity of the subject term. That is, the original English sentences present a complex subject in which two components are connected in a particular way. One must take the exam, *and* one must pass the exam. Both components of the subject must be true if the subject is true. This complexity is lost in the translations "All S are P" and "Some S are P."

If we use the techniques we have studied to deal with the third sentence, we also end up with a loss of meaning. We may translate this sentence into propositional logic by letting p stand for "Brian takes the advanced-placement exam in history," q for "Brian passes the advanced placement exam in history," and r for "Brian will receive credit for History 101." We would then rewrite the sentence as (p & q) ⊃ r. In this translation, we lose sight of the relationship between p and q, as well as how they relate (besides conditionally) to r.

Simply saying (p & q) ⊃ r does not show that the same person is taking the exam, passing the exam, and receiving credit for History 101.

Furthermore, some arguments in English are obviously valid, but when they are translated into propositional logic, their validity is not revealed. Consider, for example, the following argument:

9.3c

A student will receive credit for History 101 if he or she takes and passes the advanced-placement exam in history. Therefore, if Brian takes the advanced-placement exam in history and passes it, he will receive credit for History 101.

Given our assignments for p, q, and r, and given that s stands for "A student takes the advanced-placement exam in history," t stands for "A student passes the advanced placement exam in history," and u stands for "A student will receive credit for History 101," we would translate this argument as follows:

$$\frac{(s\ \&\ t) \supset u}{\therefore\quad (p\ \&\ q) \supset r}$$

Unfortunately, our translation does not show the relationship between "a student" and "Brian." Moreover, the obvious validity of the argument in English is not at all indicated by the symbolic representation of it in propositional logic. We therefore need to develop a new approach.

We will use the connectives of propositional logic—that is, &, ~, ∨, ⊃, and ≡. But for predicate logic, we will make two major changes: We will introduce two new symbols, which stand for quantifiers, and we will make a new list of sentence members.

There are two types of quantifiers in predicate logic. **Universal quantifiers**, which we symbolize by ∀, represent English words such as *all, every,* and *each.* **Existential quantifiers**, which we symbolize by ∃, represent English words such as *some, one,* and *a.*

In addition to connectives and quantifiers, sentences of predicate logic contain **individual constants**, which denote particular things that actually exist; **predicate constants**, which stand in relation to individual constants; and **variables**, which function like placeholders in algebra. We use lowercase Roman letters *a* through *o* to identify individual constants, which may include sets, properties, and events, as well as physical objects. The uppercase Roman letters *A* through *Z* are used to symbolize predicate constants, which are identified by removing individual constants from an English sentence; whatever is left is the predicate constant. For example, in "Shelby loves Brian," if we remove the individual constants (Shelby and Brian), we are left with "loves," which is the predicate constant.

Some predicate constants are *monadic*: They stand in relation to a single individual constant (e.g., "Brian jumped":_____, where the blank represents the individual constant). Others are *polyadic*: They stand in relation to two or more individual constants (e.g., "Mandie kissed Jason":_____ kissed _____, or "5 is halfway between 1 and 10":_____ is halfway between _____ and _____). Predicate constants are placed before the individual constants of the sentence (e.g., Jb, Kmj, and Bfot).

Variables are symbolized by the lowercase letters *w* through *z*.

A well-formed statement in predicate logic is equivalent to a complete sentence in English: It has a subject and a predicate and expresses a complete thought. Some statements of predicate logic, such as Kmj, are simple, while others, such as (Jo & Kmj) ⊃ Bfot are complex. Simple statements may contain more than one subject, each of which is either an individual constant or a variable; in both situations, the subject is represented by a lowercase letter. Any subject can stand in relation to more than one predicate; an example is o in (Jo & Kmj) ⊃ Bfot. However, a simple well-formed statement in predicate logic contains only one predicate, which is represented by an uppercase letter. While we cannot quantify a predicate, the predicate is the cement of the statement.

Before illustrating the translation of English sentences into predicate logic, we need to clarify the scope of a quantifier. The quantifier is placed before the sentence it ranges over. The scope of the quantifier is determined by parentheses or brackets other than the parentheses around the quantifier itself. Thus, in the following sentences, the scope of each quantifier is the entire sentence:

9.3d

(∀x) (Px); (∀x) (Px & Sx); (∀x) [(Px & Sx) ∨ Tx]

However, in (∀x) (Px & Sx) ∨ Tx, the universal quantifier does not range over Tx, since the quantifier's domain is limited to the parentheses. Either brackets must be supplied to extend the domain, or a quantifier must be provided to range over Tx. In its present form, the sentence is not a well-formed statement of predicate logic.

We can easily translate categorical sentences into predicate logic by using the following patterns:

9.3e

All S are P. :: (∀x) (Sx ⊃ Px)
No S are P. :: (∀x) (Sx ⊃ ~Px)
Some S are P :: (∃x) (Sx & Px)
Some S are not P. :: (∃x) (Sx & ~Px)

9.4 EXERCISE: TRANSLATING

*1.   Since no professors attended the party and all of the students did attend, it is safe to conclude that no students are professors.

*2.   Some sports cars are not American made, for no Italian cars are American made and all Italian cars are sports cars.

3.   Since no gillygongs are visible, we can conclude that no dogs are gillygongs, for all dogs are visible.

4. Some students do not take the LSAT, for no one who takes the LSAT fails, but some students do fail.

5. Since all computers are helpful and some typewriters are not helpful, no typewriters are computers.

6. No students at DBU are heavy drinkers, for some heavy drinkers are teetotalers and some students at DBU are teetotalers.

7. Since all homes in Texas are air conditioned and some homes in Indiana are not air conditioned, some homes in Texas are not homes in Indiana.

8. All players on our basketball team are over 6 feet tall. No baseball player is over 6 feet tall. Hence, no baseball player plays on our basketball team.

9. Some students are not female, but some males are not students; thus, some males are not females.

10. All those who do well in categorical reasoning will enjoy reading Aristotle. No contemporary logician enjoys reading Aristotle. Hence, no contemporary logician will do well in categorical reasoning.

As with most translations, 9.3e is not the only way to translate categorical sentences. The following chart provides some alternatives:

9.4a

All S are P.	::	$(\forall x)\,(Sx \supset Px)$	::	$\sim(\exists x)\,(Sx \,\&\, \sim Px)$
No S are P.	::	$(\forall x)\,(Sx \supset \sim Px)$	::	$\sim(\exists x)\,(Sx \,\&\, Px)$
Some S are P.	::	$(\exists x)\,(Sx \,\&\, Px)$	::	$\sim(\forall x)\,(Sx \supset \sim Px)$
Some S are not P.	::	$(\exists x)\,(Sx \,\&\, \sim Px)$	::	$\sim(\forall x)\,(Sx \supset Px)$

Try rewriting some of the problems just given, using these alternative translations.

While predicate logic can capture many expressions of ordinary language in a symbolic fashion that we can evaluate deductively, the translation of complex expressions is beyond the scope of an introductory text. Hence, we will not discuss such translation here, but simply recommend that you take advanced courses in formal logic. We leave this subject with an expression that will be of interest to most people. Consider how you might translate it:

9.4b

Nobody loves somebody without someone getting hurt.

9.5 PREDICATE LOGIC AND TRUTH TREES

Unlike truth tables, truth trees are easily imported (with minor modifications) into predicate logic. The decomposition of an argument in predicate logic requires four additional rules, which fall into two categories: rules for dealing with negations attached to a quantifier and rules of instantiating variables. Those rules are as follows:

9.5a

~∀ Rule

Whenever we encounter a sentence with a negated universal quantifier (e.g., ~(∀**x**)
(. . . **x**. . .)), we rewrite the sentence as (∃**x**) ~(. . . **x**. . .).

9.5b

~∃ Rule

Whenever we encounter a sentence with a negated existential quantifier (e.g., ~(∃**x**)
(. . . **x**. . .)), we rewrite the sentence as (∀**x**) ~(. . . **x**. . .).

9.5c

∃ Rule

For sentences of the form (∃**x**) (. . . **x**. . .) that have not been decomposed and that
are in one or more open paths, examine each of the paths and determine whether it
contains the individual constant **y**. If **y** does not appear, list . . . **y** . . . in that open
path. If **y** does appear, choose an individual constant that does not appear.

9.5d

∀ Rule

For sentences of the form (∀**x**) (. . . **x**. . .) that are in one or more open paths, examine all
of the paths and determine the individual constants that appear in them. Write . . . **y** . . .
for each individual constant that appears. If no constant appears, choose one.

Unlike the case with existential quantifiers, there is an infinite number of possible
instantiations of universally quantified sentences. As a result, sentences of the form (∀**x**)
(. . . **x**. . .) are never totally decomposed. The following is a valid argument, together with
a proof of its validity:

9.5e

$$\begin{array}{ll}
& \sim(\exists x)\,(Px\ \&\ Ax) \\
& \underline{(\forall x)\,(Sx \supset Ax)} \\
\therefore & \quad (\forall x)\,(Sx \supset \sim Px)
\end{array}$$

1.	~(∃x) (Px & Ax)	sm
2.	(∀x) (Sx ⊃ Ax)	sm

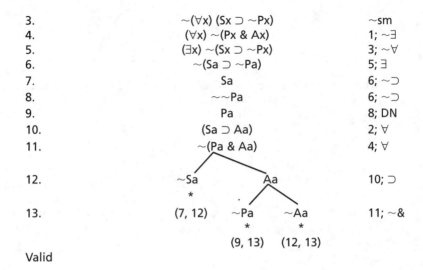

3.	~(∀x) (Sx ⊃ ~Px)	~sm
4.	(∀x) ~(Px & Ax)	1; ~∃
5.	(∃x) ~(Sx ⊃ ~Px)	3; ~∀
6.	~(Sa ⊃ ~Pa)	5; ∃
7.	Sa	6; ~⊃
8.	~~Pa	6; ~⊃
9.	Pa	8; DN
10.	(Sa ⊃ Aa)	2; ∀
11.	~(Pa & Aa)	4; ∀

12.   ~Sa   Aa   10; ⊃
                *

13.   (7, 12)   ~Pa   ~Aa   11; ~&
                        *   *
              (9, 13)   (12, 13)

Valid

(Note that we generally instantiate an existential quantifier before addressing a universal quantifier.)

The next three arguments are accompanied by proofs of their validity.

9.5f

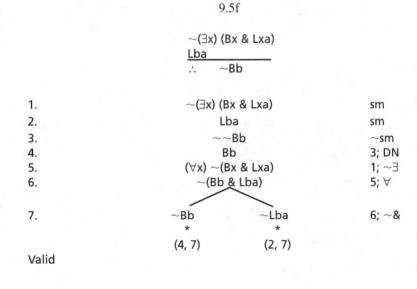

~(∃x) (Bx & Lxa)
Lba
∴   ~Bb

1.	~(∃x) (Bx & Lxa)	sm
2.	Lba	sm
3.	~~Bb	~sm
4.	Bb	3; DN
5.	(∀x) ~(Bx & Lxa)	1; ~∃
6.	~(Bb & Lba)	5; ∀

7.   ~Bb   ~Lba   6; ~&
              *   *
           (4, 7)   (2, 7)

Valid

9.5g

(∀x) (Jx ⊃ ~Px)
(∀x) (Aax ⊃ Jx)
(∀x) (~Px ⊃ Lbxa)
∴   (∀x) (Aax ⊃ Lbxa)

1.	(∀x) (Jx ⊃ ~Px)	sm
2.	(∀x) (Aax ⊃ Jx)	sm
3.	(∀x) (~Px ⊃ Lbxa)	sm
4.	~(∀x) (Aax ⊃ Lbxa)	~sm
5.	(∃x) ~(Aax ⊃ Lbxa)	4; ~∀
6.	~(Aac ⊃ ~Lbca)	5; ∃
7.	Aac	6; ~⊃
8.	~Lbca	6; ~⊃
9.	Aac ⊃ Jc	2; ∀

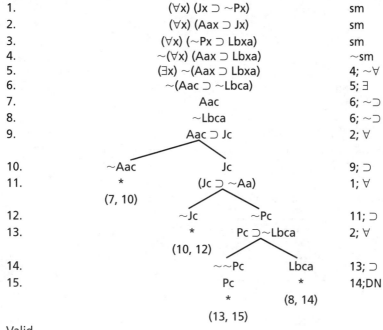

10.	~Aac	Jc	9; ⊃
11.	*	(Jc ⊃ ~Aa)	1; ∀
	(7, 10)		
12.		~Jc ~Pc	11; ⊃
13.		* Pc ⊃~Lbca	2; ∀
		(10, 12)	
14.		~~Pc Lbca	13; ⊃
15.		Pc *	14;DN
		* (8, 14)	
		(13, 15)	

Valid

9.5h

$$(\forall x) [Px \supset (\forall y) (Ty \supset Cxy)]$$
$$\underline{(\forall x) [Tx \supset (\forall y) (Cxy \supset Jy)]}$$
$$\therefore \quad (\forall x) [(Px \,\&\, Tx) \supset Jx]$$

1.	(∀x) [Px ⊃ (∀y) (Ty ⊃ Cxy)]	sm
2.	(∀x) [Tx ⊃ (∀y) (Cxy ⊃ Jy)]	sm
3.	~(∀x) [(Px & Tx) ⊃ Jx]	~sm
4.	(∃x) ~[(Px & Tx) ⊃ Jx]	3; ~∀
5.	~[(Pa & Ta) ⊃ Ja]	4; ∃
6.	Pa & Ta	5; ~⊃
7.	~Ja	5; ~⊃
8.	Pa	6; &
9.	Ta	6; &
10.	[(Pa ⊃ (∀y)(Ty ⊃ Cay)]	1; ∀

11.	~Pa	(∀y)(Ty ⊃ Cay)	10; ⊃
12.	*	Ta ⊃~Caa	11; ∀
	(8, 11)		
13.		~Ta Caa	12; ⊃
14.		* Ta ⊃ (∀y)(Cay ⊃ Jy)	2;∀
		(9, 13)	
15.		~Ta (∀y)(Cay ⊃ Jy)	14; V6, 21

16.   *   Caa ⊃ Ja   15; ∀
                        (9, 15)   ╱╲
17.   ~Caa   Ja   16; ⊃
                                                      *   *
                                                  (13, 17) (7, 17)

Valid

9.5A EXERCISE: PREDICATE LOGIC

Test the validity of the following arguments, using truth trees (you should recognize these arguments):

*1.   ~(∃x) (Px & Ax)
      (∀x) (Sx ⊃ Ax)
      ∴   (∀x) (Sx ⊃ ~Px)

2.   (∀x) (Ix ⊃ ~Ax)
      ~(∃x) (Ix & ~Sx)
      ∴   (∃x) (Sx & ~Ax)

*3.   (∀x) (Gx ⊃ ~Vx)
      (∀x) (Dx ⊃ Vx)
      ∴   ~(∃x) (Dx & Gx)

4.   (∀x) (Tx ⊃ ~Fx)
      ~(∀x) (Sx ⊃ ~Fx)
      ∴   (∃x) (Sx & ~Tx)

*5.   (∀x) (Cx ⊃ Hx)
      ~(∀x) (Tx ⊃ Hx)
      ∴   (∀x) (Tx ⊃ ~Cx)

6.   ~(∀x) (Dx ⊃ ~Tx)
      (∃x) (Sx & Tx)
      ∴   (∀x) (Sx ⊃ ~Dx)

7.   ~(∃x) (Tx & ~Ax)
      (∃x) (Ix & ~Ax)
      ∴   (∃x) (Tx & ~Ix)

8.   (∀x) (Kx ⊃ Ox)
      ~(∃x) (Ex & Ox)
      ∴   (∀x) (Ex ⊃ ~Kx)

9.   (∃x) (Sx & ~Fx)
      (∃x) (Mx & ~Sx)
      ∴   ~(∀x) (Mx ⊃ Px)

10.   (∀x) (Cx ⊃ Ax)
      (∀x) (Lx ⊃ ~Ax)
      ∴   ~(∃x) (Lx & Cx)

Frank and Ernest

I THOUGHT I HAD THE ANSWER TO THE MEANING OF LIFE, BUT EVERYTHING CANCELLED OUT.

THAVES

9.5B EXERCISE: PREDICATE LOGIC

Use truth trees to test the validity of the following arguments (these are more complex than those in the previous exercise):

*1. Ta & Ua
     (∀x) [Tx ⊃ (Vx ∨ ~Wx)]
     ∴   (∃x) Vx

2.   (∀x) Tx ⊃ (∀x) Ux
     ∴   (∀x) (Tx ⊃ Ux)

*3. (∀x) (Tx ⊃ Ux)
     (∀x) [Ux ⊃ (Ux ∨ Wx)]
     (∀x) (Tx ⊃ ~Wx)
     ∴   (∀x) (Tx ⊃ Ux)

4.   (∀x) (∀y) [(∃z) Tyz ⊃ Txy]
     ~Taa
     ∴   ~Tab

5.   Ta
     (∀x) [Tx ⊃ (Ux ∨ Vx)]
     (∀x) (Vx ⊃ Tx)
     ∴   Va

6.   (∀x) (∀y) (~Txy ∨ Uxy)
     ~(∃x) (∃y) Uxy
     ∴   (∀x) (∀y) ~Txy

7.   (∀x) (Tx ⊃ Ux)
     (∃x) (Tx & Vx)
     ∴   (∃x) (Ux & Vx)

8.   (∀x) [Tx ⊃ (Ux ⊃ Vx)]
     (∃x) [Ux & (Wx & ~Xx)]
     (∀x) [(Tx ⊃ Vx) ⊃ (Yx ⊃ Xx)]
     ∴   (∃x) (Wx & ~Yx)

*9. (∃x) (Tx & Ux)
     (∃x) (Vx & ~Tx)
     (∃x) (Wx & ~Ux)
     ∴   (∃x) (Vx & Wx)

10. (∀x) (∀y) (∀z) [(Txy & Tyz) ⊃ Txz]
     ~(∀x) Txx
     ∴   (∀x) (∀y) (Txy ⊃ ~Tyx)

11. (∃x) (Tx & Ux)
     (∀x) (Ux ⊃ Vx)
     ∴   (∃x) (Tx & Vx)

12. ~(∀x) Tx
     (∀x) (Tx ⊃ Ux)
     ∴   ~(∃x) (Ux & Tx)

13. (∀x) ~(∃y) Txy
     (∀w) (∀y) (Uwy ∨ ~Twy)
     ∴   ~(∃x) (∃z) Uxz

14. (∀x) (∃y) (Txy ⊃ Uyx)
     (∀x) (∃y) Txy
     ∴   (∀y) (∀x) Uyx

15. ~(∃x) (∀y) (Txy ⊃ Uyx)
     (∀y) (∀x) ~Uyx
     ∴   (∃x) (∃y) ~Txy

16. (∀x) (∃y) (Txy ≡ Uay)
     (∀x) Uax
     ∴   (∀x) (∀y) Txy

17. ~(Ta ∨ Tb)
     (∃x) (Uxc & Tx)
     Uac ⊃ Ta
     ∴   (∀x) ~Tx

18. (∀x) Tx
     (∀x) (∃y) Uxy
     ∴   (∃x) Uax ⊃ ~(∃y) Ty

19. (∀x) (∀y) (Txy ⊃ Tyx)
     (∀x) (∀y) (∃z) [(Txy & Tyz) ⊃ Txz]
     ∴   (∀x) Txx

20. Tab ∨ Tac
     (∀x) (∃y) ~Txy
     ∴   Tab

9.6 EXERCISE: TRANSLATION AND PREDICATE LOGIC

Translate the following arguments into predicate logic, and then test them for validity by using truth trees:

*1.   Nothing is going right. So Mary will have a bad day, since if nothing is going right, then Mary will have a bad day.

2.   If idealism is true, then everything is a delusion caused by God. However, not everything is a delusion caused by God. Hence, idealism is not true.

3.   Everything is lighter than something else. Therefore, gold is lighter than something.

4.   Snooper is not a person, because God loves everybody and God does not love Snooper.

*5.   Charlie must be a liberal, since old teachers are all liberals, and Charlie is an old teacher.

6.   No young men are lonely if they are intelligent and good looking. DeWayne is lonely. Therefore, DeWayne is not intelligent.

*7.   If Brian understands all things, then he can program in C++. Clearly, Brian doesn't understand something, since he cannot program in C++.

8.   Someone who has not met Bill loves and admires him. Everyone who has met Bill admires him, but they do not love him. Jamie admires Bill. Everyone that Jamie admires, Peter also admires. Peter loves everyone that he admires. Therefore, Peter has not met Bill.

*9.   Everybody attracts somebody. Therefore, somebody is attracted to Lisa.

10.   Jamie knows nothing about Fresno. Peter knows everything about Fresno. Karita knows something about Fresno. Phil knows something about Fresno that Karita does not know. Jamie knows something that Phil does not know. Therefore, Peter knows more than Phil.

11.   Peter's only female friends are Susan, Lisa, Mary, and Janie. Some of his female friends do not understand themselves. Susan understands herself, as does Mary. Therefore, Lisa or Janie does not understand herself.

Part III Application

COURSE PROJECT

In the application for Part I, you identified arguments within your chosen article. In Part II, you evaluated some of those arguments. For this application, you have two options. Check with your instructor to determine the one you are to do.

Option 1: Evaluate the deductive reasoning in your article. First examine the overall argument and its structure. Then look for key words (e.g., *if . . . then . . .*). Finally, consider whether any of the inductive reasoning can be rewritten for deductive evaluation.

Option 2: Develop an argument that illustrates deductive reasoning which supports *your* position on the issue introduced in your chosen article. Then write a brief essay (four to five pages) supporting your position. (See Section 7.3.) Of the examples that follow, the first illustrates Option 1 and continues to focus on Mayor Koch's article, while the second, an actual student paper, illustrates Option 2.

EXAMPLE 1

Continuing our work with the article by Edward Koch, we first look at the overall argument and its structure. In the application for Part I, we saw the following overall structure:

> If the death penalty is barbaric, and no other major democracy uses the death penalty, and an innocent person might be executed by mistake, and capital punishment cheapens the value of life, and the death penalty is applied in a discriminatory manner, and the Bible says, "Thou Shall Not Kill," and the death penalty is state-sanctioned murder, then we must not support capital punishment.
> However, the death penalty is not barbaric, and it is not relevant that no other major democracy uses the death penalty, and that an innocent person might be executed by mistake is improbable, and capital punishment does not cheapen the value of life, and the death penalty is not applied in a discriminatory manner, and "Thou shalt not kill" does not apply to the issue of capital punishment, and the death penalty is not state-sanctioned murder.
> ∴   We must support capital punishment.

To test this argument for validity, we translate it into formal language as follows:

p = The death penalty is barbaric.

q = No other major democracy uses the death penalty.

r = An innocent person might be executed by mistake.

s = Capital punishment cheapens the value of life.

t = The death penalty is applied in a discriminatory manner.

u = Thou shalt not kill.

v = The death penalty is state-sanctioned murder.

w = we must support capital punishment.

{[((((p & q) & r) & s) & t) & u] & v} ⊃ ~w
{[((((~p & ~q) & ~r) & ~s) & ~t) & ~u] & ~v}
∴   w

1.	{[((((p & q) & r) & s) & t) & u] & v} ⊃ ~w	sm
2.	{[((((~p & ~q) & ~r) & ~s) & ~t) & ~u] & ~v}	sm
3.	~w	~sm
4.	[((((~p & ~q) & ~r) & ~s) & ~t) & ~u]	2; &
5.	~v	2; &
6.	((((~p & ~q) & ~r) & ~s) & ~t)	4; &
7.	~u	4; &
8.	(((~p & ~q) & ~r) & ~s)	6; &
9.	~t	6; &
10.	((~p & ~q) & ~r)	8; &
11.	~s	8; &
12.	(~p & ~q)	10; &
13.	~r	10; &
14.	~p	12; &
15.	~q	12; &

16.	~{[((((p & q) & r) & s) & t) & u] & v}	~w1; ⊃

Even though the left branch is not decomposed, we find Koch's argument to be invalid because the right branch will never close. (After all, it is a form of denying the antecedent.)

In the application for Part II, we suggested that the following argument might be rewritten in deductive fashion:

If government functioned only when the possibility of error did not exist, government would not function at all.
Human life deserves special protection, and one of the best ways to guarantee that protection is to assure that convicted murderers do not kill again. The only way to accomplish this is with the death penalty. Examples of Biegenwald and Smith.

Example of 91 police officers killed in 1981; 7% of those solved cases had been arrested for previous murders.
Example of 85 persons arrested in New York City for homicide who had previous arrests for murder. During those two years, New York police arrested for murder persons with a previous arrest for murder on an average of one every 8.5 days.

∴   If we do not have capital punishment, then innocent persons might be killed.

Whether we interpret Koch's argument as deductive reasoning depends on the second premise. Specifically, the second member of the conjunct is crucial. If the following translation does not violate the meaning of the text, we have a valid argument.

If we protect the lives of innocent persons, then we have capital punishment.

∴   If we do not have capital punishment, then innocent persons might be killed.

p = we protect the lives of innocent persons

q = we have capital punishment

1.	$p \supset q$	sm
2.	$\sim(\sim q \supset \sim p)$	$\sim$sm
3.	$\sim p \qquad q$	$1; \supset$
4.	$\sim q \qquad \sim q$	$2; \sim \supset$
5.	$\sim\sim p \qquad \sim\sim p$	$2; \sim \supset$
6.	$p \qquad\qquad p$	$5; \sim\sim$
7.	$* \qquad\qquad *$	

EXAMPLE 2[21]

Teaching Young Readers

To become better readers, children need to be taught using a mixture of phonics and whole-language. In order to see this relationship, I will show the correlation between this teaching method and why it will produce better readers. Many methods have been proposed as the best method for teaching beginning readers. The three methods currently supported by the experts within early education are phonics, the whole-language approach, or a balance of the two methods. I agree with a balanced approach.

If explicit phonics instruction combined with the whole-language approach is used with beginning readers, then we will have better readers. Children must first be taught the principles of phonics. "Current research indicates that a strong foundation in letter–sound relationships is important to success with reading and writing development." (Marrow, Lesley, and Diane Tracey. "Strategies Used for Phonics Instruction in Early Childhood Classrooms." *The Reading Teacher* May 1997: 650.) Phonics helps children see the relationship between written words and the sounds they make. With this knowledge children actually start to read earlier than without phonics instruction. In the long run children taught using only phonics fall behind the children taught with a combination of techniques.

The whole-language approach is a context-based method. It helps the child to use clues within the text to guess at unfamiliar words. This can help the child read with more fluency, but this method relies on word memorization. By starting children with phonics and moving into a broader approach, children will have more tools to work with and therefore become good readers.

James Collins states in "How Johnny Should Read" (*Time* 27 Oct. 1997: 79–81) that "it has been established almost beyond doubt that early, systematic phonics instruction is necessary for a large proportion of beginning readers. Hundreds of studies in a variety of fields support this conclusion." This is not new information. In Jeanne Chall's 1976 book, *Learning to Read*, she reports "that beginning readers who were systematically taught phonics performed better than those who were not." (Collins 79.) Marilyn Adams, author of *Beginning to Read: Thinking and Learning about Print*, has found that using phonics and a meaning emphasis works best. (Collins 80.)

Whole-language advocates claim that it takes too long to sound out each letter and the phonics method breaks the fluency of reading. "Eye-movement studies show that readers do fixate on virtually every letter in the text. It has also been shown that readers 'sound out' words unconsciously." (Collins 80.) Using phonics would only enhance what people already do, not slow them down.

Martin Turner and Tom Burkard in "Get it Right From the Start" (*Times Educational Supplement* 9 May 1997: 12) argued "that children should be taught phonics before being introduced to reading schemes and 'real' books. Context [should] only [be] used to resolve ambiguity and improve fluency." They based this on a study performed in Scotland where children were first taught to use phonics and were sixteen months ahead of the control group after only two terms of school.

In a study by David Doake, it was shown that a group of eleven-year-olds, who had been taught using only phonics, were totally inadequate readers. They were then taught using the whole-language approach for two years. Mr. Doake found that their reading abilities had improved dramatically. This is one of many studies proving that phonics is not enough. It gives children a place to start, but then they need to be introduced to a broader method to take them the rest of the way.

It has been shown that poor readers rely on context, whereas good readers do not. This is another reason phonics is not enough. These poor readers need to learn more techniques not available to them with phonics only. Using the whole-language approach, children are taught to try to figure out unknown words using pictures and clues within the text.

"While phonics knowledge is essential for children's success with reading and writing, children must also be taught to read for purpose and meaning." (Marrow and Tracey 645.) Phonics and the whole-language approach go hand in hand. Children need a phonics base to start with and build upon. After they gain knowledge of the letter–sound relationship, they are better able to draw meaning from the text. We will have better readers when we follow these steps.

Notes for Part III

[1] Plato, *The Collected Dialogues of Plato*, ed. Edith Hamilton and Huntington Cairns (Princeton, NJ: Princeton University Press, 1978).

[2] Aristotle, *The Basic Works of Aristotle*, ed. Richard McKean (New York: Random House, 1941).

[3] *Ibid.*

[4] *Ibid.*

[5] Plotinus, *The Essential Plotinus*, ed. Elmer O'Brien (New York: Mentor Books, 1964).

[6] Ockham, *Philosophical Writings: William of Ockham*, trans. Philotheus Boehner (Indianapolis: Bobbs-Merrill Company, Inc., 1964).

[7] William James, *Pragmatism and Other Essays* (New York: Washington Square Press, 1970). © 1963, 1991 by Simon & Schuster, Inc.

[8] In Chapter 8, we will discover additional argument forms, such as hypothetical syllogisms, that make use of conditional sentences.

[9] Aquinas, *Truth*, trans. Robert Mulligan (Chicago: Henry Regnery Company, 1952).

[10] The next chapter suggests additional options that use deductive reasoning.

[11] Alfred N. Whitehead and Bertrand Russell, *Principia Mathematica*, 3 vols. (Cambridge, U.K.: Cambridge University Press, 1910–1913).

[12] Because of the works of E. Post, P. Bernay, J. Lukasiewicz, and L. Wittgenstein in the early nineteen twenties, truth tables are now a standard method for understanding truth-functional statements.

[13] The fascinating notion of possible worlds occupies much of contemporary deductive logic and metaphysics, and interpretations vary concerning the content of a possible world. Leibniz, the grandfather of possible-world talk, held that each entity in a possible world is essential to that world. The notion of possible worlds as "a way things could . . . " is a weaker interpretation than is often presented in more advanced studies of the subject.

[14] The material conditional is a weak conditional in which the antecedent need bear no real relationship to the consequent (as, for example, in the statement "If walruses have tusks, then the moon is made of green cheese"). A biconditional is just that: a conjunction of two conditionals in which the antecedent of one is the consequent of the other and vice versa.

[15] From now on, we will drop the outermost grouping symbol in a wff. Thus, we say ~p & q for (~p & q). This is a standard convention in symbolic logic, and we follow it for convenience.

[16] Richard Purtill, *Logic for Philosophers* (New York: Harper & Row, 1971), pp. 64–65. These problems also appear in his *A Logical Introduction to Philosophy* (Englewood Cliffs, NJ: Prentice Hall, 1989), pp. 45–47. Reprinted by permission of Richard Purtill.

[17]Richard C. Jeffrey, *Formal Logic: Its Scope and Limits* (New York: McGraw-Hill Book Company, 1967).

[18]*Ibid.*, p. 72.

[19]Natural deduction does have some limitations. For example, it should not be used to judge an argument *in*valid.

[20]These translations are based on a Boolean interpretation, not an Aristotelian interpretation. In an Aristotelian interpretation, it is assumed that the subject class contains at least one member; a Boolean, or modern interpretation does not make this assumption. Since our discussion of categorical logic is geared toward laying a foundation for predicate logic, we adopt the Boolean approach. The rules for testing categorical syllogisms also assume a Boolean interpretation.

[21]Gail Mayberry, "Teaching Young Readers," an essay submitted in partial fulfillment of the course requirements of critical reasoning (English 3), November 1997. The article Gail originally worked with dealt with the issue of teaching language and reading skills to young students. Used by permission of Gail Mayberry.

PART FOUR

Application

CHAPTER TEN

Pulling It All Together

10.1 COURSE PROJECT

The purpose of this exercise is to apply your critical-reasoning skills to an issue that you consider important. In Part I, you selected an article from a professional journal in your major field and identified the overall argument, as well as a number of internal arguments. In Part II, you evaluated several of the inductive arguments contained in your article. You also raised crucial questions and pursued answers to those questions. This pursuit guided your research. In Part III, you either evaluated any deductive arguments contained in the article or presented, in the form of a deductive argument, your position on an issue relevant to the article you examined.

In this final stage of your course project, you will pull the three previous parts together and produce a ten- to twelve-page paper. The paper should have three distinct parts, in addition to the introduction and conclusion. Pay attention to the transitions between sections. Because of the limited length of the paper, do not expect to completely resolve the issue or issues introduced in the original article. In the introduction to your paper, present your thesis statement carefully, and indicate how you will support that thesis within the paper. (Make sure that your thesis statement reflects the scope of your claim in the third section.) Your instructor may modify the assignment, so check with him or her before beginning the project.

Note that the process you follow in writing this paper can be adapted to the writing of any extended paper. The first step in writing any paper is to identify an issue worth researching; reading articles in professional journals is excellent for this purpose. The second step is to evaluate some of the reasoning that has already been published on that issue. This evaluation should raise questions that lead you to do research in an effort to find answers. Once the research has been done, you are in a position to carry out the third step: taking a personal stance on the issue.

10.2 STUDENT PAPERS

PUT THE BLAME
WHERE IT BELONGS[1]

From the beginning of time women have been physically beaten and sexually abused by men. In a study done by Leslie L. Feinauer and Daniel A. Stuart the focus was on recovery [from] abuse. ("Blame and Resilience in Women Sexually Abused as Children." *The American Journal of Family Therapy*, Spring 1996, 31–40.) The question is "What is the relationship between the ways adult women survivors of sexual abuse attributed responsibility (blamed themselves, blamed fate, blamed both or blamed the perpetrator) for their abuse experience and their resilience as measured by their current lack of trauma symptoms?" The research suggests that blaming the perpetrator is the most successful form of recovery. During this paper we will research the verity of this finding. If the research can substantiate the authors claim then we will agree that blaming the perpetrator is the most successful form of sexual abuse recovery of the four mentioned above concerning blame. I believe we also need to look into the concept of responsibility; I believe that if recovery is to be complete there needs to be an acceptance of responsibility on the part of the abused.

I have divided the analysis of this claim into three sections. First we will identify the claims being made by Feinauer and Stuart. Second we must evaluate the claims to see if the argument is fallacious and third we will look at outside opinions on this issue to see if other professionals agree or disagree with the findings on the issue of blame and of responsibility. Only then can I agree or disagree with findings from the study. This analysis will also support or deny my belief that blame and responsibility [go] hand in hand during recovery.

I

I looked first at the major argument from the article by Feinauer and Stuart. I then identified a few of the minor arguments. I wanted to be sure that each claim had sufficient evidence to substantiate an argument.

Major Argument

Respondents who blame themselves for the abuse had a significantly higher Trauma Symptom Checklist (TSC) score, which reflects poorer functioning and more symptoms of distress, than respondents who did not blame themselves. Respondents who blamed fate for the abuse had significantly higher TSC scores than those who did not blame fate. This suggests blaming fate is also a debilitating way of making sense of an abuse experience.

Subjects who blamed both fate and self for the abuse had a significantly higher TSC than those who did not blame both. In fact the score for blaming both is the highest mean of all four categories, suggesting that this may be the most debilitating way of making sense of sexual abuse victimization. Subjects who blamed neither fate nor self but rather the perpetrator had a significantly lower TSC score than those subjects who blamed self or fate. In fact the score for blaming the perpetrator is the lowest of all four categories, suggesting that of these four ways this may be the most empowering way of making sense of sexual abuse victimization.

∴   A very powerful indicator of resilience and recovery is how sexual abuse survivors attribute responsibility or blame for the abuse.

I found through the identification of the major claim that there are many premises to support the claim, I will now identify the evidence for a few of those minor claims.

Minor Arguments

Blaming self is not a way [of] making sense of the abuse that contributes to recovery.
Blaming oneself for being sexually victimized during childhood had a debilitating effect on functioning, which may hinder the recovery process.

∴   Respondents who blame themselves for the abuse had a significantly higher Trauma Symptom Checklist (TSC) score, which reflects poorer functioning and more symptoms of distress, than respondents who did not blame themselves.

∴   Internal attributions are more debilitating that external attributions.

When survivors blame self, fate, or both self and fate, they score much higher on the TSC.
They experience many more symptoms related to the abuse than those who do not blame themselves or fate.

∴   Survivors who blamed the perpetrator seemed to experience much less distress as indicated by their TSC score.

∴   Blaming the perpetrator may be the most empowering way of making sense of sexual abuse victimization.

Each of the claims, when put into standard form, [is] supported by arguments. We can visually see what the claims are, and what evidence is offered to support each claim. As stated in the beginning I wish to focus my attention [on] the claim concerning placing blame [on] the perpetrator.

II

In part two I will evaluate a few of the identified arguments from section I to see if any fallacies occur within the argument. If a fallacy does occur then automatically I have a weak argument. I have chosen to focus on a few on the minor arguments that pertain to my interests and evaluate them. If the minor arguments are strong then the major argument mentioned above will also be strong.

Blaming self for the sexual abuse may hinder the recovery process. Respondents who blame themselves for the abuse had a significantly higher Trauma

Symptom Checklist (TSC) score, which reflects poorer functioning and more symptoms of distress, than respondents who did not blame themselves.

∴   This appears to support the claim that internal attributions are more debilitating than external attributions.

Analysis

Simple Enumeration

Total evidence and sample diversity need to be evaluated as criteria for the simple enumeration argument. This study looks at many outside theories and even contradicts some of those theories. In some studies documented by J. Conte ((1985) The effects of sexual abuse on children: A critique and suggestions for future research *Victimology*, 10, 110–130) the belief is that internalizing the blame of sexual abuse can be empowering and contribute to recovery. Feinauer and Stuart have found that the Trauma Symptom Checklist mean in their study for the women who blamed themselves was high which indicates "poorer functioning and more distress." I believe total evidence has been adequately added. I say adequately because there is no way for every possible piece of evidence [to] be looked at and considered. What is needed is a significant amount of the evidence introduced and evaluated.

Sample diversity: The study wanted to know if the group of women that had been selected was composed of women whose life experiences were similar or dissimilar. First, to examine the effect the severity of the abuse has on the overall function, a multiple regression was run on the severity of the abuse score, which included these factors: age of onset, identification of perpetrator, frequency and duration of abuse and type of abuse. Second a one-way ANOVA was run on demographic factors (age, income level, years married, number of divorces, and education levels). This was to determine if there were significant differences among the women. With all the precautions to find out this information about the women and implementing it into the study I feel there was great effort in achieving sample diversification.

I do not believe the fallacies of incomplete evidence or biased statistic[s] occurred within this argument. I feel the argument is strong because the claim is weak. If the claim had said that the *only* way of dealing with sexual abuse is to externalize the blame then it would have been a weak argument. The authors have made an effort to show that internalizing blame for sexual abuse is debilitating and not a successful way of recovering from sexual abuse.

We have looked at blaming self and aggreed with the authors and it is not a healthy way of coping and recovering from sexual abuse. We will now look at blaming the perpetrator to see if the TSC score is lower and to determine if this is a course of recovery that is successful.

Survivors who blamed the perpetrator seemed to experience much less distress as indicated by their TSC score.

∴   Blaming the perpetrator may be the most empowering way of making sense of sexual abuse victimization.

Analysis

Statistical Syllogism

Sample Size: with regard to the sample size the article states that four thousand names of women between [the] ages of 18 and 65 were randomly selected from a voter registry, An extensive questionnaire was sent out to these women. Of the four thousand, four hundred were returned and of the four hundred, 276 met the criteria for inclusion in the study. My question is, What [were] the criteria for being included into the study? My conclusion is that the respondent needed to have experienced some form of traumatic sexual abuse and [the respondent] needed to be willing to understand where [he or she was] in recovery [from] that experience. From the evidence offered that 276 women participated in the study and from my knowledge on sample size I believe that the sample size is adequate for this study. It might have been a stronger study if more women had participated in the study but I do not believe a violation of sample size has occurred.

Total Evidence: The Trauma Symptom Checklist (TSC) was administered. It was designed to measure traumatic impact, focusing in on the long term effects of child sexual abuse. It also has five subscales of anxiety, depression, disassociation, post-sexual abuse trauma and sleep disturbance. To determine the extent to which subjects blamed themselves, fate or others, four items from the Williams McPearl Coping Scale and one other item were used. I feel that total evidence was covered. While no one can cover all evidence to a question I think that in this study there was enough of the evidence covered and offered to back up the claim that blaming the perpetrator is the most empowering way of making sense of sexual abuse.

Fallacy: I do not believe any fallacies occurred. I do think that a larger sample size would have made me feel more secure in the study, but that is just for my benefit. There was [no] violation of [the] hasty generalization [variety].

I feel the argument is strong on the grounds that the claim is weak. "Blaming the perpetrator *may* be the best way . . . " I also feel that many of the other alternatives of blame were looked at and evaluated as destructive ways of placing blame in recovery.

III

Throughout the study Feinauer and Stuart looked at many channels of blame: blame self, blame fate, blame both self and fate, and blame the perpetrator. The subjects of the survey were administered a test to determine how effectively they [were] able to cope with the abuse experience. "By comparing the level of functioning of abused survivors who attribute blame in each of these four ways, this study provided information about which attribution influenced recovery positively and which did not contribute significantly" to the recovery of the abuse.

The Trauma Symptom Checklist (TSC) was administered. It was designed to measure traumatic impact, focusing in on the long term effects of child sexual abuse. It also has five subscales of anxiety, depression, disassociation, post-sexual abuse trauma and sleep disturbance. To determine the extent to which subjects blamed themselves, fate or others, four items from the Williams McPearl Coping Scale and one other item were used. While no one can cover all evidence to a question I think that in this study there was enough of the evidence covered and offered to back up the claim that blaming the perpetrator is the most empowering way of making sense of sexual abuse.

I believe there is more to the recovery process than just blame and in this section I would like to focus for a moment on the [evidence] that supports my belief. I believe that to have a successful recovery of childhood abuse one needs to accept some degree of responsibility.

Sharon Lamb, Ed. M., from the Department of Child Psychiatry, Massachusetts General Hospital believes that "attributing all responsibility to the perpetrator may diminish the child's sense of efficacy and power in a world perceived as threatening and unpredictable" but Lamb also claims that believing the victimization was one's own fault may contribute to a lower recovery outcome (Lamb, 1986). Marianne P. Celano from the Emory University School of Medicine wrote an article stating that internalization and externalization may be interrelated in empowering the child and thereby leaving the child with [a] sense of control over the abuse (Celano, 1992). David Finkelhor, Ph.D., and Angela Browne, Ph.D., found when a victim of sexual abuse has a feeling of powerlessness there is greater anxiety and fear [and] there is a feeling of inability to control "noxious events" (Finkelhor & Browne, 1985). An article by Carolyn Moore Newberger and Edward De Vos claims, "A child who interprets fear as a response to frightening aspects of the victimization experience may be less likely to suffer enduring anxiety than a child who interprets the fear as a confirmation of his or her own powerlessness as a child" (Newberge & De Vos). "The way victims make meaning or sense out of the abuse affects their perceived power or feelings of control in the recovery process. In other words, their sense of personal efficacy in recovery is largely influenced by the meanings they attribute to the experience. This attribution [of] blame is a critical component in how a child makes sense of [the] abuse experience" (Conte, 1985; Lamb, 1986).

When we look closely at the different theories of power and blame we see the importance of the abused having authority and responsibility over the abuse and the recovery. Recovery should help sexual abuse survivors develop meaning that is not self-deprecatory. It is important that meaning leaves the victim with a feeling of empowerment. According to J. Conte this may be accomplished by separating blame for the abuse from responsibility for recovery.

These theories were addressed by Feinauer and Stuart throughout their study and were found to back up the finding that blaming the perpetrator may be the most empowering. Feinauer and Stuart do not claim that placing the blame on the perpetrator exclusively is the only successful form of recovery, I believe that is why the claim is so acceptable. There is room for other options of recovery to be added.

The research of Lamb, Celano, and Finkelhor and Browne were conducted before this research on blame and resilience. Therefore I was unable to find any other authorities' opinions on the subject of solely placing blame on the perpetrator. My conclusion is that the previous research and the evidence therein back up the claim being made by Feinauer and Stuart that placing the blame on the perpetrator instead of internalizing the blame contributes to a healthier recovery [from] the blame, while at the same time confirming my belief that such feelings of responsibly and power are just as important in the recovery [from] childhood sexual abuse.

A CRITICAL EVALUATION OF
ARGUMENTS ON ECONOMIC METHODS[2]

On September 20, 1990, at the sixtieth annual meeting of the Southern Economic Association, Dr. Charles R. Plott of the California Institute of Technology delivered the Presidential Address entitled "Will Economics Become an Experimental Science?" (*Southern Economic Journal* January 1991: 901–918.) This issue, the methodological nature of economics, is currently a hot topic within the field. Because of the respect given to scientific disciplines as well as the authority granted to scientific statements, many economists have sought to render their discipline more scientific. Thus, within the field discussion and debate regarding the philosophy of science, particularly the study of methodology, has emerged in a large amount of economic literature. Dr. Plott presents an argument in this address which purports that the discipline of economics will increasingly use laboratory techniques, altering its past methods, and approach scientific practice. His argument, which is inductive, follows and will be analyzed according to the relevant criteria and against a background of other arguments current in economics.

I

Dr. Plott opens his argument by stating the historical fact that economics has been a non-laboratory science for several hundred years. He then proposes that certain steps have been taken within the field to incorporate laboratory experimentation. He concludes that economists as a whole have begun to use laboratory techniques to further their discipline's body of knowledge. His argument is stated below in standard form:

Specific classes of economists have (in historically recent times) discovered the effectiveness of laboratory techniques in evaluating and measuring the performance of experimental markets, in gauging the effects of institutions on market performance, and regarding game theory.
Modern economists have produced dozens of new concepts whose only practical source of data that can be obtained within an appropriate time frame is the laboratory.
Almost all subfields of economics have been similarly affected by laboratory techniques.

∴   Economists have altered their methodological approach such that laboratory techniques are necessary to isolate principles which govern economic behavior.

This argument contains no apparent fallacies dealing with relevancy and clarity. His terms are clear in meaning and identify certain classes of study within the field. The evidence is relevant for it attempts to support the conclusion. The argument moves from particulars to generalization (from specific areas of economic inquiry to all practitioners as a whole). Thus, it is an inductive generalization. That is, if at least one of the premises could be falsified, the conclusion would be falsified. Because its conclusion includes the whole field, it is a universal generalization. The applicable criteria for such an argument are sample size and diversity of sample.

Thus, the first consideration is the size of [the] sample. Dr. Plott asserts that steps have been take in almost every subfield of economics to incorporate laboratory experimentation. As stated, he cites three specific areas of inquiry and elaborates extensively on the effectiveness of laboratory [experimentation] within their pursuits. By including such an expansive range of inquiry, he engages a sample of sufficient size. If, however, it can be shown that these fields need not employ laboratory techniques but may rather conduct all necessary research by simply observing economies "in the wild," his conclusion is falsified. The second consideration involves the diversity of this sample. Dr. Plott's argument also satisfies this [criterion]. His sample ranges from the study of game theory, including specific examples such as the sealed bid auction, to the study of experimental markets, including specific examples such as the application of cost/benefit analysis. Further, if his claim that nearly all subfields have been affected is true, his sample satisfies its diversity requirement. Thus, no fallacies concerning sample size and diversity exit.

In [the] final evaluation, this argument appears to be moderate. Several factors must be considered. Dr. Plott has engaged in a historical look at the field of economics. His statement that the discipline has been a non-laboratory social science for several hundred years is not controversial. Early economists such as Adam Smith and John Maynard Keynes formulated their theories in relation to real economies existing "in the wild." Keynes, for instance, examined the operation of capitalistic economies against the backdrop of the Great Depression. (McConnell, Campbell R. *Economics: Principles, Problems, Policies* (St. Louis: McGraw-Hill, 1987), 197.) Laboratory experimentation within the field of economics is a historically recent development. Thus, Dr. Plott has established a valid historical context for his argument. Furthermore, he has not violated the [criterion] for a universal generalization.

His conclusion, however, is strong. He concludes that a recent historical development has occurred within economics: namely, economists now incorporate laboratory methods in their research. That is, economics is becoming an experimental science. If, however, it is the case that only a section of the discipline operates as an experimental science using the lab while another section does not utilize the lab in any significant manner, then the laboratory is not the only practical source of data, and his conclusion about the evolving nature of economic method for all practitioners would be falsified. Thus, the strength of his conclusion weakens his overall argument. Taking into account all the factors involved in the final evaluation of his argument, it appears to be a moderate argument.

In analyzing Dr. Plott's argument certain questions arise. Have economists as a whole changed their methods to include laboratory experimentation? In what ways and for what reasons does economics attempt to be scientific? To what extent must such considerations involve issues within the philosophy of science? What diversity of opinion exists among current theorists regarding the state of economic methodology? Why is methodology important to economics? As stated above, because economics attempts to gather a body of scientific knowledge, it tries to employ scientific methods. The body of literature within the field regarding such issues continues to grow with the positive effect that the discipline reflects upon issues that have developed within the philosophy of science.

II

In his book *Research Methodology for Economists: Philosophy and Practice* (New York: MacMillan, 1986), Glenn L. Johnson cites the expanding role of economists in policy decisions since World War II, the increase in research funding and activity, and the rapid advances in research methods such as econometrics and cybernetics. This extension of research capabilities has paralleled rapid changes in the philosophic orientation of economists toward research. Such a tumultuous climate, he believes, calls for a present reexamination of methods. Dr. Richard Schmalensee of The Council of Economic Advisors furthers such a description in his article "Continuity and Change in the Economics Industry." (*The Economic Journal* 101 1991: 115–121.) Of particular interest, he points out the gulf between academic researchers, who are continually less willing to provide policy-relevant research, and economists working outside the university whose work, although "a quantitatively important part of the professions' output," (117) does not appear in professional journals. He also states that economics will have to continue to evolve as a discipline to adapt to changes in the world economy.

Bruce J. Caldwell echoes such sentiment and thoroughly engages such subject matter in his illuminating book *Beyond Positivism: Economic Methodology in the Twentieth Century*. (Boston: George Allen and Unwin, 1984.) He defends the position of methodological pluralism; that is, no single method can tell all. He engages ideas ranging from the growth of knowledge tradition such as Thomas S. Kuhn's normal science and paradigm to Paul Samuelson's operationism and descriptivism. The work of Johnson and Caldwell are cited here to illustrate the present state of turbulence concerning economic methodology and to hint that Dr. Plott may have taken a slightly simplistic view [of] economic methodology.

Dr. William J. Baumol of New York University and Princeton University argues that every method within the social sciences contains shortcomings. Thus, Dr. Plott may have trouble holding onto his proposition that laboratory techniques serve as the only practical source of data for new theories. Dr. Schmalensee offers a warning to the predictive implications of Dr. Plott's conclusion, stating that "history suggests that long-term forecasts of almost anything are more likely to provide amusing quotes for future readers than examples of acute foresight." (120)

Such concerns and discussions are vital to the activity of economics because, as Lawrence A. Boland states in *The Foundations of Economic Method* (Boston: George Allen and Unwin, 1982), some common framework is necessary for the coordination of the efforts within the field. (191) This need for a common framework applies to all scientific activity and thus appears in the works of the likes of Thomas S. Kuhn (normal science and paradigm) and Imre Lakatos (hard core and protective belt).

This discussion does not attempt to resolve the issues at hand but to illustrate the background of the subject of Dr. Plott's argument. By arguing that a specific methodological change has occurred throughout economics as a field, Dr. Plott has engaged these issues. The large amount of current literature on these subjects prevents their resolution here, and certain questions will have to remain unanswered. For instance, is there a best method? Is there a universally applicable method? Answers to such questions can only be generated through further debate within the field.

III

In light of the previous discussion regarding the diversity of opinion concerning economic methodology, Dr. Plott's argument seems too committed to laboratory experimentation. An argument with greater strength would have to take into account the methodological diversity within the field of economics.

A deductive argument could proceed in the following manner. Economies in the world continuously evolve, and economics must evolve accordingly to maintain its predictive and explanatory power. Thus, economics is in a sense a dynamic, continuously changing discipline. That economists use different methods in different situations to resolve different types of problems suggests that more than one acceptable method exists. Furthermore, since economics is a continuously evolving science, its methodology must also undergo evolution. A methodology characterized by continual change and containing more than one acceptable method implies that no single method exists which can resolve all economic questions. Therefore, because world economies continuously evolve, no single research method can be used by economists to address and answer all research questions. This argument is translated into propositional logic below:

p =   Economies in the world continuously evolve
q =   Economics, as a discipline, must adapt and evolve with real-world economies
r =   Economists utilize more than one method in conducting their research
s =   More than one acceptable economic method exists
t =   Economic methodology has changed
u =   No one method exists which can resolve all economic questions

The argument, once placed into proper form, follows:

$$
\begin{array}{l}
p \\
p \supset q \\
r \\
r \supset s \\
q \supset t \\
\underline{(t\ \&\ s) \supset u} \\
\therefore \quad\quad p \supset u
\end{array}
$$

After the argument has been translated into propositional logic, its validity may be tested using the truth-tree method. This process follows below:

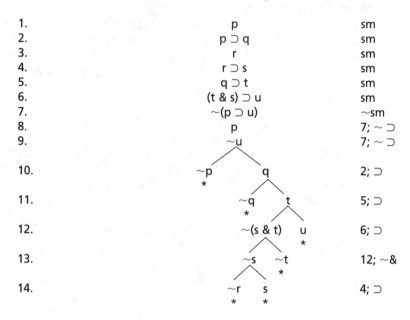

1.	p	sm
2.	p ⊃ q	sm
3.	r	sm
4.	r ⊃ s	sm
5.	q ⊃ t	sm
6.	(t & s) ⊃ u	sm
7.	~(p ⊃ u)	~sm
8.	p	7; ~ ⊃
9.	~u	7; ~ ⊃
10.	~p q	2; ⊃
11.	~q t	5; ⊃
12.	~(s & t) u	6; ⊃
13.	~s ~t	12; ~&
14.	~r s	4; ⊃

Thus, since all branches close, this argument is valid.

The above argument is deductively valid. The conclusion is absolutely claimed to be true assuming the truth of the premises. This argument was assessed by its form and structure rather than by its content and found to be valid, or of acceptable form. Unlike Dr. Plott's argument, this one accounts for methodological diversity as well as the dynamic nature of economic science.

Reason, indeed, may oft complain
   For Nature's sad reality,
And tell the suffering heart how vain
   Its cherished dreams must always be;
And Truth may rudely trample down
The flowers of Fancy, newly-blown:

But thou art ever there, to bring
   The hovering vision back, and breathe
New glories o'er the blighted spring,
   And call a lovelier Life from Death,
And whisper, with a voice divine,
Of real worlds, as bright as thine.[3]

Notes for Part IV

[1]Kristin Snow, "Put the Blame where It Belongs." A term paper submitted in partial fulfillment of the course requirements of critical reasoning and writing (English 3), December 2, 1997. Used by permission of Kristin Snow.

[2]Joel L. Bush, "A Critical Evaluation of Arguments on Economic Methods." A term paper submitted in partial fulfillment of the course requirements of critical reasoning (Philosophy 2103), December 5, 1991. Used by permission of Joel L. Bush.

[3]From "To Imagination," by Emily Brontë (1846).

APPENDIX: Scientific Confirmation

INTRODUCTION

In this section, we briefly touch upon one of the most fascinating fields of our quest for knowledge. Since the Copernican Revolution (Nicolaus Copernicus, d. 1543), scientific reasoning has been a major means of acquiring knowledge. Unfortunately, many of us lack an understanding of the nature of scientific reasoning. Frequently, we refer to this reasoning process as the *scientific method*, a method for confirming scientific theories. In the past, we were told that "underlying . . . all scientific work (is) a basic pattern of inquiry, a general scheme of attacking problems."[1] This scientific method has three distinct steps. First is observation occurs. Second, based on the observation, a generalization is made. Finally, a test is performed to check the accuracy of the generalization. This test is conducted by means of additional observations. Indeed, "Observations of the material world are at the beginning and the end of scientific reasoning. Observed facts serve both as the foundation on which a scientist builds his theories and as the ultimate check on the correctness of the theories."[2]

While this description of the scientific reasoning process may be accurate, as critical reasoners, we must realize that it is only one of several competing views. In this appendix, we will review what is commonly perceived to be the scientific method. We will then briefly present two competing positions, which have similarities to the common view, but result in different views of science. The latter two approaches are not the only major competing views, but are offered as illustrations that, at the fundamental levels of what constitutes science and how science progresses, basic philosophical and logical problems exist. As critical reasoners, we need to be aware that there are different theories concerning how scientists confirm their hypotheses. Throughout this text, we have discovered that critical reasoning does not consist merely of working through a process that guarantees an obvious answer. There are few easy answers for the critical reasoner, even in the area of science.

THE RECEIVED THEORY[3]

The most common approach to scientific confirmation has its roots in the eighteenth century and the philosophical school that dominated the period. This school of thought was empiricism. John Locke (1632–1704) laid the foundation for the movement by claiming that all knowledge is derived from experience (i.e., it is *a posteriori*). Locke claimed that, at birth and prior to experience, the mind is like a *tabula rasa*—a blank slate. But with experience, our knowledge grows. The theory of confirmation developed by the empiricist was known as the *justificational model*. According to this model, we begin with observation or the empirical process. From this process, we develop a hypothesis that leads to a theory. Finally, it was maintained that the theory would result in truth. During the early part of the twentieth century, the justificational model was adopted by the group broadly referred to by several names, including the Vienna Circle, logical positivists, and verificationalists. While members of the Vienna Circle developed varying positions, they did place themselves squarely in the tradition of empiricism.[4]

The received theory of confirmation suggests that scientific development is a cumulative process. Newer theories clarify older ones. There is a logical progress to science and the process of scientific confirmation. All these notions are embodied in the *hypothetico-deductive method*, which is commonly presented as a form of the scientific method.[5] According to this method, every scientific investigator follows three distinct steps. First is the formulation of a hypothetical generalization in response to some empirical phenomenon. Second is the deduction of particular observational statements from the generalization. Last is the testing of the observational statements to determine whether they confirm or falsify the generalization.

To illustrate this procedure, let us consider a study investigating the connection between increased fares for public transportation and the number of users of those systems. The first step for our researcher would be to formulate a hypothetical generalization. This will be a working hypothesis. Let us suppose that she proposes the following: When fares on any type of public transportation are increased, the number of people using such transportation decreases immediately. Notice that she is proposing this as a hypothetical statement; she is not claiming it to be true, nor is she concerned with its truthfulness. Furthermore, it is a generalization—a claim about all members of the given class of things. While the question the research is investigating may have arisen because of some empirical situation, step one does not occur in the laboratory. Rather, the scientist is in her office, probably sipping coffee.

Step two also does not require her to leave the office. At this stage, she simply assumes the hypothesis to be true and asks, "If it is true, then what specific consequences does it entail that I could check to confirm or disconfirm my hypothesis?" The statement she will develop at this stage must be a statement that (1) deductively follows from the generalization and (2) can be empirically tested. It will not be another hypothesis. She may deduce the following statements:

1. When the Detroit buses raised their fares last year, the bus company saw an immediate decline in passengers.
2. When the Chicago Transit Authority increased the fares for its trains two years ago, it experienced an immediate decline in passengers.

3.   When the taxicabs in Dallas increased their base fare last month, the number of taxi users immediately decreased.

4.   When the ferryboats that go out to Staten Island increase their fares next month, they will experience an immediate drop in the number of passengers.

5.   When the projected fare increase in the airline industry takes effect next year, it will experience an immediate decline in the number of passengers.

Notice that these proposed statements must be true if the hypothesis is true. Furthermore, the rescarcher has attempted to provide some diversity in her samples, not only in terms of types of public transportation, but also in terms of geographical regions.[6]

Once she has completed step two, our scientist is ready to leave her office and begin testing. During step three, she will be concerned only with testing those observational statements she listed in step two. If she finds that her test does not confirm the observational statement, then its disconfirmation is sufficient for proving that the generalization in step one is false. If her testing does confirm the statement, then she simply moves on to the next observational statement. At what point can she cease her investigations and be confident in her hypothesis? Obviously, the process ends when a counterexample is discovered. But if none ever is, the process could continue indefinitely. The *number* of observational statements tested is not as crucial as *how* step two is applied. Generally, the effort the scientist undertakes to list observational statements that could be counterexamples, yet that fail, will be more important, as in the foregoing illustration concerning public transportation. If the investigator examines instances of fare increases in communities that typically are not dependent upon public transportation, then her case would not be as strong as it would be if she cited cases where public transportation is a way of life or the only means of transportation. Notice how this procedure fits in with the "scientific method" presented in the opening paragraph of our discussion of scientific confirmation: Science is orderly and potentially ends in truth.

FALSIFICATIONALISM

Not every philosopher of science agrees with the optimism that science progresses in a logical fashion until it arrives at truth. A second theory of confirmation is presented by Karl Popper and is frequently referred to as *falsificationalism*. Popper's position is best presented in his book *The Logic of Scientific Discovery*.[7] While Popper does believe that science progresses in a logical fashion and his approach is similar to the hypothetico deductive method, his view of the end results is different.

With an emphasis on the deductive nature of science, Popper's theory of confirmation does not seek to prove a hypothesis to be true. Rather, he focuses on the notion of a counterexample (i.e., an example that proves a claim to be false. For example, consider the claim "All swans are white." Popper suggests that, instead of attempting to prove the claim to be true, we look for a swan that is not white—a swan that will prove the claim to be false. If we cannot produce a counterexample, then we have increased the likelihood of the claim being true. (Note that the failure to produce a counterexample does not mean that we have proven the claim to be true; we have only failed to falsify the claim.) However, if we can produce an Australian swan (i.e., a black swan) then we know something for sure: Our claim (the hypothesis) is false.

Part of Popper's concern is that which Immanuel Kant raised concerning eighteenth-century empiricism: Verificationalism, or proving a theory to be correct, will work only if one can observe nature without being dependent upon some framework of a theory. If we could get outside of a theory completely, verificationalism would be fine. Like Kant, Popper claims that such an observational point is impossible; we always operate within some theory. The end of the scientific enterprise will always result in theory, not truth. Science will always be theory laden.

PARADIGMS

In 1962, Thomas Kuhn published *The Structure of Scientific Revolutions*, in which he suggested that "normal science" occurs only in a worldview:

> Effective research scarcely begins before a scientific community thinks it has acquired firm answers to questions like the following: What are the fundamental entities of which the universe is composed? . . . Normal science, . . . , is predicated on the assumption that the scientific community knows what the world is like.[8]

For Kuhn, normal science operates within a given paradigm. Hence, the theory of confirmation offered by Kuhn is referred to as a *paradigm model*. Kuhn states that a scientific paradigm has two essential characteristics:

> Their achievement [is] sufficiently unprecedented to attract an enduring group of adherents away from competing modes of scientific activity. Simultaneously, it [is] sufficiently open-ended to leave all sorts of problems for the redefined group of practitioners to resolve.[9]

It is because a scientist accepts a given paradigm that she can move ahead to new discoveries. For without a paradigm, Kuhn claims, the scientist would need to spend her time rebuilding her field, always starting from step one and then giving a justification for each move. The paradigm is a position the scientist takes for granted and simply chooses to work within. As a result, normal science is a process of working out the implications of a given paradigm.

Occasionally, as the scientist is doing her research, she will obtain results that do not fit into the paradigm. These are cases known as *anomalies*. When anomalies arise, they are put aside and ignored because they do not fit the paradigm. However, eventually, the number of anomalies that exist is so great that a *paradigm shift* occurs. That is, one paradigm is replaced by another. An example is the replacement of the Newtonian paradigm of gravitation by the Einsteinian paradigm. At the point in time at which a paradigm conversion is about to take place, a number of rival theories may exist. Kuhn claims that the theory that becomes the new paradigm is not necessarily better than its rivals in all facets: "Paradigms gain their status because they are more successful than their competitors in solving a few problems that the group of practitioners has come to recognize as acute."[10] The new paradigm only needs to better address the problems that are currently viewed as the most important ones. Furthermore, the shift from one paradigm to another need not be a logical extension of the preceding paradigm. Often it "is not only incompatible, but . . . actually incommensurable with that which has gone before."[11] But once the conversion occurs, the scientist, looking at the same world as before, will now see new ways to approach her subject. She experiences a change in worldviews that Kuhn describes as analogous to a religious conversion.[12]

The paradigm model, as a theory of confirmation, takes Kant seriously when he states that science is theory laden. Kuhn's model, hence, is similar to that of Popper; but whereas Popper claims that there is a logical progression—a system for doing science—Kuhn claims that there is no overarching system. Rather, science only reflects worldviews. The decision to accept one worldview over another is more of a matter of subjective and aesthetic considerations.[13] Nor does the conversion process occur overnight, such that all scientists accept the new worldview:

> At the start a new candidate for paradigm may have few supporters. . . . Nevertheless, if they are competent, they will improve it, explore its possibilities, and show what it would be like to belong to the community guided by it. . . . More scientists will then be converted, and the exploration of the new paradigm will go on. Gradually the number of experiments, instruments, articles, and books based upon the paradigm will multiply.[14]

It seems that the new paradigm wins, not because it is more reasonable or accurate than its competitors, but because it has developed a better public-relations program. Within Kuhn's model, scientific confirmation is not the confirmation of a theory about the way the world is, but the confirmation of a theory within a theory of the way the world is. In the received theory, the confirmation of a theory tell us something about the world itself. For Kuhn, by contrast it tells us something about the worldview in which the scientist is working. Kuhn has taken us far from the "scientific method" that this appendix first presented. Gone is the notion of an objective researcher starting simply with the world about her—her empirical experiences. Gone is the notion that science is even capable of discovering truth. As a critical reasoner confronts science or is confronted by science, the scientific process and its end results are not the only problems to be grappled with.

OTHER CONSIDERATIONS

Besides the scientific method, another element the critical reasoner must take into account as he evaluates the evidence presented by science is the *role of the controlled experiment*. That is, the results given by science are considered to be more reliable if they are obtained by an experiment that conforms to a given set of criteria. In a controlled experiment, two groups are tested. Group one is known as the control group, group two as the experimental group. Both groups ought to be as similar as possible; however, the experimental group is exposed to the suspected causal condition being tested, and the control group is not exposed to that condition. For example, if the scientist is testing the effects of fluorescent lighting upon plants, we must have two groups of plants. Both groups will be composed of the same kinds of plants, but only one group, the experimental one, will be exposed to fluorescent lighting. As much as possible, the experimental group should be representative of the kind of things that are exposed to the condition being tested, and the control group should be representative of the kind of things that are not exposed to the condition in question.

As critical reasoners evaluating a given controlled experiment, we need to be concerned with several problems. As with inductive generalizations, we need to be concerned with the sample size and the diversity or representativeness of the sample. Furthermore, we must realize that there may be certain nonobvious external influences on the experiment. For example, the experimenter himself may have adverse effects upon the experiment, or the psychological influence of those being tested can affect the results. Because of this last problem, many experiments make use of a placebo that results in a *double-blind experiment*. That is, the experimenter himself does not know which group is the control group and which is the experimental group, and neither do the participants in the experiment know which group they belong to. Yet another problem that confronts the critical reasoner is the analogy often made between animal studies and humans. Is the analogy relevant? Just because a particular stimulus produces a given effect in animals, does that mean it would produce the same effect in humans?

A final concern for the critical reasoner in relation to science is the distinction between science and pseudoscience. *What exactly counts as science?* What characteristics must science have to distinguish itself from pseudoscience? For example, why is it commonly thought that astronomy is science, but astrology is pseudoscience? Imre Lakatos[15] suggests that, in order for a hypothesis to be considered scientific, the investigator must be able to state exactly what would cause him to reject the hypothesis. If the investigator cannot or does not spell out what that condition might be, then his position is merely pseudoscience. Furthermore, if a position is to be considered scientific, then the hypothesis must provide a novel prediction. Do you agree with Lakatos? Why or why not? What other considerations help distinguish science from psuedoscience?

Endnotes

[1]Konrad B. Krauskopf and Arthur Beiser, *Fundamentals of Physical Science*, 5th ed. (New York: McGraw-Hill, 1966), pp. 54–55.

[2]*Ibid.*, p. 55.

[3]For an excellent discussion of the background and development of the received view, see Frederick Suppe, ed., *The Structure of Scientific Theories*, 2d. ed. (Urbana, IL: University of Illinois Press, 1977), pp. 6–56.

[4]One of the clearest advocates of this school of thought was Alfred Jules Ayer (1910–1989), and his book *Language, Truth and Logic*, 2d ed. (New York: Dover Publications, 1946) set forth the theses of logical positivism.

[5]For a discussion of the connection between the received view and the hypothetico-deductive method, see Karel Lambert and Gordon Brittan, Jr., *An Introduction to the Philosophy of Science*, 2d ed. (Reseda, CA: Ridgeview Publishing Company, 1979), p. 91.

[6]Notice the correlation between the hypothetico-deductive method and inductive generalizations.

[7]Karl Popper, *The Logic of Scientific Discovery* (New York: Harper Torchbooks, 1968); originally published as *Logik der Forschung* (Vienna: J. Springer, 1935).

[8]Thomas Kuhn, *The Structure of Scientific Revolutions*, 2d ed. (Chicago: University of Chicago Press, 1970), pp. 4–5.

[9]*Ibid.*, p. 10.

[10]*Ibid.*, p. 23.

[11]*Ibid.*, p. 103.

[12]*Ibid.*, p. 122.

[13]*Ibid.*, p. 158.

[14]*Ibid.*, p. 159.

[15]"Introduction: Science and Pseudoscience," in John Worrall and Gregory Currie, *The Methodology of Scientific Research Programmes* (New York: Cambridge University Press, 1978), pp. 1–7.

Answers to Selected Problems

2.1A Identifying Types of Definitions

2. Denotative
4. Operational
8. Ostensive
10. Synonymous
14. Connotative
17. Denotative
20. Ostensive
22. Operational
23. Connotative

2.1B Identifying Usage of Definitions

3. Lexical
6. Stipulative
9. Precising
14. Legal
15. Persuasive
18. Theoretical

2.1C Evaluating Definitions

1. Noncircularity
3. Affirmative and accuracy
4. No problem
7. Clarity
11. Accuracy
17. Clarity
20. Affirmative
22. Noncircularity

3.3 Identifying Arguments

(Remember, the task is *identification*, not evaluation. Many of the arguments below are not *good* arguments, and the reason they are not is the issue of the remainder of this text.)

2.   Yes

> John received an A.
> Betty received an A.
> Peter received an A.
> John, Betty, Peter, and Paula were in class, and the four normally receive the same grades.
> ∴   Paula received an A.

4.   No, if understood as a command.

> Possibly yes, if understood as follows:
> It is raining.
> ∴   You need to take your umbrella.

7.   Conditional

9.   Temporal use of "since" statement

14.   Statement (conditional)

16.   Yes:

> Last year I visited the Fort Worth Zoo, the Dallas Zoo, and the Fort Wayne Zoo.
> I especially enjoyed the exotic-bird section at each zoo.
> Next week I visit the Miami Zoo.
> ∴   I am looking forward to the exotic-bird section.

18.   No, if understood as simply a command to read. However, it is probably best understood as an argument:

> The man who never reads will never be read.
> He who never quotes will never be quoted.
> He who will not use the thoughts of other men's brains proves that he has no brain of his own.
> ∴   You need to read.

22.   Statement: merely an example

29.   Yes, it has an implied conclusion:

> The statistics prove that such a building as the one proposed have provided durable housing in other parts of the country.
> It is highly energy efficient and relatively inexpensive to construct and maintain.
> It would be very adequate for both our present needs and our projected future needs.
> ∴   We should build this structure.

3.5 Exercise: Identifying Assumptions

3.   Recently, a large number of elm trees on our street died.
     Either the trees died because of lower-than-average rainfall for the past
     three years, or someone must have used a chemical and poisoned the
     trees.
     (Assumption: these are the only two possible explanations)
     The trees did not die because of the lack of rain, since other elms in the
     area were not affected.
     ∴   Someone poisoned the trees.

Notice that this assumption is questionable, since other explanations are quite
possible. For example, perhaps the elms on our street are older than any
others in the area and thus are dying a natural death, or perhaps they are more
susceptible to droughtlike conditions. Or perhaps the trees on the other streets
were watered by the residents, whereas no one watered the trees on our street.
While the conclusion may be true, as it stands, the argument is quite weak.

3.7 Exercise: Identifying and Interpreting Arguments

3.7-A

2.   Carolyn Bessette Kennedy's prescription bottle and her sister Lauren's
     luggage tag confirmed that the plane had gone into the ocean.
     ∴   It was important to know that those items had washed upon the
           beach.

3.7-B

2.   No, conditional
6.   Not an argument
10. When either objects external to us, to our organs change their modes of
     existence in such a way that the first equality of similitude does not
     remain constant, then the ideas are altered, and there is a feeling of
     change.
     The ideas are the same exactly.
     In every case our ideas refer to the difference between the new state and
     the old, and not to the absolute change.
     ∴   Whether the stars move around the Earth, or the Earth and
           ourselves move in the opposite direction around them, the ideas are
           the same, and there is the same sensation.

3.7-C

3.   Not an argument
6.   Probably not an argument
10. Long experience has shown that very close breeding of the same variety
     for a long time fixes the kind, but weakens the stock, especially in fertility.
     Judicious crossing of varieties strengthens the stock, increasing its fertility
     and especially producing plasticity or variability.

∴   If breeders wish to preserve a valuable variety, breed close; but if
       they wish to make new varieties, crossbreed.

3.7-D

1.   A belief which gains extensive reception without critical examination, is
       thereby proved to have a general congruity with the various other beliefs
       of those who receive it.
       ∴   This (whatever *this* refers to) is not true.

5.   Religion under all its forms is distinguished from everything else in this,
       that its subject matter is that which passes the sphere of experience.
       ∴   If knowledge cannot monopolize conscious, then there can never
              cease to be a place for something of the nature of religion.

6.   Not an argument

3.7-E

2.   The efforts of the hyper-orthodox in the past have increased the gap
       between Christianity and the scientists.
       They have embittered the scientists, and have done little to provide a
       working theory of any creative dimensions for the rapproachment of
       science and evangelicalism.
       ∴   It is impossible for us to follow the pattern set by the hyper-orthodox
              in their proposed relationship of Christianity.

4.   The theological, the ethical, and the practical are so conjoined in the Bible
       with the statements about Nature or creation that it is impossible to
       separate them, and to impugn one is to impugn the other.
       ∴   It is suicidal for the hyper-orthodox to pass by the findings of science
              which cannot but have a most important bearing on the Biblical
              references to Nature and matters of fact.

                                         and

       The theological, the ethical, and the practical are so conjoined in the Bible
       with the statements about Nature or creation that it is impossible to
       separate them, and to impugn one is to impugn the other.
       ∴   It is inconsistent for the neo-orthodox to try to separate neatly the
              theological elements of the Bible from the statements about Nature
              and facts.

10.   No argument, just an example

3.9 Exercise: Extended Arguments

Remember, there is a difference between identification and evaluation.

5.   **Bloody 'Beauty'**

       [1]Assuming the National Rifle Association is wrong, and [2]there really is a
"Rhino-Ammo" bullet that fragments on impact and [3]leaves a grapefruit-sized
hole in a human body, and [4]a "Black Rhino" bullet that penetrates bullet-proof
vests and *then* fragments, [5]the outcry is justified.
       [6]Police chiefs and other law enforcement officials around the nation are
alarmed, especially as police are the ones wearing the vests. [7]Sen. Pat

Moynihan, D-N.Y., said he will introduce legislation to ban such bullets if regulators with the federal Bureau of Alcohol, Tobacco, and Firearms do not stop their manufacture.

Why? Well, harken to the [8]promotional claims of David Keen, whose Huntsville, Ala., company wants to make and market the bullets: [9]"The beauty behind it," he told The Associated Press, "is that it makes an incredible wound. [10]There's no way to stop the bleeding. [11]I don't care where it hits. [12]They're going down for good."

[13]The packaging for the Rhino bullets says [14]each of the fragments "become lethal shrapnel and is hurled into vital organs, lungs, circulatory system components, the heart and other tissues. [15]The wound channel is catastrophic. [16]Death is nearly instantaneous."

[17]Attractive, no? [18]We think a society already awash in violence, and suspicion does not need the "beauty" of "incredible wounds." [19]We don't think loonies should be lured by the appeal of "catastrophic" wound channels and "instantaneous" death.

[20]Somebody—the ATF, Congress, whoever—needs to head this one off at the pass.

(*Fort Worth Star-Telegram*, December 30, 1994.)

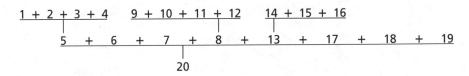

3.11 Identifying Fallacies Caused by Unclear Thinking
2.   Relevance: Appeal to the people
4.   Clarity: Equivocation
9.   Relevance: Fallacy of abusiveness
13. Relevance: Accidental
27. Relevance: Complex question

3.13 Exercise: Basic Types of Reasoning
1.   Deductive
4.   Deductive
9.   Inductive

4.4 Exercise: Single-Event Probabilities
2. $\dfrac{f}{p} = \dfrac{1}{52}$

5. $\dfrac{f}{p} = \dfrac{2}{400}$

4.6 Exercise: Conjunction of Independent Events
2. $\dfrac{f}{p} \times \dfrac{f}{p} \times \dfrac{f}{p} \times \dfrac{f}{p} \times \dfrac{f}{p} = \dfrac{1}{2} \times \dfrac{1}{2} \times \dfrac{1}{2} \times \dfrac{1}{2} \times \dfrac{1}{2} = \dfrac{1}{32}$

5. $\dfrac{f}{p} \times \dfrac{f}{p} \times \dfrac{f}{p} \times \dfrac{f}{p} = \dfrac{3}{6} \times \dfrac{3}{6} \times \dfrac{3}{6} \times \dfrac{3}{6} = \dfrac{81}{1,296}$

4.8 Exercise: Conjunction of Dependent Events

1a. $\dfrac{f}{p} \times \dfrac{f}{p} = \dfrac{3}{10} \times \dfrac{2}{9} = \dfrac{6}{90}$

1d. $\dfrac{f}{p} \times \dfrac{f}{p} \times \dfrac{f}{p} = \dfrac{3}{10} \times \dfrac{2}{9} \times \dfrac{1}{8} = \dfrac{6}{720}$

4.10 Exercise: Mutually Exclusive Alternative Events

4. $4 \ \& \ 6 = \dfrac{f}{p} \times \dfrac{f}{p} = \dfrac{1}{6} \times \dfrac{1}{6} = \dfrac{1}{36}$

$6 \ \& \ 4 = \dfrac{f}{p} \times \dfrac{f}{p} = \dfrac{1}{6} \times \dfrac{1}{6} = \dfrac{1}{36}$

$5 \ \& \ 5 = \dfrac{f}{p} \times \dfrac{f}{p} = \dfrac{1}{6} \times \dfrac{1}{6} = \dfrac{1}{36}$

$\dfrac{f}{p} + \dfrac{f}{p} + \dfrac{f}{p} = \dfrac{1}{36} + \dfrac{1}{36} + \dfrac{1}{36} = \dfrac{3}{36} = \dfrac{1}{12}$

4.12 Exercise: Mixed Probabilities

2. Alternative probabilities $\dfrac{6}{2,197}$

4. Conjunction of dependent events $\dfrac{650}{2,652}$

6. Single events $\dfrac{5}{10}$

8. Conjunction of independent events $\dfrac{1}{4}$

4.14 Exercise: Bayesian Confirmation

1. Jones: 36 total   Smith: 42 total
             12 large   20 medium
             12 medium   22 small
             12 Small   21 brown
             24 white   21 white
             12 brown   basket
             basket
    Bruce: 48 total   Klein: 36 total
             48 large   24 large
             6 brown   12 medium
             42 white   24 white
             box   12 brown
                                        basket

a.   What is the Pr J, given 1 dz large?

$$\text{Pr}(h \mid e) = \frac{\text{Pr}(h) \times \text{Pr}(e \mid h)}{[\text{Pr}(h) \times \text{Pr}(e \mid h)] + [\text{Pr}(\sim h) \times \text{Pr}(e \mid \sim h)]} =$$

$$\text{Pr}(J \mid lg) = \frac{\text{Pr}(J) \times \text{Pr}(lg \mid J)}{[\text{Pr}(J) \times \text{Pr}(lg \mid J)] + [\text{Pr}(\sim J) \times \text{Pr}(lg \mid \sim J)]} =$$

$$\frac{\frac{1}{2} \times \frac{1}{3}}{\left(\frac{1}{2} \times \frac{1}{3}\right) + \left(\frac{1}{2} \times \frac{2}{3}\right)} = \frac{\frac{1}{6}}{\frac{1}{6} + \frac{2}{6}} = \frac{\frac{1}{6}}{\frac{3}{6}} = \frac{1}{3}$$

5.5A Exercise: Simple Enumeration

1.   1.   Joe received an A in British literature
            Betty received an A in British literature
            <u>John received an A in British literature</u>
            ∴   Bill received an A in British literature

      2.   p to p: simple enumeration.

      3.   **Sample Diversity:** It is unclear whether the sample is diverse, since we do not know anything about the other students (if any). We can assume that diversity is not an issue if we discover certain information as we look at total evidence.
            Total Evidence: This argument raises a number of serious questions. Did the four individuals all attend the same school? Did they take the class the same semester? Did they have the same instructor? Do the four students generally receive similar grades? Are these four a random selection of students, or are they close friends? While we have no reason to believe that any evidence has been withheld, we definitely have some questions.

      4.   Since the criteria are not obviously violated, we cannot identify a fallacy.

      5.   This argument is a moderate argument. Even though the argument does not explicitly show how it satisfies the criteria and the claim of the conclusion is very strong, I believe the argument is moderate. The reason for this is the assumption that such an argument would typically be offered *only* in cases where those involved are friends who have taken a particular class together and know of each other's progress throughout the semester. It would be ridiculous to offer such an argument if this assumption was not implied.

5.6A Exercise: Inductive Generalization

4.   You're right! This is deductive reasoning, but why?

6.   1.   The first time I used XYZ on ants in the house, it took care of the problem.
            The second time I used XYZ, it worked.
                                        .
                                        .
                                        .
            The tenth time I used XYZ, it worked.

XYZ worked the eleventh time I used it.

∴   Every time in the future that I use XYZ on ants in the house, it
       will take care of the problem.

2.   p to g: inductive generalization.

3.   **Sample Diversity:** While the samples are not diverse in terms of the loca-
       tion of previous applications, such diversity is not required, since the pro-
       jected usage also is in the house. This argument does represent a sort of
       diversity in that there are eleven separate instances of the product being
       used. While it is not clear that these instances did not occur at essentially
       the same time, a normal reading of the argument would suggest some time
       lapse between applications. Diversification also suggests the question
       whether the application of XYZ in the past was isolated to a single part of
       the house or whether previous applications were in different parts of the
       house. Furthermore, did the previous applications involve a variety of ants?
       Let's assume that diversification is well satisfied.
       Sample Size: Sample size does not initially appear to be problem-
       atic. Eleven successful applications or occurrences of an event often
       are adequate for the establishment of a pattern. However, the claim is
       for *every* future usage of the product, and it is questionable whether
       the eleven successful applications are large enough to support the
       claim. In spite of my skepticism, I cannot say that sample size is
       clearly violated.

4.   Since there are no clear violations of the criteria, there are no fallacies.

5.   This argument is weak because of the problems I identified in terms of
       sample size, especially given the strong claim in the conclusion.
       Furthermore, even if the sample size were unproblematic, it is possible
       that the ants may develop a resistance to XYZ. Thus, it may not work
       every time in the future. If the conclusion simply had claimed that XYZ
       might work in the future, the argument could have been assessed as
       strong.

5.7A Exercise: Argument from Analogy

8. 1.   In 1985, the USSR tested weapons and, as a result, produced
          megacuries of KR-85.
          In 1985, the United States tested weapons and, as a result, produced
          megacuries of KR-85.
          In 1985, several major Western European countries and Japan tested
          weapons.

    ∴   We can assume that those Western countries and Japan also
             produced megacuries of KR-85.

    2.   p to p: Argument from analogy.

    3.   **Relevance of Analogy:** Relevant similarities: All of the countries men-
          tioned in the passage performed weapons testing in 1985. All of the coun-
          tries were major world countries (i.e., none of the countries were small
          third-world countries). This is important because they all potentially have
          the same weapons to test.

Relevant dissimilarities: Even though all of the countries potentially have the same weapons capabilities, the USSR and the United States were the only countries in 1985 that were considered super powers. Given the argument, it is not clear that this dissimilarity is actually relevant, but it may be. Furthermore, there is no indication that the weapons tested in all cases were the same kind. That is, the weapons tested by the two super-powers could have been nuclear, whereas those tested by the other nations could have been conventional. We just do not have sufficient information to say either way.

4.   The argument cannot be said to be fallacious, because, at this point in time, we do not have any clear violation of the rules. If, upon carrying out some research, it was discovered that the weapons were of different kinds, then we could have a fallacy. However, at this time, we can claim only that no fallacies are evident.

5.   If the author of this argument had told us that the weapons were in fact the same kind and that no other conditions were present, other than the location of the testing, I would have evaluated the argument as strong. Unfortunately, this information was not given. Also, if we had been told that the weapons were completely different, then we would have assessed the argument as weak. Again, though this scenario did not occur. Because the argument could go either way, depending upon the results of additional research, I will assess it as moderate.

5.8A Exercise: Statistical Syllogism

2.   1. $96^+\%$ of the cards in the stack are black.
         The top card is in the stack.
         ∴   The top card is black.

     2.   g to p: statistical syllogism.

     3.   **Sample Size:** The sample size is over 96%; hence, it is as high as it can be, given the situation, without being 100%. Hence, I believe that the sample size is very good.
         Total Evidence: Even though Las Vegas has had problems with running fair tables in the past, given the current regulatory agencies, I do not think we can say that total evidence is violated.

     4.   No fallacies.

     5.   Since it is Wertz's money, I would encourage him to make a large bet, for the argument seems to be a strong one.

5.9A Exercise: Appeal to Authority

5.   1.   The surgeon general says, "Smoking by pregnant women may result in fetal injuries, premature birth, and low birth weight."
         Susan is a female smoker.
         ∴   Probably, her next child will be born prematurely.

     2.   Appeal to authority.

     3.   **Expertise:** Generally, the surgeon general is considered to be an expert in health-related issues, and this is one such issue.

Consensus: Contrary to the advertisements of the 1950s and 1960s in which doctors (other experts in health-related issues) offered their support to the tobacco industry, most doctors today would agree with the surgeon general's position.

4. No fallacies.
5. Unlike a similar argument in Section 5.8A, this argument appears to be quite strong. We should note the relative strength of the conclusion. It does not say, "Her next child will be born prematurely." Nor does it say, "Possibly, her next child will be born prematurely." The argument's conclusion lies between the two in terms of its strength.

5.10A Exercise: Appeal to Experience

1. 1. The other night, I walked on air to the ground from my office window on the second floor.

    ∴   Walking on air must be possible.

   2. Appeal to experience.
   3. **General Reliability:** People who know me will attest that I am generally very reliable. I am not prone to stretch the truth, nor do I attempt to deceive others. Furthermore, I've never been known to hallucinate because of drugs or alcohol or for any other reason. Generally, if I say something is true, it can be accepted as true.

      Consistent: A "minor" problem is that my experience with walking on air violates several laws of physics, such as the law of gravity. My experience also is inconsistent with the experience of other individuals. While these inconsistencies do not prove that I did not walk on air, they do force me to acknowledge the violation of this standard. As a result, *my* experience should not be used as evidence for the possibility of walking on air. If, in the future, we find that gravity is some times violated and that others have similar experiences, then my experience could be used as support. However, at the present time, the criterion is violated.

   4. Fallacious appeal to experience.
   5. The argument is weak because it is fallacious.

5.12 Exercise: Mixed Enumerative Induction

1. This passage can be interpreted two different ways:

   First
   1. Model 1 of finned boat: 2-1/2 ft long, 3/4 ft/sec.
      Model 2 of finned boat: 5 ft long, 1-1/2 ft/sec.
      Waves in both cases were 4 inches high.

      ∴   Anytime one doubles the length of a boat, its speed will increase accordingly.

   2. p to g: inductive generalization.
   3. **Sample Size:** While we have two models in the argument, there actually is only one case of the doubling of length resulting in a doubling of speed. Clearly, this sample size is a violation of the standard.

Sample Diversity: The diversity in this argument is equally problematic. The evidence concerns only "finned boats" in a swimming pool, but the claim seems to go beyond the pool and beyond simply finned boats. Again, we have a clear violation.

4. Both hasty generalization and biased statistics are committed.

5. The argument is weak because it is fallacious.

Second

1. Model 1 of finned boat: 2-1/2 ft long, 3/4 ft/sec.
   Model 2 of finned boat: 5 ft long, 1-1/2 ft/sec.
   Waves in both cases were 4 inches high.
   ∴   If one doubles the length of model 2, then the new model will possibly go twice as fast as model 2.

2. p to p: simple enumeration.

3. **Total Evidence:** Assuming that the third model will also be a finned boat constructed of similar materials and tested under the same conditions, it appears that total evidence is not violated. Furthermore, assuming that no laws of physics are violated, we might claim that this criterion is fully satisfied.

   Sample Diversity: Since the third model is a boat like those mentioned in the premises, it follows that, given the stated assumptions, diversity is unproblematic.

4. No fallacies.

5. This argument is moderate to strong, based on the preceding reasoning. In addition, the conclusion is extremely weak, making the argument strong.

3. 1. Cost for testing every worker is high.
      Concern for the employees' privacy
      Concern for the federal laws dealing with discrimination against people with AIDS.
      ∴   The courts uphold ban on AIDS.

   2. p to p: simple enumeration. (While the conclusion appears to be a generalization, it is actually referring to a specific test and a specific law.)

   3. **Diverse Sampling:** The evidence seems extremely diverse. The premises offer diversity in that monies, individual rights, and federal laws are all taken into account. This criterion is well satisfied.

      Total Evidence: Is there any omission of evidence in this argument? Is the argument an accurate representation of the reasoning used by the court as it determined its position? If the argument is not a misrepresentation, the line of reasoning is flawed. If it is an accurate account of the reasoning that the court used, then we must point out that the court violated total evidence. While the court took into account diverse evidence, it seemed either to ignore or simply overlook a very crucial piece of evidence. The reasoning ignores the serious implications of acquiring AIDS and that hospital workers routinely handle body fluids, the method by which the disease is transported. It appears that the court chose not to include this information in the reasoning. Whether this exclusion was intentional or simply an oversight, the argument is flawed.

4. The fallacy of incomplete evidence has been committed.

5. The argument is weak because it is fallacious.

6. According to the chart, there were 20 million in 1990, around 23 million in 1995, and an estimated 25 million in the year 2000. The problem is that the chart does not actually tell us just *what* the 20 million refers to. The title of the chart suggests that the reference is to the number of Hispanics; however, the data presented by the chart does not tell us for sure. As critical reasoners, we must beware of reading information that is lacking into charts, graphs, and pictures.

8.   1. With sexual harassment policies in place, a school board will know what to do if sexual harassment occurs.
   If a sexual harassment case reaches the courts, the grievance and rectifying procedures provide some legal protection, proving that your board made a good-faith effort to prevent sexual harassment among employees.
   <u>Sexual harassment policies may help prevent sexual harassment.</u>
   ∴   Every school board needs sexual harassment policies.

    2. p to g: inductive generalization.

    3. **Sample Size:** While there are only three premises, the nature of these premises seem easily to justify the conclusion. There is a "qualitative" factor present in the evidence. Each premise, by itself, has adequate quality to support the conclusion. (Interestingly, sample size typically is satisfied quantitatively, but here it is satisfied qualitatively.)
   Sample Diversity: The diversity of this argument is excellent. Notice that the first premise deals with present sexual harassment, the second deals with past cases, and the third addresses future cases of sexual harassment.

    4. No fallacies.

    5. The argument seems to be strong. It is true that the conclusion is a strong claim, which might suggest a weakening of the argument. However, given the subject of the argument, a weaker claim seems inappropriate. Because of the diversity in the evidence and the qualitative nature of that evidence, the argument is strong.

12.   1. According to the Bible, it is morally wrong to have sex outside of marriage.
   <u>Condoms are for sexual activities.</u>
   ∴   We should not be passing out condoms in our public schools.

    2. Appeal to authority.

    3. **Expertise:** Is the Bible considered an expert or authority in moral issues? Yes, even those who disagree with the Bible would acknowledge that it is an authority (at least for Westerners).
   Consensus: Is there a consensus among experts that the position advocated by the Bible is correct? Notice the audience to which the argument is presented: the general public. In today's society, those recognized as

authorities by the general public would not necessarily agree. This is illustrated by the fact that today, in light of AIDS, "safe sex" is promoted. Therefore, the criterion is violated.

4.   Fallacious appeal to authority.

5.   The argument is weak because it is fallacious.

(Consider what might occur if the audience were changed. Instead of presenting this argument to the general public, consider what might happen if the audience were a group of conservative Christians. The same argument probably would be viewed as strong. This shows us that part of evaluating an enumerative argument should take into account the intended audience. This statement should not be something new, for your English composition instructor probably told you that, as a writer, you need to know your audience.)

6.4 Exercise: Causal Reasoning
1.a   Remote

1.d   Probabilistic and remote

6.6 Exercise: Mill's Methods
1.   Joint

2.   Difference

3.   Agreement

5.   Concomitant Variation

7.1A Exercise: Conditional Statements
4.   If one turns in all of the assignments, then he or she will pass this course.

9.   If a tree falling in the forest makes a sound, then someone is there to hear it.

21.   Not a conditional statement; "then" is used as a transition word.

27.   If both the relations of the subject and predicate are particular, then there cannot be a syllogism.

32.   If there is not something which causes the movement from potency unto actuality, then there is no other cause here.

43.   If I have these premises, then I shall prove the main conclusion as follows.

49.   If you allow that religion can be pluralistic or merely melioristic in type, then you see that pragmatism can be called religious.

7.2A Exercise: Conditional Arguments
2.   If Peter finishes his dissertation, then he will have a teaching position. Peter has a teaching position.
∴   Peter has finished his dissertation.
Affirming the consequent; invalid

11.   If Peter and Joan attend the party and are dressed in their normal fashion, then the party will be extremely successful.

The party was not extremely successful.

∴   Peter and Joan either did not attend the party or did not dress in their normal fashion.
Denying the consequent; valid

18.   If Ted is not allowed to chair the committee, then the findings of the committee will be significant.
Ted does not chair the committee.

∴   The findings will not be significant.

Even though it appears that this argument is affirming the antecedent, we cannot assess the argument as valid or invalid. Since the conclusion has changed—which does not happen in affirming the antecedent—the argument does not fit any of our models. Hence, we cannot, at this point, say whether it is valid or invalid.

27.   If this argument preserves truth, then it is valid.
This argument does not preserve truth.

∴   This argument is not valid
Denying the antecedent; invalid

(This argument is fallacious, for it violates the criterion of truth preservation. But is the argument an example of poor reasoning? If our examination of the argument ends here, then we will conclude that it is an example of poor reasoning. However, such a conclusion should cause us to have an uneasy feeling, for surely the argument makes sense! But why? While it clearly is not a good deductive argument, what can be said about it if we understand it as an example of inductive reasoning? [For example, is it a statistical syllogism?])

30.   If the universe is quasi-Euclidean and its radius of curvature is therefore infinite, then σ would vanish.
It is improbable that the mean density of matter in the universe is actually zero, or σ would vanish.

∴   The universe is not quasi-Euclidean.
Denying the consequent; valid

8.2A Exercise: Order of Interpretation

(Why can there be more than one order of interpretation in some cases?)

2.   ~(p & ~q) ⊃ (p ⊃ q)
      3   2 1   5   4

4.   [(p & q) & ~r] ∨ [(~p & q) & r]
       1   3 2 7 4 5   6

7.   ~[~(~p & ~q) ∨ (s ⊃ ~t)]
    8 4 2 3 1 7 6 5

9.   ~~(r & ~s)
    4 3 2 1

8.3A Exercise: Truth Tables and Consistency

1.

p q r	p ⊃ (q ∨ r)	~(~p ∨ r)	~q r
T T T	T T	F F T	F T

p q r							
T T F	T	T	T	F	F	F	F
T F T	T	T	F	F	T	T	T
T F F	F	F	T	F	F	T	F
F T T	T	T	F	T	T	F	T
F T F	T	T	F	T	T	F	F
F F T	T	T	F	T	T	T	T
F F F	T	F	F	T	T	T	F

Inconsistent

2.

p q r s	p ∨ q	q & s	q ⊃ r
T T T T	T	T	T
T T T F	T	F	T
T T F T	T	T	F
T T F F	T	F	F
T F T T	T	F	T
T F T F	T	F	T
T F F T	T	F	T
T F F F	T	F	T
F T T T	T	T	T
F T T F	T	F	T
F T F T	T	T	F
F T F F	T	F	F
F F T T	F	F	T
F F T F	F	F	T
F F F T	F	F	T
F F F F	F	F	T

Consistent

18.

p q r s	~s	p ⊃ ~q	~p ⊃ (r ⊃ ~q)	(~s V ~r) ⊃ q	q	~r
T T T T	F	F F	F T F F	F F F	T	F
T T T F	T	F F	F T F F	T T F	T	F
T T F T	F	F F	F T T F	F T T	T	T
T T F F	T	F F	F T T F	T T T	T	T
T F T T	F	T T	F T T T	F F F	T	F
T F T F	T	T T	F T T T	T T F	F	F
T F F T	F	T T	F T T T	F T T	F	T
T F F F	T	T T	F T T T	T T T	F	T
F T T T	F	T F	T F F F	F F F	T	F
F T T F	T	T F	T F F F	T T F	T	F
F T F T	F	T F	T T T F	F T T	T	T
F T F F	T	T F	T T T F	T T T	T	T
F F T T	F	T T	T T T T	F F F	T	F
F F T F	T	T T	T T T T	T T F	F	F
F F F T	F	T T	T T T T	F T T	F	T
F F F F	T	T T	T T T T	T T T	F	T

Consistent

8.3B Exercise: Consistency of a Single Statement

2.

p q	[(p ⊃ q) & ~q] & ~p
T T	T F F F F
T F	F F T F F
F T	T F F F T
F F	T T T T T>

Consistent

8.4A Exercise: Logical Equivalence and Truth Tables

6.

p q	(p ⊃ q) ≡ (~p ∨ q)
T T	T T F T
T F	F T F F
F T	T T T T
F F	T T T T

Equivalent

10.

p q	~(p ⊃ q) ≡ (~p ⊃ ~q)
T T	F T F F T F
T F	T F T F T T
F T	F T T T F F
F F	F T F T T T

Not equivalent

8.5A Exercise: Statements and Truth Tables

2.

p	(~p ⊃ p) & (p ⊃ ~p)
T	F T F F F
F	T F F T T

Contradiction

4.

p q	p & (p ∨ q)
T T	T T
T F	T T
F T	F T
F F	F F

Contingent

8.

p q	p ⊃ (q ⊃ p)
T T	T T
T F	T T
F T	T F
F F	T T

Tautology

8.6A Exercise: Arguments and Truth Tables

4.

p q	p & q	~p	~q
T T	T	F	F
T F	F	F	T
F T	F	T	F
F F	F	T	T

Valid (notice that while there are no counterexamples, the argument, as a set of statements, is inconsistent)

10.

p q r	p ⊃ q	q ⊃ r	r ⊃ p
T T T	T	T	T
T T F	T	F	T
T F T	F	T	T
T F F	F	T	T
F T T	T	T	F
F T F	T	F	T
F F T	T	T	F
F F F	T	T	T

Invalid

Counterexample:

p q r
F T T
F F T

12.

p q s t	~(p ⊃ t) & q	~(q V p) ⊃ t	~(p & q) V s	~t
T T T T	F T F	F T T	F T T	F
T T T F	T F T	F T T	F T T	T
T T F T	F T F	F T T	F T F	F
T T F F	T F T	F T T	F T F	T
T F T T	F T F	F T T	T F T	F
T F T F	T F F	F T T	T F T	T
T F F T	F T F	F T T	T F T	F
T F F F	T F F	F T T	T F T	T
F T T T	F T F	F T T	T F T	F
F T T F	F T F	F T T	T F T	T
F T F T	F T F	F T T	T F T	F
F T F F	F T F	F T T	T F T	T
F F T T	F T F	T F T	T F T	F
F F T F	F T F	T F F	T F T	T
F F F T	F T F	T F T	T F T	F
F F F F	F T F	T F F	T F T	T

Valid

21.

p	q	r	s	t	~[(s & t) ⊃ (r V ~p)]					p ⊃ s	q ⊃ t	~[(p & q)⊃ r]		
T	T	T	T	T	F	T	T	T	F	T	T	F	T	T
T	T	T	T	F	F	F	T	T	F	T	F	F	T	T
T	T	T	F	T	F	F	T	T	F	F	T	F	T	T
T	T	T	F	F	F	F	T	T	F	F	F	F	T	T
T	T	F	T	T	T	T	F	F	F	T	T	T	T	F
T	T	F	T	F	F	F	T	F	F	T	F	T	T	F
T	T	F	F	T	F	F	T	F	F	F	T	T	T	F
T	T	F	F	F	F	F	T	F	F	F	F	T	T	F
T	F	T	T	T	F	T	T	T	F	T	T	F	F	T
T	F	T	T	F	F	F	T	T	F	T	T	F	F	T
T	F	T	F	T	F	F	T	T	F	F	T	F	F	T
T	F	T	F	F	F	F	T	T	F	F	T	F	F	T
T	F	F	T	T	T	T	F	F	F	T	T	F	F	T
T	F	F	T	F	F	F	T	F	F	T	T	F	F	T
T	F	F	F	T	F	F	T	F	F	F	T	F	F	T
T	F	F	F	F	F	F	T	F	F	F	T	F	F	T
F	T	T	T	T	F	T	T	T	T	T	T	F	F	T
F	T	T	T	F	F	F	T	T	T	T	F	F	F	T
F	T	T	F	T	F	F	T	T	T	T	T	F	F	T
F	T	T	F	F	F	F	T	T	T	T	F	F	F	T
F	T	F	T	T	F	T	T	T	T	T	T	F	F	T
F	T	F	T	F	F	F	T	T	T	T	F	F	F	T
F	T	F	F	T	F	F	T	T	T	T	T	F	F	T
F	T	F	F	F	F	F	T	T	T	T	F	F	F	T
F	F	T	T	T	F	T	T	T	T	T	T	F	F	T
F	F	T	T	F	F	F	T	T	T	T	T	F	F	T
F	F	T	F	T	F	F	T	T	T	T	T	F	F	T
F	F	T	F	F	F	F	T	T	T	T	T	F	F	T
F	F	F	T	T	F	T	T	T	T	T	T	F	F	T
F	F	F	T	F	F	F	T	T	T	T	T	F	F	T
F	F	F	F	T	F	F	T	T	T	T	T	F	F	T
F	F	F	F	F	F	F	T	T	T	T	T	F	F	T

Invalid

Counterexample:

p	q	r	s	t
T	F	F	T	T

8.7A Exercise: Translating Sentences

2. p = Joan will take philosophy of science
   q = Joan does like science

   p & ~q

4. p = Mandie has taken art classes

   ~p

6. p = I will teach symbolic logic next semester
   q = I will teach philosophy of science next semester

   (p V q) & ~(p & q)

8.   p = Professor Peters teaches critical reasoning
      q = I will take critical reasoning next semester
              p ⊃ q

10.   p = I will do well in critical reasoning
      q = The professor simply gives me an A just for showing up
              q ⊃ p

12.   p = Jamison will play tight end next week
      q = Brown is still sick
              (q ⊃ p) & (~q ⊃ ~p)

14.   p = You will benefit from this course
      q = You fail this course
              p & q
      ("even if" translates as "even though")

16.   p = We will go to Iowa
      q = We will go to Illinois first
              ~p ⊃ q or ~q ⊃ p or p ∨ q

18.   p = Peter will attend the meeting
      q = Mary will attend the meeting
              (p ∨ q) & ~(p & q)

8.7B Exercise: Translating Arguments

2.   p = It will rain
      q = The sun will shine
              [p ∨ (~p & q)] & ~[p & (~p & q)]
              ~p
              ∴   q
              Valid

4.   p = passing a class
      q = enjoying a class
              p ≡ q
              ~p
              ∴   ~q
              Valid

6.   p = John enjoyed the music
      q = Mary enjoyed the music
              ~[(p ∨ q) & ~(p & q)]
              ~p
              ∴   ~q
              Valid

8.   p = Earth is round
      q = The moon is out
              ~(p ≡ q)
              p
              ∴   ~q
              Valid

10. p = truth
     q = our ability to recognize truth
     r = error
     s = our ability to recognize error

         p ⊃ q
         s ⊃ r
     ∴   r ⊃ p
                    Invalid
                        Counterexamples:
                            p q r s
                            F T T T
                            F T T F
                            F F T T
                            F F T F

12. p = my perceiving the desk
     q = I have good vision
     r = I am wearing glasses
     s = I am hallucinating

         ~(p ⊃ q) & r
         ~[(r V p) & ~(r & p)] ⊃ q
         [~(p & r) V s] & ~[~ (p & r) & s]
     ∴   ~q
                    Valid
                    (However, the set composed of the statements of the
                    argument is inconsistent.)

14. p = Truth is liberation from falsehood
     q = We are never free
     r = Freedom is the essence of truth
     s = Truth is an illusion

         r
         r ⊃ p
         (p V s) & ~(p & s)
         s ⊃ q
     ∴   p & q
                    Invalid
                        Counterexample:
                            p q r s
                            T F T F

8.8A Exercise: Truth Trees and Validity

1.

1.	p ⊃ q	sm
2.	p	sm
3.	~q	~sm
4.	~p q	1; ⊃

                            ~p   q
                             *   *
                            2,4   3,4
                    Valid

3.

1.	~(p & q)	sm
2.	~p	sm
3.	~q	~sm

4.   ~p   ~q   1; ~&

Invalid

5.

1.	~(p ⊃ q)	sm
2.	p	sm
3.	~~q	~sm
4.	q	3; ~~
5.	p	1; ~⊃
6.	~q	1; ~⊃

                *
              4,6

Valid

7.

1.	p ≡ q	sm
2.	p	sm
3.	~q	~sm

4.   p   ~p   1; ≡
5.   q   ~q   1; ≡
          *   *
        3,5   2,4

Valid

9.

1.	~q ⊃ r	sm
2.	~p ⊃ t	sm
3.	t ⊃ ~r	sm
4.	~(q ∨ p)	~sm
5.	~q	4; ~∨
6.	~p	4; ~∨

7.   ~~q   r   1; ⊃
8.   q   7;~~
9.   *   ~~p   t   2; ⊃
10.   5,8   p   9;~~
11.   *   ~t   ~r   3; ⊃
             6,10   *   *
                   9,11   7,11

Valid

11.

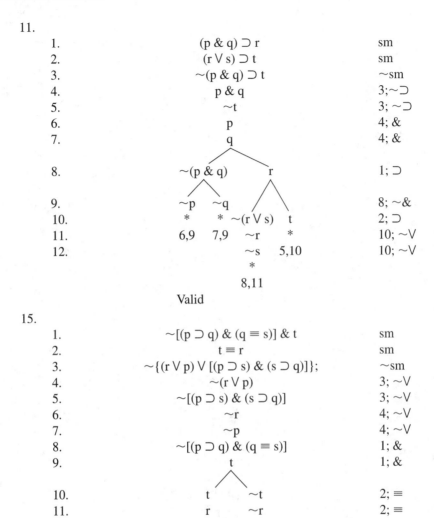

1.	(p & q) ⊃ r	sm
2.	(r ∨ s) ⊃ t	sm
3.	~(p & q) ⊃ t	~sm
4.	p & q	3;~⊃
5.	~t	3; ~⊃
6.	p	4; &
7.	q	4; &
8.	~(p & q) r	1; ⊃
9.	~p ~q	8; ~&
10.	* * ~(r ∨ s) t	2; ⊃
11.	6,9 7,9 ~r *	10; ~∨
12.	~s 5,10	10; ~∨
	*	
	8,11	

Valid

15.

1.	~[(p ⊃ q) & (q ≡ s)] & t	sm
2.	t ≡ r	sm
3.	~{(r ∨ p) ∨ [(p ⊃ s) & (s ⊃ q)]};	~sm
4.	~(r ∨ p)	3; ~∨
5.	~[(p ⊃ s) & (s ⊃ q)]	3; ~∨
6.	~r	4; ~∨
7.	~p	4; ~∨
8.	~[(p ⊃ q) & (q ≡ s)]	1; &
9.	t	1; &
10.	t ~t	2; ≡
11.	r ~r	2; ≡
	* *	
	6,11 9,10	

Valid [The argument is valid because all paths close, even
though not all lines have been decomposed (i.e., lines 5 and 8).]

8.8B Exercise: Truth Trees and Consistency

1.

1.	p ⊃ (q ∨ r)	sm
2.	~(~p ∨ r)	sm
3.	~q	sm
4.	r	sm
5.	~~p	2;~∨
6.	~r	2;~∨
	*	
	4,6	

Inconsistent

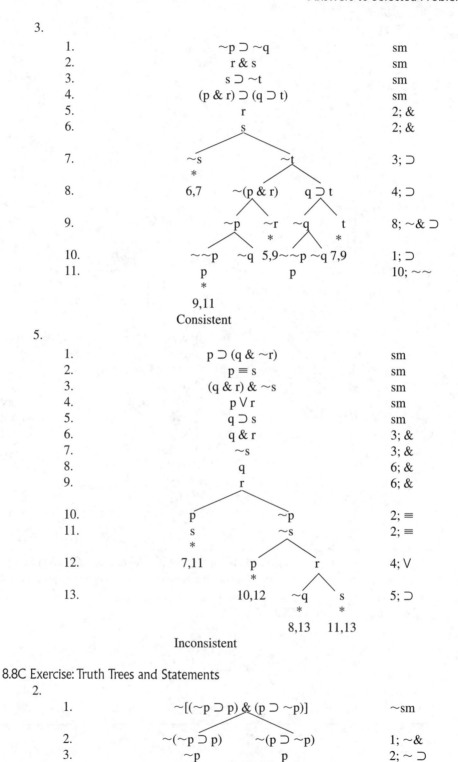

3.

1.	~p ⊃ ~q	sm
2.	r & s	sm
3.	s ⊃ ~t	sm
4.	(p & r) ⊃ (q ⊃ t)	sm
5.	r	2; &
6.	s	2; &
7.	~s ~t	3; ⊃
8.	6,7 ~(p & r) q ⊃ t	4; ⊃
9.	~p ~r ~q t	8; ~& ⊃
10.	~~p ~q 5,9~~p ~q 7,9	1; ⊃
11.	p p	10; ~~

9,11
Consistent

5.

1.	p ⊃ (q & ~r)	sm
2.	p ≡ s	sm
3.	(q & r) & ~s	sm
4.	p ∨ r	sm
5.	q ⊃ s	sm
6.	q & r	3; &
7.	~s	3; &
8.	q	6; &
9.	r	6; &
10.	p ~p	2; ≡
11.	s ~s	2; ≡
12.	7,11 p r	4; ∨
13.	10,12 ~q s	5; ⊃

8,13   11,13
Inconsistent

8.8C Exercise: Truth Trees and Statements

2.

1.	~[(~p ⊃ p) & (p ⊃ ~p)]	~sm
2.	~(~p ⊃ p) ~(p ⊃ ~p)	1; ~&
3.	~p p	2; ~ ⊃

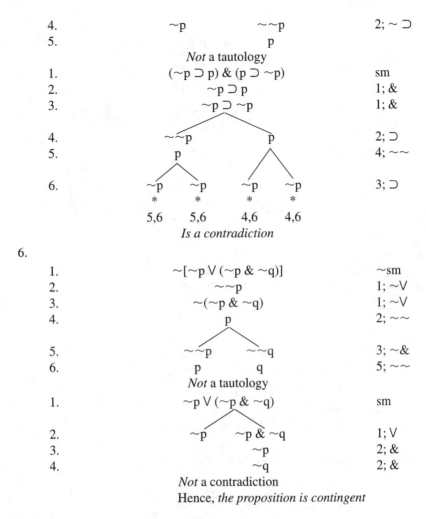

4.	~p	~~p	2; ~ ⊃
5.		p	

Not a tautology

1.	(~p ⊃ p) & (p ⊃ ~p)	sm
2.	~p ⊃ p	1; &
3.	~p ⊃ ~p	1; &
4.	~~p p	2; ⊃
5.	p	4; ~~
6.	~p ~p ~p ~p	3; ⊃
	* * * *	
	5,6 5,6 4,6 4,6	

Is a contradiction

6.

1.	~[~p ∨ (~p & ~q)]	~sm
2.	~~p	1; ~∨
3.	~(~p & ~q)	1; ~∨
4.	p	2; ~~
5.	~~p ~~q	3; ~&
6.	p q	5; ~~

Not a tautology

1.	~p ∨ (~p & ~q)	sm
2.	~p ~p & ~q	1; ∨
3.	~p	2; &
4.	~q	2; &

Not a contradiction

Hence, *the proposition is contingent*

8.8D Exercise: Truth Trees and Equivalence

2.

1.	~[~(p & q) ≡ (~p ∨ ~q)]	~sm
2.	~(p & q) ~~(p & q)	1; ~ ≡
3.	~(~p ∨ ~q) (~p ∨ ~q)	1; ~ ≡
4.	~~p p & q	3; ~∨: 2; ~~
5.	~~q p	3; ~∨: 4; &
6.	p q	4; ~~: 4; &
7.	q	5; ~~
8.	~p ~q	3; ∨
9.	~p ~q	
	* * 5,8 6,8	
	6,9 7,9	

Equivalent

10.

| 1. | $\sim[\sim(p \supset q) \equiv (\sim p \supset \sim q)]$ | | | | $\sim sm$ |

```
1.          ~[~(p ⊃ q) ≡ (~p ⊃ ~q)]                        ~sm
2.        ~(p ⊃ q)              ~~(p ⊃ q)                   1; ~ ≡
3.        ~(~p ⊃ ~q)            ~p ⊃ ~q                     1; ~ ≡
4.           ~p                   p ⊃ q                     3; ~ ⊃: 2; ~~
5.           ~~q                                            3; ~ ⊃
6.           q                ~~p        ~q                 5; ~~: 3; ⊃
7.           p                  p                           2; ~ ⊃: 6; ~~
8.           ~q                                             2; ~ ⊃
9.           *               ~p   q   ~p   q                4; ⊃
            6,8               *          *
                            7,9        6,9
```

Not equivalent

8.9A Exercise: Natural Deduction and Replacement Rules

4. $\sim(p \& q) \& \sim(t \equiv s)$ DeMorgan
8. $(p \& q) \& p \supset (q \supset r)$ Exportation
13. $\sim(p \equiv r) \lor [(s \& t) \supset (\sim s \lor \sim r)]$ Implication

8.9A-2 Exercise: Natural Deduction and Ordinary Language

3. p = doing well on this assignment

q = doing well all semester

$\sim(p \supset q) :: p \& \sim q$ Implication

One can do well on this assignment and not do well all semester.

8.9C Exercise: Natural Deduction and Justification

2.

1.	$(p \supset r) \& (q \supset v)$	given
2.	$p \lor q$	given
3.	$(r \supset q) \& (v \supset t)$	given
4.	$\sim(q \lor t) \lor s / \vdash s$	given
5.	$r \supset q$	3; Simpl
6.	$v \supset t$	3; Simpl
7.	$p \supset r$	1; Simpl
8.	$q \supset v$	1; Simpl
9.	$r \lor v$	2,7,8; Cons Dilem
10.	$q \lor t$	5, 6, 9; Cons Dilem
11.	s	4, 10; Dis Syll

7.

1.	$\sim p \& q$	given
2.	$(r \supset p) \& (s \& t)$	given
3.	$r \lor U$	given
4.	$\sim u \lor v / \vdash v$	given
5.	$u \supset v$	4; Impl

6.	r ⊃ p	2; Simpl
7.	v ∨ p	3,5,6; Cons Dilem
8.	~v ⊃ p	7; Impl
9.	~p	1; Simpl
10.	v	8,9; MT

12.

1.	~p ∨ r	given
2.	r ⊃ q	given
3.	~q / ⊢ p ≡ q	given
4.	~r	2,3; MT
5.	~p	1,4; DS
6.	~p & ~q	3,5; Conj
7.	(p & q) ∨ (~p & ~q)	6; Add
8.	p ≡ q	7; Bicon

17.

1.	(s ∨ p) ⊃ q	given
2.	(t ∨ r) ⊃ u	given
3.	v ⊃ ~(q & u)	given
4.	s & t / ⊢ ~v	given
5.	s	4; Simpl
6.	t	4; Simpl
7.	s ∨ p	5; Add
8.	t ∨ r	6; Add
9.	q	1, 7; MP
10.	u	2,8; MP
11.	q & u	9, 10; Conj
12.	~v	3, 11; MT

19.

1.	~(v & ~v) ⊃ ~(w ⊃ v)	given
2.	(u ⊃ p_1) ∨ (w ⊃ v)	given
3.	[u ∨ (t & q_1)] ∨ v	given
4.	(u ⊃ p_1) ⊃ (t ⊃ x)	given
5.	~p ⊃ ~(p_1 ∨ x)	given
6.	v ≡ w / ⊢ (~ q_1 ⊃ u) & p	given
7.	(v ⊃ w) & (w ⊃ v)	6; Bicon
8.	w ⊃ v	7; Simpl
9.	v & ~v	1, 8; MT
10.	~v	9; Simpl
11.	u ∨ (t & q_1)	3, 10; DS
12.	(u ∨ t) & (u ∨ q_1)	11; Distr
13.	u ∨ q_1	12; Simpl
14.	q_1 ∨ u	13; Comm
15.	~q_1 ⊃ u	14; Impl
16.	v	9; Simpl
17.	w	6, 16; Bicon Elim
18.	w & ~v	10, 17; Conj

19.	$\sim(w \supset v)$	18; Impl
20.	$u \supset p_1$	2, 19; DS
21.	$t \supset x$	4, 20; MP
22.	$u \lor t$	12; Simpl
23.	$p_1 \lor x$	20,21,22; Const Dil
24.	p	5,23; MT
25.	$(\sim q_1 \supset u) \& p$	15, 24; Conj

8.9D Exercise: Natural Deduction and Reductio ad Absurdum

8.

1.	$(t \lor q) \supset (u \& r)$	given
2.	$(r \lor p) \supset s$	given
3.	$t \lor p / \vdash s$	given

4.	$\sim s$	assume
5.	$(r \lor p) \supset s$	2; Reiter
6.	$\sim(r \lor p)$	4, 5; MT
7.	$\sim r \& \sim p$	6; DeMor
8.	$\sim p$	7; Simpl
9.	$t \lor p$	3; Reiter
10.	t	8,9; DS
11.	$t \lor q$	10; Add
12.	$(t \lor q) \supset (u \& r)$	1; Reiter
13.	$u \& r$	11, 12; MP
14.	r	13; Simpl
15.	$\sim r$	7; Simpl

| 16. | s | 4–15; Reductio |

10.

| 1. | $\sim p \supset \sim(q \& \sim r)$ | given |
| 2. | $(q \& \sim r) \lor r / \vdash \sim r \supset p$ | given |

3.	$\sim(r \supset p)$	assume
4.	$\sim r \& p$	3; Impl
5.	$\sim r$	4; Simpl
6.	$(q \& \sim r) \lor r$	2; Reiter
7.	$(q \& \sim r)$	5,6; DS
8.	$\sim p \supset \sim(q \& \sim r)$	1; Reiter
9.	p	7,8; MT
10.	$\sim p$	4; Simpl

| 11. | $\sim r \supset p$ | 3–10; Reductio |

8.9E Exercise: Natural Deduction and Conditional Proofs

7.

| 1. | $[(p \lor r) \& (s \& \sim q)] \supset t$ | given |
| 2. | $\sim(u \& v) \supset \sim(s \supset q)$ | given |

3.	$(s \ \& \sim q) \supset (\sim p \supset r)$	given
4.	$\sim t \lor q \ / \vdash \sim v \supset t$	given

5.	$\sim v$	assume
6.	$\sim u \lor \sim v$	5; add
7.	$\sim (u \ \& \ v)$	6; DeM
8.	$\sim (u \ \& \ v) \supset \sim (s \supset q)$	2; Reiter
9.	$\sim (s \supset q)$	7,8; MP
10.	$s \ \& \sim q$	9; Impl
11.	$(s \ \& \sim q) \supset (\sim p \supset r)$	3; Reiter
12.	$\sim p \supset r$	10,11; MP
13.	$p \lor r$	12; Impl
14.	$(p \lor r) \ \& \ (s \ \& \sim q)$	10,13; Conj
15.	$[(p \lor r) \ \& \ (s \ \& \sim q)] \supset t$	1; Reiter
16.	t	14,15; MP

_____

17.	$\sim v \supset t$	5–16; CP

9.

1.	$(p \lor q) \supset (r \ \& \ s)$	given
2.	$(s \lor t) \supset (u \ \& \ v)$	given
3.	$q_1 \equiv p_1 \ / \vdash (p \supset u) \ \& \ (\sim q_1 \lor p_1)$	given

----

4.	p	Assume
5.	$p \lor q$	4; Add
6.	$(p \lor q) \supset (r \ \& \ s)$	1; Reiter
7.	$r \ \& \ s$	5,6; MP
8.	s	7; Simpl
9.	$s \lor t$	8; Add
10.	$(s \lor t) \supset (u \ \& \ v)$	2; Reiter
11.	$u \ \& \ v$	9, 10; MP
12.	u	11; Simpl

_____

13.	$p \supset u$	4–12; CP
14.	$(q_1 \supset p_1) \ \& \ (p_1 \supset q_1)$	3; Bicond
15.	$q_1 \supset p_1$	14; Simpl
16.	$q_1 \lor p_1$	15; Impl
17.	$(p \supset u) \ \& \ (\sim q_1 \lor p_1)$	13, 16; Conj

10.

1.	$(q \supset p) \ \& \ s$	given
2.	$(q \ \& \ p) \supset r$	given
3.	$(t \ \& \ r) \supset \sim u \ / \vdash q \supset (t \supset \sim u)$	given

----

4.	q	Assume

5.	t	Assume
6.	$(t \ \& \ r) \supset \sim u$	3; Reiter
7.	$t \supset (r \supset \sim u)$	6; Export

8.	(r ⊃ ~u)	5,7; MP
9.	q	4; Reiter
10.	(q ⊃ p) & s	1; Reiter
11.	(q ⊃ p)	10; Simpl
12.	p	9,11; MP
13.	q & p	9,12; Conj
14.	(q & p) ⊃ r	2; Reiter
15.	r	13,14; MP
16.	~u	8,15; MP

17.	t ⊃ ~u	5–16; CP

18.	q ⊃ (t ⊃ ~u)	4–17; CP

8.9F Exercise: Natural Deduction and Validity

6.

1.	~(p ⊃ t) & q	given
2.	~(q ∨ p) ⊃ t	given
3.	~(p & q) ∨ s / ⊢ ~t	given
4.	~(p ⊃ t)	1; simplification
5.	p & ~t	4; implication
6.	~t	6; simplification

13.

1.	~[(p & q) ≡ (r & s)]	given
2.	p ≡ r / ⊢ ~(q ≡ s)	given

3.	q ≡ s	Assume
4.	(q ⊃ s) & (s ⊃ q)	3; biconditional
5.	q ⊃ s	4; simplification
6.	s ⊃ q	4; simplification
7.	(p ⊃ r) & (r ⊃ p)	2; biconditional
8.	p ⊃ r	7; simplification
9.	r ⊃ p	7; simplification
10.	[(p & q) & ~(r & s) ∨ ~(p & q) & (r & s)]	1; biconditional

----

11.	[(p & q) & ~(r & s)]	Assume
12.	p & q	11; simplification
13.	~(r & s)	11; simplification
14.	p	12; simplification
15.	q	12; simplification
16.	~r ∨ ~s	13; DeM
17.	r	8,14; MP
18.	~s	16,17; DS
19.	~q	5,18; MT

20.	~[(p & q) & ~(r & s)]	11–19; Reductio

21.	~(p & q) & (r & s)	10,20; DS
22.	~(p & q)	21; simplification
23.	r & s	21; simplification
24.	r	23; simplification
25.	s	23; simplification
26.	~p ∨ ~q	22; DeM
27.	p	9,24; MP
28.	~q	26,27; DS
29.	~s	6,28; MT
30.	~(q ≡ s)	3–29; Reductio

28.

1.	(p ∨ q) ⊃ r	given
2.	r ⊃ (p & q) / ⊢ (p & q) ⊃ (p ∨ q)	given
---	------------------------------	
3.	~[(p & q) ⊃ (p ∨ q)]	assumption
4.	(p & q) & ~(p ∨ q)	3; implication
5.	p & q	4; simplification
6.	~ (p ∨ q)	4; simplification
7.	p	5; simplification
8.	~p & ~q	6; DeMorgan
9.	~p	8; simplification
10.	(p & q) ⊃ (p ∨ q)	3–9; reductio

38.

   One of the shortcomings of natural deduction is that it is incapable of showing an argument to be invalid. As the following tree indicates, this argument is invalid:

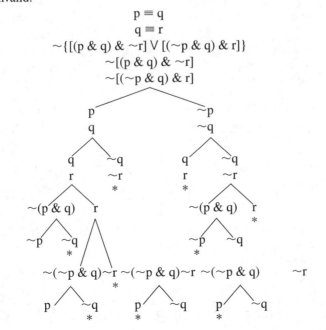

9.1A Exercise: Categorical Statements
1.   All S* are P (UA)

9.1B Exercise: Nonstandard Categorical Statements
1.   All who are expected to attend the lectures are seniors.
3.   Some pacifists are not political types.

9.2A Exercise: Categorical Arguments
1.   No professors attended the party.
      All students attended the party.
      ∴   No students are professors.

      No P* are M*
      All S* are M
      ∴   No S* are P*
      Valid, no violations

3.   No gillygongs are visible
      All dogs are visible
      ∴   No dogs are gillygongs

      No P* are M*
      All S* are M
      ∴   No S* are P*
      valid, no violations

9.2B Exercise: Categorical Arguments
2.   Some fun things are dangerous.   Some M are ____
      Some fun things are free.   Some M are ____

      Since the middle term cannot be distributed at least once, any conclusion
      drawn from these premises is erroneous, since the resulting argument
      would be invalid. However,. . .

      Some fun things are dangerous.   Some P are M
      All dangerous things are free.   All M* are S
      ∴   Some free things are fun.   ∴   Some S are P

4.   All perfect trees are evergreens.   All S* are M
      All evergreens are hardwood.   All M* are P
      ∴   All perfect trees are hardwood. ∴   All S* are P

6.   All non-English sentences are those that should be removed from this
      book.
      No Spanish is English.
                        or
      All sentences in this book are English.   All S* are M
      No Spanish is English.   No P* are M*
      ∴   No sentences in this book are Spanish   ∴   No S* are P*

9.4 Exercise: Translating
   1.   (∀x) (Px ⊃ ~Ax)
       (∀x) (Sx ⊃ Ax)
       ∴   (∀x) (Sx ⊃ ~Px)

   2.   (∀x) (Ix ⊃ ~Ax)
       (∀x) (Ix ⊃ Sx)
       ∴   (∃x) (Sx & ~Ax)

9.5A Exercise: Predicate Logic
   1.

1.	~(∃x) (Px & Ax)	sm
2.	(∀x) (Sx ⊃ Ax)	sm
3.	~(∀x) (Sx ⊃ ~Px)	~sm
4.	(∀x) ~(Px & Ax)	1; ~∃
5.	(∃x) ~(Sx ⊃ ~Px)	3; ~∀
6.	~(Sa ⊃ ~Pa)	5; ∃
7.	~(Pa & Aa)	4; ∀
8.	Sa ⊃ Aa	2; ∀
9.	Sa	6; ~ ⊃
10.	~~Pa	6; ~⊃
11.	Pa	10; DN

12.   ~Pa   ~Aa   7; ~ &
         *
13.   (11,12) ~Sa   Aa   8; ⊃
              *   *
           (9,13) (12,13)
          Valid

   3.

1.	(∀x) (Gx ⊃ ~Vx)	sm
2.	(∀x) (Dx ⊃ Vx)	sm
3.	~~ (∃x) (Dx & Gx)	~sm
4.	(∃x) (Dx & Gx)	3; DN
5.	Da & Ga	4; ∃
6.	Ga ⊃ ~ Va	1; ∀
7.	Da ⊃ Va	2; ∀
8.	Da	5; &
9.	Ga	5; &

10.   ~Ga   ~Va   6; ⊃
       *
11.   (9,10) ~Da   Va   7; ⊃
          *   *
        (8,11) (10,11)
       Valid

5.

1.	(∀x) (Cx ⊃ Hx)	sm
2.	~(∀x) (Tx ⊃ Hx)	sm
3.	~(∀x) (Tx ⊃ ~Cx)	~sm
4.	(∃x) ~ (Tx ⊃ Hx)	2; ~∀
5.	(∃x) ~ (Tx ⊃ ~Cx)	3; ~∀
6.	~(Ta ⊃ Ha)	4; ∃
7.	~(Tb ⊃ ~Cb)	5; ∃
8.	Ta	6; ~⊃
9.	~Ha	6; ~⊃
10.	Tb	7; ~⊃
11.	~~Cb	7; ~⊃
12.	Cb	11; DN
13.	Cb ⊃ Hb	1; ∀
14.	Ca ⊃ Ha	1; ∀

15.   ~Cb   Hb   13; ⊃
                  *

16.   (12,15) ~Ca   Ha   14; ⊃
                                  *
                               (9,16)
                   Invalid

9.5B Exercise: Predicate Logic

1.

1.	Ta & Ua	sm
2.	(∀x) [Tx ⊃ (Vx V ~Wx)]	sm
3.	~(∃x) Vx	~sm
4.	(∀x) ~Vx	3; ~∃
5.	Ta	1; &
6.	Ua	1; &
7.	Ta ⊃ (Va V ~Wa)	2; ∀
8.	~Va	4; ∀

9.   ~Ta   Va V ~Wa   7; ⊃
           *

10.   (5,9)   Va   ~Wa   9; V
                   *
                 (8,10)
                  Invalid

3.

1.	(∀x) (Tx ⊃ Ux)	sm
2.	(∀x) [Ux ⊃ (Ux V Wx)]	sm
3.	(∀x) (Tx ⊃ ~ Wx)	sm
4.	~(∀x) (Tx ⊃ Ux)	~sm

5.	(∃x) ~ (Tx ⊃ Ux)	4; ~∀
6.	~(Ta ⊃ Ua)	5; ∃
7.	Ta	6; ~⊃
8.	~Ua	6; ~⊃
9.	(Ta ⊃ Ua)	1; ∀

10.
```
        ~Ta        Ua         9; ⊃
         *          *
       (7,10)     (8,10)
       Valid
```

9.

1.	(∃x) (Tx & Ux)	sm
2.	(∃x) (Vx & ~Tx)	sm
3.	(∃x) (Wx & ~Ux)	sm
4.	~(∃x) (Vx & Wx)	~sm
5.	(∀x) ~(Vx & Wx)	4; ~∃
6.	(Ta & Ua)	1; ∃
7.	(Vb & ~Tb)	2; ∃
8.	(Wc & ~Uc)	3; ∃
8.	Ta	6; &
10.	Ua	6; &
11.	Vb	7; &
12.	~Tb	7; &
13.	Wc	8; &
14.	~Uc	8; &
15.	~(Vb & Wb)	5; ∀

```
16.      ~Vb          ~Wb                    15; ~&
17.       *        ~(Vc & Wc)                5; ∀
       (11,16)
18.                ~Vc      ~Wc              17; ~&
                             *
                          (13,18)
                 Invalid
```

9.6 Exercise: Translation and Predicate Logic

1.

Nothing is going right.
If nothing is going right, then Mary will have a bad day.
1.   Mary will have a bad day.

~(∃x) (Rx)
[~(∃x) (Rx)] ⊃ Bm
∴   Bm

1.	$\sim(\exists x)\,(Rx)$	
2.	$[\sim(\exists x)\,(Rx)] \supset Bm$	
3.	$\sim Bm$	

4.	$\sim\sim(\exists x)\,(Rx)$ Bm	2,$\supset$
5.	$(\exists x)\,(Rx)$ *	4, DN
6.	Ra (3,4)	5, $\exists$
7.	$(\forall x)\sim Rx$	1, $\sim\exists$
8.	$\sim Ra$	7, $\forall$
	*	
	(6,8)	

Valid

3.   Everything is lighter than something else.
   $\therefore$ Gold is lighter than something.

$(\forall x)\,(\exists y)\,Lxy$
$\therefore \quad (\exists y)\,Lgy$

1.	$(\forall x)\,(\exists y)\,Lxy$	
2.	$\sim(\exists y)\,Lgy$	
3.	$(\forall y)\sim Lgy$	2, $\sim\exists$
4.	$(\exists y)\,Lgy$	1,$\forall$
5.	Lga	4, $\exists$
6.	$\sim Lga$	3, $\forall$
	*	
	(5,6)	
	Valid	

5.   All old teachers are liberals.
   Charlie is an old teacher.
   $\therefore$ Charlie is a liberal.

$(\forall x)\,Tx \supset Lx$
Tc
$\therefore \quad Lc$

1.	$(\forall x)\,Tx \supset Lx$	
2.	Tc	
3.	$\sim Lc$	
4.	$Tc \supset Lc$	1,$\forall$

5.	$\sim Tc$ Lc	4,$\supset$
	* *	
	(2,5) (3,5)	
	Valid	

7. If Brian understands all things, then he can program in C++.
    Brian cannot program in C++.
    _____
    ∴   Brian doesn't understand all things.

(Notice that predicate logic is not needed with this problem, and we can call
the argument valid, since it is denying the consequent.)

9. Everybody attracts somebody.
    _____
    ∴   Somebody is attracted to Lisa.

    (∀x) (∃y) Axy
    _____
    ∴   (∃x) Alx

    1.   (∀x) (∃y) Axy
    2.   ~(∃x) Alx
    3.   (∃y) Aly   1,∀
    4.   Ala   3, ∃
    5.   (∀x) ~Alx   2,~∃
    6.   ~Ala   5,∀
                              *
                           (4,6)
                           Valid

Additional Readings

(This list does not include works cited in the text.)

Chapter 1: **Introduction to Critical Reasoning**

Hansen, Hans. "An Informal Logic Bibliography." *Informal Logic* 3 (Fall 1990): 155–184.
Kahane, Howard. "The Proper Subject Matter for Critical Thinking Courses." *Argumentation* 3 (May 1989): 141–148.
Paul, Richard. *Critical Thinking: What Every Person Needs to Survive in a Rapidly Changing World*. Rohnert Park, CA: Sonoma State University, 1990.
Siegel, Harvey. *Educating Reason: Rationality, Critical Thinking, and Education*. New York: Routledge, 1988.

Chapter 2: **Foundations**

Ammerman, Robert, and Marcus Singer. *Belief, Knowledge, and Truth: Readings in the Theory of Knowledge*. New York: Charles Scribner's Sons, 1970.
Ayer, Alfred. *Language, Truth and Logic*. New York: Dover Publications, 1946.
Barthes, Roland. *Elements of Semiology*. New York: Hill and Wang, 1984.
Battersby, Mark. "Critical Thinking as Applied Epistemology." *Informal Logic* 11 (Spring 1989): 91–100.
Davidson, Donald. *Inquiries into Truth and Interpretation*. Oxford: Clarendon Press, 1984.
Devitt, Michael, and Kim Sterelny. *Language and Reality: An Introduction to the Philosophy of Language*. Cambridge, MA: MIT Press, 1987.
Garfield, Jay, and Murray Kiteley. *Meaning and Truth: The Essential Readings in Modern Semantics*. New York: Paragon House, 1991.
Gardner, Howard. *The Quest for Mind: Piaget. Levi-Strauss, and the Structualist Movement*. Chicago: University of Chicago Press, 1981.
Harman, Gilbert. *Thought*. Princeton, NJ: Princeton University Press, 1973.
Hawkes, Terence. *Structuralism and Semiotics*. Berkeley, CA: University of California Press, 1977.
Lehrer, Keith. *Knowledge*. Oxford, U.K.: Clarendon Press, 1978.
Kirkham, Richard. *Theories of Truth: A Critical Introduction*. Cambridge, MA: MIT Press, 1995.
Pappas, George, and Marshall Swain. *Essays on Knowledge and Justification*. Ithaca, NY: Cornell University Press, 1978.
Pojman, Louis. *What Can We Know? An Introduction to the Theory of Knowledge*. Belmont, CA: Wadsworth Publishing Company, 1995.
Popkin, Richard. *The High Road to Pyrrhonism*. San Diego: Austin Hill Press, Inc., 1980.

Quine, Willard. *From a Logical Point of View*. New York: Harper Torchbooks, 1961.

Ricoeur, Paul. *Interpretation Theory: Discourse and the Surplus of Meaning*. Fort Worth: Texas Christian University Press, 1976.

Russell, Bertrand. *An Inquiry into Meaning and Truth*. Baltimore: Penguin Books, 1962.

Schiffer, Stephen. *Remnants of Meaning*. Cambridge, MA: MIT Press, 1987.

Trigg, Roger. *Reason and Commitment*. Cambridge, U.K.: Cambridge University Press, 1973.

White, Alan. *Truth*. Garden City, NY: Anchor Books, 1970.

Wolfe, David. *Epistemology: The Justification of Belief*. Downers Grove, IL: InterVarsity Press, 1982.

Chapter 3: **Introduction to Arguments**

Govier, Trudy. "Critical Thinking as Argument Analysis?" *Argumentation* 3 (May 1989): 115–126.

Groarke, Leo. "Deductivism Within Pragma-Dialectics." *Argumentation* 13 (1999): 1–16.

Harman, Gilbert. "Logic and Reasoning." *Synthese* 60 (1984): 107–127.

MacKenzie, Jim. "Reasoning and Logic." *Synthese* 79 (1989): 99–117.

Marks, Joel. "When Is a Fallacy Not a Fallacy." *Metaphilosophy* 19 (1988): 307–312.

Toulmin, Stephen. *The Uses of Argument*. Cambridge, U.K.: Cambridge University Press, 1976.

Walton, Douglas. "What Is Reasoning? What Is an Argument?" *Journal of Philosophy* 87 (August 1990): 399–419.

Chapter 4: **Introduction to Probability**

Billingsley, P. *Probability and Measure*. New York: John Wiley and Sons, Inc., 1979.

De Finetti, Bruno. "Foresight: Its Logical Laws, Its Subjective Sources." *Studies in Subjective Probability*, ed. Henry E. Kyburg, Jr., and Howard Smokler (97–158). New York: John Wiley and Sons, Inc., 1964.

De Finetti, Bruno. "Probabilism." *Erkenntnis* 31 (1989): 169–223.

Eells, Ellery, and Brian Skyrms, eds. *Probability and Conditionals*. New York: Cambridge University Press, 1994.

Fehr, Howard, Lucas Bunt, and George Grossman. *An Introduction to Sets, Probability, and Hypothesis Testing*. Boston: D.C. Heath and Company, 1964.

Foster, Marguerite H., and Michael L. Martin. *Probability, Confirmation, and Simplicity: Readings in the Philosophy of Inductive Logic*. New York: Odyssey Press, Inc., 1966.

Hawthorne, James. "Bayesian Induction Is Eliminative Induction" *Philosophical Topics* 21 (Spring 1993): 99–138.

Howson, Colin, and Peter Urbach. "Bayesian Reasoning in Science" *Nature* 350 (April 1991): 371–374.

Jeffery, Richard. *Probability and the Art of Judgment*. New York: Cambridge University Press, 1992.

Kneale, William. *Probability and Induction*. Oxford, U.K.: Clarendon Press, 1949.

Schlesinger, George. *The Sweep of Probability*. Notre Dame, IN: University of Notre Press, 1991.

Chapter 5: **Enumerative Induction**

Boyd, Robert. "Strawson on Induction." *The Philosophy of P.F. Strawson*, ed. Lewis Edwin Hahn. The Library of Living Philosophers, Volume XXVI. Chiago: Open Court, 1998.

Burbidge, John. *Within Reason: A Guide to Non-Deductive Reasoning*. Lewiston, NY: Broadview Press, 1990.

Gardner, Michael R. "Random Walks by Semi-Drunk Bugs and Others, on the Square and on the Cube." *Scientific American* (June 1969): 122.

Grimmett, Geoffrey, and David Stirzaker. *Probability and Random Process*. Oxford, U.K.: Clarendon Press, 1988.

Hakel, Milton. "How Often Is Often?" *American Psychologist* 23 (July 1968): 533–534.

Hunter, Geoffrey. "A Possible Extension of Logical Theory?" *Philosophical Studies* 16 (December 1965): 81–88.

Logue, James. *Projective Probability*. New York: Oxford University Press, 1995.

Newman, Robert, and Dale Newman. *Evidence*. Boston: Houghton Mifflin Company, 1969.

Polya, G. *Mathematics and Plausible Reasoning*. Princeton, NJ: Princeton University Press, 1973.

Salmon, Merrilee. *Introduction to Logic and Critical Thinking*. Fort Worth, TX: Harcourt Brace College Publishers, 1995.

Simpson, Ray. "The Specific Meanings of Certain Terms Indicating Differing Degrees of Frequency." *The Quarterly Journal of Speech* 30 (October 1944): 328–330.

Von Wright, G. H. "Remarks on the Epistemology of Subjective Probability." *Logic, Methodology, and the Philosophy of Science*, ed. E. Nagel, P. Suppes, and A. Tarski. (330–339) Stanford, CA: Stanford University Press, 1961.

Walton, Douglas. "Rules for Plausible Reasoning." *Informal Logic* 14 (Winter 1992): 33–51.

Chapter 7: **Conditional Logic**

Baum, Robert. *Logic*. New York: Holt, Rinehart and Winston, Inc., 1989.

Beardsley, Monroe. *Practical Logic*. New York: Prentice-Hall, Inc., 1950.

Bonevac, Daniel. *The Art and Science of Logic*. Mountain View, CA: Mayfield Publishing Company, 1990.

Kelley, David. *The Art of Reasoning* (expanded edition with Symbolic Logic). New York: W. W. Norton and Company, 1990.

Chapter 8: **Propositional Logic**

Allen, Colin and Michael Hand. *Logic Primer*. Cambridge, MA: MIT Press, 1992.

Bergmann, Merrie, et al. *The Logic Book*. New York: McGraw-Hill Publishing Company, 1990.

Hunter, Geoffrey. *Metalogic: An Introduction to the Metatheory of Standard First Order Logic*. Berkeley, CA: University of California Press, 1973.

Pollard, Stephen. *Philosophical Introduction to Set Theory*. Notre Dame, IN: University of Notre Dame Press, 1990.

Russell, Bertrand. *Introduction to Mathematical Philosophy*. New York: Touchstone Books.

Index

Credits

Cartoon on p. vi: Reprinted by permission of Wendy Oxman. FRANK AND ERNEST cartoon on p. 3: © 1988 Thaves / Reprinted by permission. Newspaper distribution by NEA, Inc. Cartoon on p. 4: Reprinted by permission of Wendy Oxman. DILBERT cartoon on p. 5: DILBERT reprinted by permission of United Feature Syndicate, Inc. BROOM HILDA cartoon on p. 10: © Tribune Media Services, Inc. All Rights Reserved. Reprinted with permission. Cartoon on p. 15: Reprinted by permission of Wendy Oxman. THE FAR SIDE cartoon on p. 22: The Far Side ® by Gary Larson © 1983 FarWorks, Inc. All Rights Reserved. Used with Permission. Quotes from Bernard Ramm on pp. 45–46: Reprinted by permission of Eerdmans Publishing Company. Editorials on pages 50–53: Reprint Courtesy of the *Forth Worth Star-Telegram*. HERMAN cartoon on p. 52: © 1988 Jim Unger / dist. by LaughingStock Licensing Inc. Cartoon on p. 56: Reprinted by permission of Jimmy Margulies. Article by Mayor Edward Koch on pp. 69–72: Reprinted by permission of *The New Republic*. HAGAR THE HORRIBLE cartoon on p. 82: Reprinted by special permission King Features Syndicate. NANCY cartoon on page 88: NANCY reprinted by permission of United Feature Syndicate, Inc. Cartoon on page 102: © 2000; Reprinted courtesy of Bunny Hoest and *Parade Magazine*. BROOM HILDA cartoon on p. 107: © Tribune Media Services, Inc. All Rights Reserved. Reprinted with permission. Cartoon on p. 113: Reprinted by permission of Wendy Oxman. FRANK AND ERNEST cartoon on p. 118: © 1992 Thaves / Reprinted by permission. Newspaper distribution by NEA, Inc. THE FAMILY CIRCUS cartoon on p. 134: Reprinted with special permission King Features Syndicate. PEANUTS cartoon on p. 145: PEANUTS reprinted by permission of United Feature Syndicate, Inc. Cartoon on p. 151: Reprinted by permission of Jimmy Margulies. Student report on pp. 169–172: Used by permission of Linda Calandra. B.C. cartoon on p. 175: By permission of Johnny Hart and Creators Syndicate Inc. HAGAR THE HORRIBLE cartoon on p. 179: Reprinted with special permission King Features Syndicate. MOTHER GOOSE & GRIMM cartoon on p. 193: © Tribune Media Services, Inc. All Rights Reserved. Reprinted with permission. PLUGGERS cartoon on p. 213: © Tribune Media Services, Inc. All Rights Reserved. Reprinted with permission. PEPPER AND SALT cartoon on p. 234: From The Wall Street Journal—Permission, Cartoon Features Syndicate. Cartoon on p. 250: © 1998 by Sidney Harris. FRANK AND ERNEST cartoon on page 264: © 1994 Thaves/ Reprinted with Permission. Newspaper distribution by NEA, Inc. Student report on pp. 269–270: Used by permission of Gail Mayberry. Student report on pp. 277–280: Used by permission of Kristin Snow. Student report on pp. 280–284: Used by permission of Joel L. Bush.

TRUTH TREE METHOD

Rules of inference:

those which stack—

those which branch—

those which branch and stack—

| P ≡ Q | ~ (P ≡ Q) |

P   ~P   ~P   P
Q ~Q   Q ~Q

Rules for Predicate Logic:

~∀ Rule

Whenever we encounter a sentence with a negated universal quantifier (e.g., ~(∀**x**) (...**x**)), we rewrite the sentence as (∃**x**) ~(...**x**).

~∃ Rule

Whenever we encounter a sentence with a negated existential quantifier (e.g., ~∃**x**) (...**x**)), we rewrite the sentence as (∀**x**) ~(...**x**).

∃ Rule

For sentences of the form (∃**x**) (...**x**) that have not been decomposed and are in an open path(s), examine the path(s) and determine whether it contains the individual constant **y**. If **y** does not appear, list ... **y** in that open path(s). If **y** does appear, choose an individual constant that does not appear.

∀ Rule

For sentences of the form (∀**x**) (...**x**) that are in an open path(s), examine the path(s) and determine the individual constants that appear in that path(s). Write ...**y** for each individual constant that appears. If no constant appears, choose a constant.